Max Weber
& Islam

Max Weber & Islam

Toby E. Huff
Wolfgang Schluchter
EDITORS

Transaction Publishers
New Brunswick (U.S.A.) and London (U.K.)

Copyright © 1999 by Transaction Publishers, New Brunswick, New Jersey.

All rights reserved under International and Pan-American Copyright Conventions. No part of this book may be reproduced or transmitted in any form or by any means, electronic or mechanical, including photocopy, recording, or any information storage and retrieval system, without prior permission in writing from the publisher. All inquiries should be addressed to Transaction Publishers, Rutgers—The State University, 35 Berrue Circle, Piscataway, New Jersey 08854-8042.

This book is printed on acid-free paper that meets the American National Standard for Permanence of Paper for Printed Library Materials.

Library of Congress Catalog Number: 99-24272
ISBN: 1-56000-400-2
Printed in the United States of America

Library of Congress Cataloging-in-Publication Data

Max Weber and Islam / edited by Toby E. Huff and Wolfgang Schluchter ; with an introduction by Toby E. Huff
    p. cm.
Includes bibliographical references and index.
ISBN 1-56000-400-2 (alk. paper)
    1. Weber, Max 1864–1920. 2. Sociology, Islamic. I. Huff, Toby E., 1942– . II. Schluchter, Wolfgang, 1938–
BP173.25.M39   1999
306.6'97'092—dc21
                                                  99-24272
                                                      CIP

Contents

Preface   vii

Introduction
Toby E. Huff   1

1. Hindrances to Modernity: Max Weber on Islam
   Wolfgang Schluchter   53

2. The Institutionalization of Early Islamic Societies
   Ira M. Lapidus   139

3. Aspects of Islamization: Weber's Observations on Islam Reconsidered
   Nehemia Levtzion   153

4. Islamization in Late Medieval Bengal: The Relevance of Max Weber
   Richard M. Eaton   163

5. Max Weber and the Patrimonial Empire in Islam: The Mughal Case
   Peter Hardy   183

6. Paradise or Hell? The Religious Doctrine of Election in Eighteenth and Nineteenth Century Islamic Fundamentalism and Protestant Calvinism
   Rudolph Peters   205

7. Weber and Islamic Reform
   Barbara D. Metcalf   217

8. Secularization, Weber, and Islam
   Francis Robinson   231

9. Weber, Islamic Law, and the Rise of Capitalism
   Patricia Crone   247

10. Weber and Islamic Sects
   Michael Cook — 273
11. Weber's Analysis of Islam and the Specific Pattern of Islamic Civilization
   S. N. Eisenstadt — 281

   Bibliography — 295

   Contributors — 317

   Index — 321

Preface

Beginning in 1979 Professor Wolfgang Schluchter of Heidelberg University began preparations for a series of high-level conferences focused on Max Weber's studies in the sociology of religion. The intent was to bring together a renowned panel of experts—biblical scholars, Hebraists, Sinologists, Indianologists, and Islamicists—to evaluate Weber's studies. These were to be masters of the specialized scholarly materials in the particular religious tradition in question, and individuals who had enough familiarity with Max Weber's writings to offer up-to-date assessments of Weber's early twentieth-century writings about the world religions. Each conference of experts was charged with offering new interpretations and critiques of Weber's wide-ranging and monumental thought that often delved into legal and economic history, theology, as well as the political history of the civilization in question.

The first of the volumes to appear (in German) was focused on Ancient Judaism.[1] The next conference of experts took up Weber's writings about China and the religious traditions of Taoism and Confucianism.[2] Following that a distinguished panel of scholars evaluated Weber's thought on Hinduism and Buddhism.[3] This was followed by a reassessment of Weber's thought on Ancient Christianity.[4] Next came the conference (June 1984) that sought to reconstruct and evaluate Weber's widely scattered comments on the sociology of Islam. The results of that conference form the basis of the present volume.[5]

Until now, none of these conference proceedings have been available to English-speaking readers. With this volume we bring to the English-speaking world the results of the conference proceedings focused on Weber's comments on Islam and the Muslim world. Each of the original authors was contacted in order to prepare this edition of the volume.[6] Most of the original essays have been newly revised to incorporate significant developments and new understandings of Islam that had appeared since the mid-eighties conference. Given the procession of world events that have transpired since the mid-1980s, it is evident that the topic of Islam and its place in the current geopolitical context, has grown in significance. Likewise, the effort to reassess Weber's early twentieth-century pioneering efforts to understand Islam from a sociological point of view is greatly overdue. As the reader will bear witness, some of the critiques of Weber's ideas in this volume display great subtlety as well as erudition in the quest to faithfully assess Weber's sometimes oblique, but always richly flavored, comments on Islam.

Toby E. Huff

Notes

1. Wolfgang Schluchter, ed., *Max Webers Studie über das antike Judentum. Interpretation und Kritik* (Frankfurt: Suhrkamp, 1981).
2. Wolfgang Schluchter, ed., *Max Webers Studie über das Konfuzianismus und Taoismus. Interpretation und Kritik* (Frankfurt: Suhrkamp, 1983).
3. Wolfgang Schluchter, ed., *Max Webers Studie über das Hinduismus und Buddhismus. Interpretation und Kritik* (Frankfurt: Suhrkamp, 1984).
4. Wolfgang Schluchter, ed., *Max Webers Sicht des antiken Christentums. Interpretation und Kritik* (Frankfurt: Suhrkamp, 1985).
5. Wolfgang Schluchter, ed., *Max Webers Sicht des Islams. Interpretation und Kritik* (Frankfurt: Suhrkamp, 1987). A sixth volume of critical and interpretive studies focused on Occidental Christianity was also published: Wolfgang Schluchter, ed., *Max Webers Sicht des okzidentalen Christentums. Interpretation und Kritik* (Frankfurt: Suhrkamp, 1988).
6. However, two authors, Maxime Rodinson and Ernest Gellner, died in the interim, and their papers have been omitted, though they are available in other places.

Introduction

Toby E. Huff

Those who have read broadly in Max Weber's voluminous writings and understood his larger purpose have grasped the fact that he worked on a canvas much larger than the issue of "the Protestant ethic and the spirit of capitalism."[1] It is true, of course, that it was precisely to test certain implications of the relationship between *economic ethics* and *religious* orientations that Weber moved into comparative cross-cultural, historical, and civilizational frames of reference. By moving in that direction, Weber sought to establish whether or not there were any other *world religions* like Christianity, which had given birth to such unrelenting pursuit of economic rationalism which was linked to the rise of modern capitalism in the West. However, in moving to this enlarged conception of his problematic, Weber came to see his problem as one which had to account for the general emergence of Western rationalism as a whole. In that broader conception, Weber postulated that the West had not only been unique in generating modern capitalism, but also modern science, and a host of related cultural phenomena, such as modern bureaucracy, the Western legal system, and a wide range of peculiarly rationalized cultural forms in art, architecture, and music. In this connection, Weber's monograph translated as *The Social and Rational Foundations of Music*[2] merits special attention. For as Wolfgang Schluchter notes below, Weber's realization that art and music, too, were highly influenced by scientific and technological principles, was for him a major breakthrough. This realization that so-called "nonrational" forms of cultural creativity had been shaped by the Western forces of rationalism forced him to recognize that *all* forms of cultural development in the West, not just economic, are under the grip of Western *rationalism*. In the scholarly literature this tortured term, rationalism, remains controversial and I shall have something more to say about it later. For now I would simple say that Weber uses the term "rationalism" to include a variety of mental operations that serve to make symbolic systems as well as human action more systematic, logically ordered, and methodically controlled.

In so formulating the problem, Weber enlarged his problematic to focus on the types of rationalism as well as the forms of *rationalization* that unfolded in the peculiar developmental history of the West. But as he did this, he realized that the real test of the significance of such cultural development—economic, legal, political, scientific, technological, and artistic—could only be appreciated if his research agenda included both *comparative* and *historical* frames of reference. Accordingly, within a few short years his attention had broadened still further to encompass a great range of cultural developments in each of the major civilizations that were dominated by the six great world religions: Confucianism and Taoism (taken as one complex), Hinduism and Buddhism, Ancient Judaism, Christianity, and Islam. This vastly expanded canvas of cultural studies was to be the domain within which Weber would carry out his studies in the sociology of religion, a sociology and typology of rationalism, the sociology of law, as well as a sociology of economic ethics. To say the least, this was a daunting undertaking that only someone of Weber's training and genius would dare to undertake. The remarkable thing is that he did in fact carry out a major part of this plan, by writing monographs and specialized studies on all but the last of these civilizational contexts, that is, Islam. Considering the fact that Weber died at the early age of fifty-eight, it is little short of miraculous that he produced the studies that he did. At Weber's death, his writings on Islam were little more than scattered comments sprinkled throughout his monographs on law, religion, and economic organization.[3] But it is fair to say that, given the intellectual preparations and larger framework of analysis that I sketched out above, and which stood behind Weber's preliminary work on Islam, his scattered comments on this topic have taken on far greater significance than would otherwise be the case.

Before I attempt to focus on the larger developmental issues which are at the center of Weber's comparative focus on Islam, it is useful to briefly recall some essentials of the Islamic faith and its early pattern of institutionalization.

Islam and Islamization

As a religious orientation, Islam is centered around prayer five times daily. In many countries around the world, the call to prayer in the early morning, noontime and evening is still announced from the minaret or rooftop of the mosque by the muezzin, who now has the electronic amplification of a loud speaker. This simple act of five times repeated daily prayer gives the Muslim community a greatly enhanced cohesiveness unlike any other world religion.

In so far as ritual practice is concerned, Muslims attend to the so-called five pillars: (1) prayer five times daily; (2) repetition of the *shahada*, that is, the pledge by the believer that "there is no God but God, and Muhammad is his messenger"; (3) fasting during the daylight hours of the month of Ramadan; (4) giving of alms to the poor (*zakat*, "poor tax"); and (5) pilgrimage (*hajj*) to Mecca once during the believer's life time if at all possible. In addition to these beliefs, Muslims believe that the Quran is the actual speech and direct word of God, and that it contains the eternal and unchanging truth for this life and the next.

Insofar as legal prescriptions are concerned, Muslims refer to the *shari'a*, sacred law, or the religious knowledge needed to guide one in order to "pass the reckoning on judgment day."[4] This, however, is composed of the Quran on the one hand, and the collected sayings (*hadiths*) of the Prophet Muhammad, on the other. This originally oral tradition which was later written down, is also know as the *sunna*—the normative tradition of the Prophet and his early followers. Over the centuries, the interpretative structure built up around this body of writings came to form a very complex set of revelations and understandings. Not surprisingly, different interpretations of various legal prescriptions that appear in the Quran, as well as differing interpretations of the implications of the sayings attributed to Muhammad, coalesced around four "schools of law." These "schools" were named after the four great men who led them: al-Shafi'i (d. 820), Ibn Malik (d. 795), Abu Hanafa (d. 767), and Ahmad Hanbal (d. 855). Hence we get such cognomens as Shafi'i, Maliki, Hanafi, and Hanbali to refer to the contrasting schools of legal interpretation in Sunni Islam.

The major schism in Islam came with the death of Ali, the cousin and son-in-law of Muhammad, who was assassinated in 661. With that event, a faction was formed, the "followers of Ali," who believe that Ali was the rightful successor to the Prophet, and was unjustly deprived of his stewardship as caliph—successor to the Prophet. This faction is called the Shi'a or Shi'ites, which continues to the present with its largest block of followers in Iran. This factional dispute also marks the end of the spiritually defined "Golden Age" of the "Four

Rightly Guided Caliphs," to which many Muslims look back with wistful longing. But that conception of the "Golden Age" of Islam must be contrasted with the intellectually more creative period of philosophical and scientific efflorescence that lasted from about 800 to 1200 C.E.

By the end of the ninth century C.E., it is generally said, the task of legal interpretation had reached completion and there was a "closing of the gates of independent reasoning" (*ijtihad*). That is, there was a halt to the introduction of new legal *principles* and new legal *structures*, but not an end to the issuing of legal opinions (*fatwas*).[5]

It should also be noted that the Islamic legal specialists were persistent in their specification of the sources or *roots of law* (the *usul al-fiqh*), which required designating the *sources* of law (i.e., the Quran and the *hadiths*), and the *modes of reasoning* by which one arrived at new legal opinions (*fatwas*). On the one hand, the early jurists stipulated that there must be a consensus (*ijma*) of the scholars within the community on any legal point, though in practice this was very difficult to achieve. On the other, it was insisted, especially by the ninth century legist al-Shafi'i, that the only legitimate mode of reasoning for arriving at new legal insights for a particular situation where there was no preceding guidance, was the use of "analogy" (*qiyas*). But the reader should note that this is not the analogy used by Common Law lawyers, but rather a much narrower mechanism that relies upon an explicit analogy drawn from the Quran itself, or possibly, from a saying of the Prophet.[6] Those who specialized in this kind of expert legal knowledge were called *fuqaha*, legal scholars, while the general term for those who took it upon themselves to learn everything they could about Islam, its history, sacred book, and ritual were known as the *'ulama'*, the religious scholars.

It cannot be too strongly stressed that the central structure of Islamic thought is based on jurisprudence (*fiqh*). Law in the Islamic world is the sustaining source providing the believer with guidance for every aspect of daily life. Consequently, it is to law not theology that Muslims are expected to turn in times of doubt.

It is apparent that such a complex religious, legal, and social system could not come about overnight but evolved over a number of centuries. That is, the intellectual and political structure of Islam arose over a period of several centuries and entailed the assimilation of local populations and the creation of new political and religious structures, along with distinct interest groups that defined and safeguarded those political and religious institutions. It is appropriate, therefore, to refer to the process of *Islamizing* Middle Eastern culture as a special case of *institutionalizing* a new religious faith.

This is the approach taken by Ira Lapidus in his chapter in this book. For him Islam is at once a religious vision, a congeries of religious elites who espouse and safeguard that faith, and a sociopolitical system. His paper sketches the broad outlines of that Islamization process whereby the Middle East was transformed into a new kind of society and civilization, that is, the Islamic civilization. He stresses in particular the role of the religious scholars (*'ulama'*), the sufi mystics, as well as the political leaders, all of whom championed Islam on the local level, in villages, in cities, and in the newly formed Islamic state. Each of these elites, he writes,

> attempted to insinuate Islamic values and identities into an already complex civilization and to reshape that civilization in accord with their own ethos and interests. Thus the caliphs acting at the state level attempted to transform the existing imperial institutions into what we shall call Islamic states. The *'ulama'*...and the sufis acting upon the masses of the population attempted to form Islamic communal or sectarian associations, and to integrate Islamic symbols and identities into existing collectivities.[7]

By this means religious scholars (*'ulama'*) and mystically inclined spiritual adepts emerged who sought to spread the Islamic message to the unlettered believers by instructing them in proper religious conduct. Likewise the political leaders, especially the caliphs and amirs who thought of themselves as "the commanders of the faithful" sought to create a political structure that preserved and projected Islamic ideals throughout the new Islamic domains. Likewise in his reconstruction of the "basic premises" of Islamic civilization, S. N. Eisenstadt suggests that the schools of law (dominated by the religious scholars), the Sufi orders and the *waqfs* (pious endowments), constituted a nascent "public sphere" of autonomy which promoted a measure of "pluralism" within Islamic societies.[8] From the present writer's point of view this is an overstatement of the possibilities for public dialogue in Muslim societies.[9]

From this point of view, Professor Lapidus avers, Islam was not a "warrior" religion. But as we see from the writings of a number of contributors to this volume, correcting Weber's view on this matter is no easy task.

If one considers what is often called the "formative period" of Islam, its first 150 years extending from the time of Muhammad (ca. 622) to about 800 C.E., it is clear that the early history of Islam, including the many military operations carried out by the Prophet and his followers leading to the conquest of Mecca, was marked by innumerable military battles commemorated in Muslim histories. Similarly, it is evident that Islam expanded by military conquest out of the Arabian peninsula, west across Egypt to Morocco, and then north across the straits of Gibraltar to Spain, into southern France, as well as north across Iraq and Iran to Turkey.

In addition to these considerations there is the matter of military slaves, "the slaves on horses," to use Patricia Crone's phrase, who were systematically recruited by various Muslim rulers into the service of Islam and the caliphate. As Professor Crone points out elsewhere,[10] during the Umayyad dynasty (661–750) these slaves on horse back were kept in garrison cities around the empire and were prohibited from engaging in agriculture while they extracted taxes from the local population.

In any event, the systematic use of slave soldiers appears to have persisted from the ninth to the nineteenth century throughout the central heartlands of the Muslim world.[11] The Mamluk rulership (1250–1517) was but the product of this system, as its leaders were former slaves who usurped political power and took control in Egypt.

In the fifteenth century, the pattern of military conquest was renewed by the Ottoman Turks. The conquest of Constantinople in 1453 was obviously the result of a massive military effort on the part of the Ottomans. Without that military leadership it seems unlikely that Islam would have spread across the Bosphorus straits and up the Adriatic coast, gained strongholds throughout the Balkans, and arrived on the doorstep of Vienna in 1683. But conversion of the local population to Islam was a complex matter.

For conversion was not instantaneous, nor was it forcibly accomplished "by the sword" as popular imagery used to have it. Indeed, as Nehemia Levtzion points out in his chapter, during the early Umayyad dynasty the Arab conquerors "discouraged conversion of the local population...because it wanted to keep them as tax-paying subjects."[12] Accordingly Professor Levtzion affirms Weber's judgment that the continuation of the non-Muslims within the Muslim community was (quoting Weber), "considered desirable because of the financial contribution they could make."[13]

This insight, however, is tied to Weber's image of Islam and its putative method of violent propagation. While Weber no doubt shared the Christian view that religious conversion ought to be a deeply felt religious awakening, he was aware that the Islamic view was significantly different, placing more weight on the performance of ritual than on heartfelt conformity to theological doctrine. This follows from the legalistic approach that Islam took which places all human acts into one of five categories: required, encouraged, permissible, discouraged, or forbidden.

Consequently Levtzion points out in this connection that Weber placed too much stress on "the violent propagation of the true Prophecy." Yet, he continues, "Weber was right that the holy war was not directed for the purpose of conversion." The purpose of *jihad* was the universal spread of Islamic domination. In that respect its purpose was political and territorial not directed toward conversion.[14]

On a doctrinal and psychological level, the idea of *jihad*, of unrelenting struggle in the service of the faith was (and is) a religious duty, never to be forgotten in the history of Islam.[15] Those who die in the service of the faith were and still are considered martyrs with automatic admission to paradise. The idea of striving in the service of the faith is deeply and ambiguously built into the language of Islam. For example, the *mujtahid,* is the religious scholar who "strives" to understand the faith of Islam and to render correct legal decisions, using *ijtihad* (intellectual effort), when called upon to do so.[16] On the other hand, the *mujahideen* ("warriors," most recently called "freedom fighters" in the Afghan situation) are those who struggle in the defense of the faith by undertaking some mission, usually one of combat. Both are granted unquestioned admission to paradise and both words are derived from the Arabic word *jihad*, to struggle. The ambiguity of Islam's identity in this regard is deeply rooted in its fundamental religio-philosophical commitments.

In a word, even if we consider only the early formative period of Islamic history, its first 150 years, the historical record shows that it was spread as a political system by military means throughout a vast area of what has come to be recognized as the central lands of Islam. This occurred in a fashion unlike the pattern of any other world religion. This is not to suggest that we ought to accept Weber's characterization of it as a warrior religion, but only to remind ourselves that Weber's conception was not without historical evidence and that the self-identity of Islam remains to this day highly contested with groups, large and small, assembled under the banner of *jihad* throughout the Middle East and the Indian subcontinent.[17]

By the end of the ninth century (ca. 250 A.H.), the *'ulama'* had become the unquestioned architects of Islamic thought, and were able to exert considerable force on rulers who deviated from Islamic ideals.

But they had no legal power apart from their religious legitimation to call wayward political leaders to account (as S. N. Eisenstadt notes in his paper). Professor Lapidus's solution to this dilemma of divergent points of view within Islam is to say that Islam "is not a single religion in a single milieu but a world civilization representing a wide range of religious views and social ethics."[18]

Moreover, the story of Islam's spread throughout the world has to be balanced by the equally significant fact that during the early spread of Islam in the Middle East, Muslim rulers granted tolerance to all "peoples of the book," that is to Jews and Christians, though of course they had to pay a nonbeliever's (*dhimmi*) poll tax (*jizya*) which granted them protection. Likewise, over the centuries Islam was spread by many different groups, Sufis, religious scholars, and traders as well as warriors. At this point the issue becomes one of conversion: when and how did conversion to Islam come about. This is a subject in need of much greater study. From the scattered studies of conversion that do exit, perhaps all one can say is that the process of conversion was long and drawn out in the various areas of Islamic domination. In general the conversion process seems not to have run its course and reached something like a majority until somewhere between the middle of the tenth and the beginning of the twelfth century.[19] Professor Levtzion offers his opinion that in the new Islamic empire the number of Muslims did not equal the number of non-Muslims until "the middle of the tenth century, i.e., three full centuries after conquest."[20]

For readers of this volume, the essay by Richard Eaton on the rise of Islam in Bengal, that far eastern province of India (now part of Bangladesh), provides a fascinating contrast and set of insights into the Islamization of a distant place in the later medieval period. Professor Eaton tells us that in Bengal, Islam was propagated by charismatic individuals dedicated to Islam who spread their faith among rural peasant cultivators. Here there was no coercion but a quiet emulation of a pious ideal. In addition, this charismatic authority soon followed the path of "routinization" as Weber conceived it. The provision of land grants to the charismatic individuals (on behalf of the Mughal rulers) led to the emergence of religiously identified communities, which in later generations resulted in strictly political leadership on both the local and regional levels by *descendants* of the original charismatic leaders. This was followed by the transformation of the charismatic authority into bureaucratic domination.

Viewed from this longer perspective, it is apparent that Islam was spread around the world by many different impulses and groups, including landholders and long-distance traders.

In the chapter by Peter Hardy, we see another aspect of the institutionalization of Islamic rulership under the Mughals of India. Here the use of the organizational techniques of patrimonialism seen fully evident. According to Hardy "the intensely personal, man-to-man character of allegiance and the absence of any formal limit to, or condition on that allegiance"[21] were in full flower among the Mughals throughout the rise, consolidation, and decline of Mughal rule. "Once a patrimonial servant or client has acknowledged a master or a patron, then all the former's time and energy is to be devoted to service" so that "other worldly loyalties, to kin and to ethnic group" are completely set aside.[22] Thus the pattern of patrimonial domination in Mughal India confirms Weber's references to the existence of patrimonialism in the Muslim world.

Law, Economy, and Development

As I noted earlier, in the Islamic world the dominating intellectual (and social) structure was law, not theology. Consequently, Max Weber's writings in the sociology of law bear an inordinate weight in any assessment of Weber's understanding of Islam. From a Weberian point of view the great question of why modern capitalism arose in the West and not elsewhere was always a *multi*-factor problem. It has often been broken down into a *motivational* component and an *institutional* component, and Wolfgang Schluchter has referred to a set of "internal" and "external factors."[23] The domain of law obviously belongs to the *institutional* side of the equation. Under some conditions the legal and institutional arrangements may serve to facilitate or even *promote* capitalist activity as some economists would argue.[24] However, from a Weberian point of view, continuous rational economic action must be seen as highly problematic, needing some additional motivational element. Having discovered an intrinsic connection between the various forms of ascetic Protestantism and enhanced economic activity, above all the launching of modern capitalism, Weber wanted to know whether or not any of the other world religions had given rise to *economic ethics* analogous to the innerworldly asceticism of Protestantism. Accordingly he proposed to treat the problem comprehensively under the heading of "the economic ethics of the world religions." That is, he deliberately sought evidence that any of the other world religions generated something analogous to the Protestant asceticism that contained a world-transforming inner worldly impetus.

For present purposes I consider the discussion of Weber's analysis of law and its relationship to economic activity first, and then the motivational issues that are also discussed by contributors to this volume.

Weber's *Rechtssoziologie* is undoubtedly the most complex and daunting of any of his writings. Although Weber was trained as a lawyer, it seems unlikely that that training would have taken him so deeply into the comparative sociology of law as he went. For he explores not only the medieval and modern development of European law (Roman law, Canon law, Civil Law, and Common Law), but also the comparative development of law in Judaism, India, China, and Islam. But here as in Weber's comments on Islam generally, Weber's discussion of Islamic law is less than concerted, except for three specific pages on that subject.[25]

However, as Patricia Crone points out in her chapter on this subject, Weber's *Rechtssoziologie* was "formulated as a contribution to the problem of Western 'rationalism.'" But Crone thinks this formulation of the problem was a major mistake on Weber's part, since she believes that the concept of rationalism "should be abandoned."[26] This is not the first time such a recommendation has been offered, and it may be well to remind ourselves again of the larger civilizational context of Weber's problem.

As noted earlier, Weber was thoroughly convinced that a complex set of cultural phenomena, in addition to the appearance of modern capitalism, had arisen only in the West. For him, these developments in law, science, politics and political administration, art and music represented *progressive* developments. They were the outcome of a long evolutionary process, but which did not have equivalents in the older civilizations of India and China.

Clearly something very startling and unique occurred in the West and not elsewhere: we now know that from about the eighth to the beginning of the fourteenth century C.E., the Arab-Muslim world had the most advanced science of any civilization in the world, including China. In the field of astronomy, where the great theoretical breakthrough to modern science is usually located, the planetary models of the Damascene astronomer and timekeeper (*muwaqqit*) Ibn al-Shatir (d. 1375) and those of Copernicus were virtually identical, with only minor differences in some parameters, though the Arab models remained geocentric. Nor were the Arabs lacking in any technical or mathematical skills. In fact, their highly developed skills in trigonometry, which the Chinese lacked, resulted in the establishment of a Muslim bureau of astronomy in Peking in the thirteenth century. Not only that, they had pioneered several different experimental traditions. In a word, the Arab-Muslim world was positioned on the forward edge of one of the greatest intellectual movements ever but did not make the great leap from "the closed world to the infinite universe."[27]

Consequently, in his introduction to the *Collected Essays in the Sociology of Religion* (which was prefaced to *The Protestant Ethic and the Spirit of Capitalism* by Talcott Parsons), Weber wondered out loud: "Why did not the scientific, the artistic, the political, or the economic development there enter upon that path of rationalization which is peculiar to the Occident?"[28] Carrying the argument a little further, Weber suggested that "in all the above cases it is a question of the peculiar rationalism of Western culture"[29] which is at issue. "It is hence our first concern to work out and to explain genetically the special peculiarity of Occidental rationalism, and within this field that of the modern Occidental form."[30] Weber recognized at the outset that "very different things" would be meant by this term, "rationalism," and that social, legal, and economic processes could be "rationalized," that is, systematically developed, according to very different criteria. According to Weber,

> There is, for example, rationalization of mystical contemplation...just as much as there are rationalizations of economic life, of technique, of scientific research, of military training, of law and administration. Furthermore, each one of these fields may be rationalized from many different ultimate points of view and toward many different ultimate ends, and what is rational from one point of view may be irrational from another. Hence rationalizations of the most varied character have existed in various departments of life in all civilizations.[31]

Crone grants that the term "rationality" considered in these many broad domains entails "being rule-bound, regular, systematic, logical, calculating, purposive, controlled by the intellect," etc.,[32] but she finds it difficult to see all these processes as subsets of a general process of rationalization. The point is, however, that Weber was pointing to a uniquely progressive development of *thought* and *action* that entailed systematic *self*-control as well as methodical and systematic use of a variety of logical operations that clearly are intended to arrive at more accurate and more efficient outcomes. Weber was far from believing that the final outcome of these processes was ideal from any point of view. As Rogers Brubaker put it, "Rationalization...is far from automatically promoting human welfare [but] is a morally and politically problematic development."³³ It remains for us to come up with a better term than "rationalization" to cover all the "departments of culture" in which Weber saw these progressive movements occurring if we dissent from his conceptual apparatus.³⁴

In the specific case of law, Weber's typology for classifying legal systems was based on two criteria: the degree of "rationality" of the system, and the degree of its "formality." These two terms are so intermeshed, however, that it is virtually impossible to discuss one without the other. Nevertheless, it can be said that a legal system is "rational" to the degree that all of its duly recognized rules form a logically consistent whole, and that legal decisions are logically derived "applications" of those uniform and universalistic rules. Likewise, *law-finding* is "rational" to the degree that the process is guided by the intellect, as opposed to the emotions or mystical impulses. "Legal rationality" could either be "formally rational" in which logical considerations are paramount, or law could be "substantively rational," in which case rules and laws are chosen to maximize a set of substantive values, values which are external to law itself.³⁵ Professor Crone, however, finds Weber's typology of law based on formal versus substantive rationality inadequate.

Whether or not one retains Weber's typology of law, it is evident, Crone affirms, that "Islamic law is less systematic"³⁶ than European law, especially less systematic than the Pandectist tradition of civil law that Weber viewed as most "formally" rational. This legal tradition attempted to make all legal norms into a completely uniform and "gapless" system of rules and norms.³⁷

The question is, however, how do we define the kind of rationality that motivated the architects of Islamic law? Crone does not pursue this issue since she has dismissed all concern with the idea of rationality. But clearly the Islamic *fuqaha* (legists) were motivated (in Weber's terminology) by *substantive* considerations. They sought to create a system of law that maximized the consistency between the ethical injunctions of the Quran, the sayings of Muhammad (the *sunna*) and the actual *fatwas* issued by individual religious specialists in their day-to-day rulings. In addition, as noted earlier, they specified precisely the modes of logic, that is, analogy (*qiyas*), not personal opinion or individual discretion (*istihsan*), etc., which were to be used in the fashioning of *fiqh*, the legal science of religious knowledge.³⁸ Accordingly, there is good reason to apply the term "rational" to Islamic law: those who designed its construction and interpretation had strong ideals in mind according to which they shaped it. It was clearly *substantively* rational, at the same time that it ruled out other legal possibilities. In a word, though Weber's frequent use of the term "*qadi* justice" gives the impression that Islamic law was irrational in development and application, it followed its own rules of development that were generally recognized by specialists in Islamic law. This was especially so after the great synthesizing work of al-Shafi'i in the early ninth century. But it is true, as Crone points out, that Islamic law did not develop a variety of legal ideas and structures "simply because nobody seems to have thought of them"[39] (on which more below).

Professor Crone usefully points out that the term "*qadi* justice" was not invented by Weber but by another legal scholar (R. Schmidt), and that Weber did not use this term exclusively for Islamic law. For example, Weber referred to the procedures of the justices of the peace in the common law system as "qadi justice."[40]

Nevertheless, it must be said that the great Islamic jurists believed that the *shari'a* (the Quran and the *sunna*) had been given incorruptibly once and for all, and that the revelation and example of their Prophet was the unchanging legal foundation for Islamic civilization. Of course it had to be applied and adapted to new circumstances, but the Quran (in conjunction with the *sunna*) was said to contain *all* the principles and precepts for resolving every conceivable situation to be faced by the Muslim community. This stands in contrast to the case of European law, where, by the medieval period, there was a strong sense that law and society were *evolving*. As Harold J. Berman put it, in the twelfth and thirteenth centuries,

> there first developed the modern Western belief in the autonomy of law, its professional character, its integrity both as a system of institutions and as a body of learning, its capacity for growth over generations and centuries, its conscious historicity, and its ultimate supremacy over political authorities.[41]

Law and Capitalism

But let us turn to the issue of Islam and capitalism. It was evident to Weber, as it is to all participants in a modern economy, that there is a need for "a certain degree of legal rationalization," just as there was a need for a minimum of economic activity in order for modern capitalism to arise in the first place. As Patricia Crone puts it, the bourgeoisie need "a rational, that is, calculable law" for the full flowering of capitalist activity.[42] It is also suggested that "the more systematic the law, the more calculable it will be."[43] Just how such presumably greater calculability is related to economic action is not transparent. Crone debates the putative greater calculability of a legal outcome in a *formally* rational legal system such as the European civil law, but she seems to suggest that a *case law* (a "casuistically formulated") system would be more predictable than one based strictly on logical formality.

Crone argues, however, that Weber's assumption of greater calculability brought about by formal legal rationality is just plain wrong. Insofar as Weber argued that there was an inherent affinity between a formally rationalized legal system and the rise of capitalism, Crone points to the fact that English common law was less formally rational (according to Weber's account) than European civil law, but modern capitalism first appeared in England. This interpretation of the economic utility of common law versus civil law with respect to the rise of modern capitalism has been much debated, and one suspects that the debate will continue. Indeed, Professor Crone admits that another interpretation of Weber's views on this matter could be constructed, and indeed has. Sally Ewing, for example, has suggested that Weber did indeed specify what was needed for the rise of capitalism in England (a formal justice system coupled with the unfettered *freedom of contract* guaranteeing bourgeois rights), and that Weber's comments in general do not suggest that he actually thought the civil system more congenial to capitalism.[44] In addition, Harold Berman extended Ewing's commentary by suggesting that both she and Weber "neglected to say, that, the doctrine of precedent which was developed in England and the United States in the seventeenth through nineteenth centuries probably produced *more* [original emphasis] calculability than the system of codes and commentaries—the *Pandektenrecht*—of the Continental jurists."[45]

The point of the discussion, however, ought to focus on the reasons why modern capitalism did not arise in the Islamic world. While one could say that some Islamic laws supportive of "bourgeois interests" do exit and assisted capitalist activity, the scale appears to be weighted in favor of the negative elements inhibiting modern capitalism. In enumerating these positive and negative elements, Crone suggests that Islamic law created a uniform set of economic units, the principle of full ownership, and the distinction between ownership and possession: all positive elements for capitalist activity. On the countervailing side of the scale, however, one finds the following:

> the law is unconducive to capitalism in that it is highly protective. There is no freedom of contract, specifically no freedom to engage in transactions involving

risk or other features enabling one party to extract unearned profit from another...there was neither aleatory nor promissory contracts, no contracts involving things uncertain, unidentified, or unknown, no sale of future, unseen, unspecified goods except in so far as concessions were made to practice, and no interest except in so far as the prohibition could be circumvented.[46]

Crone also notes that the attitude towards "negotiable instruments and assignments to contractual rights" was restrictive. More worrisome still is the absence of certain enabling juridical functions, that is, "no damages, no corporations and no juristic persons."[47] Taken together these prohibitions and restrictions give the appearance of a formidable straight jacket placed over economy activity, especially entrepreneurship. Without freedom of contract and indeed the possibility of embarking upon highly risky enterprises such as all great innovative economic ventures entail, along with the absence of a juristic person in the form of legally autonomous *corporations*, it is difficult to see how *modern* capitalism could have arisen in the Muslim world.

Crone asserts, nevertheless, that "these restrictive rules clearly did not inhibit economic activity in medieval times." But the issue is not whether premodern capitalist economic activity existed, nor even whether it achieved high levels in the Islamic world, but whether or not Islamic law and its administration could support the development of *modern* capitalism, with all its requirements for cash flows, requisite legal autonomy, stable markets and currencies, and returns on investments through regularized interest payments. Studies in the United States, for example, over the past half century, suggest very high rates of business failure over periods of five years.[48] Eliminating risk in business as Islamic law does is not a recipe for facilitating modern capitalist enterpreneurship.

This is a question not only for the medieval and early modern periods, but for contemporary Islam as well. With the absence of an Islamic "Hong Kong," "Singapore," "Taiwan" or "Japan," the question of just what it is in Muslim societies that has so impeded economic growth continues to puzzle not just the disinterested reader, but Muslims around the world who suffer from the results of low levels of per capita income, high levels of poverty, illiteracy, and so on.[49] One thing is evident: those Muslim countries (both with and without massive oil reserves) which seek to embark upon the path of economic development have had to jettison virtually all aspects of Islamic law that relate to business and commercial activities, notwithstanding calls for adopting principles of "Islamic Banking." This is especially true of those countries which now show promise of economic development such as Malaysia and Indonesia but also Egypt, Tunisia and Turkey. The reform of Islamic law for all commercial and public administrative purposes was carried out beginning in the late ninteenth century and accelerated after World War II.[50]

At this point Professor Crone attempts to reformulate Weber's problematic, having consigned his concept of "rationality" to the "dustbin." But she concedes that behind Weber's great effort there is a "genuine vision" about the evolution of modern societies and civilization.

In her reformulation, the progressive development of Europe, leading to what all would agree is some kind of "modernity," Professor Crone declares that Europe was a failure: "Europe was trying to be traditional according to *three* quite different models and so failed in the attempt altogether."[51] This conclusion rests on the assumption that there is a three (or four) stage model of evolutionary development that characterizes the West uniquely, and according to Professor Crone, negatively, because only the West went down this path while the rest of the world did not. According to Crone, this evolutionary model evolved through various stages in which rulers and priests arose and joined together as the new dominant elite. These gave birth to (1) the emergence of a state apparatus which assigned the duties of internal and external control to rulers; (2) the emergence of organized religion and its functionaries; and (3) the emergence of the organization of production in the hands of specialists, thereby giving birth to industrial society. This last stage is said to be conjoined with the emergence of organized science (a fourth stage). Each class of specialists/rulers was accompanied by the invention of a specialized institution, namely, the state, church, factory, and university.[52] It is only through an immense Nietzschean "transvaluation of values" that one can read these developments as a "failure." Conversely, it is difficult to understand why, from this vantage point, the Arab-Muslims, who where clearly on the path of modern scientific development and ahead of the West until the fourteenth century, should withdraw from the effort and this should be seen as a "success."[53] In any event, Crone places considerable weight on the influence of the state in the historical development process and declares that Weber's idea of "rationality" is but the "final outcome of that process which began with the emergence of the state."[54] In the end, according to Crone,

> the modern world is no more rational, rule-bound, calculating, purposive (let alone reasonable) than any other, but the purpose is now determined from *within* the

activity in question, not from the vantage point of some overall aim: science must progress even if it is going to blow us up.[55]

This, then, is another version of Weber's conception of the "disenchantment of the world," and the pervasive development of humankind in a world gone "cold, heartless, bureaucratized and meaningless."[56] Crone has dismissed Weber's intellectual framework but has taken on all of his pessimism: "the world...remains as rational and disenchanted as Weber perceived it to be."[57]

* * *

Let us turn to the "internal" motivational side of the problem of capitalist activity. In his paper on "Islam and Fundamentalism," Rudolph Peters offers some important insights into the relationship between Islamic fundamentalism, charismatic leadership, and worldly asceticism. At the outset he notes that the term "fundamentalism" is perhaps not the best for describing the Islamic situation, but he suggests that if a form of "scripturalism and rejection of historical criticism" are integral parts of Christian fundamentalism, then Islamic fundamentalism shares these characteristics along with others.

Focusing mainly on eighteenth and nineteenth century fundamentalist movements, Peters suggests that these "are typically missionary movements" whose mission is to "spread and implement" their vision, since they are committed "to chang[ing] the world to make it conform to their ideals based on *sunna* [the tradition of the Prophet] and *tawhid* [the unity of God]."[58] Such movements are "missionary" movements because they take seriously the traditional Islamic injunction to do "what is reputable and forbid what is disreputable"[59]—ideas that remain highly contested in the Muslim world today.

According to his analysis, these movements "promoted inner worldly asceticism, rationalism, and austerity."[60] They incorporated a unique element of rationalism in that they insisted on their right to exercise *ijtihad*, that is original interpretation of the Quran and *sunna*, instead of obeisance to tradition (*taqlid*). There was also a measure of egalitarianism since they believed that all reasonably intelligent individuals could undertake this intellectual mission.

Secondly, Peters sees a doctrinal similarity in the belief (held by both Muslims and Calvinists) in an inscrutable transcendent God, one who also predestined all things. Peters notes that the question of freewill versus determinism is not resolved in Islam. In the citation that he uses from the work of Ibn Taymiyya (d. 1328), *both* God and man are responsible for man's acts: on the one hand, a sura from the Quran says that "No affliction befalls on the earth or on yourselves but it is in [the] Book, before We create it" (57:32); while Taymiyya says "that men act in reality, whereas God creates their deeds."[61] This phrasing is almost identical to that of al-Ash'ari, the ninth century theologian who solidified so-called Islamic "occasionalism"—the doctrine that God controls all events, at every moment.[62] But whereas the Muslim is "reasonably certain of his ultimate salvation"[63] he does not experience the anguish of the Calvinist. The latter, on the other hand, is "enjoined to act as if he were elected,...not to resign himself passively to his fate."[64] So while it may be said that the Muslim committed to such fundamentalist movements are enjoined to "act ethically" in the service of the faith, it seems doubtful that it can be said that such motivation is converted into an inner worldly asceticism of diligent hardwork, serving to transform the world, "for the greater glory of god" as the Calvinist was inclined to do. Likewise, recalling the institutional context of Islamic law outlined in Crone's work discussed above, it seems highly unlikely that such religious motivation would be sufficient to overcome all the institutional impediments blocking the rise of *modern* capitalism. Peters concludes that there were many doctrinal parallels between Islamic fundamentalism and Calvinism, though "it is true, they did not exit in exactly the same form or [to] the same degree."[65] But let us turn to the broader issues of reform and revivalism in Islam.

Reform and Revivalism

From the eighteenth century to the present the Muslim world has experienced a variety of reform and revivalist movements. There have been indigenous efforts to turn particular Muslim countries in a secular direction, ones that sought to incorporate what Muslim intellectuals and political leaders took to be positive elements in the modernist model of the West. Similarly, there have been many Muslim movements devoted to reforming society, hoping to reorganize particular states and polities around a more rigorist interpretation of the teachings of the sacred sources of Islam. Although it may be said that all of these movements arose in a broader context that was defined by the presence of Western powers, the degree to which these movements have borrowed intentionally from the West is not so evident.

In her chapter on "Weber and Islamic Reform," Barbara Metcalf gives us both an overview of the thrust of several reformist movements and a more detailed account of a particular Islamic reformist group, the Deobandi of northern India. In doing so she adds more dimensions to our understanding of Weber's problematic and the question of the relationship between Islam, innerworldly asceticism, and economic ethics.

The Deobandi movement, named after the city of that name, emerged in northern India in the 1860s, and in Barbara Metcalf's account, is but one "of many broadly similar reformist, scripturalist movements" which arose in various Muslims societies over the last two hundred years. One document she analyses from this group is called "The Jewelry of Paradise," which contains an allusion to the rewards of heaven granted to those of stalwart faith and good deeds. Though it was written for female readers, it was also read by others. What seems remarkable about this document is the appearance of so many elements that resonate as "puritan" injunctions. These include injunctions to the believer to lead an active and vigorous life, to treat household duties with efficiency and spiritual cultivation, to exercise thrift, to arise early in the morning, to avoid idleness, in short, to follow a frugal, sober, and disciplined life.[66] Similarly, the believer is enjoined to avoid ostentation, habitual intake of fine food and drink, while it encourages scrupulosity in the acquisition of wealth.

Whether or not one sees this as a possible analog to the Protestant ethic, Professor Metcalf stresses the rootedness of this reformist movement in religious doctrine. It created "a fellowship of believers, each enjoined to take individual responsibility, guided by the learned and wise, in living what can only be called a godly, righteous and sober life, characterized by frugality and hard work."[67] The "profit" to be gotten from such a life was salvation in the afterlife, not mundane possessions of this world. At the same time, Metcalf observes that this new religious ethic "served well the more mobile and politically integrated population"[68] that was then emerging in cities of the region, not in rural areas. But in her view this was no accommodative reaction, but a genuine, deeply felt response to the disparities of the world and the felt need to reform it.

Considering the many similar reformist groups of southeast Asia and Africa that have been recently documented, Metcalf sees three common traits: (1) the leaders were drawn from the classical academies and Sufi brotherhoods; (2) the groups "seek invariably to redress some injustice in the world"; and (3) among Sunni movements since the time of the great medieval reformer, Ibn Taymiyya (d. 1328), reformers have focused on "the corruption of the true faith." Consequently she argues that it is "misleading to conclude that the reformist teachings were even implicitly supportive of an accommodation to capitalism."[69]

In the pages that follow, Metcalf reviews the development of these movements, such as the Wahhabis of Saudi Arabia, the Padri of Indonesia, the Fulani of West Africa, and others. In all these movements, she see movements that "saw the world to be awry, and blamed current problems, whatever their nature, on a failure to adhere to the pristine teachings of Islam."[70] To one conversant with Weber's writings about the "theodicy problem," this pattern seems to be a striking illustration of the "ultimate metaphysical question" faced by prophets and reformers. For them, the

> ultimate question of all metaphysics has always been something like this: if the world as a whole and life in particular were to have a meaning, what might it be, and how would the world have to look in order to correspond to it?[71]

Thus Muslims like all other sincere believers are caught in the metaphysics of that "insoluble problem of the imperfection of the world in the light of God's omnipotence."[72]

From this point of view, Metcalf stresses the role of religious doctrine and the need to recognize that *ideas* can indeed become "ideal interests." Moreover, Metcalf urges that in undertaking to study reformist groups and the search for "functional equivalents" to the Protestant ethic, the researcher needs to attend to the *sequence* of events, and thereby not fall prey to taking the conjunction of economic interests and religious innovation as cause and effect.

Finally, in laying out some parallels between the themes of reformist movements in Islam and European precursors, Metcalf points to a fascinating difference between the European and Islamic situations. Despite the many "puritan" themes seen in the Deobandi's, "only in exceptional cases does Islamic reform give rise to the kind of psychological tension that generates sustained rationalized action in the political, let alone, economic sphere."[73] If this is true, she has provided us with an invaluable clue about the differences between Christian and Islamic reformist impulses insofar as they champion "active mastery" of the world. This conclusion stands as a corrective amplification of the conclusion reached by Rudolph Peters discussed above.

Perhaps it is here that one should consider Michael Cook's efforts to apply Weber's "church-sect" typology to Islam. He finds it difficult to apply that model under the strict definitions that Weber offered. Of course, the church/sect typology was originally set out by Ernst Troeltsch in his classic work on *The Social Teachings of the Christian Churches,*[74] and Weber was willing to follow his lead. The reader will also be aware that throughout the papers of this volume, the various contributors did indeed use the term "sect(s)" and "sectarian" to refer to a variety of distinguishable Islamic groups. And clearly, as in Metcalf's paper, the reader learns of those who "set themselves apart from"[75] the unfaithful believers and their deviant practices. Some observers, perhaps Muslims, might think that the very idea of separatist groups is doctrinally alien to Islamic thought, as it implies disunity within the Muslim community and is to be avoided by all means, at least ideally.[76] This flows from the universally proclaimed Muslim idea of reciprocity: "a believer is a believer only when he wants for his brother what he wants for himself." [77] But it flows as well as from the injunction not to get mired in intellectual debates about ambiguous passages in the Quran (Sura 3:7). Nevertheless, Rudolph Peters discusses such groups as the Wahhabis of eighteenth-century Saudi Arabia, the followers of Taraqi-yi Muhammadi in India of the same time, the Sanusi of ninteenth-century Sudan, Mawdudi's Jamâ'at-i Islami of twentieth-century Pakistan, as well as the Muslim Brotherhood and the *Takfir wa'l-Hijra* ("excommunicate and exile") group of twentieth-century Egypt. So the question is not whether sectlike groups exist, but how it is that they should be described.

We should be reminded that, as with all of Weber's concepts, he consciously used what he called "ideal types," that is, conceptual idealizations that rarely exist in pure form. Hence the ideal type of the "church" as of the "sect" "aims to give unambiguous means of expression to" what would otherwise be an unreflective description of some discrete set of facts.[78] Consequently "historical research faces the task of determining in each case, the extent to which this ideal-construct approximates to or diverges from reality."[79]

Professor Cook notes that in this dichotomy between church and sect, the church as a pure type leans toward compulsory membership, hierarchical authority, and political involvement. The sect leans in the other direction, towards voluntary membership (as a community of the "pure" in Christianity), and towards an antipolitical stance in the community at large. And it is with this latter axis that Cook finds the greatest difficulty. For he suggests that the groups that Islamic scholars would most assuredly call "sects" are also strikingly *political*.

It is a question of some interest as to whether or not this observation would be taken by Weber, or any of his interpreters, as a rejection of the concept. For surely historians (and sociologists) focusing on Christian "sects" would point to those that did in fact adopt a political strategy, sometimes stridently so. In general sociologists have assumed (apparently believing that Weber did too) that the various identifiable sects in the Christian world have often sought to *change* it, both through exhortation in a straightforward sense and in an overtly political fashion. Americans still debate the question of where to draw the line between "religious exhortation" and political campaigning, especially when it concerns sectarian groups with well known leaders such as those Protestant denominations that are frequently lumped together under the labels of the "New Religious Right," "Southern Fundamentalists," etc.

Perhaps the most obvious such case of sectarian sponsored political activism is that of the Puritans in England who recruited Oliver Cromwell to lead their great revolutionary overturn of the political status quo. One would not need to look far for many other examples, including the Prohibitionists in the United States in the early twentieth century, who succeeded handsomely in getting the laws changed.[80] Likewise, the European continent's history is full of sectarian groups who adopted a variety of strategies for settling their scores with the political and religious status quo.

It therefore seems that Michael Cook is onto something very important in focusing on the Khârijites, those "Seceders" of the late seventh century C.E., who display "notable parallels to the sectarian Christian idea of an *eccelesia pura*."[81] It seems to be a universal religious impulse of prophets and reformers to call the faithful back to a purer state of being and to shed the impediments of the contaminating world. For Muslims, this is described as *jahiliya*, the pagan times of ignorance before the Word arrived—but also a state of spiritual waywardness. But just as surely, those who experience success in the initial call are often driven to reinsert their ideal images back into the mainstream of society, thereby re-entering civil society.

If we accept the view that there are historical situations in which sects *do* embark upon political action, then Cook seems to be telling us that "these Khârajite groups would be well worth considering as Weberian sects."[82] Rather than assuming that one has uncovered "hidden historical premises,"[83] we would instead be on the way to discovering those historical conditions which are productive of sectarian behavior, whether it is politically quiescent or active, whether it occurs in

Islam or in Christianity. Moreover, S. N. Eisenstadt, taking his cue from the work of Ernst Gellner, suggests that "sectarian-like movements...often led not only to the overthrow, or more frequently, [the] downfall of existing regimes."[84] Rudolph Peters noted in his chapter, echoing Barabara Metcalf's similar observation, that "fundamentalist movements often arise from a widespread feeling of malaise" suggesting communal decline, and that such movements are strongly committed to bringing the surrounding society back into conformity with pure religion. Research on this whole cycle of developments is of great importance. In a word, Islamic developmental history is littered with all sorts of separatist groups, some led by charismatic figures, some not, and any systematic study of them would greatly enrich our understanding of sect formation in the Islamic world, as well as clarify what Weber barely began to probe.

Islam and Secularism

As we saw in the last section, the developmental history of Islam is hardly over. From the late nineteenth century to the present the Muslim world has experienced a variety of reform movements and revivalist movements. There have also been indigenous efforts to move particular Muslim countries in a secular direction, one that incorporated what Muslim leaders perceived to be positive aspects of modernization. Turkey is the most notable example of this, but Egypt as well began taking this path in the twentieth century and, some would say, earlier.

Although all of these movements arose in a broader context defined by the presence of Western colonial powers, the degree to which these movements have borrowed intentionally from the West is not uniform. For example, in her chapter on the Deobandi movement in northern India in the late nineteenth century, Barbara Metcalf describes a group undergoing a religious awakening that contains strong ascetic elements, but which, Metcalf's analysis suggests, stems from indigenous Islamic roots.

Nevertheless, in his chapter, "Secularization in Islam," Francis Robinson suggests that over the last two hundred years there has been a parallel secularization process going on which contains many elements of Weber's image of that process. Most conspicuously in this account, there has been a "disenchantment of the world" whereby the sacred and magical connection of all things has been torn asunder. In place of these religious and magical connections, a cold calculating bureaucratic mentality, seemingly bent on achieving greater economies of scale and efficiency, has become increasing dominant. It seems unlikely, however, that such developments in the Muslim world should be placed on the same scale as in the West, though leanings in that direction can be discerned.

To pursue this theme, Robinson turns to South Asia and the distinction between "structural" and "subjective" secularization. The former applies to the institutional arrangements of society and the latter to the subjective experience of secularizing forces by individuals.[85]

According to Robinson the arrival of the British in India resulted in a structural secularization whereby the traditional sacred core of Islamic culture was displaced, especially in law and in education. That is, within a hundred years of so after the British arrived, Islamic law had largely been displaced and Western law (the common law tradition) had been put in its place. This led to a sort of fragmentation so that, apart from the application of Islamic personal law to the family, all legal matters were placed in the formally rationalized system of common law, and above all, the introduction of the legal idea of precedent.[86]

In educational institutions Robinson suggests that a new emphasis was introduced, one that stressed efficient intellectual functioning in a regularized bureaucratic setting as opposed to one geared toward religious enlightenment ("peaks of achievement in *tafsir* [Quran commentary] or *fiqh* [jurisprudence]).[87] The introduction of this model seems at once to have reduced the production of old-style religious specialists and fragmented education, since the old-style education pattern persisted in some areas, while it was eliminated entirely in others, especially in government circles. Thus a significant amount of *structural secularization* took place in British India, and more so in a country like Turkey by the end of the reign of Atäturk. In such cases, and others, the original religious vision of Islamic cultural unity was fragmented and greatly dissipated.

With regard to "subjective" secularization, Francis Robinson again sees a parallel process very much in Weberian terms. He sees this as the appearance of what he calls a "Protestant or Puritan" Islam as illustrated by Barbara Metcalf's study on the Deobandi (see chapter 8). Following Robinson's interpretation, we witness the rise of

> an Islam based on scripture; it is one which is rationalizing in the sense of making religion self-conscious, systematic and based on abstract principles. Groups of Muslims come forward who, while they do not in the main reject saints and Islamic mysticism (sufism), increasingly see themselves as following religious prac-

tice which is different from that of the sufi shrines, indeed, they often define their Islam in contrast to the parochial forms of the shrines. Theirs is a universal form in which Muslims all over India, indeed, all over the Muslim world, could share. It is one, moreover, whose growth and development is closely interwoven, as in the emergence of European protestantism, with the translation of scripture into the vernacular languages and the harnessing of the printing press to the spreading of religious knowledge.[88]

Thus in this interpretation, Robinson sees a "rationalizing" disenchantment occurring *within* the religious realm itself. For these Muslims the world was less

penetrated through and through by sacred beings and forces. God was firmly transcendent and humans had no comfort, no guidance except God's revelation through Mohammad to help them live in this world so that they might be judged favorably in the next. These Muslims increasingly seemed to find the world a cold, bleak, disenchanted place.[89]

This line of analysis clearly suggests that "we find within the Islamic world much evidence of the growth of secularization along the lines that Weber traced in Christian Europe."[90]

But once said, further reflection takes one in another direction. Robinson suggests that this fragmenting and disenchanting process was largely "forced on Muslim societies," that it was in part "a consequence of the projection of Western capital and power." And if that is the case, one could read this secularization process as a "Western model," *not* an Islamic model of secularization. He then suggests that the yardstick for viewing the secularization of Muslim societies is the degree to which they operate independent of the *shari'a*. For, the *shari'a*, using H. A. R. Gibb's phrase, "stands for all that the Constitution stands for in the United States of America and more."[91] This then provokes the realization that for a great part of Muslim history, Muslims have not known just what the "do's and don'ts" of Islam are. The absence of easily available written documents, combined one should probably add, with a vast illiteracy, meant that "patterning of society after some version of the *shari'a* has been painfully slow."[92] On the contemporary scene, Robinson sees "an extraordinary thirst for Islamic knowledge" especially in a society like Turkey. No doubt one should extend this observation to other parts of the Muslim world, and stress as well, that there has been a major improvement in levels of literacy in many parts of the Muslim world. Even though illiteracy rates are still high, this advance has enabled many young people to master written Arabic and to gain access to sacred documents hitherto available only to the tiny elite of religious scholars who knew classical Arabic. Some observers point out that this increased literacy has resulted in the religious scholars being thrust aside, though it has also been aided by the widespread use of such modern technologies as the audio and video cassette as well as the Internet.[93] Thus, the paradoxical influence of the West, that is, the secularization and fragmentation of the Islamic religious vision, has "helped to draw many Muslims closer to the *shari'a* than before."[94] Perhaps it is too soon to tell whether the effort to impose the Shari'a has now crested or whether there will be more vigorous calls for its imposition. For Francis Robinson, however, there has been a discernible drift toward a "willed Islam," a distancing from Sufi mysticism, and an embrace of an Islam focused on worldly achievement, tinged with a new sense of human agency. For him this is a new "individualism," perhaps related to European influences, yet possibly the harbinger of a new thrust toward secularization.

Reconstructing Weber on Islam

I turn now to the effort to reconstruct Weber's sociological thought on Islam. The previous discussion assessed the degree to which Weber's image of Islam needs to be expanded to meet the standards of contemporary research on the Muslim world. The present discussion focuses primarily on Wolfgang Schluchter's effort to reconstruct Weber's fundamental approach to comparative analysis of Islamic civilization. Schluchter's analysis highlights the conceptual framework implicit in Weber's general study of the world religions, while it assembles many of Weber's comments on Islam and its social structure.

The Basic Framework

In his chapter, "Hindrances to Modernity," Wolfgang Schluchter provides a deeply reflective and hermeneutically precise reconstruction of the developmental trajectory of Weber's thought regarding Islam. He shows in great detail the connections between Weber's writings on the *Agrarian Sociology of Ancient Civilizations*,[95] *The Protestant Ethic and the Spirit of Capitalism*, and all of the intermediary monographs and essays that set the stage for Weber's broader inquiry into the connections between the world religions and economic ethics. Schluchter also provides us with a fascinating detective story centered on the possibility that Weber had written more about Islam than the published record contains. His suggestion is that these additional writings were in a text that was inexplicably lost from the posthumous papers found in Weber's literary estate at his death.[96]

From these reflections and protracted internal analyses Schluchter arrives at four important conclusions. First, Weber's basic knowledge of Islam was probably arrived at between 1911 and 1914, before World War I. Second, despite his intentions otherwise, Weber was not able to return to the study of Islam between the outbreak of war and his death in 1920. Third, while Weber's interest in Islam was keen, and he included Islam in the developmental complex that included all three religions of the Book, he probably would not have treated Islam as extensively as he did the other world religions. Fourth, according to Schlucher, Weber's interests in Islam were more analytical and conceptual as he saw intriguing "puritan" and ascetic parallels between Islam and ascetic Protestantism, especially its Calvinist expression. Consequently his focus was more "typological" than empirically detailed in its presentation.

However, it should be added that Weber probably was not aware of the important and impressive Arabic achievements in the natural sciences up until the fourteenth century, and hence their consequences for the intellectual development of the West. For example, the amazing similarities between the planetary models of the Arab astronomer and timekeeper, Ibn al-Shatir and those of Copernicus were only discovered, largely by American historians of science, in the 1950s.[97] Likewise, it seems doubtful that Weber was aware of the experimental traditions in Arabic-Islamic science especially in the writings of Ibn Sina (d. 1037), Ibn al-Haytham (d. 1040), or Kamal al-Din al-Farisi (d. ca. 1320), and their impact on late medieval Europeans.[98] Thus Weber should be credited with having perceived the great significance of the unique development of modern science in the West, and probably forgiven for not having uncovered more about the specific history of Arabic science, which constitutes a puzzle even more intriguing than the absence of modern capitalism in the Muslim world.

In laying out this developmental outline of Weber's intellectual evolution, Schluchter stresses the fact that Weber's point of view was always *multifocal*, that he recognized the existence of many contrasting developmental histories of the world's civilizations, and appreciated their contrasting configurations. For him there was always a need for additional developmental histories while he himself focused on those of law, science, technology, economics, political administration, and aesthetics. What brought any and all of these complementary points of view together was precisely the author's *point of view*. Most strikingly, Weber's own point of view as a comparative and historical sociologist gave his work an unparalleled vision for inquiry, one that remains as compelling today as when Weber originally gave expression to it earlier in this century.

Granted that Weber's remarks on Islam are fragmentary and that a more finished text may have once existed, Professor Schluchter asks, how is it possible to reconstruct an outline of what Weber's framework of analysis would have included? Schluchter follows the sound understanding that for Weber the emergence of modern "rational capitalism" was (and continues to be) the most fateful force of the modern world. Since this development occurred uniquely in the West, the peculiar shape that Western culture and society took stands as an endlessly fascinating comparative template for asking questions about other parts of the world. To bring this unique emergence of modern capitalism in the West into focus for comparative purposes, Schluchter points out that Weber was careful to specify what he meant by an *individual capitalist enterprise*. It was one, according to this analysis, which "is a profit-oriented enterprise…is a factory enterprise…is independent from the household, and…controls its economic activity by means of double-entry bookkeeping."[99]

With these preliminaries behind, Schluchter turns to one of Weber's more fully and concisely formulated late statements of the pattern of development that brought modern capitalism about. From Weber's point of view, the emergence of modern capitalism was the outcome of both "internal" and "external" factors that are part of a broad set of features within "general cultural development" in the West. As I list these cultural features that uniquely evolved in the West, the contemporary reader at the end of the twentieth century must remember that these words were penned nearly eight decades ago, that Weber was speaking historically, and that the world looks very different now. Nevertheless, according to Weber,

> Only the Occident knows the *state in the modern sense*, with a constitution [*gesatzer Verfassung*], specialized officialdom, and the concept of citizenship. Beginnings of this institution in antiquity and in the Orient were never able to develop fully. Only the Occident knows *rational law*, made by jurists and rationally interpreted and applied, and only in the Occident is found the concept of *citizen* (*civis Romanus, citoyen, bourgeois*) because only in the Occident does the *city* exit in the specific sense of the word. Furthermore, only the Occident possesses *science in the present-day sense of the word*. Theology, philosophy, and reflection on the ultimate prob-

lems of life were known to the Chinese and the Hindu, perhaps even of a depth unreached by the European; but a rational science and in connection with it a *rational technology* remained unknown to those civilizations. Finally, Western civilization is further distinguished from every other by the presence of men with a *rational ethos for the conduct of life*. Magic and religion are found everywhere; but a religious basis for conduct that, when consistently followed, had to lead to a specific form of rationalism is again peculiar to Western civilization alone.[100]

Given this framework, Schluchter surmises that if Weber had completed his study of Islam in a fashion consistent with his other studies of the World religions, then he would have organized his analysis around just these major terms of analysis found in this citation: the *state, city, law, science, and methodical conduct*. These would have provided the major "points of comparison" for his analysis. Indeed, Schluchter claims that a careful review of Weber's comments on Islam can be organized around these major terms:

the type of religious ethic—world mastery as world conquest and world adjustment; the type of political domination—Oriental prebendal feudalism; the type of city—Oriental urban anarchy; the type of law—theocratic and patrimonial *qadi*-justice; and the interrelation of these orders and powers (their mode of "integration")—"centralism."[101]

Only the topic of science is omitted. Schluchter's rich analysis then proceeds to show what Weber's thoughts on each of these subjects were.

Motivational Elements

The first of these topics concerns the motivational factor, "one side of the causal chain," in the emergence of modern capitalism. Here the issue is whether or not Islamic religious thought engendered a "practical" economic ethic of systematic, methodical control over daily life. As is well known, Weber argued that ascetic Protestantism, above all, its Calvinist formulation, fostered the emergence of a rational economic ethic, at the center of which was a belief that the "God of Calvinism demanded of his believers not single good works, but a course of good works transformed into a *system* of life."[102] At the same time, the doctrine of the elect, that some individuals and not others are chosen for eternal life, created an insurmountable tension for the believer. This in turn created a *psychological* need for a sign, an indication of proof that the believer had indeed received the grace of God.

As Schluchter pursues this comparative theme, he reveals that Weber's thoughts on this subject were much deeper than many have surmised. For Weber was the beneficiary of a Heidelberg dissertation on the question of predeterminism and predestinationism written by F. Ulrich in 1912.[103] Ulrich's analysis served to demarcate the theological differences between *destination* and *predestination* on the one hand, and *determination* and *predetermination* on the other. It is one thing for an individual's life to be determined in *this world*, and quite another for the individual's fate to be *pre*determined in the life hereafter.

Weber was struck by the similarities between Calvinism and Islam in that in both cases God was "unconditionally transcendent" as well as unchangeable, omnipotent, and omniscient. However, following Ulrich's analysis, Islam leans toward "predeterminism," that "God guides those whom he pleases," seeming to suggest a lack of human freedom. Many observers have noted, as we saw earlier, that Islamic thought never resolved the conflict between fatalism and free will, between a full-fledged predeterminism and the merits of *self*-determinism necessary for legal purposes.[104] Nevertheless, Weber argued, that predetermination operated in Islam in *this world*: "the prevailing conception was that predestination determined, not the fate of the individual in the world beyond, but rather his singular fate in this world, the question for example, whether (and above all) the warrior for the faith falls in battle or not."[105] From this point of view, Muslims rarely experience the great ambivalence and anxiety of being "chosen" or not, such as the Calvinist experiences. For the all powerful God of Islam only requires the faithful performance of the five pillars. To this there is never conjoined, as there was in Calvinism, the demand for a logic of *proof,* an outward sign that one was included in the circle of the chosen. Schluchter concludes, following Weber's analysis, that

> Muslims were not confronted with the problem of the certainty of salvation, of the *certitudo salutis*, to as radical a degree as were the Calvinists. The belief in providence did not produce the same measure of uncertainty and fear. Admittedly, fear of death is involved in both cases; however, in one case it is the fear of death in the face of the beyond, whereas in the other it is fear of death in the face of battle.[106]

The Calvinist feared the consequences in the afterlife of a misspent life here on earth, and thereby took shelter in a life of sobriety and unrelenting hard work. But "the proof of the believer in predestination, played no part in Islam. Thus only the fearlessness of the warrior...could result, but there were no consequences for the rationalization of life, for there was no religious reward for them."[107] While it is unfortunate that Weber focuses here only on the case of the *mujahideen*, the combatant in the service of the faith, not the ordinary believer, or the *mujtahid,* "intellectual striver" for religious and legal enlightenment, the implications for the larger body of ordinary believers seems to be the same. God rewards the faithful service of all, and the requisite service is the observance of the five pillars. Very little doubt remains in the mind of the believer in "the Compassionate, the Merciful" (al-Rahman, al-Rahim), as to his fate in the hereafter.[108]

The implications of this psychological attitude of devoted trust in God for the development of capitalism, Schluchter goes on to suggest, is that Islam remained compatible with all the traditional forms—state-supported capitalism, booty-capitalism, etc, but not modern rational capitalism. "Islam does not revolutionize economic mentality...it does not provide a force to transform life from within and thus to overcome the spirit of traditionalism in economic or other areas of life."[109] This conclusion seems remarkably consistent with Barbara Metcalf's earlier observation that, "only in exceptional cases does Islamic reform give rise to the kind of psychological tension that generates sustained rationalized action in the political, let alone, economic sphere."[110]

In short, comparing the religious influences of ascetic Protestantism (Calvinism) and Islam with regard to the creation of an innerworldly practical economic ethic, Weber saw a pronounced disparity. The Calvinist doctrine of predestination combined with the psychological need for a sign, or proof, of salvation created a methodical approach to daily life that saw no release. It required a continuous pattern of disciplined daily conduct, as a "calling" in the higher service of God. This is turn, Weber observed, resulted in a utilitarianism that served the progressive rational reorganization of the social order according to God's unknown plan.

On the other hand, the Islamic religious commitments were directed toward the performance of the five daily prayers and observance of the other pillars of Islam. But this ethic of piety—of "doing good and forbidding evil"—did not become transmuted into an economic ethic of social transformation, nor did it entail *responsibility* for transforming the social order into a more *utilitarian* pattern. Contemporary Islamists seem intent on changing the present "corrupt" order into a religious order based on an imagined ideal preexisting state.

Law and the State

Schluchter next turns to the *institutional* (or external) factors that provide the preconditions that supported modern capitalist development, and proceeds to reconstruct the essentials of Weber's analysis from his scattered writings. Among these "external" conditions for the rise of modern capitalism, law and governmental structures are of paramount importance. Following Schluchter's analysis it becomes clear that Weber's writings do indeed contain many indications that Weber thought deeply about comparative *political* development. And it is to be stressed that Weber's analysis was centered on *development* over time, not on a static picture.

As we have seen in earlier discussions, Weber characterized Islamic political domination as "patrimonialism," that is, a system of rulership in which all of the subalterns of the ruler are directly and personally connected to him. He pays the subordinates from his own purse. In the Arab-Muslim world of the formative period these functionaries often became part of the ruler's household and even claimed genealogical descent from the ruling family in later generations.[111] Schluchter points out that Weber used several terms to label these political arrangements, such as "arbitrary patrimonialism," "Sultanism," "prebendal feudalism," and "free prebendal feudalism."[112]

In tracing these political and legal developments, Weber noted, it is important to remember that when Muhammad died he left no designated male successor. In the end, the political leaders worked out their own arrangement, often through military battle, while the religious scholars of a later time, the *'ulama'*, went in their own direction, taking sacred law (*shari'a*) with them. The political leaders looked to the *'ulama'* for legitimation, which they sometimes got, but which could not be gotten from the Quran directly, since it contains very little by way of legal guidance for a political empire, above all, for one as massive as the Islamic empire had become by 750 with its conquest of Spain.

According to Schluchter's analysis, Weber saw both Islam and the West as beginning in contrasting forms of patrimonialism. In the European West, the prevailing "feudalism" was "a marginal case of patrimonialism" which was more highly advanced than Islamic patrimonialism, so that it became at least "an approximation of a *Rechtsstaat*,"[113] that is, a political system governed by formal law. In contrast, Weber saw the patrimonialism of the Islamic world as one in which the ruler increasingly monopolized resources, increasing his powers and arbitrary rule. Schluchter does not stress this in his analysis, but clearly the idea that the sacred law (*shari'a*) is a God given and complete structure in Muslim eyes prevented political leaders as well as religious scholars from directly *legislating new law* that could fill the gaps, such as those that Patricia Crone says, "that nobody seems to have thought of." However, it should be noted that over the centuries political rulers did introduce laws of expediency, sometimes referred to as "government in accordance with the precepts of divine law" (*siyas shari'a*).[114] Nevertheless, these remained outside the sacred law itself.

The paramount question for developmental history, however, as Schluchter sees it, is how patrimonial domination is modified to suit the purposes of the ruling powers—and whether this is supportive of capitalism's long term development. These modifications, he argues, are "solely a legal and ethical question, not an economic one."[115] For the Islamic ruler the question was how to hold the empire together in the face of potential rivals and petty rulers, who, shepherding their local resources, might seek to overthrow the caliphal throne.

In the Europe, according to Schluchter's reconstruction, Weber saw the development towards a *Rechtsstaat* and the conditions facilitating modern capitalism's rise in three steps which borrowed the strengths of "fief-based feudalism...the help of the *Ständestaat* that represents a kind of corporate form of fief-based feudalism, and...the help of a rational bureaucratic patrimonial state that arose out of the *Ständestaat*."[116] Moreover, according to this analysis, "all of these were characterized by rule of law (*Rechtsstaatlichkeit*)."[117]

These steps are surprisingly explicit in Weber's writings. During the Christian Middle Ages, it is well known that the Christian church was the dominant political structure, at least in Western Christendom. Furthermore, canon law, Weber tells us, "occupied a relatively special position with reference to all other sacred laws."[118] Given the rise of the universities in the eleventh and twelfth centuries, and their fusion of the teaching of philosophy, logic, theology, and the natural sciences (in contrast to the Islamic colleges, *madrasas*, which omitted these disciplines in their formative years[119]), the European universities gave a unique direction to religious and legal thought. As Weber put it, "the rigorously logical and professional legal technique which was developed through both ancient philosophy and jurisprudence was also bound to influence the treatment of Canon law."[120] That is, it turned it into a formally rational system of law, which had begun under the Romans.

Secondly, "the character of ecclesiastical law making was influenced by the fact that the church's functionaries were holders of rationally defined bureaucratic offices."[121] Thus, the very idea of a bureaucratically defined administrative apparatus, that is, a methodically connected and interlocking set of offices based on the rule of law, was found in the *sacred* law itself. This was so because the canonists had rediscovered Justinian's Civil law texts, especially the *Digest* and assimilated it. This was an extraordinarily refined system of legal thought, and canon law theorists and lawyers borrowed from it freely. Furthermore, this model of methodical legal construction based on a kind of formal rationality rather than religious presuppositions, served to guide the development of *secular* law (urban law, commercial law, manorial law, etc.). As Weber put it, "In this way there arose that unique relationship between sacred and secular law in which Canon law became...one of the guides for secular law on the road to rationality."[122] Hence there was an enormous legal legacy, namely, that of Roman and Hellenistic law, which was entirely absent in Islam. In addition the sacred Christian law (infused by Roman law) became the pattern for *secular* legal development (on which more below).[123] Islamic sacred law preempted the emergence of secular law, while in the Western Europe Church law itself became the model for positive legislation and progressive legal development. According to Weber,

> the most significant contributions of Canon law were the recognition of informal contracts, the promotion in the interest of pious endowments of freedom of testation, and the Canonist conception of the corporation.[124]

With regard to contracts, we saw earlier the many restrictions that Islamic law placed on all commerical contracts. Second, regarding testation, *Sura* 4 of the Quran spells put the rules of testation, the proportions that males, females, and other relatives are to receive, thereby constricting the freedom of testation of which Weber speaks. Indeed, Islamic law gave birth to that hybrid occupation of *faradi*, that is, the mathematically trained legal expert who supervised the division of inheritance and sometimes contributed to the science of astronomy.[125] Thirdly, the idea of a *corporation*, a legally autonomous entity was unknown to Islamic law, as Joseph Schacht and others have pointed out.[126] Furthermore, the corporation as a "whole body" was an entity with a bundle of legal rights: to sue and be sued, to buy and sell property, the right to create one's own laws and regulations, the right to have representation both within the corporation and before the King's court, and the principle of decision-making based on election by consent or "the greater and sounder part."[127] There was even the elective principle of "what touches all should be considered and be approved by all (*Quod omnes tangit omnibus tractari et approbari debet*)."[128] These principles, it is fair to say, were lacking in Islamic law and were not acknowledged until contact with Western legal systems in the nineteenth and twentieth centuries. With regard to the idea of a legal "institution," (*Anstalt*), Joseph Schacht wrote toward the end of his career, that "the whole concept of an institution is missing" in Islamic law:

> The idea of a juridic person was on the point of breaking through but not quite realized in Islamic law, and this did not happen at the point where we should expect it, with regard to the charitable foundation or *waqf*, but with regard to the separate property of a slave who is being sold not as an individual but together with his business as a running concern.[129]

In a word, European law underwent remarkable development in the medieval period. As this occurred the model of canon law imparted a surprisingly forward momentum to the development of secular law, though it must be said that the Romanists (specializing in Roman civil law) did their part in this, as they were unhindered by the canonists.

But there is still another fundamental insight to be gained from Weber's writings, though he does not make it explicit. That is, there was a fundamental rupture in the development of Western law (that I just outlined above) centered on the concept of the corporation. Weber says, "the churches were, indeed, the first 'institutions' in the legal sense, and it was here that the legal construction of public organization had its point of departure."[130] Weber seems to recognize what Harold Berman calls "the legal revolution" of the twelfth and thirteenth centuries but he does not stress the fact that when the church declared itself to be a "whole body," a *corporation*, it established the principle of the *separation* of the sacred and secular domains. In effect, the church's action (under Pope Gregory VII) in the Investiture Controversy (1075–1122) created a *formal* legal separation of sacred and secular law with the expectation that the jurists in the secular domain would create a legal structure parallel to the sacred law. This is what Weber suggests when he refers to the fact that "public organization had its point of departure" in this episode, which concerns the formalization of the idea of a "juristic personality," that is, the corporation and the "institution" (Anstalt), to which discussion Weber directs the reader's attention.[131]

In short, the Christian church itself in the eleventh and twelfth centuries initiated a separation between sacred law and all forms of secular law. This bifurcation gave a great impetus to the development of law, taking it for granted that the legal system is itself a constantly *evolving* structure. In the Islamic world, however, no such departure occurred. In the nineenth century, under the Turkish reforms (*tanzimat* reforms) and the pressure to provide a suitable legal framework for interacting with the West, the domain over which Islamic law was allowed to operate was greatly constricted. In the end, Western legal conceptions were imported to fill the gaps, in administrative as well as commercial law, which Islamic law could not satisfy without major changes to the *shari'a*, which was not imaginable.[132]

But there is one final set of considerations that needs to be mentioned in the context of Weber's comparison of Western and Islamic forms of legal and political organization. For there is another principle and related set of powers connected to the concept of a corporation which has immense significance but which is not articulated by Weber. That is the principle of "jurisdiction," that is, the principle of the *legitimate domination* of legal action within the properly bounded domain of the corporate entity whether it be a city, town, state, university or commercial guild. Corporate entities in the twelfth and thirteenth centuries were permitted to enact their own *ordinances* and *statutes*, which means that they could enact new laws and regulations for the purpose of regulating and controlling their corporate members. The idea was that each corporate entity had its *rightful sphere of jurisdiction* over which it had *sovereignty*—another fundamental legal concept underlying modern nationalism as well as international law.

In the Islamic world the concept of legal jurisdiction was never worked out on any level. Each of the four schools of law had "agreed to disagree" and each could be applied wherever a *qadi* or *faqih* (judge or lawyer) was present to render a judgment. Moreover, the individual plaintiff could go to as many legal scholars as he chose, settling on the legal decision of his choice.[133] At a higher level, lawyers were not an autonomous legal profession, and the jurisdictional boundaries of rulers was always in doubt. As Farhat Ziadeh put it,

> The Shari'a had never developed the necessary procedures or writs that would bring the prince or executive power to account for actions committed outside the law. Throughout Islamic history the judiciary, composed of the *'ulama'* exercised its functions as a result of delegation by executive power and therefore was dependent on it.[134]

This analysis suggests that the paths of political and legal development of Islamic civilization and the West were on very different trajectories.

To complete his analysis of the Islamic side, Schluchter turns to a number of additional matters, including the slave soldiers, their tax farming, and the problems these customs created for a stable unified empire. Schluchter concludes that, according to Weber's analysis, "Oriental feudalism is less 'typified,'" apparently meaning less formally stipulated, than its Occidental counterpart. "It is also less decentralized...and lack[s] the idea of contract in the Western sense and the concept of the Anstalt."[135] Even with all these contrasts in the "external" environment, Schluchter thinks it "a mistake...to take Weber's comparative analysis as a direct explanation of the external aspects that favored rational capitalism in the West."[136] This is apparently because the "highly developed" feudal ethic of the West can be "considered an anti-capitalist force par excellence. Nothing is so distant from capitalist business morals, from a vocational ethic defined in terms of functions performed, as a heroic ethic that is deeply hostile to all means-ends rationality."[137]

Law and Cities

Although Weber wrote a monograph on the city, thereby dramatizing its importance in comparative historical development, it could be argued that it properly belongs to a special chapter in Western *legal* history. In either case, as Schluchter points out, Weber saw the development of the Western city in its full-blown sense as a revolutionary development. As urban settlements, the Occidental and the Oriental "city" share a variety of functions, such as those of a market place, a military fortress, an administrative center, and sometimes a location of courts. However, in the case of the Western city, Weber asserted that

> the urban citizenry...usurped the right to dissolve the bonds of seigneurial domination; this was the great—in fact, the *revolutionary*—innovation which differentiated the medieval Occidental city from all others.[138]

The result was the emergence of a new type of social organization which enjoyed political and administrative autonomy, whose inhabitants were "free citizens" governed by a "*special law* exclusively applicable to them and who thus form a legally autonomous status group."[139] These elements together form what Schluchter calls additional "historical prerequisites" for the development of modern capitalism. For him these elements include "the democratic principle of legitimation;

the organizational principle of the corporate urban commune; and the market-oriented bourgeoisie."[140]

Insofar as legal structure is concerned, each of these elements seems to be a product of the evolving legal theory of corporations, or "whole bodies," which applied equally to merchant guilds, universities, cities, and towns, and even charitable organizations.[141] The rise of legally autonomous cities and towns as well as universities seems to be deeply intertwined, preventing a clear separation of the paths of mutual influence. What is certain is that the legal revolution of the medieval period produced major changes in the legal structure of the West, and these legal changes came about considerably before modern capitalism made its appearance, if we follow Weber's own definition of the essential elements. There is much to be said for Harold Berman's view that the larger process was indeed the "Papal revolution" of the twelfth and thirteenth centuries that set off all the radical legal innovations of this period. However the story is told, the European West clearly did undergo a major restructuring during this period of time.

European cities as legally autonomous, self-governing entities were indeed unique in developmental history, and they fully partook of the new freedoms and new forms of agency that the evolving Western legal system made possible. They could create their own laws and courts, as well as raise armies and mint coins. Thus the rise of cities, and eventually city-states, virtually guaranteed a decentralized, polycentric political climate in Europe. But just as this could induce many forms of economic competition, thereby aiding economic development, so too autonomous and competing political entities could fall into military encounters, casuing great fractures rather than social cohesion. In any event, Weber's analysis rightly pointed to these emerging structures in law, governmental, and civil administration.

If, on the other hand, we consider the Islamic world, no such legal or urban revolution occurred. From an Islamic point of view, the "revolution" had taken place with the arrival of the Quran, the uncorrupted speech of God. When supplemented by the life and practice of Muhammad (the *sunna*), the blueprint was established. The task was to adjust the community to the precepts of sacred law, not to undertake bold new departures. Likewise, the idea of *two* or more competing legal structures, one sacred and one secular, was utterly foreign to Islamic thought.

There is much more to be said about Weber's comments on the contrasts between Western and Islamic legal development, as shown by

Schluchter's detailed exposition. For present purposes, the contrast is clearly evident. Considered in this broader framework of political and social organization, there can be little doubt but that *law* played a major role in creating the conditions for both *political* and *economic* development in the West. The same can be said, as I have shown elsewhere, for the rise of modern science.[142] The markedly different configurations of legal and political development (including the emergence of the city as a new type of social organization) goes far to explain why modern capitalism was able to make the breakthrough in the West but not in the Muslim world. Similarly, the different economic ethics of Islam and the West, hedged about as they were by contrasting structures of legal domination and agency, had very different consequences for economic development in the two civilizations. Despite the obvious need to correct and amplify Weber's scattered comments on Islam, the theoretical framework within which he set out to make his comparison with Islam has a great deal of merit. Thanks to Wolfgang Schluchter's effort to reconstruct that theoretical framework for comparative civilizational analysis, the merit of it is far easier to appreciate.

Criticism of Weber

Finally I turn to the critics of Weber's thoughts on Islam that Schluchter singles out for comment. These include the book by Maxime Rodinson, *Islam and Capitalism*,[143] and Bryan S. Turner's *Weber and Islam*.[144] It is interesting that both of these books, written as they were in late 1960s and early 1970s, were deeply influenced by Marxist thought. It is therefore not surprising that they both under estimated the influence of religious *ideas*. While Rodinson had a deep knowledge of Islam, and self-consciously adhered to Marxism, his comments on Islam and the singularity of the Quran often verge on apologia. For example, comparing the writings of Thomas Aquinas and the Quran, he says that "the rationalism of the Koran is rock-like."[145] Likewise the Quran is said to be a book "in which rationality plays a big part. In it Allah is continually arguing and reasoning…" and he claims that the revelation of the Quran "is guaranteed authentic by the fact that it is substantially identical with previous revelations, which in turn seem to [Muhammad] guaranteed by history."[146]

Rodinson was aware of the fundamental civilizational problem that Weber articulated: "Why in fact did capitalism triumph in modern times in Europe and not in the Muslim countries (among others)?"[147]

Schluchter's engagement with Rodinson's perspective focuses largely on the question of "ideology," that chimera of Marxist thought. From Rodinson's point of view, ideas are but "ideology," elements to be explained away. In the case of Islamic thought, recast as "ideology," Rodinson seeks to neutralize it, to remove it as a possible influence on the social world. Likewise, if there are ideas in the West (or elsewhere) that are presumed to be special, to have "causal" efficacy, then they too must be explained away. The standard Marxist mode in this case is to ignore the actual content of the "ideology," and to claim instead that the ideas in question are nothing but a "reflection" or a superficial product of the underlying social conditions. These latter are sometimes termed "substructure," and sometimes described as the "prevailing mode of production." In either case, the ideas (or ideology) are said to "correspond" to this constellation of social and economic conditions.

Rodinson follows just these dual procedures in the case of Islam. On the one hand, he asserts,

> it can be said that no tendency discernible among Muslims is to be explained by the constraint exercised by a body of sacred writings existing previously and acting as a force...[on them].[148]

Similarly,

> it is perhaps worth taking the trouble to show...that post-Koranic ideology did not, in the Middle Ages, present that sharp contract with the ideology of the Christian world which might...seem to give support to Weber's thesis.[149]

On the other hand, if these denials do not seem sufficient, then Rodinson claims that the ideational items in question are not in reality what they seem, that is, they are not really *Islamic* elements, but something else:

> If Weber were right, and capitalism did not develop in the Islamic world because the ideology prevailing there was inimical to the rationalism needed for such a development, the cause would therefore seem to have not lain in Islam itself, the Muslim religion, but in all the factors that underlay that ideology.[150]

By this means Islam as a meaningful system of thought is anesthetized, exempted as it were, from all influence on the world.

With regard to the rationality question, Schluchter points out that Weber did not distinguish between "high" and "low" *levels* of rationality, but to *types* of rationality. Islamic religious law was for Weber a good illustration of *sacred* law as a type of *substantive* law, and it had its own virtues and limits. Schluchter does not point it out, but it is evident that Western law, in its pursuit of *formal* rationality in Weber's specific sense, made a concerted effort to incorporate the wisdom of many other kinds of law, under the assumption that the European legal system was *evolving*, moving toward a more universal and, yes, "rational," structure. As Western legal historians have pointed out, the jurists specializing in Roman civil law and those specializing in ecclesiastical law (the canonists) sought to integrate the best of German folk law, Roman civil law, divine law, and canon law. Beyond that, they believed in natural law as an extension of divine law, which was to be a guide for both church and civil law. Such an integrative effort was no mean feat, nor could it be accomplished without the use of carefully considered legal procedures against which each additional piece of law was to be accepted or rejected. Yet incredibly Rodinson claims that the medieval *qadi* "was himself guided, in principle, by a huge corpus of the *fiqh*, which was much more thoroughly systematized, unified, and rationalized than was" Western law and custom.[151] No matter how systematic and complete Rodinson wants to claim that Islamic jurisprudence was, it was essentially a closed system in the sense that it did *not* intentionally borrow (or seek to incorporate) principles from Roman law, canon law, Hebrew law, Greek law, or Persian law, or any of the other legal systems existing at the time of Islam's rise in the Middle East. Of course, one *can* find borrowings from Judaic and probably Persian law, but Islamic legal scholars would rarely have claimed that they intentionally borrowed such ideas, or that it was proper to do so. The "material roots" of Islamic law are the Quran and the *sunna*—nothing more. Nor was there an imperative to logically arrange Islamic law in terms of "higher principles," such as Natural law, a hierarchy of jurisdictions, or logical consistency.[152]

Accordingly, when Rodinson claims, as stated above, that a medieval Islamic judge and a European legal scholar of the same time were operating in just the same fashion and with the same conceptual tools and assumptions, he stretches credulity. As we have seen, Islamic law was missing a whole range of legal concepts and forms of legal agency, especially the concept of the corporation as a legally autonomous entity in which a group of individuals was treated as "a whole body," with one will. It was missing the right of corporate entities to *create their own* laws and *courts*; to have legal representation, as well as the concept of election by consent. It lacked the principle of jurisdiction and most important of all, the separation of sacred and secular law and jurisdictions; and not least of all, freedom of testation.

To Rodinson's claim that Weber's reasoning is circular, that "the period in which modern Europe took its decisive step along the path of modern capitalism," was also the one in which Europe "was more rationalistic than other civilizations,"[153] Schluchter points out that Weber was hardy a neophyte when it comes to thinking about historical causation, or the logic of concept formation. On the other hand, it could be pointed out, as Schluchter did earlier in his paper, that Weber specified many historical *preconditions* that had to be established before the "decisive" turn and unique conjoining of worldly asceticism and the evolving institutional structure of Europe occurred. The whole set of legal and institutional innovations that created the technical possibilities of the modern bureaucratic state, along with those legal devices necessary to facilitate capitalist development and accumulation belong to these preconditions. These were also connected to the rise of legally autonomous cities and towns. The point should be made, therefore, that all these innovations were set afoot long *before* the Reformation. In one of those passages where Weber spelled out the importance of the separation of the household from the business enterprise, he made this evolving path very clear:

> But the factor of decisive importance in this development is not the spatial differentiation or separation of the household from the work-shop and the store.... What is crucial is the separation of household and business for accounting and legal purposes, and the development of a suitable body of laws, such as the commercial register, elimination of dependence of the association and the firm upon the family, separate property of the private firm or limited partnership, and appropriate laws of bankruptcy. This fundamentally important development is the characteristic feature of the Occident, and it is worthy of note that the legal forms of our present commercial law were almost all developed as early as the Middle Ages—whereas they were almost entirely foreign to the law of Antiquity with its capitalism that was quantitatively sometimes much more developed.[154]

In a word, Rodinson's suggestion of circular reasoning stems from the lack of clarity in his own account of the structural development of the West.

With regard to what Schluchter calls "Weber's first main thesis," that is, "the traditional character of Islamic economic ethics," he concludes that the thesis is undisturbed by Rodinson's more detailed discussion of Muslim teaching and practice. Given Rodinson's base-superstructure framework, he is ill-equipped to distinguish between the logical and the psychological levels of analysis and their effects on human behavior. Likewise, none of the papers in this volume provide evidence that classical or reformed Islamic moments produced the inner worldly economic ethic analogous to the Protestant ethic, though some came close.

Regarding Weber's "second main thesis," Schluchter concludes "that the institutional conditions that prevailed in the Islamic states were favorable for commercial capitalism but not for industrial capitalism as an economic system."[155]

No doubt more criticisms of Rodinson's book on Islam and capitalism could be stated, but for present purposes it is evident that his criticisms of Weber are wide of the mark, and that Rodinson's understanding of the preconditions for the rise of modern capitalism, especially those that Weber located in European legal history, was deeply flawed. Despite Rodinson's deep knowledge of Islam and its history, he is neither a reliable critic of Weber on these issues nor a helpful guide to the internal structure and motivational blockages within Islam insofar as they bear on the question of why modern capitalism did not arise in the Muslim world.

In the case of Bryan Turner's book on Weber and Islam, Schluchter takes a more positive attitude. At the same time he rejects Turner's suggestion that Weber changed his position from one accenting *ideational* factors to *institutional* factors. Turner should be given credit for raising the issue of whether or not sociologists have any contribution to make to the study of Islam and the Muslim world at a time when very little attention was given to it by Western sociologists. His approach to Weber's writings, however, entail a mix of unsteady insights and less than objective reporting. Turner's major thesis was that "for Weber it was the patrimonial nature of Muslim political institutions which precluded the emergence of capitalist pre-conditions, namely rational law, a free labor market, autonomous cities, a money economy, and a bourgeois class."[156] Turner was correct to emphasize the pervasive influence of patrimonial structures in the history of Islam, but many other assumptions that Turner adduces seem to be at odds with the papers in this volume, and sometimes at odds with Weber's own writings. No doubt a significant part of the problem was that Turner gave as much attention to the analysis of the ideas of Karl Marx, especially the so-called "Asiatic mode of production," as he did to Weber's own writings. This diverted energy that ought to have gone into greater analysis of Weber's writings on Islam as well as the developmental history of intellectual and social structures in the Muslim world. This leads Turner to draw misleading conclusions, such as his belief that "when Weber attempted to show that...Islam as a religion of warriors produced an ethic which was incompatible with the 'spirit of capitalism,' he was hopelessly incorrect in purely factual terms."[157] It is difficult to reconcile that sweeping judgment with the discussions above, above all, those pointing to the persuasiveness of military conquest during the formative period of Islam's world wide dissemination. Likewise, it is difficult to reconcile Turner's conclusions with the more subtle analysis provided by Nehemia Levtzion.

Still another difficulty is Turner's claim that Weber "regards Islam... in many respects as the polar opposite of Puritanism..." and "that asceticism was absent in Islam."[158] Weber wrote that, "In the Quran, Muhammad is represented as completely rejecting every type of monasticism, though *not* all asceticism, for he did accord respect to fasting, begging, and penitential mortification."[159] Furthermore, Weber pointed out that "Islam imposed such requirements for everyday living as the wearing of distinctive clothing (a requirement that even today has important economic consequences...)...and the avoidance of certain unclean foods, of wine, and gambling."[160] Thus Weber was hardly unaware of those forms of asceticism that were most obvious in the Muslim community.

On the other hand, Weber quite rightly, Turner's opinion not withstanding, attempted to compare "the typical" behavior of the Puritan and the Muslim with regard to sensuality and personal luxury, which did indeed seem to stand in contrast to each other in earlier history. Insofar as sexual sensuality is concerned, contemporary Muslim feminists have rather pointedly singled out for criticism the traditional Islamic idea that women are meant to serve the sexual impulses of men, and that lack of sexual gratification—for both men and women—is a danger to the community.[161] Clearly that attitude is far removed from that of all the ascetic Protestant sects, as Weber suggests. According to Weber's summary of eighteenth century Puritan atttidues toward sexuality, "sexual intercourse is permitted, even within marriage, only as the means willed by God for the increase of His glory according to the Commandment, 'Be fruitful and multiply,' Along with a moderate vegetable diet and cold baths, the same prescription is given for sexual temptations as is used against all religious doubt," that is, "Work hard in your calling."[162] All this stands in profound contrast to those references in Islamic thought to the sensual delights that await the (male) Muslim believer in paradise.

More surprisingly, one can even find expressions in the contemporary Muslim community that, were Christ to reappear today, he would return as a polygamist. In a word, all of these sensual privileges were given unequally to male believers and today Muslim feminists have raised profound objections to these ideas, especially as they apply to polygamy, the unqualified guardianship of men over women, the right of men to scourge their wives, to unilaterally repudiate their wives, the unequal gender-based division of inheritance, and the reservation of the public sphere for men alone. It was precisely these elements of Islam that were rejected by the Turkish modernizers in the early part of this century, and which now are contested by female Muslims.[163] They are hardly outdated critiques of Islam of nineteenth-century Europeans that Turner would have us believe.[164]

Similarly, Turner prematurely criticizes Weber's contrast between the normative daily life of asceticism desired by the Puritan with the *sunna*-derived injunction, "when god blesses a man with prosperity he likes to see the signs thereof visible upon him."[165] Surely this idea of conspicuous display of blessings is apposite to that of the Puritans, Calvinists, and other Protestant sects.

Happily several of the discussion of this volume, those of Peters and Metcalf in particular, help to give greater subtlety to the discussion of the evident "puritan" themes in Islam and Calvinism. Nevertheless, they seem to lead to Weber's earlier conclusion that the "innerworldly" ethic of activist mastery did not emerge in Islam, though other forms of asceticism did. This is most evident in the contribution by Metcalf (chapter 8).

With regard to Schluchter's dissent from Turner's thesis about a switch in Weber's own theoretical emphases from ideational to institution factors, the first emphasis would presumably be found in Weber's essay on the Protestant ethic, while the latter stress appears in Weber's later writings. Schluchter maintains that "the fact that Weber later treats the other side [the institutional conditions], which he had deliberately neglected in the *Protestant Ethic*, implies neither the abandonment of the 'first' side nor a 'later discovery or recognition' of the other."[166] Otherwise Schluchter suggests that much of Turner's reconstruction of Weber's thought on Islam is "congruent" with the thrust of his paper in this volume. Nevertheless, it remains to be said that Turner's book frequently becomes bogged down in a fruitless debate about "materialism" versus "idealism" that advances neither sociological contributions to the sociology of Islam nor our appreciation of what Weber accomplished in framing the questions of comparative historical sociology as he did. The reader will be in a greatly enhanced position to draw his or her own conclusion about that after reading the individual essays that follow.

Notes

I should like to thank several individuals who read earlier drafts of this chapter for their judicious and helpful comments. These include Leif Stenberg and Roland Robertson and two dear friends, Elfie Raymond and Herman Schneider, who offered exceptional editorial assistance.

1. Max Weber, *The Protestant Ethic and the Spirit of Capitalism*, translated by Talcott Parsons (New York: Charles Scribners' Sons, 1958).
2. Max Weber, *The Social and Rational Foundations of Music,* ed. and trans. by Don Martindale, Johannes Riedel, and Gertrude Neuwirth (Carbondale: Southern Illinois University Press, 1958).
3. The possibility that Weber had written a more extended analysis of Islam is taken up below, 26f, 60–64.
4. Concerning Islamic law, the reader may consult some of the following sources: Joseph Schacht, *An Introduction to Islamic Law* (Oxford: Oxford University Press, 1964); N. J. Coulson, *A History of Islamic Law* (Edinburgh: Edinburgh University Press, 1964); idem, *Conflicts and Tensions in Islamic Jurisprudence*, revised edition (Chicago: University of Chicago Press, 1969); Fazlur Rahman, *Islam* (Chicago: University of Chicago Press, 1968); Asaf A. A. Fyzee, *Outlines of Muhammadan Law*, third edition (Lahore, and Oxford: Oxford University Press, 1964); among others.
5. See Schacht, *Introduction*, chapter 10. For a modification of Schacht's view see Wael B. Hallaq, "Was the Gate of Ijtihad Closed?" *International Journal of Middle East Studies*, 16 (1984): 3–41; and Haim Gerber, *State, Society and Law in Islam. Ottoman Law in Comparative Perspective* (Albany: State University of New York, 1994).
6. For this distinction cf. Majid Khadduri, trans. *Islamic Jurisprudence. Shafi'i's Risala* (Baltimore, MD: The Johns Hopkins University Press, 1961), esp. 38ff and 305–309; Edward H. Levi, *An Introduction to Legal Reasoning* (Chicago: University of Chicago Press, 1949); and Melvin A. Eisenberg, *The Nature of the Common Law* (Cambridge: Harvard University Press, 1988). For a similar conclusion see Wael Halleq, "The Logic of Legal Reasoning in Religious and Non-Religious Cultures: The Case of Islamic Law and the Common Law," *Cleveland State Law Review* 34 (1985/86): 79–96.
7. Lapidus, "Institutionalization," (p. 141f)
8. Eisenstadt, "Weber's Anaylsis of Islam and the Gestalt of Islamic Civilization," 287.
9. For the basis for this judgment, see Huff, "Science and the Public Sphere: Comparative Institutional Development in Islam and the West," *Social Epistemology* 11 (1997): 25–37.
10. P. Crone, "The Rise of Islam in the World," in *The Cambridge Illustrated History of the Islamic World*, ed. Francis Robinson (New York: Cambridge University Press, 1996), 2–31. Also see Crone, *Slaves on Horses: The Evolution of the Islamic Polity* (Cambridge: Cambridge University Press, 1980) and Daniel Pipes, *Slave Soldiers in Islam* (New Haven, CT: Yale University Press, 1981). Slavery, per se, continued into the twentieth century.
11. Daniel Pipes, *Slave Soldiers and Islam*, 45–50.

12. Levtzion, "Aspects of Islamization," 154.
13. Weber, *Economy and Society*, ed. G. Roth and C. Wittich (Berkeley: University of California Press, 1978), 474.
14. "Aspects of Islamization," ibid.
15. It may be noted that among the belongings of the group of assassins responsible for the death of President Sadat of Egypt in 1981 a pamphlet was found with the title, "The Neglected Duty," that is, *jihad*. In recent years this principle has been referred to by some Muslims as the "sixth pillar" of Islam. In any event, the document contains an impressive compilation of historical references justifying and advocating jihad. See Johannes J. G. Jansen, *The Neglected Duty: The Creed of Sadat's Assassins and Islamic Resurgence in the Middle East* (New York: Macmillan, 1986). For a compilation of the documents explaining and specifying the occasions for jihad, see Rudolph Peters, *Jihad in Classical and Modern Islam: A Reader* (Princeton, NJ: Markus Wiener Publishers, 1996).
16. See Bernard Lewis, *The Politial Language of Islam* (Chicago: University of Chicago Press, 1991), 30 and 229n11.
17. The tensions dervived from this theological conception are nicely captured in the title of a contemporary set of inteviews with Muslim leaders by Joyce M. Davis, *Between Jihad and Salaam. Profiles in Islam* (New York: St Martin's, 1997).
18. "Institutionalization," 142.
19. For a useful overview of the pattern of conversion and the spread of Islam see Lapidus, *A History of Muslim Societies* (New York: Cambridge University Press, 1988), 242–52; as well as *Conversion to Islam*, ed. N. Levtzion (New York: Holmes & Meier), 197. For a recent review of the various conversion studies, see Michael Morony, "The Age of Conversion: A Reassessment," in *Conversion and Continuity: Indigenous Christian Communities in Islamic Lands Eight to Eighteen Centuries,* eds. Michael Gervers and Ramzi Jibran Bikhazi (Toronto: Pontifical Institute of Medieval Studies, 1990), 135–150.
20. "Aspects of Islamization," 155.
21. Hardy, "Islamic Patrimonialism in the Mogul empire," 186.
22. Ibid.
23. "Hindrances," 68, 80f, 84ff, 87f, 94f, 101, 129n52.
24. Douglass C. North, *Institutions, Institutional Change and Economic Performance* (New York: Cambridge University Press, 1990).
25. Weber, *Economy and Society,* 2: 818–822.
26. "Weber and Islamic Law," 248.
27. Toby E. Huff, *The Rise of Early Modern Science: Islam, China, and the West* (New York: Cambridge University Press, 1993), 48–54. The phrase I borrow from Alexandre Koyré.
28. Weber, *The Protestant Ethic and the Spirit of Capitalism* (New York: Charles Scribner's Sons, 1958), 25.
29. Ibid., 26.
30. Ibid.
31. Weber, ibid., 26.
32. See below, 248.
33. Rogers Brubaker, *The Limits of Rationality. An Essay on the Social and Moral Thought of Max Weber* (London: George Allen & Unwin, 1985), 4.
34. For a very useful outline of the continuing rationalization of modern social life (through the extension of efficiency, calculability, predictability and social control) over more and more aspects of American social life (but also the globe),

see the improbably titled book, *The McDonaldization of Society*, revised edition (Thousand Oaks, CA: Pine Forge Press, 1996). Remarkably, the fast-food business has incorporated and perfected the integration of bureaucracy, "scientific management" and assembly line technology in such a fashion that it has become a universal model of how to "rationally" organize any kind of ongoing activity from food products to education, healthcare, and other domains.

35. Weber, *Economy and Society,* 2: 656–7.
36. "Weber and Islamic Law," 251.
37. For a modern treatise on the Civil Law tradition, see John Henry Merryman, *The Civil Law Tradition. An Introduction to the Legal Systems of Western Europea and Latin America* (Stanford, CA: Stanford University Press, 1985).
38. On this see Schacht, *Introduction to Islamic Law*, 37ff.
39. "Weber and Islamic Law," 255.
40. *Economy and Society*, 891.
41. H. J. Berman, "Conscience and Law: The Lutheran Reformation and the Western Legal Tradition," *Journal of Law and Religion* 17 (1987): 177–202, at 177. This is a summary of the thesis of his *Law and Revolution* (Cambridge, MA: Harvard University Press, 1983)
42. "Weber and Islamic Law," 252.
43. Ibid.
44. Sally Ewing, "Formal Justice and the Spirit of Capitalism: Max Weber's Sociology of Law," *Law and Society Review* 21 (1987): 87–512.
45. Harold J. Berman, "Some False Premises of Max Weber's Sociology of Law," *Washington University Law Quarterly* 65, 4 (1987): 758–770, at 769 n28.
46. "Weber and Islamic Law," 255.
47. "Weber and Law."
48. C. Wright Mills was one of the first to point this out in the U.S. for the period before World War II; see *White Collar* (New York: Oxford University Press, 1951), 23.
49. This portrait of the Muslim world as burdened by all these social and economic ills, in addition to severely depressed levels of scientific and technological achievement, was carefully set out by a number of the Muslim participants at the International Conference on "Values and Attitudes Toward Science and Technology" (VAST '96) held in Kuala Lumpur, Malaysia in September 1996. See Mumtaz Ali Anwar and Ahmad Bakeri Abu Bakar, "Current State of Science and Technology in the Muslim World," in *VAST '96 Papers*, (Kuala Lumpur: International Islamic University Malaysia), vol. 1: 304–327; and Ghulam Hannif, "The Challenge of Science and Technology to the Muslim World," ibid., 284–302. For a focused comparison of the *economic* differences between the Arab Muslim countries of the Middle East and several Asian NICs (newly industrialized countries), see Tufan Kolam, "Scientific Manpower and Economic Development," in *Science and Technology Manpower for Development in the Islamic World*, ed. F. A. Daghastani (Amman: Islamic Academy of Science, 1992), 69–85.
50. See the essays in *Law in the Middle East*, eds. M. Khadduri and H. Liebesny, (Washington, DC: The Middle East Institute, 1955); esp. Liebesny, "The Development of Western Legal Privileges," 309–333; as well as Norman Anderson, *Law and Reform in the Muslim World* (London: Athlone Press, 1976). For the inner struggles of such reformers, see Malcolm Kerr, *Islamic Reform: the Political and Legal Theories of Muhammad 'Abduh and Rashid Rida* (Berkeley: University of California Press., 1966). Saudi Arabia of course claims to follow the *Shari'a*.
51. "Weber and Law," 260.

52. Ibid.
53. A fuller account of this general thesis is in Crone, *Pre-Industrial Societies* (Oxford: Basil Blackwell, 1989), 161ff; which draws on Ernest Gellner's ideas in his, "A Social Contract in Search of an Idiom: The Demise of the Danegeld," in *Spectacles and Predicaments* (Cambridge: Cambridge University Press, 1979), 277–306.
54. "Weber and Law," ibid.
55. Ibid., 259.
56. Ibid. 259.
57. Ibid.
58. Peters, "Islam and Fundamentalism," 210.
59. Ibid., 211.
60. Ibid.
61. Ibid., 212.
62. On this see *The Theology of Ash'ari*, ed. and trans. Richard J. McCarthy (Beirut: Imprimerie Catholique, 1953); and M. Fakhry, *Islamic Occasionalism and Its Critique by Thomas Acquinas* (London: Allen & Unwin, 1958), among others.
63. Peters, "Islam and Fundamentalism," 212.
64. Ibid.
65. Ibid, 215.
66. "Islamic Reform Initiatives," 220.
67. Ibid.
68. Ibid.
69. Ibid. 223.
70. Ibid.
71. Weber, *The Sociology of Religion*, trans. Ephraim Fischoff (Boston: Beacon Press, 1964) 59.
72. Ibid, 142.
73. "Islamic Reform Initiatives," 225.
74. Ernst Troeltsch, *The Social Teachings of the Christian Churches*, 2 vols. (New York: Harper Torch, 1960 [1911]).
75. Metcalf, ibid., 220.
76. See Richard P. Mitchell, The *Society of the Muslim Brothers* (New York: Oxford University Press, 1993, reprinted), 2216ff.
77. As cited in Ibn Khaldun, *The Muqaddima*, trans. F. Rosethal (Princeton, NJ: Princeton University Press) 3: 169.
78. Weber, *The Methodology of the Social Sciences,* ed. and trans. Edward Shils and Henry Finch (New York: Free Press, 1949), 90.
79. Ibid.
80. Peter H. Odegard, *The Story of the Anti-Saloon League* (New York: Columbia University Press, 1928).
81. "Weber and Sects," 277.
82. Ibid.
83. Ibid. 275, 278.
84. "Weber's Anaylsis of Islam and the Gestalt of Islamic Civilization, " 291.
85. Robinson draws on the work of Peter Berger, *The Social Reality of Religion* (Harmondsworth: Penguin Books, 1973).
86. "Secularization," 233; and see Herbert Liebesny, "English Common Law and the Islamic Law in the Middle East and South Asia: Religious Influences and Secularization," *Cleveland State Law Review* 34 (1985/6): 19–33.
87. "Secularization," 234.
88. Ibid., 235.

89. Ibid., 236.
90. Ibid., 238.
91. Ibid., 239.
92. Ibid., 240.
93. Among others see Oliver Roy, T*he Failure of Political Islam* (Cambridge: Harvard University Press, 1994); and Ibrahim M. Abu-Rabi', *Intellectual Origins of Islamic Resurgence in the Modern Arab World* (Albany: State University of New York Press, 1996); and Dale Eickelman, "Mass Higher Education and the Religious Imaginatiuon in Contemporary Arab Societies," *American Ethnologist* 19 1994 (4): 643–655.
94. Robinson, "Secularization," 241.
95. Max Weber, *Agrarian Sociology of Ancient Civilizations,* trans. R. I. Frank (London: New Left Books, 1976).
96. Schluchter, "Hindrances," 60ff.
97. E. S. Kennedy and Victor Roberts, "The Planetary Theory of Ibn al-Shatir," *Isis* 50 (1959): 227–235; E. S. Kennedy, "Late Medieval Planetary Theory." *Isis* (1966) 57: 365–78; and for a useful overview of this development, George Saliba, "Arabic Astronomy and Copernicus," *Zeitschrift fur Geschichte der Arabish-Islamischen Wissenschaften* Band 1: 73–87; reprinted in *A History of Arabic Astronomy. Planetary Theory During the Golden Age of Islam* (New York: New York University Press, 1994), chapter 15.
98. For more on this see Huff, *The Rise of Early Modern Science*, chapters 2 and 5.
99. "Hindrances," 66.
100. Weber, *General Economic History*, Schluchter's emphasis, as cited in "Hindrances," 67.
101. "Hindrances," ibid.
102. Weber, as cited in "Hindrances," 71.
103. F. Ulrich, *Die Vorherbestimmungslehre im Islam und Christentums. Eine religionsgeschichtliche Parallele* (Gütersloh: C. Bertelsmann, 1912).
104. E.g., W. Montgomery Watt, *Free Will and Predestination in Early Islam* (London: 1948) ; idem, "Islamic Alternatives to the Concept of Free-Will," in *La Notion de liberté au Moyen Age: Islam, Byzance, Occident* (Paris: Societé d'Edition, 1985), 15–24; and R. M. Frank, "Two Islamic Views of Human Agency,", in ibid., 37–49. Also see Harry Wolfson, *The Philosophy of Islam* (Cambridge, MA: Harvard University Press, 1976).
105. Weber, *Economy and Society*, as cited below, 78.
106. "Hindances," 78.
107. Weber, *The Protestant Ethic*, as cited by Schluchter, below, ibid.
108. As noted in our discussion earlier regarding jihad, "holy struggle," the reader should understand that the Muslim must "struggle" in all ways, intellectual (i.e., though *ijtihad*) and militarily (if called upon) in the service of the faith. But some Muslims would say that any kind of *exertion* in the service of the faith, such as calling others back to the faith or otherwise proselytizing in the name of the faith through peaceful intellectual and political means, can be termed "*jihad*." See Tyan, "Djihad," *EI*[2] vol. 2: 538ff.
109. "Hindrances," 80.
110. "Islam and Reform," 225.
111. Crone, *Slaves on Horses.*
112. "Hindrances," 92.
113. Ibid.
114. N. J. Coulson, *A History of Islamic Law* (Edinburgh: Edinburgh University Press, 1964), 129.

115. "Hindrances," 95.
116. Ibid.
117. Ibid., 96.
118. Weber, *Economy and Society,* 828.
119. See George Makdisi, *The Rise of the College in Islam and the West* (Edinburgh: Edinburgh University Press, 1981).
120. *Economy and Society*, ibid.
121. Ibid.
122. Ibid., 829. This path of development has been spelled out with great insight and much more detail by Harold J. Berman, *Law and Revolution: The Formation of the Western Legal Tradition.*
123. It should be noted, however, that, following Islamic scholars of the late nineteenth century, Weber assumed that there had been a "reception" of Roman law, which there had not been. See *Economy and Society*, 834, n24.
124. Weber, Ibid., 829.
125. See A. I. Sabra, "The Appropriation and Subsequent Naturalization of Greek Science in Medieval Islam: A Preliminary Statement," *History of Science* 25 (1987): 223–243; and idem, "Science and Philosophy in Medieval Theology: The Evidence of the Fourteenth Century," *Zeitschrift für Geschichte der Arabisch-Islamishen Wissenschaften* 9 (1994): 1–42.
126. Schacht, *An Introdcution to Islamic Law.*
127. I have discussed these issues in *The Rise of Early Modern Science,* chapters 4, 5 and 6; and see Berman, ibid. chapter 2 and passim.
128. See Berman, *Law and Revolution*, 608 n58; as well as Gaines Post, *Studies in Medieval Legal Thought: Public Law and the State, 1150–1322* (Princeton, NJ: Princeton University Press, 1964), chapter 3.
129. Schacht, "Islamic Religious Law," in *The Legacy of Islam*, 2nd ed. (New York: Oxford University Press, 1974), 398. Likewise D. Santillana expressed the same view: "Muslim jurists do not know–and that is easy to understand if we think of the political and social differences between the Islamic state and those of the Roman type–neither the juridical personality of municipalities, nor of that of collectives of persons such as guilds" (*Istituzioni di diritto musulmano malichita* 1, 170–1, as cited in S. M. Stern, "The Constitution of the Islamic City," in *The Islamic City*, ed. A. Hourani (Philadelphia: University of Pennsylvania Press, 1970), 49.
130. *Economy and Society,* 829.
131. That is, to part ii, section 6 (in the chapter on the Sociology Law, VIII), of *Economy and Society*: "Associational Contracts—Juristic Personality," 705ff.
132. See Khadduri and Liebesney, *The Law of the Middle East,* and Norman Anderson, *Law and Reform in Muslim World,* among others.
133. Makdisi, *The Rise of the College*, 277; F. Ziadeh, *Lawyers: The Rule of Law and Liberalism in Modern Egypt* (Stanford, CA: Stanford University Press, 1968), 9; and M. K. Masud, B. Messick, and D. S. Powers, "Muftis, Fatwas, and Islamic Legal Interpretation," in *Islamic Legal Interpretation* (Cambridge, MA: Harvard University Press, 1996), especially 25–26.
134. Farhat Ziadeh, *Lawyers,* 149.
135. "Hindrances," 99.
136. Ibid., 100.
137. Ibid.
138. *Economy and Society*, 1239.
139. Ibid., 1240, original emphasis.
140. "Hindrances," 103.

141. Cf. Michaud-Quantin, Pierre, *Universitas: Expressions du movement communautaire dans le moyen-Age Latin* (Paris: J. Vrin.; 1970); G. Post, *Studies*; and Berman, *Law and Revolution*.
142. Huff, *The Rise of Early Modern Science*.
143. Maxime Rodinson, *Islam and Capitalism*, trans. Brian Peace (Austin: University of Texas, 1978).
144. Bryan S. Turner, *Weber and Islam* (London: Routledge, 1974).
145. *Islam and Capitalism*, 90.
146. Ibid., 78.
147. Ibid, 3
148. Ibid., 102.
149. Ibid., 103.
150. Ibid.
151. Ibid, 106.
152. How radically different the spirit now is, for example, in Malaysia to "upgrade" Islamic law, is revealed in Donald Horowitz, "The Qur'an and The Common Law: Islamic Law Reform and the Theory of Legal Change," *The American Journal of Comparative Law* 42, 2–3 (1994): 233–293, and 545–580. The result might be characterized as a new hybrid law, as Horowitz suggests, that yields both an upgraded and authentic new *Islamic* legal system, and one that is fully consistent with the principles of British Common Law.
153. Ibid., 77.
154. Weber, *Economy and Society*, 387.
155. "Hindrances," 119.
156. Turner, *Weber and Islam*, 2.
157. Ibid.
158. Ibid., 12.
159. *Economy and Society*, 624, emphasis added.
160. Ibid.
161. These themes are vivdly explored by Fatima Mernissi in her many books, especially, *Beyond the Veil* (Reading, MA: Addison Wesley Press, 1987); and *The Veil and the Male Elite. A Feminist Interpretationn of Women's Rights in Islam* (Reading, MA: Addison Wesley Press, 1991).
162. Weber, *Protestant Ethic*, 158f.
163. Regarding the Turkish situation see Nilüfer Göle, *The Forbidden Modern* (Ann Arbor: University of Michigan Press, 1996); and Yesim Arat, "The Project of Modernity and Women in Turkey, " in *Rethinking Modernity and National Identity in Turkey*, eds. Sibel Bozdogan and Resat Kasaba (Seattle: University of Washington Press, 1997), 95–112.
164. Turner, *Weber and Islam*, 140.
165. As cited by Weber in *Economy and Society*, 624.
166. Ibid., 121.

1

Hindrances to Modernity: Max Weber on Islam

Wolfgang Schluchter

> *Industrialization was not impeded by Islam as the religion of individuals...but by the religiously conditioned structure of the Islamic state formation, its officialdom, and its implementation of law.*
> —Max Weber, Economy and Society

The Fate of Weber's Study of Islam

While working on his comparative and developmental analyses of the major religions, on their relations to the nonreligious—especially the economic and political orders and powers—Max Weber also took up Islam. It is one of the six major religions that interested him most.[1] As in the case of these other religions, he was especially attracted to its inception and early development: the "birth" of Islam in Mecca and Yathrib (later Medina), its "heroic age" during the rule of the early caliphs (632–61) and the Umayyads (661–750), and its "maturation" during the period of the Abbasids (750–1258), generally regarded as the golden age of Islam. This coming-of-age is reflected in the canonization of the crucial religious sources, the consolidation of the most significant orthodox and heterodox movements, and the establishment of religious stratification between the masses and the virtuosi. It also found expression in a lessening of the dynamism characteristic of its initial drive toward world conquest and in a subsequent religious, and, above all political, polycentrism that stands in contrast to the originally unifying, national-Arabic movements. Of course, none of this is intended to deny the fact that important secondary movements followed in the wake of these primary ones. On the contrary, Weber clearly recognizes the effect of such secondary movements of "empire-building" power in the Ottoman and Mogul periods, without which Islam would be unimaginable. However, his comments remain rather scanty here, which, at least with regard to Indian Islam, is somewhat surprising given his thorough analysis of Hinduism and Buddhism. Admittedly, even in the case of early Arabic Islam, there exists no coherent text that could serve as the basis of interpretation. Before attempting such an interpretation, I think it is appropriate to say a few words about the fate of Weber's study of Islam, a study that certainly would have included not only Arabic and Persian, but also Turkish and Indian Islam.

Weber's interest in non-Christian religions and in the civilizations (*Kulturkreise*) influenced by them[2] appears to have intensified around 1910. It was presumably awakened earlier, not least of all in Eranos, the Heidelberg circle on religion in which interdisciplinary scholarship was writ large.[3] Religious scholarship of the time favored comparative studies of religion,[4] and Weber was a strong adherent of this approach.[5] Moreover, 1910 appears to be the beginning of a new phase in his work. In 1909, he had published his large and comprehensive study *The Agrarian Sociology of Ancient Civilizations (Agrarverhältnisse im Altertum)* (Weber 1924a, 1976) and completed publication of the series of essays "Psychophysics of Industrial Labor" ("Psychophysik der industriellen Arbeit") (Weber 1995). With the "Anticritical Last Word" ("Antikritisches Schlußwort") (Weber 1978d, 1978a), which appeared in 1910, he closed the debate in the wake of *The Protestant Ethic and the Spirit of Capitalism* (Weber 1921, vol. 1; 1958b).[6] The new phase was marked by a return to the sociology of religion (already implicit in the two countercritiques of Rachfahl) and by the planning and execution of the large-scale "Handbook on Political Economy" ("Handbuch der politischen Oekonomie," later "The Outline of Social Economics" ["Grundriss der Sozialökonomik"]). This is also confirmed by Marianne Weber in her biography (Marianne Weber 1926). There she wrote, in view of the conclusion of the essays on "Psychophysics," the last part of which appeared on September 30, 1909:

> Now that all of this has been cleared up, Weber is returning to his studies in universal sociology, and in a twofold manner. He wants to continue the essays in the sociology of religion and is at the same time preparing, in response to the prompting of his publisher, Paul Siebeck, a major collective work: "The Outline of Social Economics." He is designing its plan, recruiting its coauthors, and has allotted to

himself, in addition to the organizational work, the most important contributions. The writings in the sociology of religion draw in part from the same sources as this new work and are being brought along hand in hand with it.[7]

Apparently, in this new phase Weber initially follows the lead given by his previous findings. *Agrarian Sociology* contains an economic theory of the ancient world, a sort of economic and political sociology of ancient Mediterranean-European civilization and its development. It can be viewed as a preliminary stage to Weber's later sociology of economics and domination.[8] In the "Anticritical Last Word," Weber formulated the "truly most urgent questions"[9] for a sociology of religion:

1. The investigation of the different effects of the Calvinist, Baptist, and Pietist ethics on methodical conduct.
2. The investigation "of the beginnings of similar developments in the Middle Ages and in early Christianity."
3. The investigation of the economic side of the process or, in later formulations, the investigation of the other side of the causal chain—after the investigation of the conditioning of economic mentality by religion now the investigation of the conditioning of religion by the economy, especially by class constellations.[10]

This undertaking amounted to a sociology of the bourgeoisie *(Bürgertum)*, a depiction of the elective affinities between bourgeois class constellations and religiously conditioned modes of conduct, affinities provided not only but certainly "most consistently by ascetic Protestantism."[11]

If the conclusion of *Agrarian Sociology* is read in conjunction with these programmatic statements, it appears that in this new phase Weber intended to clarify above all the historical preconditions of modern capitalism. These included both the "subjective" and the "objective," the motivational and the institutional ones.[12] This new phase also included the analysis of obstruction, indifference, or reinforcement among these preconditions.[13] This required the reconstruction of Occidental development from a necessarily one-sided viewpoint, based on a theoretical relation to values. It also required a comparative perspective, especially with regard to Judaism and Islam, because both contributed to this development.

Admittedly, Weber gave no indication of such an intention in his "Anticritical Last Word." He did, however, make plain his desire to show, by elaborating further upon the *Protestant Ethic* and *Agrarian Sociology,* to which preconditions modern capitalist development—in the interplay between form and spirit, subjective and objective, motivational and institutional factors—owes its existence. It is worth noting the parameters of Weber's solution in 1910, as formulated in the closing passages of the "Anticritical Last Word." Weber first distances himself from any purely technological explanation of modern and indeed of any capitalist development. His purpose, however, is not merely to reject monocausal approaches, but to reject as well those multicausal approaches that take only one side of the causal chain into account. He writes:

> The capitalism of antiquity evolved *without* technical advances and in fact occurred simultaneously with the cessation of such advances. The technical progress of the Continental Middle Ages was surely of no little importance in creating the *possibility* for the development of modern capitalism, but certainly it constituted no decisive stimulus for development. Objective factors such as certain aspects of climate, which influence conduct and labor costs, count among the most significant pre-requisites, along with the inland culture that shaped the political-social organization of medieval society and therefore the medieval city, particularly the continental city and its bourgeoisie. (See my previously cited article in the *Handwörterbuch der Staatswissenschaften*.) In addition, new forms of productive organization in, for example, cottage industries, were specific economic influences; although not entirely alien to ancient culture, they displayed a unique structure, diffusion, and importance. The great process of development that lies between the highly unstable late medieval developments toward capitalism and the mechanization of technology, which is so decisive for capitalism in its present form, culminated in the creation of certain objective political and economic pre-requisites that are so important for the emergence of the latter. It culminated particularly in the creation and diffusion of the rationalist and antitraditionalist spirit and the whole mentality that absorbed it. Major insights into this phenomenon may be furnished by the history of modern science and its recent practical relation to the economy and by the history of the modern *conduct of life* and its practical meaning for the economy.[14]

The developmental history of political and economic organization, and also of science and conduct, must be written in such a way that the writer does not hastily degrade one into a mere function or consequence of the other.[15] It needs to be written with a view to the qualitative transformations that occurred in antiquity, in the Middle Ages, and in the period between the late Middle Ages and modernity. This reconstruction of Western development, especially of capitalism, must be carried out not only in terms of a specific viewpoint; it must be "dissolved" into a series of partial developments that have to be continuously and repeatedly interrelated. This calls for a value-related, ideal-typical developmental construct as a prerequisite for the realization of this project. Indeed, Weber does not object to developmental constructions as such, but only to those that operate with models of complete and all-inclusive stages based on normative criteria that are then reified. That he subsequently repeatedly raised the question of why rational industrial capitalism arose only in the West, and that he responded to it with the constellation of conditions that existed only here, does not imply that other constellations could not also have produced such a result or that other civilizations that later followed the path to industrial capitalism had to pass through the same "stages" into which one can "dissect" Western development. For Weber, universal history dissolves into a plurality of developmental histories in and between civilizations.[16] However, this plurality does not imply that the dimensions one chooses for their reconstruction are arbitrary. The recourse to organizational forms, especially to economic ones, is never sufficient,[17] for these are only some of the important elements shaping conduct. Other important elements are normatively based conceptions of duty. They are, at least in precapitalist times, embedded in religious world views and ethics. Therefore, one needs to take into account not only economic but also cultural, especially religious, forces if one aims to reconstruct Western and non-Western developmental histories.[18]

It quickly becomes clear that this new phase of work coincides with a qualitative transformation of Weber's approach.[19] He made a discovery, and it too is documented in Marianne Weber's biography. Although its dating is unclear, its nature is not. It is the insight that the development of modern scientific rationalism demonstrates connections not only with economic but also with aesthetic developments, especially with the Western development of music.[20] Marianne Weber provided the following description:

> The times hurl abuse at rationalism and many artists in particular consider it an inhibition of their creative powers. For this reason this discovery [of the connection between scientific and aesthetic development] especially excites Weber. He has now also planned a sociology of art, and sometime around 1910 undertook as a first attempt in the midst of his other studies, the investigation of the rational and sociological foundations of music. It led him into the most remote areas of ethnology and into the most difficult investigations of tonal arithmetic [*Tonarithmetik*] and symbolism. Nevertheless, as soon as this part was provisionally established, he forced himself to return to those writings promised and already in progress.[21]

The discovery did not only lead to "detours"; it was also of far-reaching significance for Weber's twofold project. It motivated him to broaden the scope of his analyses. Certainly, the distinctive character and development of Occidental capitalism remained at the center; however, this was now but one of several Western cultural phenomena of universal significance.[22] This broadened scope meant that one cannot confine oneself to the investigation of religious and economic development. Analyses of domination and law, of social organizations ranging from the family to the "state," have to be included as well. Moreover, if one seeks to define and explain the distinctive character of the *whole* of Western culture in terms of its rational-methodical conduct, its rational capitalist enterprise, its rational *Anstaltsstaat,* its formally rational law, its rational science, and its music of harmonic chords, it is necessary to compare this civilization with others and to show why these phenomena did not occur there. In order to do this, one needs criteria and concepts. These criteria and concepts are, as Weber emphasized with all the clarity one could ask for, based on the cultural values of the civilization to which he belonged. Although this basis leads, in accordance with the postulate of theoretical value relation, to a heuristic Eurocentrism, it does not entail normative Eurocentrism. To make these comparisons, one also needs basic knowledge of other civilizations, especially of the religions and the forms of economy, domination, and law that helped shape them. This knowledge must go at least as far as is necessary to find "the points of comparison" with Occidental development,[23] and thus, at least far enough to work out the similarities and differences vis-à-vis Western development.

That rational industrial capitalism and other Occidental cultural phenomena arose only in the West, or more precisely, that they occurred here for the first time, is a historical fact for Weber. These phenomena do not necessarily interest everyone, nor does everyone consider them the most important of phenomena; nevertheless, no one can deny their reality. But exactly because they aroused Weber's interest, he was compelled to go beyond the limits of his own civilization and, not to be forgotten, beyond the limits of his own scholarly discipline to investigate these phenomena.[24] There are three chief reasons for this: the clarification of the problems of identification (demonstration of the unique features), the clarification of the problems of causal attribution (demonstration of the historical preconditions), and the clarification of the problem of diagnosis (demonstration of the "sacrifices," of the "lost" possibilities); for the comparison does not merely show the unique features of the West and facilitate causal attributions, it also makes clear what was, in contrast to other cultures, not realized here. Thus, in addition to theoretical and historical dimensions, cultural science also possesses a practical dimension.[25] Weber apparently first took the step beyond the limits of his own civilization in connection with his research on music, but this step continued to have consequences. As his wife reported, "When (sometime around 1911) he resumes his studies in the sociology of religion, he is drawn to the Orient: to China, Japan, and India, and then to Judaism and Islam."[26]

No later than 1911, Weber worked through those "sources" important for his twofold project. For non-Western civilizations, these sources were largely secondary, to an even greater extent than those he used to analyze Western development.[27] For Islam, it appears that outside of his knowledge of the holy sources (Quran, *sunna*, *shari'a*), presumably gathered from secondary literature, he based his analysis primarily on the work of German Islamicists of the time, such as Carl Heinrich Becker, Julius Wellhausen, Ignaz Goldziher, and Joseph Kohler, whose studies have not lost their relevance even today. These were supplemented by the works of Christian Snouck Hurgronje and probably one or another English or French author.[28] This accords with the impression one gains of Weber's analysis of other civilizations. His comparative studies reflect above all the contemporaneous German scholarship in sinology, Indology, Semitics, Egyptology, and Islamic studies, as well as in Protestant theology insofar as it was oriented toward comparative religion (*Religionswissenschaft*). Differences that do arise here depend on the extent to which Weber approached the monographic presentation of his findings.

How then did the two projects develop, in which Islam—alongside Confucianism, Hinduism, Buddhism, Judaism, and Christianity (and its "internal" subdivisions)—plays an important role? By the end of 1913, Weber had apparently brought to paper large parts of *both* projects. In the meantime, the one project had been entitled "The Economic Ethics of the World Religions" ("Die Wirtschaftsethik der Weltreligionen"), whereas the other was called "The Economy and the Societal Orders and Powers" ("Die Wirtschaft und die gesellschaftlichen Ordnungen und Mächte"). As Marianne Weber's comment shows, the sources tapped during this new phase of work were used for both projects. As Weber himself later put it, the two projects—at least in terms of the parts on the sociology of religion—serve mutually to interpret and supplement each other and were meant to be published simultaneously.[29] Let us look at two letters that yield a relatively clear picture of the state and substance of the two manuscripts at the end of 1913. On December 30, 1913, Weber wrote to his publisher Siebeck of "The Economy and the Societal Orders and Powers" that he had worked out a complete theory and exposition that relates the major forms of social groupings to the economy: from the family and household to the enterprise, the kin group, the ethnic community, religion (encompassing all the major religions of the world: a sociology of salvation doctrines and religious ethics—what Troeltsch did, now for *all* religions, only much more concise), finally a comprehensive sociological theory of the state and domination. I can claim that nothing of the kind has ever been written, not even as a precursor.[30]

On June 22, 1915, Weber offered Siebeck a series of essays, "Economic Ethics of the World Religions," for publication in the *Archiv für Sozialwissenschaft und Sozialpolitik*. He said he had had them "since the beginning of the war" and that they encompassed "Confucianism (China), Hinduism and Buddhism (India), Judaism, Islam [and] Christianity," and furthermore represented the successful "generalization and realization of the method" proposed in the *Protestant Ethic*. He went on to say that four essays were involved, of four to five press sheets each, "preliminary studies toward, and commentaries on, the systematic sociology of religion" for the "Outline of Social Economics," and thus for that manuscript spoken of in the letter of December 30, 1913. The essays—according to Weber—could at some point, along with others and in revised form, be published on their own. In this way, he anticipated the *Collected Essays in the Sociology of Religion (Gesammelte Aufsätze zur Religionssoziologie)* (Weber 1921). They did in fact start appearing in 1920, with a first volume that Weber himself had prepared for print.[31] At least a part of this series, however, must have dated from 1913 rather than the beginning of the war. This follows from the footnote that Weber added to the publication of the first article. The latter appeared, along with an "Introduction" to the complete series, on October 14, 1915. This note stated that the subsequent essays were being published "unchanged" in the manner "in which they were written down two years ago and were read aloud to friends."[32] Thus, one can infer that by the end of 1913, at the latest by the beginning of the war, voluminous manuscripts existed on both projects, and Islam was included in their analyses.

One of these manuscripts, entitled "The Economy and the Societal Orders and Powers," was not published during Weber's lifetime. It was part of his literary estate and was published after his death (along with a later manuscript that he himself had completed for publication) as parts 2 and 3 (later only part 2) of *Economy and Society*. The latter included—from the time of the second edition of this highly problematic "book construct" created by the editors[33]—four texts in which Islamic civilization is discussed: those on the sociologies of religion, domination, law, and the city. Although the other of the two manuscripts was published by Weber himself under the title "The Economic Ethics of the World Religions" (Weber 1921), it was published only in part and (after the printing of the "Introduction," the first two articles on Confucianism, and the "Intermediate Reflections") in a version different from the one to which the letter of June 22, 1915, gives witness. Weber revised the articles on Hinduism prior to first publication. This was also true of the articles on Buddhism and ancient Judaism.[34] More important, though, the series of articles reaching fruition by January 1920 did not go beyond ancient Judaism. Weber never managed to publish the parts on Islam and Christianity mentioned in the letter.

This provokes two questions: Did Weber still want to publish these articles? And what became of that part of the "Economic Ethics" manuscript dealing with Islam and Christianity? An unequivocal answer can be given to the first question: there can be no doubt that Weber intended to incorporate studies of Islam and Christianity (though no longer into the *Archiv* series) into the "Collected Essays on the Sociology of Religion." This is not only confirmed in the second version of the "Introduction" of 1920,[35] but above all in the announcement that Weber himself wrote in September 1919. Here he presented the public with the contents of the planned four-volume "Collected Essays on the Sociology of Religion" (cf. Weber 1921). He commented that two of these volumes were in press. These would include a revision of those essays on the sociology of religion already published, that is, the essays on ascetic Protestantism, Confucianism and Taoism, Hinduism and Buddhism, and Judaism, to be supplemented by analyses not yet published of Egyptian, Mesopotamian, and Zoroastrian religious ethics and of "the development of the European bourgeoisie in antiquity and the Middle Ages." These would then be followed by two further volumes consisting solely of unpublished studies (and, one must add, of studies largely not yet written): a third volume treating "early Christianity, talmudic Judaism, Islam, and Oriental Christianity," then a "concluding volume" on "Christianity of the Occident."[36] In my view, this announcement makes two things clear: First, the treatment of Islam would definitely have been shorter than that of Confucianism, Hinduism, or ancient Judaism. Second, it presumably would have been twofold in purpose, pursuing developmental and typological aims, for similar to Judaism, Islam belonged to the context of the historical "pre-conditions" of Western development and at the same time represented a development of historical significance in its own right vis-à-vis that of the West.[37] This is also implied by the placement of Islam in the project: within the context of both its historical predecessors and its most important rivals.

In contrast, it is not as easy to supply an unambiguous answer to the second question, which concerns the manuscript. An indirect approach is required, unless one simply answers that Weber never had a manuscript on Islam and that his remarks to the contrary can only be understood as a projection. In fact, if the statement in the letter of June 22, 1915, were accurate, would there not have to be a manuscript among his posthumous papers? Furthermore, does not the fact that the *General Economic History*, which some like to see as Weber's "last words,"[38] contains no lengthy passages on Islam imply that it no longer interested him after the war began? It can hardly be denied that no manuscript entitled "Islam" was found in the literary estate or that Weber no longer intensively dealt with Islam after the war broke out. But I still consider the statement made in the June 1915 letter truthful. What manuscript is Weber then referring to in this letter? I will offer a confessedly speculative solution to this riddle.

In my view, the only manuscript that could be considered is found today in the sociology of religion section of *Economy and Society*. In chapter 6, it is entitled "XV. The Great Religions and the World" (Weber 1978b: 611–34; in German: "Die Kulturreligionen und die 'Welt'"). It is preceded by the text (chap. 6: XII–XIV; Weber 1978b: 576–610) that Weber refined into his famous "Intermediate Reflections." In another essay I have shown that *Economy and Society* and "The Collected Essays in the Sociology of Religion" are shaped by an increasing division of labor.[39] Just as parts XII–XIV were used in the "Economic Ethics of the World Religions," so too was part XV. Whereas parts XII–XIV remained as they were in *Economy and Society*, a section of part XV is missing. An indication of this is its beginning. It is not the direct continuation of XIV, but instead that of a text or part of a text that is no longer found in the sociology of religion section of *Economy and Society*. It is that text or part of a text, I claim, that Weber incorporated in the revision of the studies of Confucianism and Hinduism. The beginning of part XV in *Economy and Society* reads:

> Judaism in its postexilic and particularly its talmudic form (the only forms we are interested in here), is the *third* of those religions that are in some sense accommodated to the world. Judaism is at least oriented to the world in the sense that it does not reject the world as such but only rejects the prevailing social rank order in the world.

We have already made some observations concerning the sociological classification of Judaism.⁴⁰

After this opening sentence, the religiously motivated relation to the world of talmudic Judaism is described and compared to that of the Catholics, the Puritans, and the early Christians. This is then followed by a description of Islam. It is classified as the fourth world-accommodating religion. The analysis then turns to the relations to the world of world-rejecting religions. Here, early Buddhism and early Christianity are treated. At this point the manuscript breaks off. It was intended to be continued. But much more important is that its beginning, which apparently once existed, is missing. Moreover, the remaining manuscript contains sketches of all religions mentioned in the letter except Confucianism and Hinduism. As is known, Weber considered Confucianism, but also parts of Hinduism (at least before 1915) as "religions that are in some sense accommodated to the world." This missing section, however, could mean that not only were the first parts of the manuscript "The Great Religions and the World" in fact used for the "Economic Ethics," but the remaining truncated portion would have served as the basis of the continuation of the series. It is in any case not improbable that Weber was also thinking about this manuscript when he offered his publisher a series of essays in 1915. And it is just as probable that he would have made use of other parts of the sociology of religion for the "Economic Ethics." Thus, after 1915 at the latest, he probably considered the manuscript in the edited posthumous form in which we have it today to be only a preliminary version of the sociology of religion.⁴¹

What can be concluded from the fate of the Islam study? Four points can be made:

1. By the beginning of the First World War, Weber had attained a basic knowledge of Islamic civilization, which he had chiefly made use of in the context of the sociologies of religion, domination, and law. However, this research did not result in a monographic essay. His intention was to write this essay in the framework of the "Economic Ethics of the World Religions," initially for inclusion in the *Archiv* series, later for the "Collected Essays in the Sociology of Religion."

2. Although Weber intended to do so, he evidently did not deal intensively with Islamic civilization from the outbreak of the war until his death. The remarks found in his work about Islam basically rest on preliminary work done from 1911 until 1914 at the latest, terminologically also reflecting Weber's approach of this period.

3. The monographic essay envisioned would hardly have equalled

the size of the studies of Confucianism and Taoism, Hinduism and Buddhism, or ancient Judaism. Without a doubt, Islam belonged to the same extended context of historical prerequisites of Western development as talmudic Judaism, early Christianity, and oriental Christianity—prerequisites that Weber apparently hoped to treat as a whole in the concluding volume of his "Collected Essays in the Sociology of Religion." However, Islam, as a "comparatively late product... in which Old Testament and Jewish-Christian elements played a very important role," could hardly have the same genetic significance for Weber as ancient Judaism or ancient or medieval Christianity.[42]

4. Weber's real interest in Islam is typological. As will be shown, it demonstrates similarities with ascetic Protestantism and especially with Calvinism—similarities, however, of a purely external character. Weber would certainly have centered the essay around this thesis.

Thus, if one seeks to reconstruct the basic outlines of Weber's study of Islam, attention has first to be directed to the manuscript entitled "The Economy and the Societal Orders and Powers" and especially to the discussions in the sections on religion, domination, law, and the city. Insofar as the later version of the sociology of domination, which Weber himself was still able to submit to publication in 1920, builds upon the earlier version, there are also references to Islam. The latter, however, do not represent an advance over 1913–14. The same holds for the second version of the *Protestant Ethic* and for the *General Economic History,* in which scattered remarks on Islam are also found.

An Outline of Weber's Analysis of Islam

Methodological Considerations

How can Weber's remarks on Islam be tied together, how can a relatively coherent overall picture be derived from them? Some preliminary methodological considerations, starting from a thought already presented, are useful here. Weber's comparative studies are subject to a *heuristic* Eurocentrism and they are not *comprehensive* cultural analyses. What interested him were Western cultural phenomena—their distinct character, and the "combination of circumstances" that brought them about.[43] The clarification of the questions of identification and causal attribution raised in this context is the ultimate purpose of the comparison. For this reason, all comparisons for Weber were governed by the goal of uncovering the contrasts (the points of opposition or difference) to those cultural phenomena that held his interest. These interests can range over a variety of areas; to establish this range is a theoretical task.

As the letter of June 22, 1915, points out, the comparative essays on the "Economic Ethics of the World Religions" are intended to generalize the method found in the *Protestant Ethic*. Thus, the religious conditioning of economic attitudes is doubtlessly involved. Yet, the class conditioning of religion must also play a part. This class question, however, is at the same time a question of the "structure of society."[44] In other words, more is involved than just economy and religion; the analysis also takes up domination (including law), and it concerns all these orders and their interrelations. This is the widening of scope that resulted from the discovery that ushered in a new phase of work: that Western culture is not only distinct from other civilizations in its economic development, but also in its scientific and artistic development, and above all in its political and legal development. In short, its configuration of order is different from others in its most important features. Accordingly, in the "Economics Ethics of World Religions" both sides of the causal chain are treated despite its repeatedly emphasized limited objective; moreover, attention is brought not only to differences in religion, but also to differences in domination and law, and, in the cases of India and China even, at least in passing, in science.[45]

Weber provides not only a typological classification, but also a genetic reconstruction of Western cultural phenomena. These are linked in a series of causal relations, the recognition of which presupposes the subclassification of overall development into partial developments and developmental phases. I cannot retrace Weber's complex analysis of Occidental cultural development here.[46] However, this development clearly "culminates" in the elective affinity between rational capitalism and the rational *Anstaltsstaat*.

For Weber rational capitalism is (still!) the more fateful of the two forces. What definition of rational capitalism does he provide? From the first version of the *Protestant Ethic* to the economic sociology in the second version of *Economy and Society* (chapter 2), Weber uses many definitions that are not completely identical but have a common core. It is first of all important to separate the definitions referring to the *individual enterprise* from those referring to the *economic system*. A rational-capitalist enterprise, for example, can be distinguished from a large-scale household (*oikos*), a large workshop (*ergasterion*), and a craft shop through the combination of four characteristics: it is a profit-oriented enterprise, it is a factory enterprise, it is independent of the household, and it controls its economic activity by means of double-entry bookkeeping. The other three units lack at least one of these features. The craft shop comes the closest to the rational-capitalist enterprise, but it lacks mechanized technology and fixed capital. In order for an individual enterprise to rationally calculate its activity, however, a legal order guaranteeing free property and contractual freedom is presupposed, for rational calculation presupposes that the material means of production (*Beschaffungsmittel*) are appropriated as "free property by autonomous, private, profit-oriented enterprises" and that market freedom exists in the labor market (formally free labor!) and in the commodity and capital markets. Moreover, decisions of justice and administration must be predictable. This presupposes the priority of procedural rationality, of legal security, before substantive rationality, before "justice."[47] Of course, all of this does not suffice to establish a capitalist economic system. This exists only when numerous such enterprises produce mass goods for expanded markets—goods that serve to fulfill everyday needs—and when this is the dominant mode of want satisfaction. Admittedly, the rational-capitalist mode of want satisfaction never exists to the exclusion of all other modes. Nonetheless, one can speak of a capitalist epoch only "if want satisfaction is primarily capitalist; if we think away this kind of organization, want satisfaction as such would collapse."[48]

This makes two things clear. First, rational profit-oriented enterprises in expanded markets can exist without capitalist want satisfaction predominating. In this case, this mode competes with others, such as craft shops or manors, and is constantly in danger of "death by suffocation" if markets shrink. Second, there are attitudinal as well as political and legal presuppositions for this mode of capitalist want satisfaction that are *not* required by other modes of capitalist want satisfaction, such as trading, tax farming, lease and sale of offfices, plantations and colonial enterprises, provisioning of the state, and the financing of wars. Under certain circumstances, these modes can flourish with traditional economic attitudes and ethics.[49] For Weber, this kind of ultimately politically oriented capitalism has existed throughout the world. Not its historical prerequisites but rather those of rational capitalism as an economic system are of interest.

These historical preconditions were already fully described by Weber in his "Anticritical Last Word" of September 1910. This can be seen by comparing it with later formulations, such as that of the *Gen-*

eral Economic History, which in any case, given its complicated textual status, always has to be taken with a grain of salt. Nevertheless, the formulation reported in this connection is too similar to others to be a distortion of Weber's conception. It is of special interest because here the step mentioned previously is at least implicitly taken from a purely typological to a more genetic treatment of distinctly Western cultural phenomena. Weber first describes the distinct character of Western capitalism in terms similar to those mentioned earlier; then he "explains" why it emerged only in the West. To do this, he names "certain features of its general cultural development":

> Only the Occident knows the *state in the modern sense*, with a constitution [*gesatzter Verfassung*], specialized officialdom, and the concept of citizenship. Beginnings of this institution in antiquity and in the Orient were never able to develop fully. Only the Occident knows *rational law,* made by jurists and rationally interpreted and applied, and only in the Occident is found the concept of *citizen (civis Romanus, citoyen, bourgeois)* because only in the Occident does the *city* exist in the specific sense of the word. Furthermore, only the Occident possesses *science in the present-day sense of the word.* Theology, philosophy, and reflection on the ultimate problems of life were known to the Chinese and the Hindu, perhaps even of a depth unreached by the European; but a rational science and in connection with it a *rational technology* remained unknown to those civilizations. Finally, Western civilization is further distinguished from every other by the presence of men with a *rational ethos for the conduct of life.* Magic and religion are found everywhere; but a religious basis for conduct that, when consistently followed, had to lead to a specific form of rationalism is again peculiar to Western civilization alone.[50]

State, city, law, science, and methodical conduct provide both the key terms and the "points of comparison" for the "Economic Ethics." It is contingent upon these cultural phenomena whether the developments toward rational capitalism—the beginnings of which indeed exist in all civilizations—meet resistance or not.[51] The structures of political domination and law are decisive for the extent of external resistance, whereas the religiously anchored conceptions of duty and the modes of conduct associated with them are decisive for the extent of inner resistance. Just as in the case of the other studies, Weber's essay on Islam would have concentrated above all on these.

In fact, Weber's scattered remarks on Islam can be organized around these points of comparison: the type of religious ethic—world mastery as world conquest and world adjustment; the type of political domination—Oriental prebendal feudalism; the type of city—Oriental urban anarchy; the type of law—theocratic and patrimonial *qadi*-justice; and the interrelation of these orders and powers (their mode of "integration")—"centralism." Science is the only key term about which nothing can be found in these remarks. In the other studies, too, it is largely neglected, as is art. This neglect, however, is certainly not an oversight but is connected to the limited aim of the studies. Admittedly, this is a failing if one adheres to Weber's own theoretical approach as presented in the "Intermediate Reflections," which distinguishes religious, economic, political, aesthetic, erotic, and intellectual spheres, or as presented in the "Author's Introduction" to the "Collected Essays in the Sociology of Religion," which lists the distinct Western cultural phenomena according to spheres, or even as presented in the aforementioned quotes from the "Anticritical Last Word" of the *General Economic History*. In accordance with this theoretical approach, the development of science in particular belongs to those factors constitutive of each and every cultural development.

The Religious Ethic: World Mastery Between World Conquest and World Adjustment

One side of the causal chain of development toward rational capitalism concerns the relationship between religious ethics and conduct, something that had intrigued Weber since the turn of the century at the very latest and that remained undiminished thereafter. He had pursued this interest in the comparative framework of "The Protestant Ethic and the 'Spirit' of Capitalism" (1904–5), although he admittedly limited it to pre- and post-Reformation Christian movements. Here Weber established that the relationship between religious ethics and conduct is, to begin with, an internal one. Even though this internal relationship can be supported, distracted, or obstructed by its external aspects, it is to be analyzed independently of the latter.[52] The "ability and disposition of men to adopt certain types of practical rational *conduct*"—so Weber's thesis—is also dependent upon the belief in the exemplary status of duties formulated in religious-ethical terms. This in any case holds true for a "precapitalist era" in which religion was still a force in life.[53] But orientation to values, especially to ethical values, is to be regarded as a general feature of human beings. A person acts not only according to purposes, but also according to values. Whereas a purpose is the conception of success that becomes the cause of an action, a value is the conception of validity that becomes the cause.[54] Admittedly, human action is undoubtedly determined over large stretches by utilitarian motives and supported by doctrines of prudence. Human beings are also moral beings, however, and therefore capable of making the axiological turn.⁵⁵

This was the educational achievement of the great religions: that they affected—with different degrees of radicalness—this axiological turn among their respective followers. This, for example, distinguishes them from magic in all its expressions. Of course, the axiological turn can not only vary in degree of radicality, it can also differ in *direction*. This decides which stance to the world a religion supports. In a different context I have shown how Weber's comparative sociology of religion leads to a typology of religiously-motivated stances toward the world and to related modes of conduct.⁵⁶ His study of Islam also would have focused on this line of thought.

In order to conceive of Islam as precisely as possible and to "bring... out the points of comparison with our Occidental religions as well as possible,"⁵⁷ it is reasonable to start with Christianity and with its most important representative in terms of Weber's central question, Calvinism. It is well known that Weber also regarded his quickly famous historical study of ascetic Protestantism as a contribution "to the understanding of the general manner in which ideas become effective forces in history."⁵⁸ Because of this he justified its publication in the *Archiv*, which "generally did *not* [involve itself] with purely historical work."⁵⁹ Interestingly enough, Weber explicitly distances himself in this context from two explanatory approaches, one that attributes the creation of ideas exclusively to economic situations and another that attributes the development of created ideas exclusively to inborn forces. For an idea such as the duty of calling, constitutive as it is for the "spirit" of rational capitalism, to be selected at all and to be able to function as a superstructure, however, "it had to originate somewhere, and not in isolated individuals, but as a way of looking at things [that is] common to whole *groups*";⁶⁰ for it to become an effective historical force, it had to "fight its way to supremacy against a whole world of hostile forces," a struggle that in no way always ends with the "best" surviving.⁶¹ Here the twofold significance of Weber's later frequently used concept of autonomy (*Eigengesetzlichkeit*) comes into view: ideas and worldviews (*Weltbilder*) do not always originate as functions or results of material interest constellations, and in some circumstances they survive by struggle, even when they have become "dysfunctional." The foe, however, against which the spirit of rational capitalism was created and which it had to overcome, was the spirit of traditionalism. To oust the latter, a truly "revolutionary force" from within was necessary.⁶² Weber's claim was that this could not have been achieved by a doctrine of prudence (*Klugheitslehre*), no matter how elaborate. It required a *religious* ethic and a group of individuals with *heightened* interest in salvation for whom this ethic offered a convincing doctrinal basis.

Ideas must work their way through the minds and hearts of actors. Two different relations have to be kept separate in order to understand the way this process works: the subjective appropriation of such ideas can be weak or strong, passive or active; and ideas do not always come to match interests, they can provoke "practical entanglements of interest."⁶³ The more active the appropriation and the greater the discrepancy between ideas and interests, the greater the practical psychological tensions ensuing from the ideas. The greater the tensions, the greater the tendency that such practical entanglements or conflicts of interests will be provoked, in the wake of which the meaning of the subjective appropriation is altered. It is for this reason that Weber always emphasized that one must distinguish strictly between the dogmatic and the pragmatic-psychological effects of a given ethic when the relation between ethics and conduct is taken up for study. The logical and the pragmatic-psychological consequences following from the doctrinal basis of a given ethic need not point in the same direction, because as a rule they are two different things. This has sometimes been interpreted as if the substance of the doctrinal justification, the doctrine in itself, were immaterial. This is not the case. Just because two processes are not identical does not mean they are unrelated to each other.

In spite of the distinction, basic to his entire approach, between the logical and pragmatic-psychological consequences arising from the doctrinal basis of a given ethic, Weber emphasized the following point in the context of an instructive criticism of William James: the latter's pragmatic approach failed to take up the significance of the substance of thought in its own right, which "captures and moulds the immediate experience of religion in its own way."⁶⁴ Anyone who on principle classifies ideas according to the way in which they prove themselves in life ultimately proceeds in a reductionist manner. He can offer no explanation whatsoever as to why practical entanglements of interests arise. They can in fact mean two different things: that religious interests "capture" religious ideas for their own purposes (instead of vice versa), or that religious interests are captured by other interests—salvational interests being put into the service of social honor, political power, or material wealth.

For Weber, the doctrine of election by grace belongs to the foundations of Calvinism. It is not the only dogma, and not even the most important, but it is the one—when actively appropriated—that most heightens those psychological tensions ensuing from Calvinism. Were a religiously motivated person to believe unconditionally in this dogma and in it alone, that person would be compelled to fatalism. The pragmatic-psychological effect of Calvinism, however, was just the opposite, namely, unceasing activity.

One reason for this is that the notion of predestination does not stand alone. Rather, it is connected to the notion of proving oneself, of justifying faith, according to which the believers have to prove themselves and their actions before God by adhering to His commandments. This idea is more important than that of the doctrine of election by grace.[65] Instead of lessening the tension, however, this combination heightens it, for it prevents the believer from taking two well-traveled and natural paths to salvation. It negates both the mystical solution, the unification with God, and the "traditional" solution, the fulfillment of duty in the expectation of reciprocity. The very principles of this doctrine prevent good works from being the source of salvation. Such works must be done simply for their own sake, or more accurately, solely for the glorification of God, that being the purpose of the world. Moreover, such works do not "count" in themselves, but only as part of the overall way one conducts one's life. "The God of Calvinism demanded of his believers not single good works, but a course of good works transformed into a *system* of life."[66] He further demanded the continuous and persistent transformation of one's entire being, an overall methodological way of conducting one's life from within toward without, confident and self-disciplined.

However, as much as the idea of proof provides practical instruction, setting the basis for activity, it is constantly upset, in psychological terms, by the doctrine of election by grace, with its unchangeable and unknowable wisdom of God. This instability provides the second reason why Calvinism impels its followers toward unceasing activity. The theory of predestination produces in every believer enormous insecurity about the fate of his salvation, and this creates fear. The logical need of the dogmatist is confronted in stark and unreconcilable fashion by the apprehensive believer's need for security. This would ultimately have resulted in inhibition of action, in fatalism, if this need for security, for *ceritudo salutis,* were not satisfied in some manner. Thus, precisely at this point a practical entanglement of interests arises.

The interest in the certainty of salvation captures, as it were, the dogma. In addition to its manifest meaning, the idea of proof is attributed a latent one. Although the idea is thus left in its dogmatic framework, it is in fact partly reinterpreted. The good works performed by the individual, with which he increases God's glory and not his own, must continue to hold their validity as not only willed by God but ultimately effected by God. Nevertheless, they are simultaneously reinterpreted to be signs of election.

Weber uses a certain type of theological literature that could be named "response literature"[67] as evidence that this practical entanglement of interests did in fact exist and have dogmatic repercussions. By reproducing the decisive theological responses to the need of the faithful for salvational certainty, these sources provide a striking display of the "process of mutual adjustment" between ideas and interests. Their choice as an object of analysis thus also allows one to follow the course by which ideas make their way into life. Decisive for Weber is the mutual and reciprocal quality of this process of alignment. Ideas and interests tend to work upon each other. Neither a reductionism of ideas nor of interests is supported. This is the exact meaning of the famous later formulation according to which material and ideal interests directly determine man's action, but ideationally defined worldviews very often, like switchmen, determine along which tracks "action has been pushed by the dynamic of interest."[68] Without the combination of the ideas of predestination and proof and without the maintenance of the dogmatic core of this combination even after its reinterpretation, the "collapse into a purely utilitarian doctrine of good works with a solely inner-worldly orientation" would have been probable.[69] Without this combination the tension produced by the linkage with one's fate beyond would largely be lacking, a tension that was the occasion for the "greatest possible systematic focusing of the ethic of conviction imaginable."[70] Because reinterpretation does not do away with the original dogmatic foundations, because success in action as the sign of election is the means "not of purchasing salvation but of getting rid of the fear of damnation,"[71] it results in the pervasive Christianization of all of life, producing self-certain saints in the form of the "Puritan merchant men of steel of that heroic age of capitalism."[72] These were men for whom otherworldly salvation and not thisworldly prosperity was important.

The fact that the idea of proving oneself before God for His greater glory concretized itself as the "idea of methodically proving oneself in one's vocation in economic life"[73] also has dogmatic grounds. According to the Calvinist doctrine, the field of proof is, strictly speaking, the whole world created by God. This follows for Weber from the objective impersonal conception of the idea of love of one's neighbor such that the fulfillment of "the vocational tasks resulting from the *lex naturae* [law of nature]" can be decisive for action willed by God and pleasing to His sight.[74] Admittedly, such a concretization of religious duty as vocational duty is in accordance with the nonreligious ideal and material interests of a rising bourgeois stratum. Moreover, the connection of these nonreligious interests with the religious ones and the worldview that serves to interpret the latter is important for an appropriate sociological understanding of the process of dissemination, whereby the idea of vocational duty proves itself in its struggle with other ideas. Nevertheless, this connection is not primary and also not decisive for understanding the inner or intrinsic relation between the religious ethic and the mode of conduct. Interests in themselves are in any case blind, and nonreligious interests in precapitalist eras do not produce any forces that radically transform life from within.

Weber thus shows with regard to Calvinism the factors that play a decisive role in the relationship between religious ethics and conduct: the religious foundations or substance of ideas on the one hand, and the need for consistency in dogma and the need of assurance of one's salvation on the other. The latter could also be termed the need for religious legitimation. Weber links it with the nonreligious need for legitimation, interconnected but nonetheless not identical with the religious need; this nonreligious need is related to the justification of the distribution of worldly goods such as power, social honor, and wealth.[75]

Against the backdrop of this analysis and the thesis of the possible difference between the logical and pragmatic-psychological effects of religious foundations, two interesting patterns emerge. On the one hand, thoroughly similar psychological effects could occur on the basis of differing religious foundations, and on the other, the psychological effects could be different given similar religious foundations. The first case is exemplified by the Baptists, the second by the Islamic religious ethic. The religious ethic of the Baptists—even without a doctrine of predestination—had psychological consequences similar to those of Calvinism, whereas Islam, though it possessed such a doctrine, produced psychological effects in contrast to those of Calvinism.[76]

In order not to misconstrue this first main thesis of Weber's analysis of Islam from the very start, it must be emphasized in just what way the religious foundations of Calvinism and Islam are not essentially different, namely, in the way in which the unconditionally transcendent character (*Überweltlichkeit*) of the *one and only* God of creation is maintained.[77] In contradistinction not only to all Asiatic religions but also to all religions of antiquity with the exception of Judaism, God is here "endowed with [the traits of] absolute unchangeableness, omnipotence, and omniscience—that is to say, with an absolutely transcendental character."[78] He is "a transcendental unitary God who is universal," whose powers are immeasurable.[79] This makes unbridgeable the gap between God and humans. In terms of the question of individual salvation, such a conception of God limits the significance of all mediators, be they personal or institutional in nature. Mohammed is a prophet, the *last* of the prophets through whom God, Allah, proclaims his will to man for the final time. He is "an instrument for proclamation, who on the strength of the mission given him demands obedience as an ethical duty"; in short, he is the prototype of an ethical prophet.

He is, however, neither the son of God nor one who dies sacrificially for the sake of the salvation of a humanity burdened by original sin.[80] Thus, the idea of the church as an institution of sacramental grace administering salvation always remained totally foreign to Islam. It is a creation of the Christianity of late antiquity and the Middle Ages. Calvinism also limits the salvational significance of all mediators: Jesus died only for the chosen, and the idea of salvation via ecclesiastical sacrament falls under the suspicion of magic.[81] In fact, the conception of God and the idea of predestination are most intimately connected. The more radically the transcendence of God is conceived, the more the individual's salvational fate tends to appear to be predestined; the more consistently the faithful are followers of the idea of predestination, the greater the tensions between God and man. In view of ancient Judaism (Job), early Islam, and early Calvinism, Weber described this general relationship in the following manner:

> Belief in providence is the consistent rationalization of magical divination, to which it is related, and which for that very reason it seeks to devaluate as completely as possible, as a matter of principle. No other view of the religious relationship could possibly be as radically opposed to all magic, both in theory and in practice, as this belief in providence which was dominant in the great theistic religions of Asia Minor and the Occident. No other so emphatically affirms the nature of the divine to be an essentially dynamic activity manifested in God's personal, providential rule over the world. Moreover, there is no view of the religious relationship which holds such firm views regarding God's discretionary grace and the human creature's need of it, regarding the tremendous distance between God and all his creatures, and consequently regarding the reprehensibility of any deification of "things of

the flesh" as a sacrilege against the sovereign God. For the very reason that this religion provides not rational solution of the problem of theodicy, it conceals the greatest tensions between the world and God, between the actually existent and the ideal.[82]

As in Calvinism, so too in Islam do Old Testament and Judeo-Christian motifs continue to play an important role, especially in the conception of God.[83] As in Calvinism, the belief in providence perhaps initially provided a rational solution to the theoretical but not the practical problem of theodicy. As we saw, in Calvinism this was made possible by means of the idea of proof and its two-fold interpretation. What does the process of mutual "adjustment" look like in early Islam?

To determine Weber's answer to this question, one must risk conjecture. Nevertheless, Weber did provide indications of the direction in which the answer is to be sought. In the 1920 version of the *Protestant Ethic*, two passages are found that make positive reference to F. Ulrich's Heidelberg dissertation in theology. Moreover, in the systematic sociology of religion, a short comparison is made between Calvinist and Islamic predestination and their respective consequences.[84] These indications do provide an orientation, yielding a relatively clear picture once they are elaborated on.

Let us begin with Ulrich's dissertation. It starts by making two distinctions, between destination and predestination and between determination and predetermination. Which of these concepts is chosen to describe the religious foundations of belief is contingent on whether omnipotence and absolute dominion (*Allwirksamkeit*) (determination) or absolute goodness and mercy (destination) predominate and whether God's acts of will are consigned to primeval or prehistorical times (representing predetermination and predestination, respectively, in each of the two alternatives). The concepts of God in both Islam and Calvinism arise from similar sources: in both cases the accent tends to fall more on the God of the Old rather than the New Testament. In the Christian tradition, however, the God of the New Testament, of redemption and mercy, is never totally sacrificed to the God of the Old Testament, the omnipotent God. This holds even for Calvinism, whose concept of God is perhaps the closest of all religions within the Christian tradition to that of ancient Judaism and Islam. Weber too had already pointed to the tension in Calvinism's conception of God in the first version of the *Protestant Ethic*. It knew a double God, "the gracious and kindly Father of the New Testament...and behind him the *Deus absconditus* [the hidden God] as an arbitrary despot" of the Old Testament.[85]

Islam lacked this tension. God's most outstanding feature here is His omnipotence and, linked to it, His benevolence and bestowal of favor, not, however, His granting of a "sin-pardoning grace."[86] This whole realm of thought—encompassing as it does ideas such as original sin, life in its entirety beset by guilt, the incapability of being good, and saving grace—remained peripheral to Islam. Metaphysical, cosmological, and teleological interpretations of God's effectiveness, and not ethical and soteriological ones, occupy the foreground of this religion. In its worldview, cognitive components are generally given priority over evaluative ones. The relationship between faith and reason is much less problematic in Islam than in Christianity. Admittedly, Islam recognizes the ethical relation between God and man. It also recognizes sin and final judgment. But sin is not original sin and final judgment is not the site of a grace that pardons sins. No one is incapable of being good, and final judgment functions in a certain sense according to the principles of bookkeeping. The ethical relation, similar to that of Judaism, has a legal-moral orientation, with works being ultimately conceived of as the basis for salvation. Of course, whether one is saved or not is determined by God—"*God guides* whom he pleases," as one *sura* reads, but he guides those "who show themselves open to his revelations and adopt them in faith."[87] Those who do not do so, who are unrepentant and unmoved, take upon themselves guilt for which they are accountable. To err is the result of one's own activity, and God punishes this fault. But He does not punish without warning. Concepts such as error and offense, just punishment, and obedience on the basis of understanding, not those of (original) sin, saving grace, and love, are the focus of thought. It was apparently with these facts in mind that Weber wrote: "The ethical concept of salvation is actually alien to Islam. Its God is one of unlimited power but also of mercy, and the fulfillment of his commandments is certainly not beyond the powers of humans."[88]

Thus, the God of Islam is above all one of absolute power, whereas the God of Christianity is above all one of absolute benevolence and mercy. These different accents affect the belief in providence. In Islam, where it is one of the most important dogmas, according to Ulrich,[89] this belief undergoes a cosmological and teleological turn rather than a soteriological one; it tends more toward predetermination than toward a doctrine of predestination. But, more important, neither in the *sunna* nor in the Quran is the doctrine developed consistently and conclusively. Instead, two lines of thought appear with little connection made between them: on the one hand, the absolute power of God that can also bring about evil, and on the other, the self-determination and responsibility of man for his own salvation. The theoretical development never reaches the conclusiveness and consistency of Calvinism. Weber views this similarly when he writes: "Islamic predestination knew nothing of the 'double decree'; it did not dare attribute to Allah the predestination of some people to hell, but only attributed to Him the withdrawal of His grace from some people, a belief that admitted man's inadequacy and thus His inevitable transgression."[90]

Thus, in Islam, as compared to Calvinism, the belief in providence not only has a deterministic bias, but it also never attains the same rational coherence as in the latter. Moreover, it is not linked to the idea of proof. The relationship of man to God is one of subject to lord, a relation of submission and of worship from a position of subordination. It provides support for faith in Allah and the prophets and for obedient adherence to divine law, but not for setting the proof of one's ethic of conviction in terms of overall conduct as the "central and constant quality of personality."[91] The contrasts between dutiful fulfillment of the law and its fulfillment out of a sense of duty, between fulfillment as the real foundation (*Realgrund*) and as the mere indication (*Erkenntnisgrund*) of grace appear to be the most important typological distinctions between the Islamic and the Calvinist religious ethics. They are rooted in the respective contents of their faiths. In spite of the Islamic providentialism, the basic beliefs did not contribute to the religious undergirding of innerworldly vocational calling. Thus, as in lay Catholicism or Lutheranism, though of course for other reasons,[92] no systematization of salvation by works emerges in Islam. Instead, it suffers, as do the others, from the constant threat of collapsing into an unsystematic and utilitarian salvation by works.

The matter could have rested there. However, Weber's analysis goes beyond an interpretation compatible with Ulrich's comparative remarks.[93] Weber is convinced that the belief in providence also had *special* consequences in Islam—consequences that one can conceptualize only by looking into the tensions precipitated by the doctrine and the practical "solutions" arising from them. The idea of predestination, as we have seen, is actually one of predetermination, and it is not linked to any idea of proof. This undoubtedly weakens the ethical character of the doctrine and lessens the compulsion to systematize life that is inherent in Calvinism. Nevertheless, even in this weakened form, it is able to bring about the "complete obliviousness to self in the fighter for the faith in his allegiance to the religious commandment of the holy war for the conquest of the world."[94] Why is this so?

Weber claims the following: in Islam, predestination, or better, predetermination, is ultimately related above all to one's fate not in the world beyond but in this world: "The prevailing conception was that predestination determined, not the fate of the individual in the world beyond, but rather his singular fate in this world, the question, for example (and above all), whether the warrior for the faith falls in battle or not."[95] In contrast, one's fate in the beyond is secured by observing the five pillars of faith: belief in Allah and the prophets, prayer five times daily, the month of fasting (Ramadan), the pilgrimage to Mecca, and the giving of alms (*tawhid, salat, sawm, zakat,* and *hajj*). Not least because of the largely unconnected juxtaposition of deterministic and nondeterministic lines of thought in the Quran and the *Sunna*, but also because of the simplicity, even the parsimony of the early Islamic vision,[96] Muslims were not confronted with the problem of the certainty of salvation, of the *certitudo salutis*, to as radical a degree as were the Calvinists. The belief in providence did not produce the same measure of uncertainty and fear. Admittedly, fear of death is involved in both cases; however, in one case it is the fear of death in the face of the beyond, whereas in the other it is fear of death in the face of battle. In this context, deterministically interpreted providence—due to its fatalistic bias—is an interpretation that actually impedes rather than produces fear, for it provides the warrior for the faith the certainty that he will only experience that which Allah has predetermined for him. It is precisely this certainty about one's fate in the beyond that transforms the faithful Islamic warrior's fear of death into a proud, thisworldly spirit. It is this basic deterministic feature of the dogma that represents a motivational source of his invincibility and equips him with world-conquering military discipline.[97] In the later version of the *Protestant Ethic* Weber summarizes this first major thesis in a pointed fashion. He discovers that in Islam the fatalistic consequences of the belief in providence, which were never completely eradicated in Calvinism either, have actually come into force. He asks why and then responds:

> Because the Islamic idea was that of predetermination, not predestination, and was applied to fate in this world, not in the next. In consequence the most important thing, the proof of the believer in predestination, played no part in Islam. Thus only the fearlessness of the warrior (as in the case of *moira* [personal destiny]) could result, but there were no consequences for the rationalization of life, for there was no religious reward for them.[98]

Thus, we find that in Islam religious interest "confiscates" religious doctrine in such a way that it brings forth logical consequences that the doctrine itself does not draw on its own. It is a kind of "practical entanglement of interests" that provides these consequences with both an active and a passive accent, so to speak. In no way does the doctrine lead to a renunciation of activity. What it does instead is to give fearlessness in war a religious foundation. Conversely, in those situations involving one's fate in the everyday life of this world and not extraordinary circumstances such as war, the "complete obliviousness to self" is repressed in favor of an unsystematic, utilitarian salvation of works or even in favor of "lightly fatalistic characteristics (*kismet*)."[99] This is for Weber, incidentally, also the reason why Islam (similar to most religions), despite its basically antimagical orientation, did not completely eradicate magic in the religiosity of the masses.[100] Hence, Weber presents an image both divided and cyclical of the psychological effects of the Islamic doctrine. In extraordinary situations it works to unify and discipline, whereas in everyday situations it loses this influence on conduct.[101]

Prerequisites for the "confiscation" of religious foundations for the sake of an innerworldly hero and warrior ethic were naturally also found in the doctrine: in the concept of the holy war (*jihad*) and in the division of the world into the house of Islam and the house of war (*dar al-Islam, dar al-Harb*). Another prerequisite also existed in the nonreligious legitimation interests of those strata that appropriated the doctrine. These interests, however, are only at the very beginning similar to those so important for Calvinism:

In the first Meccan period of Islam, the eschatological religion of Mohammed developed in pietistic urban conventicles which displayed a tendency to withdraw from the world. But in the subsequent developments in Medina and in the evolution of the early Islamic communities, the religion was transformed into a national Arabic warrior religion, and even above all into a status-oriented warrior religion. Those followers whose conversion to Islam made possible the decisive success of the Prophet were consistently members of powerful families.[102]

A warrior aristocracy with its feelings of knightly status has no sense for a worldview marked by concepts such as sin, humility, and redemption.[103] Moreover, a member is far removed from the ideal of innerworldly vocational asceticism. At most he is capable of developing "the asceticism of the military camp or of a martial order of knights, not that of monks, and certainly not the bourgeois, ascetic systematization of conduct. Moreover, this ascetism was truly predominant only periodically, and was always disposed toward turning into fatalism."[104] The Sufism of the petty bourgeoisie was even further from developing innerworldly asceticism. Instead, it moved along contemplative and mystical paths and "under the leadership of plebeian technicians of orgiastics."[105]

Similar conceptions of God and doctrinal foundations are thus found in Calvinism and Islam. Nevertheless, the psychological effects of these similar religious sources are radically distinct. They make possible, on the one hand innerworldly vocational asceticism, and on the other self-sacrifice in extraordinary situations, a heroism that disintegrates into thisworldly utilitarianism during routinization, that is, in the transition from war to everyday life. Calvinism increases the inner tension between salvational doctrine and salvational interest to an inhuman extent, and thus unleashes the motivation for constant world mastery; in contrast, Islam does not involve believers in such unbearable tension. Although it motivates them in this way to temporary world mastery as world conquest, it prevents, especially because of the marginal position of original sin and redemption, long-term world rejection.[106]

For this reason, Islam also does not revolutionize economic mentality. It remains feudal or petty bourgeois or booty capitalist. As are all world religions, Islam is compatible with all forms of traditional economic activity, including the politically oriented mode of capitalism. But it does not provide a force to transform life from within and thus to overcome the spirit of traditionalism in economic or other areas of life. Despite its antimagical and activist tendencies, in spite of its intellectual rationalism, Islam (along with Judaism, Catholicism, and Lutheranism) failed to achieve that which ascetic Protestantism alone among all the most important religions achieved, namely, the breeding of those steely merchants and entrepreneurs who did not act as economic supermen letting their acquisitional urge run free, but instead tempered this urge rationally, compelling it to take the form of a vocational duty, and in this way objectivated and objectified it.

Weber thus sees a double psychological effect of the Islamic religious ethic: it motivates its followers to world mastery, in the sense of world conquest, but also to world adjustment. He also discovers a cycle between these stances toward the world and the modes of conduct associated with them. It is a cycle that moves between extraordinary and everyday situations, between struggles of faith and "bourgeoisification."[107] Following Ibn Khaldun, others have diagnosed Islamic regimes in terms of a distinctive cycle of stability and instability on the basis of the cooperation and conflict between monocentric imperial politics and polycentric tribal politics, exacerbated by the cooperation and conflict between the ethical monotheism of high religion and the ritual polytheism of tribal religion.[108] What they apply to domination, Weber appears to espouse for the religiously conditioned mode of conduct in Islam. The fact that this cycle arises, that Islam in contrast to Calvinism does not cultivate "a systematic rational ordering of the moral life as a whole,"[109] means that, though it perhaps does not directly obstruct the "development of an *economically* rational mode of conduct,"[110] it certainly does not encourage it. There are, as we saw above, intrinsic reasons for this. The doctrinal foundations in their relation to the religious interests of the believers are decisive. They lead, in spite of a similar conception of God and a theory of predestination, to a result "divergent" from that of Calvinism. The often claimed "puritanism" of Islam is but superficially similar to Puritanism as Weber conceives it.

Although indispensable, the analysis of the internal relationship between the religious ethic and conduct is only the first step in working out the contrasts between the Islamic and Occidental civilizations in terms of their respective positions toward rational capitalism as an economic system. The investigation of the internal relations has to be followed by a study of the external ones, that is, by the study of the class-conditioned character of religion. This other aspect of the causal chain has already been touched upon in the context of the mutual "adjustment" between religious and nonreligious legitimation interests. The fact that Calvinism and with it all of ascetic Protestantism, and even beyond that, Christianity and Judaism, were specifically bourgeois religions (*bürgerliche Religionen*) from the very beginning and remained so, whereas Islam, like Asiatic religions, ultimately came into being as a religion of the ruling stratum (*Herrenreligion*), is of utmost importance here. However, the external relations encompass more than social stratification. They also involve orders and organizations. Whereas in the case of the concept of order the emphasis is on rules, in the case of the concept of organization it is on the administrative staff in charge of applying sanctions in order to enforce these rules.

Weber insists on the two aspects of the causal chain, because, in my view, he makes a claim for a double-sided relationship between motives and institutions. There is just as much an institutionally formative power of motives or interests as there is a motivationally formative power of institutions.[111] For this reason the analysis must proceed both from within toward without and from without toward within until that point is reached where the linkage between the two sides becomes visible. Every analysis that seeks to satisfy the premises of an interpretive sociology understood as a theory of action and order has to proceed in *both* ways in the analysis of those "historical individuals" selected and constituted by means of the theoretical value relation ("individuals" that can represent single persons or entire cultures).[112] Thus, "explanations" in Weber are never purely motivational or purely institutional. This insight, which in a methodological sense renders the contrast between materialism and idealism obsolete, is nothing new in Weber.[113] It marked the first version of the *Protestant Ethic* of 1904–5. This insight is seen not only in Weber's envisioned supplemented and extended project at the conclusion of this study or in his methodological foundation of cultural science of 1903–4; it is above all given witness to by the well-known closing lines of this historical study itself:

> For although modern man is on the whole usually incapable, even with the best of will, of conceiving the true importance which religious beliefs have had for conduct, culture, and national character, it nevertheless cannot be our intention to substitute for a one-sidedly "materialist" interpretation an equally one-sidedly "spiritualist" interpretation. Both are equally possible, but both are of equally little service to the interests of historical truth if they claim to be not preliminaries to enquiry, but its conclusion.[114]

A nonreductionist approach can never derive the "spirit" from the "form" nor the "form" from the "spirit," even though there are certainly historical situations in which one of these "factors" loses its relative independence vis-à-vis the other. This, however, is not a methodological statement; it is a statement about a historical pattern, where the form "produces" the spirit or the spirit the form. It is therefore important to sharply distinguish two different cases: the case of a one-sided and the case of a mutually favorable relationship. Furthermore, there are also the relations of indifference and obstruction. Which of these relations holds is a historical question. In routinized long-term formations, one-sided relations are especially frequent. Here, as a rule, form produces its corresponding spirit, as is said of modern capitalism in its "iron age." Here, the relations sometimes prevail that are generally postulated by naive historical materialists and Darwinists. But this approach is unsuitable for explaining the genesis of modern capitalism. Here, Weber argues, we are faced with a case of a mutually favorable relationship, of an elective affinity between a religio-ethically motivated conduct and the early capitalist institutions, which originated in European inland cities.

External relations do not exist only between religio-ethically generated motivation and economic or political institutions. They already exist within the religious sphere. In the *Protestant Ethic*, with special clarity in the later version, Weber draws attention to the independent importance of "church organization" (*Kirchenverfassung*)[115] vis-à-vis doctrinal foundations, devoting a separate essay, "The Protestant Sects and the Spirit of Capitalism" ("Die protestantischen Sekten und der Geist des Kapitalismus"), to this aspect.[116] Here the postulated two-sided relationship between motive and institution can be shown especially clearly. For psychological reasons, the doctrine of predestination and proof was joined to organizational efforts "to separate regenerate from unregenerate Christians, those who were from those who were not prepared for the sacramental order of life."[117] This led to a system of external control imposed on the believer. It provided support for the idea of proof, by demanding from him "that he holds his own in the circle of his associates."[118] The psychological effect of this external control supporting the idea of proof could be so strong that the organization was able to replace the doctrine of predestination, that is, an important element of the internal relation in Calvinism."[119] This holds true for the Baptists mentioned earlier.

No such organizational force shaped Islam, according to Weber. Admittedly, a kind of hierocracy exists, centered on the Quran, the *Sunna*, and above all, the *shari'a*, the divine law. A kind of priesthood also exists, if one understands by this a "bearer of the systematization and rationalization of religious ethics."[120] Nevertheless, these "priests" (*'ulama'*) are, like rabbis, not cultic priests; moreover, they are closer to legal scholars than to theologians. Above all, they are not the heads of a church in the Christian sense. The Islamic hierocracy is not a charismatic institution of grace, as was the medieval Catholic Church. Neither is it an instrument of discipline, as were the churches and sects of ascetic Protestantism. Although Islam, like the other world religions, distinguishes between religious virtuosi and the religious masses and between believers and nonbelievers, the former distinction is without salvational importance and the latter is linked to the stratification of status groups, with the "economic privileging" of the adherents of Islam.[121] Islamic religious organization also offers nothing that would work in the direction of ascetic proof in everyday life. Weber is even of the opinion that early Islam, despite its strict monotheism and its conception of a transcendent creator God, like Judaism "directly repudiated asceticism, whereas the unique character of Dervish religiosity stemmed from (mystic, ecstatic) sources quite different from the relation to a transcendent God and was intrinsically quite remote from Occidental asceticism."[122] Finally, one can add that the *umma,* the Islamic community, the "best community," as it was first realized in Medina, served—on the supralocal level, in its intermediary position between religion and politics, and between particularism and universalism—more to secure a certain degree of cultural unity in the face of growing internal differentiation than to comprehensively and effectively regulate all aspects of everyday life.

Even early Islam, by the time of its codification and canonization, was not left untouched by tensions and even conflicts between religion and politics. This was the case despite its pursuit of a kind of organic unity between religion and politics and in spite of the interconnecting of religious and political functions starting with Mohammed and continuing under the early caliphs. By the time of the Umayyads this conflict had erupted openly. The tension is apparently also reflected in the *shari'a*. As Patricia Crone writes, "By the 750s...Islam had already acquired its classical shape as an all-embracing holy law characterized by a profound hostility to settled states."[123] From this point onward, at the latest, the accusation of worldliness is used as a weapon against political rulers. Admittedly, despite this conflict between religion and politics, a separation between political and hierocratic power was never effected as it was in the West. Nor did it ever come to a long-term strictly theocratic solution, much less to a purely caesaropapist solution, even though the tendency to theocracy, especially in Shi'ite Islam, always existed.

Internal and external conditions can thus always be one-sidedly or mutually favorable, indifferent, or obstructive. Such relations, however, can also exist solely among internal conditions (just as they can solely among external ones). The unifying force of the Calvinist religious ethic, so strongly emphasized by Weber, indeed consists in gathering the various internal relationships in which the believer is involved under one effective principle. On the basis of this "greatest possible systematic focusing of the ethic of conviction imaginable," religiously motivated action had effects on all areas of life.[124] What can be said about motives can also be said about institutions. They too are involved in one-sidedly or mutually favorable, indifferent, or obstructive relationships with one another. Especially in the later version of the sociology of domination, Weber treats not only the relationship of the political structure to economic mentality but also to economic structures.

The question always raised there is which constellations of conditions were favorable for the rise and development of rational capitalism and which were not. Emerging and developing rational capitalism is dependent not only on intrinsic conditions but also on extrinsic ones. It can run into institutional resistance just as much as it can be obstructed by mentality. In this context political domination and law are particularly interesting. Naturally, they too have their internal aspects. But after having proceeded from within toward without, I will now proceed in the opposite direction.

Political Domination: Oriental Patrimonialism, the Oriental City, and Sacred Law

Oriental Patrimonialism and Occidental Feudalism

Islam arose from a twofold movement, both religious and political in character. Decisive in its emergence was the "novel" combination of these two components found here. Mohammed was both an ethical prophet and a charismatic politico-military leader. He overcame tribal particularism by surpassing its polytheism and ritualism with monotheism and a legal ethic, and by transforming feuding tribes into a national-Arabic movement of conquest. In contrast to the ancient Jewish prophets, and above all to Jesus, Mohammed was, from the moment of the Hegira of 622 onwards, not a marginalized prophet of doom, and certainly not a wandering charismatic preacher; instead, he was a religio-political leader who knew how to realize his intentions step by step, especially through the skillful use of the time-honored tribal practices of the creation and resolution of conflict. Presumably following Ignaz Goldziher and Julius Wellhausen, Weber makes a clear distinction between the first Meccan period and the time in Medina: with the departure from Mecca and the successful "reception" in Medina, the transformation of Islam from an eschatological religiosity into a political religion—into a religion of national-Arabic warriors—was inaugurated.[125]

The course of Mohammed's career—his initial failure in Mecca, his "departure" for Medina, his success there, his victorious return to Mecca, and the beginning of "world conquest"—has often been recounted. The images remain basically the same. In contrast to the research of the life of Jesus, research of the life of Mohammed is impeded not only by religious reservations but also by the state of available sources. Neither the application of the methods of criticism of biblical sources to

Islamic sources, already initiated by Wellhausen, nor the application of formal biblical criticism to these sources, as carried out by Noth, have had results comparable to those for the Bible.[126] Carl Heinrich Becker once spoke of the "wild chaos of rampant religious growth and conflict"[127] in Islamic studies, while Patricia Crone speaks today of a sort of rubble heap lacking in characteristic structures.[128] This holds for the oral tradition, the *sunna*. By comparison, the Quran stands as firm as bedrock. The picture of the Prophet results from both, but above all from the *sunna*, which represents Mohammed's sayings and actions (*hadith*). Their authorization rests not on their contents, but on the constructed genealogy of the transmitters of the tradition reaching back to the Prophet. This tradition was not merely oral, it was also characterized by an atomistic quality and rapid transformations. The individual sayings and actions were handed down nearly free of context, and were used as ammunition in the religious struggle. The is a compilation that reflects these conflicts. It is more the "theology" of its compilers and their "parties" than the history of Mohammed.

This open horizon toward the past was quickly closed, however. The rapid fixation of the constructed tradition corresponded to the destruction of the sources. In the frozen form of six collections, the tradition became monolithic. By the ninth century, the canon was already largely established and consecrated.[129] This situation satisfies dogmatic needs, but not historical ones. As Patricia Crone puts it:

> There is of course no doubt that Muhammed lived in the 620s and 630s A.D., that he fought in wars, and that he had followers some of whose names are likely to have been preserved. But the precise when, what, and who, on which our interpretations stand and fall, bear all the marks of having been through the mill of rabbinic arguments and subsequently tidied up.[130]

Nevertheless, regardless how "theologically biased" the tradition might be, two presuppositions contained in Weber's statement appear to be historically "correct": that the transition from Mecca to Medina represents a decisive point in the course of Mohammed's life, and that his ethical prophecy is a decisive precondition of his political effectiveness. Subsequent to his "departure" Mohammed moved, as Wellhausen puts it, from preacher to ruler, but the model of rulership is not human kingship (*Mulk*), but rather the monarchical prophet of late Judaism:

> The authority to rule is not a private possession for the usufruct of its holder. The realm belongs rather to God; his plenipotentiary, however, who knows and carries out His will, is the prophet. The prophet is not just the proclaimer of the truth, but

also the sole rightful ruler on earth. Outside of him, there is place for no king, and no other prophet either: at any one time there is but one.[131]

The realization of this model necessitates the satisfaction of both external and internal preconditions. Let us first turn to the former. Medina offered an incomparably more favorable terrain than Mecca for Mohammed's pursuit of religio-political power. Mecca was at the Arabic religious, political, and economic center, a kind of city of the royal lineage, and in any case, firmly under the control of lineages skilled in imposing their will. They guaranteed the city's peace. It was a rich city whose profit was not unconnected to the host of religious festivities encouraged under polytheism and the trade fair linked to them. In these circumstances, Mohammed's radical monotheism must have appeared to be bad for business. The rejection of his message in Mecca was thus in part economically motivated. At the time of the Prophet's first appearance, Mecca found itself in neither a religious, political, nor economic crisis. A situation of inner and outer need that, according to Weber, opens the horizon for charismatic movements did not exist. In Medina, the situation was different. Jathrib, as it was called at the time of the Hegira, was a city on the margin, under Greco-Roman and Christian-Aramaic influence, with a strong Jewish community; from the Arabic point of view, it was, if not the periphery, at least the semiperiphery. The peace of the city had heen laid low. Feuds between rival tribes predominated, in a situation similar to that of some Southern European medieval cities. At the very least there was a political crisis situation with economic consequences, a situation of external need. It was a situation open to an arbitrator but also to an interpretation that—with the help of an order-giving "central power"—transcended the family and tribal particularism responsible for the strife.[132]

Mohammed, supported by the followers he had won in Mecca, mostly "friends, relatives, and slaves,"[133] established the *umma* in the place of the rule of families and tribes. Admittedly, he did this in accordance with the established pattern for arbitrating tribal feuds, in W. Montgomery Watt's words, as "the head of the clan of *Emigrants*."[134] Nevertheless, the "community" took the place of relatives and tribe. Here, too, Jewish and Christian examples appear to have played a role. The transition to the "community" represented at the same time a transition to the peace of the land as the peace of God. Because there is only one God and all believe in Him, the law of the feud as defined by membership in lineage, tribe, or clan no longer retained validity among members of the community. Corresponding to the duty of internal peace is the duty of war. The duty of revenge in pre-Islamic law was no longer incumbent upon one "brother for another, but upon one believer for another." As Wellhausen observes, war becomes a military operation.[135] In addition, it becomes a holy war.

However, the communitarian principle did not totally replace the tribal principle. Associations, not individuals, joined the *umma*. Similar to the ancient polis, the association lost significance in relation to the "cultic" and military association, but kinship (*sib*) solidarity was not completely broken. As Weber puts it in view of later development, "Islam...never really overcame the divisiveness of Arab tribal and clan ties, as is shown by the history of internal conflicts of the early caliphate; in its early period it remained the religion of a conquering army of tribes and clans."[136] Admittedly, just on the basis of this radical monotheism and the strict otherworldliness of the universal God, there was no possibility of distinct "cults of the gentes" existing in subordination to the "community," as they did in the ancient polis. Pre-Islamic Arab polytheism was consistently eliminated. But neither is the *umma* an oath-bound brotherhood in the pattern of Christian medieval urban communities. This was ever less the case the farther the Islamic religious and military association went beyond the city limits of Medina.

The *umma* did not initially exclude all outside it and treat all equally within it in the sense of radically excluding all heathens, Jews, or members of certain status groups. Even after the rise of Mohammed in Medina, the old relations, now pacified, remained largely the same. Similar to the Jewish communities at the time of Christ, the Medina *umma* was apparently also acquainted with different degrees of membership, probably a reflection of the ancient Arabic distinction between those with full rights ("first-class citizens") and co-inhabitants ("second-class citizens" [*Beisassen*]),[137] and more generally, a reflection of the way in which guest tribes became incorporated in larger organization throughout the ancient Orient. But Mohammed's relationship to the Jewish community in Medina changed dramatically when he realized that they did not recognize his claim to messianic prophecy. Only thereafter did he turn away from and indeed militate against Judaism. It is likely that changes in the direction of prayer, from Jerusalem toward Mecca, along with other symbolic acts, are connected to this.[138] Regardless of the actual historical facts of the situation, this shows a process of autonomization and the creation of identity on the symbolic level vis-à-vis the other two monotheistic and ethical religions of revelation, redemption, and the book, whose superiority over Arabic polytheism and ritualism obviously deeply impressed Mohammed. It also shows an important step along the road toward an Arabization of monotheism, toward defining the new doctrine as a "national-Arabic" religion.[139]

The mission of Islam that Mohammed began to develop in Mecca and that made it possible for him to create a new form of war and peace grew out of the tension caused by the cultural chasm separating the world of the Jewish and Christian transcendental and universal God and the world of the Arabic functional and local gods with their commercialized cultic sites and sacred-mundane festivities. Arab gods had permanent places of worship if for no other reason than that immense stones were usually part and parcel of their arrangement. As Wellhausen put it, as a rule, Arabic tribes wandered but their shrines did not. Along with stones, trees and water were also objects of worship at the cultic sites. The stone served as the sacrificial altar and as the representation of divinity. Originally, cults were probably without images—images being a secondary development.[140] As I mentioned earlier, the place of worship served both functional and local gods and as a commercial center. Some of these were places of pilgrimage and in this way additionally economically privileged. Mecca also possessed such a place of worship of "nationwide" importance, the *ka'ba*. As a Meccan, Mohammed was perfectly well acquainted with it.[141] He established his doctrine around it and not around unknown or newly invented shrines. Here he also formed a link with ancient Arab traditions. These he transformed in the light of monotheism by means of the cleansing, standardization, and centralization of heathen rituals. Functional and local gods were done away with, and the various places of worship were organized in terms of the *ka'ba*—made, so to speak, into branches of it.[142]

Mohammed thus related two already existing "worlds": the world of ancient Arab tradition and the world of monotheism, one connected to nomadic and urban tribal particularism, the other, to world empires, or at least to the prospect of a world empire, ruled by a powerful universal God by means of his instrument on earth. Without a doubt Mohammed is an Arabic prophet from the very beginning. The language of revelation is Arabic, the translation of the Quran into other languages being frowned upon even today. Mohammed sought to overcome Arabic particularism. Initially, however, he intended to do this in conjunction with rather than in opposition to Judaism and Christianity. They served him as "reference religions."[143] Even though he apparently was not well acquainted with them, they appeared to offer him a way out of the "regulated anarchy" of Arabic conditions. Thus, he probably originally understood himself not as a prophet superior to Moses and Jesus, but as one equal to them.[144] In Medina, this all changed. With the turn against Judaism as well as Christianity, in symbol and in fact, Islam was no longer placed in the Judeo-Christian tradition but above it, at the same time taking a place in the overall context of the Arabic history of religion that now began with Abraham's establishment of religion at the *ka'ba*.[145]

The doctrine of a transcendental, omnipotent, universal God must have appeared as an alien element in the ancient Arabic conceptual universe. It signified a radical break. To legitimize his message, Mohammed was unable to cite Arabic traditions, not even in the sense that pre-exilic Jewish prophets could in reminding the people of the commitment they had taken upon themselves, and thus of something that was part of their past. Mohammed was left with only the break with tradition and the charismatic legitimation of his new mission. What is reported of the times gives indications confirming this. They fit Weber's specifications of charismatic leadership the conversion experience; "rebirth" in a situation close to "bourgeois satiety," and, at around forty years of age, the pathological states and stances that are then rationally worked through; the break with Mecca; and finally, the proof of supernatural powers in the battle of Badr. Yet, what we have here is a rather moderate form of charisma. There is no radical break with the family ties and economic life. In this way, too, Mohammed, in comparison to Jesus, represents an intermediate position. Although he transforms the old into the new he does not completely break with the old. Instead, the latter is "raised in value": "monotheism with a tribal face."[146]

Mohammed died after he had conquered Mecca and largely unified Arabia. His fortunes in war were admittedly mixed after Badr, and apostasy, the *ridda,* already arose during his lifetime. However, as in all forms of charismatic leadership the greatest obstacle it left behind was the unresolved question of succession. The search for a solution split Islam into the Sunni and Shi'ite movements and traditionalized it quickly under the rule of Sunnism, which remained predominant outside of Persia. As Weber observed:

> The structure of Islam has been decisively affected by the fact that Mohammed died without male heirs and that his followers did not found the Caliphate on hereditary charisma, and indeed during the Umayyad period developed it in an

outright anti-theocratic manner. It is largely owing to such differences about the ruler's qualification that Shi'ism, which recognizes the hereditary charisma of Ali's family and hence accepts the infallible doctrinal authority of an imam, is so antagonistic to orthodox *Sunna*, which is based on tradition and *ijma (consensus ecclesiae)*.[147]

The earlier caliphate, in which the leaders were recruited from the circle of Mohammed's followers—from the circle of "disciples"—still kept the religious and the politico-military function unified. It employed the Arabic tribes, largely unified under Mohammed, for the purpose of world conquest. In this way, the "urban rule" in Medina developed in less than thirty years into a territorial rule of considerable scope (Syria, Iraq, Mesopotamia, Egypt, and Iran). Under the rule of the Umayyads, further areas were added (Carthage, the Indus Valley, Spain).

The incredible thrust of this movement was tied to the interconnection of politics and religion. The battle for God brings both paradise in heaven and booty on earth. Allah in his power to control and move all, in his transcendence, is suitable as the God of war of battle-experienced nomads. Thus, in a holy war the dissemination of doctrine is tied from the very beginning to the subjection and economic exploitation of unbelievers. The ideal and material interests of the holy warriors are so intimately connected that religious ends merge with politico-economic ones. Interestingly enough, this has a moderating influence. One would expect from a basically universalist ethical salvation religion, which Islam in fact represents—in conjunction with Judaism and Christianity and in contrast to the remaining major religions, that a holy war would serve either to force unbelievers to convert or to eradicate them. This certainly was a consequence of certain versions of the vision of the Christian Crusades, a consequence that did not, according to Weber, occur in Islam. The "elevation" of the believers through the "subjugation of the unbelievers to [their] political authority and economic domination [via taxation]" suffices.[148] In the interest of this "elevation," which naturally has primarily politico-economic effects, the protection of the subjugated is even required. In this manner, political and economic interests push themselves ever more into the foreground in the battle on behalf of the faith. At stake is not converting or missionizing the unbelievers, and certainly not saving their souls; what is involved are revenues, and in this way religion becomes a defining characteristic of status group stratification.[149] This led, however, to the ethical and salvational aspects receding in the face of its political aspects: "Those religious elements of ancient Islam which had the character of an ethical religion of salvation largely receded into the background as long as Islam remained essentially a religion of warriors."[150]

Along with the areas where they resided, unbelievers had not only to be conquered but also administered. The farther the area of domination expanded, the greater number of peoples brought under the rule of Allah, and the more poignantly was Islam confronted with the basic organizational problem of charismatically and traditionally legitimated authority: the problem of centralization and decentralization.[151] This universal problem of traditional configurations of order was only intensified in this particular case inasmuch as Allah's elite troops were originally tribes of nomadic tenders of herds, who, unlike settled peasants, for example, were not accustomed to a continuous territorial power to which they were to submit. They did not easily accept the constraints of this system, even as its rulers. The problem of religious, and above all, political unity, had to be resolved, however. This required both institutional differentiation and the establishment of military and civilian administrative staffs, without which a central power cannot successfully rule over large geographical areas.

The institutional differentiation involves above all the relative autonomization of religious and political functions, of hierocratic and political powers, and the separation of powers between and within them. The establishment of administrative staffs primarily involves the military troops and the organization of officials, both in structure and in spirit. According to Weber, the Arab, tribally organized, theocratic levy had already dissolved in the ninth century into the "'booty-happy' religious zeal [that] had carried the great conquests."[152] The caliphate, too, separated itself from the sultanate under the Abbasids in a kind of division of labor between spiritual and worldly tasks, both admittedly—at least according to the intent of the canon taking shape—subject to a single religious law. In comparison with the situation in Medina and then under the early caliphates, however, this represents a new structural constellation. We must turn to this constellation if we want to fully understand the relationship of the "Islamic Orient" and the "Islamic states" to rational capitalism—a relationship that was not merely unfavorable, but rather one of obstruction and resistance.[153]

Weber employs different terms to characterize this new constellation in relation to political domination: "arbitrary patrimonialism," "sultanism," "prebendal feudalism," and even "free prebendal feudalism."[154] This is initially surprising insofar as in arbitrary patrimonialism (under which sultanism can be classified) the lord has a wide realm of discretionary powers, and thus his powers are hardly stereotyped. In contrast, feudalism represents "a marginal case of patrimonialism" because the stereotyping of relations of domination is relatively far advanced.[155] For this reason, a developed feudal system is "at least an approximation of a *Rechtsstaat*."[156] It thus limits the ruler's discretion (*Eigenrecht der Herrenmacht*) through a regulated division of authority (*Herrengewalten*). Such a "rule of law" is of course not based on an objective legal order, but on "subjective" rights, on privileges. It protects the rights of individuals and, in certain circumstances, those of associations (as a kind of *Ständestaat*) as well as the resulting mode of distribution. By contrast, in patrimonialism the individual right of the ruler is increased vis-à-vis other sources of power, and the more arbitrary political domination, the greater the discretion of the ruler. This individual right is a "right to intervene" that does not spare the vested rights of others and the associated mode of distribution. Again, the more arbitrary the patrimonial formation, the more they are compromised. What patrimonialism and feudalism do share is the necessity for the central power to come to terms with the other powers. Both are territorial forms of domination that have to regulate relations of domination, in nonpatrimonial as well as patrimonial domains. They are distinguished by *how* they regulate these relations. It thus logically follows that a formation cannot be both sultanistic and feudalistic at the same time.

Now this terminological indeterminacy could simply be the result of the history of *Economy and Society*. We know that Weber wrote two versions of the sociology of domination, and that although the second one built upon the first, it was more stringently formulated and more conceptually precise. In the latter version, the Islamic Near East and the Mughal empire are classified under fiscally conditioned prebendal feudalism, not under sultanism. The latter is also described, as in the original version, in conjunction with the greatest possible power of the ruler in patrimonialism; however, it is but briefly described and characterized as a marginal and historically fairly improbable phenomenon.[157] There could also be substantive reasons for the terminological indecisiveness. Islamic state formations were perhaps both sultanistic and prebendal-feudal, depending on the object of one's attention.

In the first version of the sociology of domination (and thus in that text which, as part of "The Economy and the Societal Orders and Powers," most directly reflects his study of Islam) Weber treats Islamic feudalism in comparison with its Occidental counterpart. Once again his aim is to show that Western medieval feudalism represents a special historical case that is one of the general cultural prerequisites for the rise and development of rational capitalism. The comparison encompasses equally form and spirit, structure and ethic. Let us go briefly through this comparison.

A general consideration is helpful here. The feudal relation has in fact a highly stereotyped and legalized form in comparison to the purely patrimonial relation. In typological terms, it is both patrimonial and charismatic in origin. The patrimonial origin is connected to two facts: a ruling power requires an administrative staff in order to militarily defend and administer a territory, and this administrative staff can appropriate political rights of rule and economic opportunities, and thus take possession of military and administrative means. The administrative staff develops an autonomy (*Eigenrecht*) that it secures economically: the *beneficium*. The charismatic origin is tied to the fact that the lord is a war hero who gathers around himself followers who believe in his heroism. It is a relation of nonmaterial, purely ideal devotion. Even if this relation becomes routinized, it maintains its ideal character. A specific relation of loyalty arises between the lord and his administrative staff: one of *homagium*. In the feudal relation, both of these components, the material and the ideal, the *beneficium* and the *homagium*, become interconnected, and in such a way that "a revenue-based right to rule" is "exchanged" for a personal commitment of loyalty. This occurs by way of a contract that, strictly speaking, presupposes "free" contractual parties. A fiefholder is not a patrimonial subject, he is a freeman. On the basis of such contractual relationships—"a *revenue-bearing* complex of rights the possession of which [makes possible] a *lordly* existence" in exchange for personal fealty, especially in war—a complex system can develop, a hierarchy of fiefs with intermediary strata. This is particularly the case where such a system spans large territories. More important, though, the feudal formation has, in addition to its economic, material, and "patrimonial" character, an ideal, ethical, and "charismatic" side. The authority relation (*Herrschaftsbeziehung*) is regulated by a "very demanding code of duties and honor"— by means of a specific mentality and a corresponding mode of conduct, more specifically, by means of a chivalrous mode of conduct.[158]

There are thus internal and external aspects to the feudal relation. It requires a special ethic, a feudal ethic, centered on the concepts of fealty and honor. It is important to make clear that this ethic was more than one of filial piety. The appeal "to honor and personal fealty, freely assumed and maintained" is constitutive for the mode of conduct associated with these virtues.[159] This is connected to a specific feeling of dignity and the "permeation of the most important relationships of life with very personal bonds."[160] Weber points out the educational significance of the game for this chivalrous mode of conduct and the affinity that exists between it and an artistic mode.[161] Even a patrimonial relation—for example, in the form of a prebendal relation—has its "inner" aspect, its "ethic." It, too, is built upon the idea of loyalty. However, "filial piety," the model of which is provided by the authoritarian relationship between father and child, differs from vassal fealty. Even though the former can also be status group-oriented, emphasizing "being" over "function," it nevertheless lacks that basic aristocratic trait of vassal fealty that is born in the playful shaping of a heroically oriented life. It also lacks the legal structure upon which the feudal relation is ultimately based: the "free" contract.

A formation of patrimonial domination can thus undergo both prebendal and feudal modifications. Which kind of modification is involved is solely a legal and ethical question, not an economic one. In both cases, patrimonialism becomes *ständisch*, with powers being divided through the appropriation of rights of rule and economic opportunities by the administrative staffs. The staffs are no longer separable from the material means of administration, whether they be military or civilian in nature. This aspect is crucial for the clarification of the structural question. As we know, in this way Weber applies Marx's thesis on the centrality of the relation to the means of production to all areas of life and to all periods in history. Now the division of lordly power and the limitation of the discretion (*Eigenrecht*) associated with it serves the purpose of maintaining the undivided domain of domination, the unity of the empire. This unity is constantly threatened by the manner in which this goal is to be reached. The relatively autonomous regional powers can become opposing powers. This potential forces the central authority to take countermeasures that aim at eliminating or at least "taming" the independence of the administrative staffs, which portends, however, the expansion (or at least the "protection") of the autonomous rights of the central authority and thus the return to patrimonialism, the extreme form of which is sultanism.

According to Weber, in a typological sense, the West came to terms with this central problem of all traditional political formations in three steps: with the help of fief-based feudalism, with the help of the *Ständestaat* that represents a kind of corporate form of fief-based feudalism, and with the help of a rational bureaucratic patrimonial state that arose out of the *Ständestaat*. All these formations were characterized by rule of law (*Rechtsstaatlichkeit*), which admittedly reached full maturity only in the modern *Anstaltsstaat*. The idea of contract is joined by that of the *Anstalt* to form the core of this "rule of law." The notion of the *Anstalt* was never limited to the sphere of political territorial power, but also included the hierocratic power, the church, and the urban powers. An important aspect of Occidental political development thus involves the fact that here corporate territorial bodies arose, in part autonomously and in part out of fief-based feudalism, which came into fierce conflict with one another because each stood on its own feet. This conflict promoted decentralization and structural pluralism and made possible a hierarchy of legal and de facto autonomous units. In this way, the center of power gravitated, so to speak, toward the intermediate level, supported by a strong tendency to subject the internal and external relations of domination to the constraints of law.[162] This represents a relatively early tendency toward a rational constitution (*Satzung*), not least of all because the West was already acquainted in the Middle Ages both with a clear division—as compared to other legal systems—between sacred (canonic) and profane (Roman and Germanic) law and with a relatively formal sacred law. Ever since the Investiture Struggle, this legal demarcation between church and "state" received, moreover, support from political motives.[163]

Thus, since the Middle Ages, the West has basically ceased to employ patrimonial, much less sultanistic, strategies in coming to terms with the "problem of unity." Instead, its strategy aimed at a *ständisch* division of powers among structurally heterogenous units and their legal fixation by means of statutes. If one views the Islamic state formations in this regard, two institutions above all stand out: the army of purchased slaves and the fiscally conditioned military prebendalism. Both are connected to the "warrior" origin of the Islamic movement. In Weber's view, the Islamic state formations are first of all "military states," for the structural characterization of which the analysis of the military organization is especially important.

"Slaves on horses" as a system is apparently peculiar to Islamic state formations.[164] Of course, and this must be equally emphasized, there is no religious foundation for this system in Islam.[165] But as we shall see momentarily, it helps to understand why these states posed structural obstacles to any form of rational capitalism.

The system of "slaves on horses" appears to have already arisen in the early ninth century.[166] In any case it defined the structure of political domination at the time of the Abbasids. As Weber observes: "The Abbasids bought and militarily trained Turkish slaves who, as tribal aliens, appeared wholly tied to the ruler's domination; thus the dynasty became independent of the national levy and its loose peacetime discipline and created a disciplined army."[167] The national levy was the levy of Arab tribes that had succeeded at Islamic world conquest. The holy warriors, marked in part by the religious ethic, had proved themselves as heroes through the conquest of ever new areas and peoples. However, with the pacification of the realm, the time was over for both discipline and tribal cooperation. The tribes became—in the transition from the extraordinary situation of war to the everyday-situation of peace—subject to the cyclic movement between readiness to self-oblivious sacrifice and bourgeoisification. For this reason they were not a suitable administrative staff for securing the central power's domination of the empire. By creating a troop of purchased slaves out of tribal aliens, the central power crafted itself an instrument that freed it from dependency on the tribes and, above all, from the maelstrom of their centrifugal, anticentralistic tendencies. The administrative staff was recruited nonpatrimonially, and employed patrimonially, indeed, sultanistically. This did not prevent the dissolution of the empire, which had already occurred under the Abbasids in the ninth century. What the military slave system did provide, however, was a powerful instrument for reestablishing imperial unity after periods of breakdown into regional empires. Admittedly, this came about because Islam as a religion held alive the idea of unity: "The religious unity of the caliphate did not prevent the disintegration of the purely secular sultanate, a creation of the slave generals, into sub-empires. But the unity of the well-disciplined slave armies in turn favored the indivisibility of these sub-empires once they were established; partly for that reason hereditary division never became customary in the Islamic Orient."[168]

A large slave troop, nonpatrimonially recruited and sultanistically employed, and for this reason necessarily freed from all forms of civilian labor, cannot be provisioned by the royal household. Other arrangements have to be made. In this context, Carl Heinrich Becker put forth the thesis (in an essay that apparently deeply impressed Weber) that Oriental feudalism, the decisive development of which he placed in the time of the Crusades, arose out of tax farming. The slave generals increasingly functioned as tax collectors on their own behalf. In addition to payment for their military service they were originally provided with taxable units for which they acted as tax guarantors vis-à-vis the central authority. In exchange for the discontinuation of the service payments and in addition to the entrepreneurial profits made in tax collection, they came to appropriate the taxes for themselves. The fact of monetary payment was connected to the relatively highly developed monetary economy. In contrast, Occidental feudalism was initially based on a natural economy.[169] Weber adopts this idea but immediately links it to another:

> The extraordinary legal insecurity of the taxpaying population in the face of the arbitrariness of the troops to whom their tax capacity was mortgaged could paralyze commerce and hence the money economy; indeed, since the period of the Seljuks the Oriental economy declined or stagnated to a very great extent because of these circumstances.[170]

Thus the two institutions, the military slave system and the military fief for fiscal purposes, extended the realm of arbitrary discretion, in comparison to Western fief-based feudalism. That realm lessened the calculability of the administrative process. According to Weber this had an interesting economic consequence: the artificial immobilization of wealth, especially by means of pious foundations (*waqfs*), in order to evade arbitrary seizure by patrimonial authorities. Once again following Becker, Weber views the transfer of wealth into the restrictiveness of the *waqfs* as a reaction against the unpredictability of patrimonial domination that was conducive to an "increase of the realm bound by sacred law."[171] This transfer could also keep wealth from possibly being used for capitalist purposes. Weber views the function of the *waqfs* as similar to that of the "entailed estate" (*fidei commissum*). Support of the latter, especially in Prussia, had provoked his opposition in the strongest terms possible due to its "anticapitalistic consequences."[172]

However, the military fief for financial purposes is not a fief, strictly speaking. Even Becker had already pointed out that what is given here is a *beneficium* but not a *feudum* because *homagium,* vassalage, is lacking. Originally, the granting of the *beneficium* was not linked to military service in any way. The military, according to Becker, had forced itself "improperly and after the fact into the existing system of benefices."[173] This basic pattern is seen in ethics and in the mode of conduct attendant to it. This "base" ultimately does not permit a feudal ethic with a chivalrous mode of conduct, as Western feudalism does. Only in phases of religious war does a knighthood of the faithful emerge that approximates Occidental knighthood but without the gamelike character of the latter. As Weber points out: "In the age of the Crusades, Oriental prebendal feudalism sustained a sense of knightly status, but on the whole its character remained defined by the patriarchal character of domination."[174]

Weber thus identifies three points of comparison between Oriental, especially Islamic, prebendal feudalism, and Occidental feudalism that turn out to represent three points of contrast: the economic foundation of military organization, its social carriers, and the ethic encompassing this structure. In terms of the economic foundation, prebends that were originally usurped stand in contrast to fiefs that were originally contracted. The prebends are utilized solely for fiscal purposes; of interest are strictly the taxes, more precisely, the monetary taxes, and not the land. The predominance of this monetary orientation is possible only because of a monetary economy that is more developed in comparison to that of the West. Becker points out that there was an intensive development of limited partnership and cooperatives and that checks and bills of exchange were used for fiscal and economic purposes.[175] In terms of the social carriers, purchased slaves stand in contrast to freemen. The army of purchased slaves is a disciplined mass army, the feudal army one of knights geared toward individual heroic battle. The army of purchased slaves tends to sustain plebeian traits; the knightly army, aristocratic ones. Admittedly, even the slave troops—if sufficiently pervaded by the conceptual universe of Islam—can become an army of "noble warriors of the faith."[176] Nevertheless, a difference remains in terms of the third point of contrast, the ethic and respective mode of conduct. Here, what is ultimately an ethic of submissive piety stands in contrast to a feudal ethic. Oriental feudalism is not a feudalism of fealty, as are its Occidental (and Japanese) counterparts. In Weber's comparative typology, Oriental feudalism lacks fealty, Japanese feudalism lacks a patrimonial foundation, and only Occidental feudalism combines both—and this is what defines its singular historical character.[177]

Thus, Oriental feudalism is less "typified" than is its Occidental counterpart. It is also less decentralized. It is furthermore lacking the idea of contract in the Western sense and the concept of the *Anstalt*. The combination of the two is important for the development of Occidental feudalism into the *Ständestaat*. This leads to differences in the manner of, and especially the predictability of administrative action. One could ask, however, are these differences so decisive in answering the questions whether and in what way the form and spirit of political domination influence the developmental prospects for rational capitalism? Is it not in fact the case, moreover, that regardless of whether there is more or less arbitrary patrimonialism, prebendal or fief-based feudalism, do they not all deprive industrial capitalism of a breeding ground: For what is at stake are the developmental prospects for productive capital, not those for commercial capital. The formation of the latter, as Weber repeatedly emphasizes, "is feasible under almost all conditions of domination, especially under patrimonialism."[178] The commercial enterprise repeatedly arises under the conditions of traditional political domination in varying frequencies. At issue, however, is not commercial capital or some subsidiary modes of market production, but the capitalist economy as a system. At stake are the developmental prospects for a new structural principle: the meeting of everyday needs on the basis of industrial capitalism.[179] It involves the replacement of the principle of the household through the market principle, the replacement of a power amenable to tradition with one thoroughly antagonistic to it.[180]

Indeed, it would be a mistake in my opinion to take Weber's comparative analysis as a direct explanation of the external aspects that favored rational capitalism in the West. Within a traditional framework, administration, taxation, and as we will see, the administration of justice are nowhere so organized as to fully offer the predictability of governmental action so indispensable for the formation and utilization of industrial capital. The feudal ethic, so highly developed in the West compared to the Islamic Orient, can, like all status group-oriented ethics, be considered an anticapitalist force par excellence. Nothing is so distant from capitalist business morals, from a vocational ethic defined in terms of functions performed, as a heroic ethic that is deeply hostile to all means-ends rationality.[181] Of course, the form and spirit of traditional political domination can be so constituted that they develop toward the predictability of governmental action when additional conditions are met. This, however, was the case only in the West and not in the Islamic Orient. In my view, we have here Weber's second thesis.

Occidental feudalism contains within it, for example, two of the elements that "permit further development" but are missing in Oriental prebendal feudalism: the decentralization of political domination by means of a feudal hierarchy, which is a form of estate-type division of powers that, through compromise, makes possible a predictable distribution of burdens,[182] and the feudal contract. Both were influential in the further political development of the Occident. Otherwise, however, in its relation to rational capitalism, Occidental feudalism is not different from traditional political domination in general. The latter favors politically oriented, not economically oriented capitalism. In a refinement of the first version, Weber provided a particularly concise formulation for the exception to this rule in the later version of the sociology of domination:

> The situation is fundamentally different only in cases where a patrimonial ruler, in the interest of his own power and financial provision, develops a rational system of administration with technically specialized officials. For this to happen, it is necessary (1) that technical training should be available; (2) that there is a sufficiently powerful incentive to embark on such a policy—usually the sharp competition between a plurality of patrimonial powers within the same cultural area; (3) that a very special factor is present, namely, the participation of urban communes as a financial support in the competition of the patrimonial units.[183]

One way to summarize our analysis of external conditions is to say that in Islam the second aspect cited in the quote is but weakly developed. In Islamic civilization the political cycle of unification and disintegration does exist, but neither the continuous conflict between relatively independent territorial units nor the sharp competition of several powers within the framework of a *ständisch* division of powers, with a legal superstructure as in the West, does. This holds both for the relationship between the lord and his administrative staffs and for that between political hierocratic domination. Despite tendencies toward autonomy that are also intrinsic to prebendal feudalism, the former relationship is centralistic in the Islamic Orient, thus lessening competition; the latter relationship is conflict-ridden, but Islam lacks the church as a bureaucratic apparatus of power.[184] The first and third aspects from the quote, however, direct attention to further potential points of differences. These will be my last subjects.

Oriental and Occidental Cities

Let us begin with the third point from the passage quoted earlier, the role of urban communal organizations. Weber proceeds in the same way in the case of the city as he did in the case of feudalism. He makes a typological comparison between the Occidental city—or more precisely, the medieval, Northern European, continental, city—and the Oriental city. Interestingly enough, Mecca at the time of Mohammed and thereafter serves him as an example of the latter.[185] It is not possible for me to give a full account of Weber's comparative analysis of the city here—an analysis that is of central importance in his explanation of the rise and development of rational capitalism in the West.[186] I will cite only those ideas important in our context. The first question involves Weber's claim that the Oriental city tends to obstruct rather than favor the developmental prospects of rational capitalism, even though it also possesses the following characteristics: it is generally the site of markets attracting trade and craft; it accommodates merchant and artisan guilds with autonomous "statutes"; it has a city patron or lord, and its pattern of social stratification diverges from that of nonurban regions; and it possesses, especially under Islamic influence, religious associations to which religious inhabitants belong independently of their social position.

Weber classifies cities in part according to which social stratum rules in them (the patrician or princely city versus the plebeian city); which economic functions they primarily fulfill (the consumer or rentier city versus the producer city—or city of trade and industry); how they are geographically situated, and connected to this, which ways and means of transportation they favor (maritime versus inland cities); and which primary orientation they possess (the politically oriented versus the economically oriented city). Thus, many cities of Occidental antiquity are patrician, consumer, maritime, and politically oriented cities; in contrast, many medieval Occidental cities are plebeian, producer, inland, and economically oriented cities. One could also classify the Oriental city in this way. It would then more closely approximate the city of Occidental antiquity than that of the Western Middle Ages. But one can quickly see that this procedure does not lead very far. Weber makes his comparison on a more sophisticated basis.

First of all, Weber strictly distinguishes the economic concept of the city from the politico-administrative and legal one; these are two different things.[187] Moreover, in purely economic terms it is sometimes difficult to distinguish cleanly between city (or town) and village. Both can be the sites where traders and businessmen settle; both can possess a market for meeting everyday needs; both can act as landowning economic associations, as economic units with revenues and expenses, and as associations regulating the economy. But even in terms of politico-administrative criteria, the distinction is not always easy to make. Villages, like cities, can possess their own territory, their own authorities, or even their own fortress, or they can belong to a fortress with garrison; moreover, both a village (always) and a city (usually) are part of a greater political association. There is one thing that villages have not developed, however: political, administrative, military, and legal autonomy and autocephaly. Admittedly, not all cities did this either. A city with fully developed autonomy and autocephaly is a special historical case. The one that especially interests Weber is found in the Occidental Middle Ages and represents but a "historical interlude."[188] One sees that here, too, he unfolds his comparative analysis from the special Occidental case, which then furnishes him with points of comparison with which he can analyze Islamic cities.

Urban autonomy and autocephaly are by themselves characterizations without specific contents. Both hold for some of the ancient poleis, especially for those that were the starting point for "great power formations."[189] Thus, it is not autonomy and autocephaly as such that are important but the manner in which they are legitimated and organized— in short, the structural principle on which they are based. In these terms the city that preoccupies Weber is the corporate urban commune. The invention and realization of this structural principle was a "*revolutionary* innovation which differentiated the medieval Oriental cities from all others."[190] This structural principle breaks with the prebendally or feudally appropriated manorial, ecclesiastical, and urban powers. Because of this usurpatory aspect of medieval Occidental urban development, Weber entitled his analysis of the city "Non-legitimate Domination: A Typology of Cities" ("Die nichtlegitime Herschaft. Typologie der Städte") in his manuscript "The Economy and the Societal Orders and Powers." This is not to be understood as if urban domination in general and that of the medieval West in particular is always non-legitimate domination. What this title actually refers to is this: Weber's comparative analysis of the city is organized around the particular Occidental case. Here and only here did this new structural principle make a breakthrough of historical consequence. Only infrequently did this breakthrough involve a consciously illegitimate and revolutionary act.[191] In the majority of cases, usurpation occurred gradually or not at all. Above all, most cities arose out of completely different conditions. The usurpation theory is not a theory of the genesis of the medieval city. In addition, only a few medieval cities were able to attain complete autonomy, and those that succeeded were soon once again subject to restrictions. The interlude was sufficient, however, to create three important historical "prerequisites" for later capitalist development: the democratic principle of legitimation; the organizational principle of the corporate urban commune; and the market-oriented bourgeoisie.[192]

Thus, in Weber's view the medieval city is a "special developmental case." This becomes comprehensible only if one focuses on "the general position of the city within the framework of the medieval political and status-group organizations."[193] As important as the economic aspect is, analysis must not be restricted to it alone. Instead, it must also take into account the aspect of politics and domination, subdivided into form and spirit. It is not by chance that Weber subsumes the comparative analysis of the city under the sociology of domination and not the sociology of the economy. Political domination and the question of its relationship to the economy are the main issues here.

The medieval Western city is thus in its "full development" a corporate communal body, legitimated on the basis of the will of the governed; its burghers are politically "revolutionary" and oriented toward economic acquisition. Such a formation is not found in Occidental antiquity, despite certain lines of continuity between ancient and medieval democracy, and it is certainly not found in the Islamic world. Here urban development did not lead to a break with the prerogatives of patrimonial rule. It also did not lead to the formation of urban communes as civic communes, with politico-administrative, legal, and (under some circumstances) military autonomy directed outside the commune and fraternization directed within.

This kind of civic commune no longer followed the lines of nonurban or preurban constituted organizations, but rather those of a "freely" constituted burgher organization that one joined as an individual and that was based upon some idea of legal equality. This is what is decisive about the "fully developed" Western city: It replaces the traditional principle of the person (*Personalprinzip*) with that of the institution (*Anstaltsprinzip*) and in this way replaces the traditional statuses of lord and subject with membership status. This legal development finds support in religious convictions, for this profane legal equality has, so to speak, a symbolical substructure in the Eucharistic community of Christianity.[194] This is not to say that "the law of the land" did not continue to have effects on "the law of the town" (town charters), nor that this legal equality is incommensurable with division according to status group. It certainly does mean, however, that the urban commune as an institutional body (*Anstalt*) radically transforms the personal legal situation of the burgher vis-à-vis that of the rural inhabitant.[195] It also means that the fraternity of burghers stands above the solidarity of relatives, neighbors, and colleagues and that the solidarity with the overall urban organization stands above the solidarity with larger territorial units of which it is a part.

The special developmental case of the medieval Occidental city is further illuminated by a comparison with Arab cities, particularly Mecca. Weber follows here the description of Snouk Hurgronje, who had already dedicated a study to this city before the turn of the century.[196] As discussed earlier, Mecca was at the time of Mohammed a kind of clan city, or more precisely, a "clan settlement"[197] located in a rural territory and not legally distinguishable from it. Essentially, this remained so. Divisions according to organizations of gentes (*Gentilverbände*), tribes, and clans also remained intact; as at the time of Mohammed, they were the social carriers of military organization. Admittedly, other organizations also existed, such as the guilds. But they never attained town rule. This was in part because the competing town-resident clans later also took advantage of the institution of purchased slaves, in this case Negro troops, who here really were "the private armies of their master and his family."[198] Although the Arab city served as the location of powerful economic interests that were influential well beyond city limits, it was never a communal organization. The religious community, the *umma*, would not have obstructed such a development. But it alone was too weak to cause a break with the importance of tribal and clan bonds at the level of the city and beyond. The decisive legal institution for doing this was lacking, the concept of the corporation (*Anstalt*).

Thus, in Islamic states, city domination is an extension of territorial domination. The same principles of legitimation and organization were employed for both. It was not the case, however, as in India and in part in China that magical sib bonds prevented urban fraternity and an urban commune attendant to it. These bonds had been broken by Islam. What was actually obstructive was the mode of military organization, the prebendal feudalism connected to it, and military prebendalism: its "centralism" prevented autonomous urban development and thus also the development of a production-oriented capitalist bourgeoisie. Weber formulated the generalization: "Thus, the more unified the organization of the [larger] political association, the less the development of the political autonomy of the cities."[199]

Weber speaks of the "distinctive anarchy of the city of Mecca." But, he adds, this anarchy was not a specific trait of Islamic or Arab cities. Rather, it was a condition found throughout the world, in Occidental antiquity and even in medieval Occidental cities, especially in Southern European ones. The anarchy consisted in the fact that here "numerous claims stand side by side, overlapping and often conflicting with each other."[200] The city was perhaps a more convenient location than the countryside for pursuing economic interests, but it was not yet an independent social organization. It became one in the West, however, beginning in antiquity, just as the church would later develop into one. That neither the city nor the church rose as a corporate body in the Orient had the consequence that no heterogeneous counterforces were available to challenge Islamic patrimonialism. Of course, Islamic patrimonialism struggled continuously with the disintegration of the unity of the realm. Disintegration, however, only brought forth repeatedly the same institutions and orientations. The unity of the empire was made up of homogeneous units, and when it broke up, it broke up into homogeneous subunits. The structural heterogeneity, the structural pluralism that marks the medieval West, was lacking. In this way, however, the historical preconditions arising from it, prerequisites for the genesis and development of rational capitalism, were also missing. Thus, as opposed to the West, both in terms of form and spirit the overall constellation of political domination in the Islamic state formations was ultimately a hindrance to the developmental prospects of rational industrial capitalism.

The Role of Law

A further aspect must be considered to understand the constellation of political domination as an impediment to rational capitalism: the development of law. In the passage cited earlier, Weber emphasized that an exception to the normal effect of traditional political domination could be expected only in cases where a patrimonial ruler, due to considerations of power and finance, turns to the use of a rational system of administration with technically specialized officials. This administrative staff has to be technically, commercially, and legally trained and oriented toward a functional ethic, that is, a vocational ethic understood in terms of an ethic of performance (*Leistungsethik*).[201] Such a "secular" administrative staff was available rather early on in the West. Important contributing factors here were the "relatively clear dualism" of sacred and profane law and the development of each of these two kinds of law in accordance with their "own inner logic."[202] This dualism also had its effects on university development, which was initially under ecclesiastical influence. The patrimonial state in the West was able to take recourse to this potential source of technical specialists in the age of absolute princely power. It was able to use it for its fiscally conditioned alliance with those bourgeois capitalist strata supported by the development of the city.[203] According to Weber, this potential administrative resource did not exist to the same extent in the Islamic state formations. Admittedly, like China, Islam had universities that resembled those of the West, but "a rational and systematic pursuit of science, with trained specialists, has only existed in the West in a sense at all approaching its present dominant place in our culture."[204] This distinctive development leads us to our last question: Why did this not occur in Islam?

We pointed out earlier that no comprehensive comparative analysis of scientific and university development exists in Weber. Although comments are repeatedly found on education and educational institutions, they satisfy to only a very limited extent the theoretical requirements of his approach.[205] The comparative analysis of law and legal development is the text that comes closest to satisfying them. One object of Weber's analysis there is to arrive at the types of law and legal thought and their social carriers. This requires a short characterization of legal training. He includes here all the civilizations that interest him in his analysis: the Chinese, Indian, Jewish, Christian, and Islamic realms. Insofar as the focus is on the early developmental phases in these civilizations, special attention is paid to sacred law and its relationship to profane law. Even this specialized investigation is centered on the West's distinctive development, for, as has already been emphasized, Christian sacred law is distinguished from other examples of sacred law by its relatively clear separation of the sacred and profane spheres. In this way it works against the growth of theocratic hybrid structures: "The Canon Law of *Christendom* differed at least in degree from all other systems of sacred law."[206]

Weber distinguishes three kinds of legal training: the empirical-practical, the theoretical-formal, and the theocratic. The first type of legal training treats the empirical order from the perspective of practical problems as a craft; the second seeks to work up these problems in doctrinal terms, and thus to systematize them rationally in a legally immanent manner; in contrast, the third does not limit itself to this, instead taking recourse to norms "that represent mere idealistic religious-ethical demands on human beings or on the legal order," and that are thus based on substantive presuppositions from outside.[207] These presuppositions originate from sacred and usually fixed traditions. Thus, here too systematization takes place but, from the perspective of juridical doctrine, in an informal manner. This is characteristic of all types of sacred law: although they are the products of rationalizing doctrines, the orientation of the latter is legally transcendent rather than legally immanent. The systematization reached by such a doctrine is thus not formal-juridical, but substantive-theological in nature, for the purpose that law serves here is not primarily profane.

According to Weber, Islamic law is sacred law in this sense. It is the product of the speculative rational labors of law schools, "specifically a 'jurists' law'"[208] performed on the basis of the Quran and *sunna* and by making use of the consensus among legal scholars (*ijma*) and of argumentation by means of analogy (*qiyas*) and conceptual work (*ijtihad*). Lawmaking "in a great measure even today, [has] rested in the hands of the theologian jurists responding to concrete questions."[209] They are specialists in sacred law (*mufti*), who issue opinions (*fatwa*) on valid doctrine, in distinction to judges (*qadi*), who administer justice. The lawmakers were initially legal prophets, thereafter only commentators of the law. The transformation occurred with the end of the prophetic and charismatic age.[210] Pure casuistry began to replace the creation of law, and disputes of interpretation move into the foreground. In Weber's view, the great jurists of the four law schools definitely continued to be legal prophets. They extended and elaborated the law and legal scholarship (*fiqh*) in a creative way on the basis of the holy scriptures and the oral tradition, the Quran and the *sunna*, and by means of independent interpretation and the *consensus omnium*. Nevertheless, with the sacred tradition having become fixed, this charismatic source of law dried up. Legal development was paralyzed. The result is a "stereotyped 'jurists' law"—a jurists' law, moreover, that opposes secularization with all the means available to it.[211]

These three processes—paralysis, stereotypification, and resistance to secularization—are mutually supportive of one another, however. They permit systematization, but of an ultimately substantive-theological and not formal-juridical nature. More important, because sacred law organizes the Muslim's entire life, the real and the ideally required orders of life distance themselves from each other to an ever greater extent. As a result, the de facto validity of sacred law is limited to "certain fundamental institutions." The remaining institutions are left to profane law—a law, however, that is not guaranteed "by statutes or stable principles of a rational legal system." The gulf between sacred and profane law is "overcome" by circumventing strategies (*hijal*) and "disputatious casuistry," and thus in a largely opportunistic manner.[212] Weber views this as "paradigmatic for the way in which sacred law operates in a scriptural religion that has genuinely prophetic origin." Sacred law can consistently be neither implemented nor eliminated.[213]

If one accepts this diagnosis, it can be linked to three points relevant to our concerns. First of all, sacred law is an effective weapon in the hands of those who administer it. This is paradoxically true because it cannot be strictly implemented. The real order never corresponds to the ideal one. This brings the social bearers of the sacred law tradition into a critical position vis-à-vis the carriers of the real order, especially vis-à-vis the political rulers. Even in the early phase of Islam, the *'ulama'* were not integrated into the caliphate.[214] Second, sacred law is a decisive impediment to the establishment of a unified legal system. This is paradoxically true because, although the validity claim of sacred law as a doctrine of religious duties is unconditional for Muslims, its realm of validity is restricted to "status-group law."[215] The result, as Weber observes, was that the "legal particularism" of the subjugated peoples continued to exist "in all of its forms" and in a precarious relationship to the law of the Muslims. This made the creation of a *lex terrae* impossible.[216] Third and finally, sacred law is also a decisive impediment to the establishment of a predictable legal procedure. This is paradoxically true because, as a doctrine of religious duties that makes no distinction between law, ethics, ritual, and etiquette, sacred law did not sufficiently realize this unity in practice. In this way it promoted the dualism between the spiritual and worldly administration of justice, without, however, allowing for a formal juridical systematization of the profane side. Neither spiritual nor worldly adjudication followed an abstract logic immanent to the law; both were instead oriented toward substantive justice, toward concrete considerations of equity.[217]

This means, however, that because the separation of spheres between sacred and profane law, and between the spiritual and worldly administration of justice de facto existed, but remained normatively hierarchized, and because sacred lawmaking changed from legal creation to legal interpretation and became paralyzed in this way, profane law proliferated, so to speak, without guidance. It did not receive direction from sacred law, nor was it self-directing. Neither of the two modes of law developed into juridical formalization—sacred law, because it was rooted in presuppositions lying outside of law; and profane law, because it remained dominated by sacred law.

It is for this reason that, in typological terms, Islamic justice is theocratic and patrimonial "*qadi* justice."[218] This is due less to its individual norms than to its overall spirit. It is the spirit of material justice, based on nonlegal postulates. The social carriers correspond to this spirit. They are not "profane" specialists but rather military prebendaries and patrimonial officials with profane status-group ethics, on the one hand, and theological jurists with sacred status-group ethics on the other. This spirit generally prevented a "logical systematization of law in terms of formal juridical concepts."[219] Weber's view of the practical effects of Islamic law, therefore, can be summarized in this paradoxical formulation: because stereotypification of Islamic sacred law increased rather than diminished, sacred law intensified the already low level of stereotypification of Oriental patrimonialism. Thus, once again the points of comparison to Western development represent points of difference.

Let us summarize these points once more. We have spoken of the fact that the differentiation between sacred and profane law in the West was not simply de facto, but enjoyed a normative foundation. Naturally, it also required constructs bridging the two spheres. This was not primarily accomplished, however, as in Islam, by means of "circumventing strategies,"[220] but on a natural law basis originating in the Stoic tradition.[221] Moreover, the separation between the spheres was also reflected in teaching: "The structure of the Occidental medieval university separated the teaching of both theology and secular law from that of canon law and thus prevented the growth of such theocratic hybrid structures as they developed everywhere else."[222] Above all, however, canon law was not hindered in its development through the fixedness of the sacred tradition, and profane law stood on its own very early in terms of both its legal tradition and its social carrier stratum. Unlike Islam and Judaism, whose legal traditions resemble each other, the Occidental medieval church never fell back on responses to specific legal questions as the sole path of legal development. It had instead "created for itself organs of rational lawmaking in the Councils, the bureaucracies of the dioceses, and the Curia, and, quite particularly, in the papal powers of jurisdiction and infallible exposition of doctrine. No other of the great religions has ever possessed such institutions."[223] Moreover, the development of profane law had the Roman and Germanic legal traditions available as guides, and its social bearers were neither clerics, theological jurists, or prebendaries, but instead legal *honoratiores* in the form of Italian notaries, English attorneys, and "Occidental medieval empirical jurists of the northern European continent."[224] This autonomous development of a profane system of law was closely connected to medieval Occidental urban development. Once again, one sees how important Weber's thesis of the structural heterogeneity or pluralism of the Occidental configuration of order was for his analysis of the singularity of Occidental development.

Thus, in the West there are relatively autonomous developments of sacred and profane law that follow their own inner logic. These developments tend to be more mutually supportive than impeding of each other. These are developments that lead away from charismatic creation and judgment in law toward an orientation around formal juridical techniques for which Roman law, equally influential in both sacred and profane legal development, served as a precursor. This produces a spirit even in the social carriers of sacred law that promotes the formation of a juridically formal doctrine of law. Moreover, Roman and even Germanic law provide legal institutions that are totally alien to the Islamic legal realm. Here Weber is not thinking primarily of private or commercial law, as has been repeatedly claimed. What he has in mind is public law, for it was the Islamic legal realm that developed institutions of commercial law favorable to rational capitalism. It was from there that they made their way to the West. However—and here I follow Joseph Schacht—it is the legal institutions of the *Anstalt* that are foreign to Islamic law. In a presentation of Islamic law that follows Weber's sociology of law, although criticizing its treatment of Islamic law in points of detail, Schacht writes: "The concept of the juristic person that arose from the problem of organizations...is just as unknown in Islamic law as are corporate organization and the concept of the *Anstalt*. The only 'corporation' recognized by the *shari'a* is the sib (*aqila*) taken from ancient Arab tribal organization, which in most cases is obligated to pay blood money."[225]

As important as these points of contrast are, what was said in the comparison of Oriental prebendal feudalism with Occidental feudalism also holds here: The claims for the relatively special position of canon law among the types of sacred law and for the relatively autonomous development of profane law do not provide a direct explanation as to why rational capitalism was favored in the West. Here, too, we are dealing at most with elements that permit development and are missing in the Islamic state formations. Although they increased the predictability of administrative and legal procedures, as did feudalism and the *Ständestaat*, they still remained traditionally defined. All modes of sacred law have the tendency, as in Islam, to treat ethical, legal, ritual, and ceremonial norms "along the same lines," and like Islam, all of them have restricted the autonomy of profane legal development. All of them were also compelled to resort to circumventing strategies in order de facto to annul normatively imperative regulations, or more accurately, to be able to tolerate their being disregarded, for example, in the Occidental church's prohibition of usury.[226] But according to Weber, such "impractical" single-case regulations never hindered rational-capitalist economic activity.

The overall effect of a given normative complex, its spirit, was always decisive. This, however, was similar in all hierocracies. Like traditional political domination, traditional hierocratic domination is fundamentally anticapitalist in orientation, however. Its animosity is directed not at politically, but at economically oriented capitalism, where capitalism represents a rational, yet unethical economic system. In spite of "fundamentally different beginnings" and "different developmental destinies," after the conclusion of their "charismatically heroic ages" religions are similar in their effects on economic life. They favor traditional economic activity, the traditional economic spirit, and the traditional form of the economy. This holds for Islam just as much as it holds for the Roman Catholic Church. The most important exception to this rule is ascetic Protestantism and its "spirit of objectification" (*Versachlichung*).

This closes the reconstruction of Weber's analysis of Islam. It turned out to be a difficult puzzle to complete. Nevertheless, the pieces of the puzzle could be found and arranged in such a way that the basic features of a picture emerge. The main connecting thread was provided by Weber's analysis of Occidental development. It identifies the points of comparison that guide the analysis of Islam and of other cultural realms. These points of comparison represent above all points of difference. They come sharply into view as long as the typological comparative aspect is in the foreground. But the points of difference obtained in this way can also be considered in terms of their genesis. If Weber had still been able to write his projected study of Islam, this aspect certainly would have moved more into the foreground.

The reconstruction of Weber's analysis of Islam is not the only puzzle. His explanation of why rational capitalism only "succeeded" in the West and not in Islamic civilization is equally enigmatic. Here, too, many pieces, termed historical "prerequisites," were used in putting the puzzle together. They could arise only in the West—according to Weber's thesis—due to a chain of circumstances. Of course, a historical agent was required to put all these pieces together. This was the achievement of the methodical conduct of ascetic Protestantism, its rationalism of self- and world-mastery, something that was ultimately lacking not only in Islam but also in Lutheranism, Catholicism, early Christianity, Judaism, and in all Asiatic religions.

Weber's sociology of religion, indeed his sociology as a whole, thus culminates in a sociology and typology of worldviews and related modes of conduct. One could also term it a sociology and typology of axiological turns and the types of personality connected to them. For the sociology of religion this is demonstrated very clearly by the "Author's Introduction" and "The Intermediate Reflections"—and also in the "Conclusions" to the study of Confucianism, the end of the study of Hinduism, and the final paragraphs of the section on religion in *Economy and Society*.

The catalogue of traits that is included in the comparative typology is unusually complex. Its complexity is especially visible in those places where the analysis switches from the comparison between Asian religions and Near Eastern-Occidental religions to the comparison among the different Near Eastern-Occidental religions themselves. The treatment of Islam provides a good example of this. Its similarity especially with Calvinism makes a detailed discussion of commonalities and differences necessary. This means bringing together the most important traits of this catalogue and examining whether the characterizations of the Near Eastern-Occidental religions really allow them to be finely demarcated. Of these religions, all of which continually appear in the manuscript, "The Economy and the Societal Orders and Powers," Weber succeeded in treating only two in monographic form in the course of his lifetime—ascetic Protestantism and ancient Israelite ethics in its transition to Judaism. Nevertheless, he planned to make such monographic presentations to the very end. Thus, by compiling this catalogue of traits, one can also examine whether the most important constitutive elements for the unwritten studies were in fact all present in 1920, at the time of Weber's death. My conclusion confirms Marianne Weber's statement: The preliminary work for the studies of talmudic Judaism, ancient and medieval Christianity, and Islam were completed long before 1920 (for an overview, see table 1.1).

The Critique of Weber's Approach to Islam

Max Weber's analysis of Islam has not evoked much response in the literature of Islamic or sociological scholarship. The essay by Joseph

TABLE 1.1
A Comparison of Early Judaism, Early Christianity, Early Islam, and Ascetic Protestantism (Calvinism), According to the Original Version of Economy and Society

(All these religions are salvational, revelational, ethical, monotheistic, and theocentric, and all are scriptual religions with more or less strongly marked activistic and antimagical tendencies.)

	Early Judaism	Early Christianity	Early Islam	Calvinism
Religious ideas				
1. Social carrier of the "revelation"	Ethical Prophets as prophets of salvation and esp. as prophets of doom with political intentions (pre-exilic prophecy)	Ethical Prophets as prophets of salvation without political intentions (John and Jesus)	An ethical prophet with a political intention (Mohammed)	Recourse to Old Testament prophecy
2. Social carrier of the systematization of the "revelation"	Priests, then scriptual and legal scholars Prototype: rabbis	Theologians and bishops Prototype: church fathers	Legal and religious scholars (jurists and theologians) Prototype: *'ulama'*	Theologians Prototype: reformers
3. Religious "canons"	Torah and the interpreting tradition, as well as supplementary oral tradition, later recorded (Talmud) Relatively closed	Old and esp. New Testament and interpreting tradition, as well as supplementary church tradition (Concilia, etc.) Relatively open	Quran and the interpreting tradition, as well as oral tradition, later recorded (*Sunna*) Closed	Old and New Testament Closed
4. Concept of God	Yahweh as transcendental god of "wrath" Absolute power	God as merciful and gracious heavenly father Absolute goodness and mercy	Allah as transcendental "great" God Absolute Power and greatness	Double god: God of Old and New Testament
5. Relationship between God and man	Contractual (covenantal) relationship (Reciprocal)	Relationship of mercy and love (Reciprocal)	Relationship of submission (One-sided)	Relationship of proof (One-sided)
6. Theodicy	Messianic eschatology	Theodicy of suffering	Divine providence as predetermination	Divine providence as predestination
Structuring of religious interests				
1. Means and paths to salvation	No asceticism Knowledge (studying) and ritual activities of worship without magical significance Animosity to magic	Otherworldly asceticism Faith and ritual activities of worship with magical significance (sacraments) Involvement in magic (sublimated magic)	No asceticism Faith and knowledge (cognition) as well as ritual activities of worship without magical significance Indifference to magic	This-worldly asceticism Faith and ritual activities without magical significance Radicalized animosity to magic

TABLE 1.1 (continued)

	Early Judaism	Early Christianity	Early Islam	Calvinism
2. Goals and goods of salvation	The coming of God's kingdom on earth and collective salvation on the basis of present collective suffering "Retribution"	Individual salvation in the hereafter due to God's goodness and mercy "Forgiveness"	Individual happiness in the hereafter (paradise) on the basis of faith and bravery "Honor /Veneration" (*Verehrung*)	Individual salvation in the hereafter on the basis of God's free will "Choseness"
3. *Certitudo salutis*	Strict adherence to religious law	Adherence to God's command-ments out of faith and trust	Strict adherence to religious law	Strict adherence to God's command-ments for the glory of God
	Action as the factual basis of salvation	Action as the expression of promised salvation	Action as the factual basis of happiness	Action as the cognitive basis of salvation
	Strict reciprocity	Mitigated reciprocity	Strict reciprocity	No reciprocity
4. Religious ethical orientation	"Sacred law" Principle of legality	"Sacred conviction" Principle of morality	"Sacred law" Principle of legality	"Sacred conviction" Principle of morality
	Legal ethic	Ethic of conviction (Ethic of love)	Legal ethic	Ethic of conviction (Ethic of duty)
5. Scope of religious message	Religious traits tied to ethnic ones—ethnic stratification	No connection between religious and nonreligious traits—religious stratification	Religious traits tied to stratification traits—status group stratification	No connection between religious and nonreligious traits—religious stratification
	Dualism of the chosen people and all others	Dualism of believer and unbelievers	Dualism of believers (conquerors) and unbelievers (conquered), House of Islam and House of War	Dualism of chosen (*electi*) and damned (*reprobati*)
	Weak missionizing impulse	Strong missionizing impulse	Strong impulse to conquest, resulting in mass conversion	Weak missionizing impulse
	Nonreligious particularism	Religious universalism	Nonreligious particularism	Religious particularism
Religious organization				
1. Internal relation: hierocratic power	Community with sermon, prayer, song, scriptual reading, and interpretation under religious guidance but without priests	Church as an institution of grace with priests as dispensers of grace / Orders as ecclesiastically recognized special organistaions ("sect")	Community (*umma*) on the basis of the five pillars[a] under the guidance of legal and religious scholars as well as of religious leaders (Imam, mullahs) for public prayer and sermon	Church as disciplinary instituion with priests as proclaimers of the word (of the Holy Scriptures) and the administrators of the divine "reason of state" / Church as "sect"

TABLE 1.1 (continued)

	Early Judaism	Early Christianity	Early Islam	Calvinism
2. External relation: relationship of the hierocratic power to political power	Separation of powers in an independent polity but with a tendency toward theocracy; if dependent, an externally closed confessional organization (paria religiosity)	Separation of powers with a tendency toward theocracy	Unified, all functions as expressions of a religious law, but with a tendency toward separation of powers (caliphate and sultanate)	Theocratic with a tendency toward separation
Carrier strata				
	Plebeian strata residing in cities	Plebeian strata residing in cities	Military ruling strata	Urban entrepreneurs and merchants
Results				
1. Religiously conditioned relationship to the world	Indifference to the world	Fluctuation between world indifference and world transcendence	Fluctuation between world mastery (as world conquest) and world adjustment	World mastery
2. Religious ideal of life	Scriptual scholar well-versed in the law, "intellectual"	Virtuoso of faith	"Hero," especially the war hero	Professional man of expertise

a) Bearing witness to Allah and Mohammed, praying five times a day, fasting during Ramadan, givings alms, and making a pilgrimage to Mecca.

Schacht dedicated to the study of Islamic law represents an early exception. Schacht orients himself along the basic lines of Weber's sociology of law—he speaks of similar ways of viewing things—but criticizes both the all-too-easy application of concepts taken from the Occidental history of law to Islamic legal conditions and the lack of periodization of Islamic legal history. Certain individual statements he also considers false. For these reasons, he corrects Weber's short discussion of Islamic law in several places. Nevertheless, in his overall sociological view of Islamic law, he arrives at conclusions similar to Weber's. He points to the lack of differentiation of substantive realms of law, to the priority of substantive rationality over procedural rationality, to the succession of legal revelation by traditionalization, to the opening and closure of the canon, to the importance of the strategy of circumvention in "assimilating" the practices of the law of custom into the *shari'a*, to the hybrid character of sacred law and the restriction of its realm of validity, and to its claim to supremacy and its tendency to permeate profane law such that the latter develops along nonformal lines. Finally, he emphasizes the lack of legal concepts, such as the juristic person, the corporation, and the *Anstalt,* central to Occidental legal development. He also evaluates the role of the Islamic communal principle vis-à-vis the ancient Arab tribal principle in a manner similar to Weber. Schacht emphasizes that the ancient Arab law of custom continues to exist within the *shari'a,* but is "corrected" by the Islamic communal principle: "[P]recisely the tribal organization at the basis of those legal relationships with its civil and criminal law solidarity [is] repressed." Nonetheless, the effects of the Islamic communal principle remained limited; indeed, due to "the patriarchal character of political patrimonialism, a character established for good with the Abbasids," it even "worked *against* the corporate organization."[227]

The lack of response to Weber's analysis of Islam is not surprising. Considerable effort is required to piece together its fundamental characteristics on the basis of his scattered remarks, as this chapter demonstrates. Nevertheless, aside from a number of thematically specialized evaluations similar to Schacht's, there are two monographs that analyze Weber's general approach in connection with Islam. Both, one more generally and the other more specifically, are based on a reconstruction of Weber's view of Islam from his works. Both are critical and written from a modified Marxian perspective. One comes from Maxime Rodinson, the other from Bryan S. Turner.[228] Let me turn briefly to each of these two works.

Rodinson raises the question of why the Islamic world, in contrast to the West, did not give rise to a capitalist economic formation, and thus to a condition in which not just the majority of enterprises produce on the basis of free labor and for the sake of profit, but in which the economic system is dominated by the capitalist sector, which in turn dominates all other sectors of society. He thus poses Weber's question, even if he does so in Marxian terms. Indeed, on this point he sees—and this is certainly correct—no opposition between Weber and Marx.[229]

The differences first arise in their respective responses to the same question, for here Weber makes recourse, in contrast to a properly understood Marx, to ideas as factors obstructing or favoring development. He thus gives what in Rodinson's view is an ultimately "ideological" explanation, and this in two senses of the word. On the one hand, Rodinson claims that for Weber, ideology in the case of Islam and Quranic and post-Quranic "ideology," has a decisive influence upon economic development. On the other hand, this explanatory approach is itself an ideology. It is an ideology of the higher rationality of the West, especially of an activist and anti-magical religious ethic that is missing in Islam. Although Weber also emphasizes the importance of state and law, here too, the same Western bias prevails.[230] Rodinson goes on to say that if, however, one examines the thesis of the low level of rationality of non-Western cultures, and thus also of Islamic culture, which follows from the claim of the "specific rationality of the European"[231] (and if one does this scientifically and, so to speak, positivistically),[232] one quickly sees that this thesis cannot be upheld, neither in terms of method nor in terms of substance. In terms of method it rests on a circular argument, and substantively, it rests on an underestimation of the level of rationality of Islamic "ideology" and Islamic institutions.

The thesis is circular inasmuch as it offers examples of the higher rationality of the West that originate from an epoch that comes after that age "in which Occidental Europe very decisively placed itself on the path of modern capitalism." The asserted rational characteristic, however, can "just as well be owed to the economic development on the capitalist path, or they could have arisen in the interplay with this development and together with it have arisen from a common cause."[233] Conversely, the thesis is substantively false because Islam in no way represents an anti-activist and magic-bound "ideology." Just the opposite is the case: If one compares the Quran, for example, with the Old and New Testaments, one can even speak of the higher rationality of the Quran:

> It thus appears as if the Quranic ideology allows rational thought, rationality, to intervene to a greater degree than do the ideologies reflected in the Old and New Testaments; as if it grants the idea of predestination about the same importance as do the two other holy scriptures, but that it unambiguously exhorts one to an active orientation in individual and social life; and finally, as if it subordinates magical technique to divine will, just as the other two revelatory scriptures do, in this way maintaining the human potential for counteracting this technique regardless of how easy it is to employ.[234]

The objection to method can be disposed of quickly. It has nothing to do with the question of whether ideas can be effective in history as obstructive or favorable factors. Without doubt, circular arguments do not provide explanations. One cannot explain something in terms of something else that occurred subsequent to it, and one must always examine whether any given correlation might be based upon a third factor. These are elementary preconditions of valid explanations that

Weber was assuredly acquainted with. He possessed a much more developed understanding of the problems of causal attribution than this objection insinuates.[235]

One aim of the foregoing analysis has been to show that Weber actually pays attention to these elementary preconditions of historical explanation in his substantive investigations. Weber's difficulties are located in a completely different area. They are connected to the logic of concept formation in the cultural sciences as he adopted it from Rickert, to the simultaneity of the selection and constitution of "historical individuals," and to the ensuing question of whether he is able to stringently separate defining and explanatory conditions.[236] Such problems arise, of course, only for those who consider neither dialectical concept formation nor a "positivist orientation" as an appropriate solution to the problem of historical explanations. Weber was neither a dialectician nor a positivist.

Thus, Rodinson's methodological objections miss the point. Unfortunately, this is true for the substantive objections as well. First of all, he seems to have overlooked the fact that in his typological comparative investigations Weber does not distinguish between levels of rationality, but between types of rationalism. It is well known that his entire sociology of religion is conceived of as a contribution to a sociology and typology of religiously conditioned rationalism.[237] Then, in his discussion of the Islamic system of belief, Rodinson does not take into account the distinction between logical and psychological consequences. He also lacks the entire conceptual apparatus to do so. In the end he comes to conclusions largely in accord with those of Weber—except that he does not know it.

Weber had also underscored the "relaxed" relationship between faith and reason in Islam, the activist potential of the Islamic doctrine of predestination, and the basic antimagical character of this prophetic scriptural religion. Of course there are many details in Rodinson's analysis that could help supplement and indeed improve Weber's study. But this would in no way affect Weber's first main thesis on the traditional character of Islamic economic ethics and mentality and the economic mode of conduct connected to it. It would also in no way affect his second main thesis that the institutional conditions that prevailed in the Islamic states were favorable for commercial capitalism but not for industrial capitalism as an economic system, and that fiscally conditioned prebendal feudalism, the lack of urban autonomy, and the relationship between sacred and profane law in part caused this. One can certainly disagree as to whether Weber identified all of the important internal and external conditions and, above all, whether they add up to a convincing explanation. In Rodinson, however, one looks for such an explanation in vain. He does offer statements such as this: "Since a certain number of structural conditions and conditioning events were given, a corresponding capitalist economic formation was able to develop in Europe."[238] However, the only thing that is certain for him, and is often reiterated, is this: Whatever these structural conditions and conditioning events may in fact have been, religion and ideology were not among them.

This is actually the decisive point of difference vis-à-vis Weber. It is not a question of method or substance, but one of theory. Despite interesting modifications of the orthodox Marxist approach, especially in regard to the theory of evolution and the variable relationship between the type of appropriation (the mode of property) and the type of exploitation (the mode of extracting the surplus product), Rodinson proceeds as a materialist in terms of method and theory. For him, only the external conditions (the "base") ultimately count, not the internal ones (the "superstructure"). Religion is a reflex, an echo: an ideology. It is therefore also not independent and cannot have any independent consequences. It is, in accordance with the *German Ideology,* like all dominant thought, "nothing more than the ideal expression of the prevailing material conditions."[239] Any explanation that does not conceive of them as such is itself ideological.

As we have shown, Weber rejects this base-superstructure model from the outset. Ideas—world views—may sometimes be the ideal expression of material conditions, but this is not always true. This is the basis of Weber's crucial distance from all Marxist perspectives, regardless of how "moderate" they may be. He sought instead to go beyond these approaches, and the *Protestant Ethic* is the first demonstration that it is possible and of how it can be achieved. Rodinson simply did not understand this crucial point of the Weber thesis he cites so often. More generally, he operates against an author with whom he is at best only superficially acquainted. In his introduction to the new German edition of Rodinson's book, Bassam Tibi complains about the remnants of the base-superstructure model in Rodinson's approach. Nevertheless, Tibi emphasizes at the same time that this affects neither the "monumental results of research" nor Rodinson's judgment of Weber, in that the study of Weber's work gives proof that Weber "lacked the knowledge of the subject both in regard to the doctrine and the history of Islam that is necessary in order to be able to make a sound judgment of it."[240] The latter may be true of Weber's knowledge of Islam, but it is all the more true of Rodinson's knowledge of Weber!

The same cannot be said about Bryan S. Turner. He was the first to make a serious attempt to reconstruct Weber's view of Islam from the remarks scattered in Weber's work. In my view, however, he started from a false premise. He distinguishes two theses that Weber supposedly put forth in the context of his comparative studies: the Protestant Ethic thesis (PE), of which there are two versions, and the Weber thesis (W). Turner claims that the first thesis was formulated in the well-known essay on the Protestant ethic of 1904–5 and then repeated in revised form in 1920, whereas the second thesis defined Weber's sociological investigation of the most important distinctions between Occidental and Oriental civilizations. In Turner's view, whereas the former places religion at the center of analysis, in the latter it plays at best a secondary role. Obtained in part by expanding the first thesis and in part independently of it, the second thesis, the real Weber thesis, moves institutional conditions into the forefront. Turner views the second thesis as the sociologically more productive and more mature one.[241] He claims that this is in part because Weber moved closer to Marx and Engels in this way. This is supposedly shown precisely in terms of Weber's treatment of Islam:

> When Weber came to analyze Islam, he focused on the political, military and economic nature of Islamic society as a patrimonial form of domination. He treated the role of values as secondary and dependent on Islamic social conditions. Insofar as Weber did adhere to that position, his analysis was not far removed from Marx and Engels, who claimed that the Asiatic mode of production, characteristic of India, China and Turkey, produced an enduring social order which was incompatible with capitalism.[242]

As I have tried to show elsewhere,[243] in Weber's view spiritual conditions naturally also make up some of the stabilizing conditions of the Chinese and Indian orders. But much more important, the contrast of the two theses is itself inappropriate. There are simply no PE thesis and a W thesis that can be distinguished from it. They are only two sides of the same approach. The fact that Weber later also treats the other side, which he had deliberately neglected in the *Protestant Ethic*, implies neither the abandonment of the "first" side nor a "later discovery or recognition" of the other. As was shown earlier, the *Protestant Ethic* itself already makes points of transition from one side to the other visible. The extension in the range of his approach found in the two manuscripts "The Economy and the Societal Orders and Powers" and "The Economic Ethics of the World Religions" is substantive and theoretical, not methodological in nature. It is false to believe that Weber's approach drew nearer to that of Marx.

Turner's reconstruction of Weber's analysis of Islam thus serves above all the purpose of demonstrating the subordinate importance of ethics vis-à-vis the social structure.[244] This leads him to an interesting discussion of the institutional factors, with Weber's scattered remarks serving as the guiding thread. It is a discussion that is in many respects congruent with the analysis presented in this chapter. Moreover, the relation between religious ethics and conduct is also treated in substantive terms. Here the thesis is that this side of the Weber thesis, in comparison with the institutional side, is substantively weaker, for Weber's assertion that the Islamic religious ethic is "confiscated" for the sake of the ideal and material interests of the warriors for the faith and transformed into a warrior ethic is untenable. For Islam "was, and continued to be, an urban religion of merchants and state officials; many of its key concepts reflect the urban life of a mercantile society in opposition to the values of the desert and of the warrior. The warrior ethic described by Weber was simply one religious perspective which was regarded with suspicion and hostility by the orthodox."[245]

This may be so, but the statement is not at odds with Weber's analysis. Above all, as is shown in Weber's comparative studies, the material and the ideal interests of traders and officials do not create, even in the Christian tradition, methodical conduct and the rationalism of world mastery. The effects of religious sources are never the result simply of the interests of its social bearers; they are also dependent on the contents of the sources. This aspect of Weber's approach is completely lost in Turner's analysis. Indeed, it has to be lost if one hopes to maintain the convergence thesis of Weber and Marx.

This thesis of the subordinate, secondary importance of ethics vis-à-vis the social structure, of motivational factors vis-à-vis institutional ones, makes the decisive point of the whole story: for the sake of "reconciliation" with Marx, the central point of Weber's approach is interpreted away. Weber never spoke of primary and secondary factors, only of causally important ones. These include internal factors just as much as external ones. The fact that it is difficult or even impossible to quantify their relative weight does not speak against his approach; as he wrote in his dispute with Rachfahl: "The fact that in historical attribution no distribution ratio can be put into numbers is not my fault."[246]

There are undoubtedly gaps in Weber's analysis of Islam, which is guided by a central question the relevance of which can and must be the subject of controversy. This pertains also to concept formation. Whoever does not share the assumed value will criticize these concepts and construct others in their stead. This is thoroughly in the spirit of Weber's methodology, for the "greatest advances in the sphere of the social sciences are *substantively* tied up with the shift in practical cultural problems and take the *form* of a critique of concept formation."[247] This does not alter Weber's basic insight that any sociological analysis interested in promoting historical truth has to take into account both sides of the causal chain.

Notes

1. These six *Kulturreligionen* (major religions) are Confucianism, Hinduism, Buddhism, Judaism, Islam, and Christianity. With the exception of Judaism, all were also regarded by Weber to be world religions because they had been capable of attracting an especially great number of followers. The concept of salvational religion calls forth yet another grouping. On the interrelation of these concepts, cf. Schluchter, *Rationalism, Religion, and Domination,* trans. N. Solomon (Berkeley: University of California Press, 1989), chapter 3. *Kulturreligion* is the broadest of the three concepts. Speaking of six religions is of course problematic insofar as each of them can be further subdivided, and Weber does precisely that, especially in the case of Christianity. This subdivision is related to his general interest in the distinctive development of the West and his special interest in the distinctive shape of ascetic Protestantism; thus, in many comparisons, the latter often appears on its own. One problem in the comparative studies in the sociology of religion is that, especially in the non-Western movements, the units of analysis remain at too high a level of aggregation. This also holds for Islam. Here, cf. the essays by Ira Lapidus and Rudolph Peters in this volume.
2. Weber speaks of "cultural areas" (*Kulturkreise*) in several passages. He avoids the term "civilization" often used today (and used to translate *Kulturkreis* throughout this essay). It is well-known that "civilization" was used in turn-of-the-century Germany as a "counterterm" to the concept of culture, a connotation still alive in Weber's brother Alfred's proposal to distinguish processes of culture, civilization, and society. This contrast did not exist in Anglo-American linguistic usage. Here the concept of civilization was used in a "value-free" sense as, for example, in the contemporary works of S. N. Eisenstadt. I consider the distinction between *Kulturreligion and Kulturkreis* useful because it points to the fact that a given religion is not necessarily identical with any ethnic, political, or linguistic boundaries, and that a civilization can encompass several religions (as well as nonreligious symbolic universes).
3. Here cf. Marianne Weber, *Max Weber. Ein Lebensbild* (Tübingen: J.C.B. Mohr (Paul Siebeck, 1926), 358.
4. Cf., for example, the two large-scale projects, Schiele and Zscharnack, *Die*

Religionen in Geschichte und Gegenwart. Handwörterbuch in gemeinverständlicher Darstellung (Tübingen: J.C.B. Mohr, 1909–13), 5 vols.; and Hinneberg, ed. *Die Kultur der Gegenwart. Ihre Entwicklung und ihre Ziele* (Berlin: Teubner, 1906), esp. part I, sections 2, 4. Weber used these works extensively.

5. This is comprehensively treated in Gottfried Kuenzlen, "Unbekannte Quellen der Religionssoziologie Max Webers," *Zeitschrift für Soziologie* 7:(1978): 215–27.
6. The controversy began with H. Karl Fischer's 1907 critique. In 1909, Felix Rachfahl entered into the debate. Weber ended the controversy with an anticritical last word, the second part of which he used "to summarize once again in a few pages some of the features of my *real* 'thesis' that were stubbornly ignored by Rachfahl, solely for those who have not recently carefully re-read my essays" (cf. Weber, *Die protestantische Ethik II. Kritiken und Antikritiken*, ed. J. Winckelmann [Gütersloh: Siebenstern, 1976] 283). At the same time he emphasized "that *everything* said in my countercritique was already just as clearly located in my essays" (Weber, *Die protestantische Ethik II*, 328). I can only agree with this, if one includes the sect essays of 1906 here. It is a riddle to me how Wilhelm Hennis can claim that Weber ultimately clarified his central question for the first time in these responses to critique. In Hennis's view, it is first here, especially in the "Anticritical Last Word" that we are "finally" (!) told "what was Weber's central concern." Hennis expresses his admiration for Rachfahl, "for keeping so much countenance in the face of so much 'hide and seek' and the intentional or unintentional covering-up of 'central' intentions" (cf. Hennis, *Max Webers Fragestellung. Studien zur Biographie des Werks* (Tübingen: J.C.B. Mohr [Paul Siebeck], 1987), 16, 21–22). It was obviously a good idea in 1910 for Weber once again to summarize his thesis in the space of a few pages. It appears that even today those who read it carefully in its original version are a "tiny minority" (cf. Weber, *Die protestantische Ethik II. Kritiken und Antikritiken*, 283).
7. Marianne Weber, *Max Weber. Ein Lebensbild* (Tübingen: J.C.B. Mohr, 1926), 346.
8. Cf. Weber, *The Agrarian Sociology of Ancient Civilizations*, esp. chapter 1, "Economic Theory and Ancient Society," 35–80. On this, see, e.g., G. Roth, "Introduction," in Weber, *Economy and Society*, p l–lvii. Further, see the essays by Jürgen Deininger and Stefan Breuer, "Der okzidentale Feudalismus in Max Webers Gesellschafts-geschichte," in Schluchter, *Max Webers Sicht des okzidentalen Christentums* (Frankfurt: Suhrkamp, 1988), 437–475; and Schluchter, *Rationalismus der Weltbeherrschung* (Frankfurt: Suhrkamp, 1980), 134ff.
9. Weber, *Die protestantische Ethik II. Kritiken und Antikritiken*, 321.
10. Cf. Weber, *Die protestantische Ethik II. Kritiken und Antikritiken*, 322; Weber, *The Protestant Ethic and the Spirit of Capitalism*, trans. T. Parsons (New York: Charles Scribner's Sons, 1958), 26; Weber, *Gesammelte Aufsätze zur Religionssoziologie*, [1920–1921], 1: 12; as well as the outline to the older version of Weber, *Wirtschaft und Gesellschaft*, ed. J. Winckelmann, 5th ed. (Tübingen: J. C. B. Mohr [hereafter *WuG*]), reprinted in Schluchter, *Rationalism, Religion, and Domination*, 467.
11. Weber, *Die protestantische Ethik II. Kritiken und Antikritiken*, 322.
12. Weber, *Die protestantische Ethik II. Kritiken und Antikritiken*, 324, where Weber speaks of "objective political" and "objective economic" preconditions that he contrasts to the antitraditionalist "spirit." Here one sees that it is hardly "Weberian" to establish institutions and motives as opposing alternatives, as is often done, especially in Anglo-American literature on Weber. Cf., for example, Randall Collins, *Weberian Sociological Theory* (Cambridge: Cambridge University Press, 1986), esp. chapter 2. Here, too, one finds Weber's supposedly last word on Protestantism (ibid., 34). Cf. also Turner, *Weber and Islam* (London: Routledge, 1974); more on this book later. Even Jeffrey Alexander's at-

tempt to come to grips with the most important positions in sociological theory on the basis of the distinction between epistemological and sociological forms of materialism and idealism and to measure their "maturity" using the yardstick of multidimensionality does not do justice to Weber, as will be shown in the following. Cf. Jeffrey Alexander, *Theoretical Logic in Sociology*, 4 vols. (Berkeley: University of California Press, 1983), esp. vols. 1, 3.

13. Weber discusses these relationships in terms of three interactions: spirit-spirit, spirit-form, and form-form. Reflections of interest in this context can be found in Schmid, "Struktur und Selektion: Emile Durkheim und Max Weber als Theoretiker struktureller Evolution," *Zeitschrift für Soziologie* 10 (1981): 17–37.

14. Weber, "Anticritical Last Word on The Spirit of Capitalism," trans. W. M. Davis, *American Journal of Sociology* 83 (1978):1128–29; Weber, *Die protestantische Ethik II. Kritiken und Antikritiken*, 323–34.

15. As Weber still puts it in his *General Economic History* (New York: Collier, 1961), 17. Here, too, I find no change between 1904 and 1920. The critique of historical materialism always has two sides to it, a methodological and a substantive one. Methodologically, it involves the rejection of every form of reductionism; substantively, it concerns the underestimation of the relatively autonomous significance of the political vis-à-vis the economic, and of the spirit vis-à-vis the form. More on this follows. Further, see Schluchter, *Rationalism, Religion, and Domination*, trans. Neil Solomon (Berkeley: University of California Press, 1989), chapter 1.

16. On the degree of dissemination of the concept of developmental history at the turn of the century, cf. Roth, "Rationalization in Max Weber's Developmental History," in S. Whimster and S. Lash, eds., *Max Weber, Rationality, and Modernity* (London: Allen & Unwin, 1987), 75–91. However, the methodological status of the concept in Weber's usage remains underdefined here. To overcome this, one has to draw upon Heinrich Rickert, for in this case too, Weber primarily follows Rickert. Cf. Rickert, *Die Grenzen der naturwissenschaftlichen Begriffsbildung. Eine logische Einleitung in die historischen Wissenschaften* (Tübingen: J.C.B. Mohr, 1902) chap. 4.5, 436ff., esp. 472–73. Rickert distinguishes seven concepts of development and defines the logical structure of the fourth (the crucial one for both him and Weber) in the following manner: Here "an individual course of events (*Werdegang*) is formed into a teleological unity by having its uniqueness related to one value. In this way, the uniqueness is combined with the unity of a sequence of events to become a historical process of development" (ibid., 473). In this manner, Rickert moves the historical individual constituted by the theoretical value relation from the simultaneous into the successive and thus logically separates developmental history from mere change, but also from "progressive" development. It is easy to see that Weber adheres to this idea in the "Objectivity" essay in those passages where he discusses ideal-typical developmental constructions in terms of their relationship to history and contrasts these constructions to Marxist laws of development. Cf. Weber, *Gesammelte Aufsätze zur Wissenschaftslehre*, 4th ed. (Tübingen: J. C. B. Mohr, 1973[1922]), 203ff., esp. 205. (I will not deal with Rickert's important distinction in this context between primary and secondary historical individuals that Weber also adopts.) The refusal to identify development with progress in no way implies that the historian would not be justified in speaking of developmental stages. On the contrary: "The historian must be able first to conceive of *processes* as necessary units, and secondly, be able not only to separate them from the outside, but also to subdivide them internally into a number of stages, that is, he always has to present an assessable series of different stages that make up the essential parts of the historical course of events [in question]" (Rickert, *Die Grenzen*

der naturwissenschaftlichen, 437; cf. also the somewhat changed formulation in the second edition, 389–90). Thus, one can speak of development and developmental stages without falling prey to the errors of classical evolutionism. Admittedly, this presupposes the possibility of distinguishing between evaluation and theoretical value relation, which is at the basis of Rickert's (and Weber's) theory of the conceptualization of historical reality. (Although the possibility of making this distinction presupposes a value theory, it does not presuppose any specific one.) Rickert dealt comprehensively with the logical problems that this concept of developmental history raises for the concept of universal history in Rickert, "Geschichtsphilosophie," in W. Windelband, ed., *Die Philosophie im Beginn des 20. Jahrhunderts. Festschrift für Kuno Fischer*, second edition (Heidelberg: C. Winter, 1907), esp. 3: 396ff. Weber wrote to Rickert about it: "*Everything* in part 3 is highly appealing to me" (letter of November 3, 1907). I myself have used the concept of developmental history in *The Rise of Western Rationalism* (Berkeley: University of California Press, 1981) in order to distinguish Weber's approach from both classical evolutionism and neo-evolutionary approaches, whether they tend to be of developmental-logical (Habermas) or of functionalistic provenance (Parsons, Luhmann). Cf. esp. the introduction and conclusion. (In the English edition, I have replaced "societal or social history" [*Gesellschaftsgeschichte*] with "developmental history" [*Entwicklungs-geschichte*] throughout. Cf. "Translator's Note" in Schluchter *The Rise of Western Rationalism,* x. If Wilhelm Hennis finds it hard to understand that "such different spirits as Friedrich Tenbruck, Wolfgang Schluchter, and Jürgen Habermas cannot resist finding *evolution-theoretic* elements in Weber's work," when for Weber history occurred as a chain of circumstances (cf. Hennis, *Max Webers Fragestellung. Studien zur Biographie des Werks* [Tübingen: J.C.B. Mohr, 1987], 204), then he studiously overlooks not only the differences between these different spirits, but above all that Weber did in fact have a theory of development. That his theory is not identical with that of classical evolutionism ("an inner lawfulness and teleological determinateness of development," in Hennis's imprecise formulation) is something that I have demonstrated particularly in opposition to Friedrich Tenbruck.

Classical evolutionism, however, is not the only form a theory of development can take, despite what Hennis appears to assume. That history occurs as a chain of circumstances does not rule out its reconstruction teleologically (in Rickert's sense!). That development does not mean progress does not imply that one has to abstain from all theories of development. Hennis has here, as well as in other systematically difficult questions, little to offer outside of polemics. It is difficult for me to grasp how, with such explicit rejection of all theories of development, one can view Weber's central question as the "development [!] of humanity [in the singular!]" (cf. Hennis, *Max Webers Fragestellung. Studien zur Biographie des Werks*, 8ff). Incidentally, Rickert's concept of historical development allows one to speak of the universal history of a civilization. This history is universal if it encompasses all those developmental stages (or phases) that are essential from a given value standpoint. Weber constantly uses the concepts of developmental history, universal history, and developmental stage (or phase) in this manner. For him, too, developmental theory exists for the sake of working out the distinctive character of a historical individual and its explanation and not for the sake of constructing "general developmental schemata." Cf., inter alia, the remarks already found in Weber, *The Agrarian Sociology of Ancient Civilizations*, trans. R. I. Frank. (London: New Left Books, 1976), 288. This interconnection is not seen in Wolfgang J. Mommsen's most recent works on the concept of universal history in Weber, which results in misclassifying Weber's approach. In my view, these articles shed more darkness than light on the subject since they actively confuse such undefined terms as the "substantive theory of universal history" (in contrast to the formal theory thereof?), "evolutionism," "teleology," "neo-evolutionism," and "neo-idealism" (in contrast to neomaterialism?), only to sometimes speak then of world history. Cf. Mommsen, "Persönliche Lebensführung und gesellschaftliche Wandel. Versuch einer Rekonstruktion des Begriffs der Geschichte bei Max Weber," in P. Alter, W. J. Mommsen, and T. Nipperdey, eds., *Geschichte und politisches Handeln. Theodor Schieder zum Gedächtnis* (Stuttgart: Klett, 1985), 261–81; idem., "Max Webers Begriff der Universalgeschichte," in Kocka, ed., *Max Weber der Historiker.*(Göttingen: Vandenhoeck & Ruprecht. 1986), 51–72; and "The Antinomical Structure of Max Weber's Political Thought," in Mommsen, *The Political and the Social Theory of Max Weber* (Chicago: University of Chicago Press, 1989), 24–43.

17. My formulations are deliberately "equivocal" because one has to distinguish, as Weber's methodology shows throughout, between the logical-formal significance and the substantive significance *(Bedeutung)*, just as this distinction is made explicitly in terms of the concept of culture, the concept of cultural significance, and the concept of development (between the creation of meaning and the social bearer of meaning!).
18. Cf. the formulation in Weber, *The Protestant Ethic and the Spirit of Capitalism*, 26–27 (Weber, *Gesammelte Aufsätze zur Religionssoziologie*, 12).
19. I have previously indicated that one can divide Weber's work into three phases. Cf. the chart in Schluchter, *Rationalism, Religion, and Domination*, as well as chapters 1, 12 and 13 there. Whereas the second qualitative transformation—taking place in 1910—is of a substantive nature, the first one, connected to the publication of Rickert's fourth and fifth chapters of the *Limits of Concept Formation in Natural Science*, trans., ed., and with an introduction by Guy Oakes (New York: Cambridge University Press, 1986—an abridged version of Rickert 1902), is methodological in character. Beginning with his essay on Roscher, Weber transforms Carl Menger's distinctions between economic history, realistic economic theory, and exact economic theory, with the help of Rickert, into an approach for the cultural sciences that requires concept construction and concept application.
20. On the significance of the sociology of music for an adequate understanding of the problematic of rationalization, cf. Schluchter, *Rationalism, Religion, and Domination.*, chapter 4.1.
21. Marianne Weber, *Max Weber*, 349.
22. Weber, *The Protestant Ethic and the Spirit of Capitalism*, 17; Weber, *Gesammelte Aufsätze zur Religionssoziologie*, 4. It remained "the most fateful force" among them, however.
23. Weber, *The Protestant Ethic and the Spirit of Capitalism*, 27; Weber, *Gesammelte Aufsätze zur Religionssoziologie,* 12.
24. Thus, beyond the discipline of economics, the discipline he belonged to beginning with his appointment to Freiburg. On this, cf. also Marianne Weber, *Max Weber*, 349.
25. On this, cf. Schluchter, *Rationalism, Religion, and Domination*, chapter 8.
26. Marianne Weber *Max Weber*, 346.
27. For this reason Weber was very modest in his claims about his comparative studies. He never considered them comprehensive cultural analyses. His primary concern was the refinement of the issues raised, just as had already been the case in the "Agrarian Sociology" (cf. e.g., Weber, *Gesammelte Aufsätze zur Sozial- und Wirtschaftsgeschichte* (Tübingen: J. C. B. Mohr, 1924], 280). Moreover, in such an approach, one can never completely avoid schematic analyses (cf. Weber *The Agrarian Sociology of Ancient Civilizations*).

28. Here, cf. inter alia, Carl Heinrich Becker, *Islamstudien*, vol. 1 (Leipzig: Quelle & Meyer. 1924), esp. chapters 1, 2, 4, 9, 13, 14; Ignaz Goldziher, *Vorlesungen über den Islam* (Heidelberg: Winter, 1910); Wellhausen, *Reste arabischen Heidentums, gesammelt und erläutert*, 2nd ed. (Berlin: De Gruyter, 1927 [1897]); idem, *Das arabische Reich und sein Sturz* (Berlin: Reimer, 1902); Joseph Kohler, "Zum Islamrecht," *Zeitschrift für vergleichende Rechtswissenschaft* 17 (1905): 194–216; and Christian Snouck Hurgronje, *Mekka*, vol. 1, *Die Stadt und ihre Herren* (The Hague: Nijhoff, 1888). Studies by Goldziher and Wellhausen are still being translated into English.
29. Weber, *Gesammelte Aufsätze zur Religionssoziologie*, I: 237. (Passage omitted in corresponding English version. Cf. Weber, *From Max Weber*, trans., ed., and with an Introd. by H. H. Gerth and C. W. Mills (New York: Oxford University Press, 1958 [1946]), 267.) This writing originally appeared as early as October 1915 in the *Archiv für Sozialwissenschaft und Sozialpolitik*. For exact publication dates, cf. Schluchter, *Rationalism, Religion, and Domination*, 471–72.
30. Now also cited in Winckelmann, *Max Webers hinterlassenes Hauptwerk: Die Wirtschaft und die gesellschaftlichen Ordnungen und Mächte* (Tübingen: J.C.B. Mohr, 1986), 36.
31. Cf. Winckelmann, *Max Webers hinterlassenes Hauptwerk*, 42.
32. Weber, *Gesammelte Aufsätze zur Religionssoziologie*, I: 237. It is interesting that Weber only brings this reference up to date in 1920 instead of omitting it, even though he had in the meantime revised the "Introduction" and above all the first parts of the study of Confucianism.
33. On this, Schluchter, *Rationalism, Religion, and Domination*, chapter 13; F. Tenbruck, "Abschied von *Wirtschaft und Gesellschaft*". *Zeitschrift für die gesamte Staatswissenschaft* 133 (1977): 703–36.
34. References in this direction from the correspondence can now be found in Winckelmann, *Max Webers hinterlassenes Hauptwerk*, 42ff. In this way, the conjectures I derived from the texts on the development of Weber's work can be made more precise. Cf. Schluchter, *Rationalism, Religion, and Domination*, chapter 4.5.
35. Cf. Weber, *From Max Weber*, 267; Weber, *Gesammelte Aufsätze zur Religionssoziologie*, 1: 237–38, where Islam along with Confucianism, Hinduism, Buddhism, Christianity, and—set apart from these—Judaism, is named as a religious ethic to be treated.
36. This announcement has now also been reprinted in Winckelmann, *Max Webers hinterlassenes Hauptwerk*, 45–46.
37. Cf. Weber 1952: 5; Weber, *Gesammelte Aufsätze zur Religionssoziologie*, 3: 7.
38. As does Randall Collins, *Weberian Sociological Theory*, chapter 2, who apparently does not realize that the editors of the *Wirtschaftsgeschichte* (*Wirtschaftsgeschichte. Abriß der universalen Sozial- und Wirtschaftsgeschichte*, 1923) filled in gaps in the text with the help of Weber's published and unpublished writings. This is why there is not a thought in this reconstruction that cannot be found elsewhere in his work.
39. Cf. Schluchter, *Rationalism, Religion, and Domination*, chapter 12.
40. Weber *Economy and Society*, 611; *WuG*, 367; emphasis added. The English translation omits the reference to "third," the very point emphasized here.
41. This also follows from a formulation in the "Author's Introduction," where Weber speaks of a "systematic study of the Sociology of Religion" that has yet to be made (Weber, *The Protestant Ethic and the Spirit of Capitalis*, 30; Weber, *Gesammelte Aufsätze zur Religionssoziologie*, 1: 15).
42. Weber, *Economy and Society*, 623; *WuG*, 375; further, Weber, *Ancient Judaism*, trans. and ed. H. H. Gerth and D. Martindale (Glencoe, Ill.: Free Press, 1952), 5; Weber, *Gesammelte Aufsätze zur Religionssoziologie*, 3: 7.

43. Weber, *Economy and Society*, 13; Weber, Weber, *Gesammelte Aufsätze zur Religions-soziologie*, 1, 1.
44. Cf. Weber, *Wirtschaftsgeschichte. Abriß der universalen Sozial- und Wirtschaftsgeschichte*, S. Hellman and M. Palyi, eds. (Munich: Duncker und Humblot. 1923), 16. Incidentally, the terminological Introduction to the *General Economic History* was omitted in the English translation (cf. Weber, *General Economic History* [New York: Collier, 1961]; a translation of Weber, *Wirtschaftsgeschichte. Abriß der universalen Sozial- und Wirtschaftsgeschichte*, 1923), which means that American Weber scholars who do not read German—and their numbers are legion—are not acquainted with it. Nevertheless, this formulation is unusual insofar as Weber mostly avoids the concept of society.
45. Especially Benjamin Nelson and Friedrich H. Tenbruck—in various essays—have drawn attention to the significance of Weber's scattered remarks on scientific development. On Weber's estimation of Chinese scientific development, see Sivin, "Chinesische Wissenschaft. Ein Vergleich der Ansätze von Max Weber und Joseph Needham," in Schluchter, *Max Webers Studie über Konfuzianismus und Taoismus. Interpretation und Kritik* (Frankfurt: Suhrkamp, 1983), 342–62.
46. See the attempt by Collins, *Weberian Sociological Theory*, which, however, I do not hold to be completely successful. Cf. Schluchter, *Paradoxes of Modernity. Culture and Conduct in the Theory of Max Weber*, trans. N. Solomon (Stanford: Stanford University Press, 1996), chapter 4.
47. Cf. Weber, *Wirtschaftsgeschichte. Abriß der universalen Sozial- und Wirtschaftsgeschichte*, 239. Further, Weber, *Economy and Society,* 161–62; Weber, *WuG,* 94; and Weber, *The Protestant Ethic and the Spirit of Capitalism*, 17–23; Weber, *Gesammelte Aufsätze zur Religionssoziologie*, 1921, 1, 4–9.
48. Weber, *Wirtschaftsgeschichte. Abriß der universalen Sozial- und Wirtschaftsgeschichte*, 239.
49. Weber, *Economy and Society*, 240; *WuG,* 139. Here are similarities to Marx. Under these conditions, the category of profit-oriented or acquisitive capital (*Erwerbskapital*) leads, so to speak, an "antediluvian existence." This of course does not imply that Weber's explanation of the rise of modern capitalism is identical with Marx's explanation of primitive accumulation.
50. Weber *General Economic History*, pp: 232–33; Weber, *Wirtschaftsgeschichte. Abriß der universalen Sozial- und Wirtschaftsgeschichte*, 270.
51. Cf. Weber, *The Protestant Ethic and the Spirit of Capitalism,* 26–27; Weber, *Gesammelte Aufsätze zur Religionssoziologie*, 1: 12, where the focus is primarily on inner resistance, inner obstructions. In *Economy and Society,* however, attention is also constantly given to sources of external resistance above all those that one "structure" offers another. Cf., for example, the points defining the interaction between political domination and economy in the newer version of the sociology of domination.
52. There is still no analysis of different types of church organization in the *Protestant Ethic*. The sect essays of 1906 represent the first move in this direction. It is known that Weber revised and expanded them for vol. I of *The Collected Essays on the Sociology of Religion*; he linked them to the *Protestant Ethic* (also now revised) by inserting a passage ("Where, in spite of a different doctrinal basis, similar ascetic features have appeared, this has generally been the result of Church organization. Of this we shall come to speak in another connection" [Weber, *The Protestant Ethic and the Spirit of Capitalism,* 128; Weber, *Gesammelte Aufsätze zur Religionssoziologie*, 1: 128. This statement is followed by the reference to the sect essay). Thus, the relationship between internal and external—a relationship incidentally that in my view has a Kantian background—has first to be analyzed in terms of its field of application. On the relationship between motive and

institution, see the instructive remarks in Weber, *Gesammelte Aufsätze zur Wissenschaftslehre*, 4th ed. (Tübingen: J. C. B. Mohr., 1973[1922]), 88–89.

53. The concept "precapitalist" is used above all in the *General Economic History*. The quote is from Weber, *The Protestant Ethic and the Spirit of Capitalism*, 26; Weber, *Gesammelte Aufsätze zur Religionssoziologie*, 1: 12.

54. Weber gives the following definition in the essay on "Objectivity": "For our purposes, an end is the conception of a success that becomes the cause of an action" (cf. Weber, *Gesammelte Aufsätze zur Wissenschaftslehre*, 183). That is a definition completely in the spirit of Kant. Weber further distinguishes between teleological rules and normative rules (*Zweck-Maxime and Norm-Maxime*) in *The Critique of Stammler*, trans. Guy Oakes, (New York: The Free Press, 1977), that is, in that text at the beginning of the development of his theory of action. In this way he lays the basis, completely in the sense of a historicization of Kant, for the later distinction between means-ends (instrumental) and value rationality. For an elaboration, cf. Schluchter, *Paradoxes of Modernity*, chapter 2. The significance of this Kantian background that allows Weber to overcome the utilitarianism of economic theory is, in my view, misjudged by both Jürgen Habermas and Gregor Schöllgen. They claim that Weber in his theory of action would prioritize instrumental (or success-related) orientation and labor, respectively, and accuse him of subsuming an orientation to reaching understanding under an orientation to success and praxis under production. This would be true if Weber had remained within the limits of the economic theory of action. However, in the transition to the second phase of his work at the very latest, he went beyond these limits. The *Protestant Ethic* in particular demonstrates, through the example of a *historical* analysis, the consequences this "breakthrough" has for research strategy. It represents one long plea for recognizing that the origin of attitudes, even economic attitudes, cannot be adequately understood in terms of a utilitarian theory of action. For a critique of Weber's supposedly too narrow concept of action, cf. Jürgen Habermas, *The Theory of Communicative Action*, 2 vols., trans. T. McCarthy (Boston: Beacon Press, 1984), esp. chapter 3, "Intermediate Reflections"; and Schöllgen, *Handlungsfreiheit und Zweckrationalität. Max Weber und die Tradition der praktischen Philosophie (*Tübingen: J.C.B. Mohr, 1985), e.g., 41, 108ff. On the early beginnings of Weber's nonutilitarian action theory, cf. Weber,. *Critique of Stammler*, 105–15, esp. 112–15; Weber, *Gesammelte Aufsätze zur Wissenschaftslehre*, 328–37, esp. 334–37.

55. On this concept, closely connected to Weber's concept of personality, see Schluchter, *Rationalism, Religion, and Domination*, chapter 8 and Schluchter 1996, chapter 2.

56. Cf. Schluchter, *Rationalism, Religion, and Domination*, chapter 4.1.

57. Weber, *The Protestant Ethic*, 30; Weber, *Gesammelte Aufsätze zur Religionssoziologie*, 1: 15.

58. Weber, *From Max Weber*, 90; Weber, *Gesammelte Aufsätze zur Religionssoziologie*, 1: 82.

59. *Archiv* 20, 1905: 53.

60. Weber, *The Protestant Ethic*, 55; Weber, *Gesammelte Aufsätze zur Religionssoziologie*, 1: 37.

61. Weber, *The Protestant Ethic*, 56; Weber, *Gesammelte Aufsätze zur Religionssoziologie*, 1: 38. This was something that Weber had already sought to show in his study of agricultural laborers from east of the Elbe.

62. Weber, *The Protestant Ethic*, 196; Weber, *Gesammelte Aufsätze zur Religionssoziologie, [1920–1921]*, 1: 40n.; inserted in 1920, in order to clarify Weber's original position vis-à-vis the objections of Sombart and Brentano.

63. Weber, *The Protestant Ethic*, 232 n. 66; Weber, *Gesammelte Aufsätze zur Religionssoziologie*, 1: 111 n. (inserted in 1920). Weber apparently developed this concept in analogy to that of "entanglements of argument" (*Problemverschlingung*), which repeatedly appeared in neo-Kantian writings.
64. Weber, *The Protestant Ethic*, 233 n. 66; Weber, *Gesammelte Aufsätze zur Religionssoziologie*, 1: 111 n. 4 (in this passage the decisive points were unchanged from the early version of the text).
65. Weber, *The Protestant Ethic,* 125–26; Weber, *Gesammelte Aufsätze zur Religionssoziologie*, 1: 124–25.
66. Weber, *The Protestant Ethic,* 117; Weber, *Gesammelte Aufsätze zur Religionssoziologie*, 1: 114.
67. On this, see Weber, *Die protestantische Ethik II. Kritiken und Antikritiken,* 317. This has interesting consequences for the selection of sources. First, one needs sources that make the dogmatic foundations visible. Then, one requires sources that throw light on the psychic problems of the faithful. Only in the *Protestant Ethic* does Weber use both types of sources. In contrast, in his studies of other cultural religions, he contents himself largely with the demonstration of their dogmatic foundations.
68. Weber, *From Max Weber,* 280; Weber, *Gesammelte Aufsätze zur Religionssoziologie*, 1: 252.
69. Weber, *The Protestant Ethic,* 125–26; Weber, *Gesammelte Aufsätze zur Religionssoziologie*, 1: 125.
70. Weber, *Economy and Society,* 575; Weber, *WuG,* 348.
71. Weber, *From Max Weber*, 115; Weber, *Gesammelte Aufsätze zur Religionssoziologie*, 1: 110 (inserted in 1920).
72. Weber, *From Max Weber*, 112; Weber, *Gesammelte Aufsätze zur Religionssoziologie*, 1: 105.
73. Weber, *Economy and Society, 1978b,* 575; Weber, WuG, 348.
74. Weber, *From Max Weber,* 108–9; Weber, *Gesammelte Aufsätze zur Religionssoziologie*, 1: 101.
75. On these interests cf. Weber, *Wirtschaftsgeschichte. Abriß der universalen Sozial- und Wirtschaftsgeschichte*, 16. There he distinguishes between economic, magic and religious, political, and status group interests. They can be developed out of the combination of material and ideal interests with interests from within and interests from without. Incidentally, this combination also yields the most important areas of culture: the economic order, the religious order, the politico-legal order, and the social order. Cf. my effort at systematization in Schluchter 1981: 34–35, which I would conceive of somewhat differently today. Modifications are already found in Schluchter, *Rationalism, Religion, and Domination*, chapter 2, a revised version of Schluchter, *Max Webers Sicht des okzidentalen Christentums* (Frankfurt: Suhrkamp, 1988), chapter 2.
76. This also goes to show how unreasonable it is to link the so-called Protestantism thesis exclusively to the theory of predestination, as for example, Collins does.
77. Weber, *Economy and Society*, 572; *WuG,* 346.
78. Weber, *Economy and Society,* 518; *WuG,* 314.
79. Weber, *Economy and Society,* 518; *WuG,* 315.
80. Weber, *Economy and Society,* 447; *WuG,* 273. In another context I have suggested classifying Mohammed more as an ethical savior than as an ethical prophet, which deviates from Weber's own classifiication. Cf. Schluchter, *Rationalism, Religion, and Domination*, chapter 4.2. The justification for my approach was that Islam, like Christianity, was originally a movement of personal charisma, which is even further strengthened in Islam due to its political character. More on this follows.

81. Weber, *From Max Weber*, 104-5; Weber, *Gesammelte Aufsätze zur Religionssoziologie*, 1: 94.
82. Weber, *Economy and Society*, 523; *WuG*, 317.
83. Weber, *Economy and Society*, 623-24; *WuG*, 375.
84. Ulrich, *Die Vorherbestimmungslehre im Islam und Christentum. Eine religionsgeschichtliche Parallele* (Gütersloh: Bertelsmann, 1912). Referred to in Weber: *The Protestant Ethic*, 227 n. 36, 240 n. 106; Weber, *Gesammelte Aufsätze zur Religionssoziologie*, 1: 102 n. 2, 128 n. 1 (both passages inserted in 1920). It is not clear whether Weber had already been familiar with this dissertation while writing the first version of *Economy and Society*. The argumentation there (*Economy and Society*, 572-76; *WuG*, 346-48) in any case does not preclude this possibility. On the conception of predestination in Islam, cf. also Peters in this volume.
85. Weber, *The Protestant Ethic*, 221 n. 12; Weber, *Gesammelte Aufsätze zur Religionssoziologie*, 2: 92 n. 1.
86. Ulrich, *Die Vorherbestimmungslehre im Islam und Christentum*, 57.
87. Ulrich, *Die Vorherbestimmungslehre im Islam und Christentum*, 67-68.
88. Weber, *Economy and Society*, 623-24; *WuG*, 375.
89. Ulrich, *Die Vorherbestimmungslehre im Islam und Christentum*, 14.
90. Weber, *Economy and Society*, 574; *WuG*, 347.
91. Weber, *Economy and Society*, 573; *WuG*, 346.
92. Weber traces this back to the institution of confession in lay Catholicism and to the affectual turn of religion in Lutheranism.
93. Cf. Ulrich, 912. *Die Vorherbestimmungslehre im Islam und Christentum*, 126ff.
94. Weber, *Economy and Society*, 573; *WuG*, 347.
95. Weber, *Economy and Society*, 574; *WuG*, 347.
96. Cf. Ulrich, *Die Vorherbestimmungslehre im Islam und Christentum*, 47. On the foundations of Islamic doctrine in general, see Tibi, *Der Islam und das Problem der kulturellen Bewältigung des sozialen Wandels* (Frankfurt: Suhrkamp, 1985), esp. chapters 1, 2.
97. Weber, *Economy and Society*, 573; *WuG*, 347.
98. Weber, *The Protestant Ethic*, 227 n. 36; Weber, *Gesammelte Aufsätze zur Religionssoziologie*, 2: 102 n. 2.
99. Weber, *Economy and Society*, 575; *WuG*, 347.
100. In this sense Weber in fact considered only ancient Judaism and ascetic Protestantism successfully antimagical religions. Obviously, Islamic reform movements are also inspired by the turn away from magical practices of the masses. Cf. Metcalf in this volume.
101. Weber, *Economy and Society*, 575; *WuG*, 347.
102. Weber, *Economy and Society*, 623-24; *WuG*, 375. It is obvious from this quote that Weber does not pass judgment on Islam as such, but tries to point to a peculiar appropriation of the religious sources through a social stratum at a specific period of time. It is true, however, that he neglected contervailing tendencies strengthening the truly salvational elements in these sources.
103. Weber, *Economy and Society*, 472; *WuG*, 288.
104. Weber, *Economy and Society*, 627; *WuG*, 376.
105. Weber, *From Max Weber*, 269; Weber, *Gesammelte Aufsätze zur Religionssoziologie*, 1: 240.
106. Naturally, even long-term world rejection need not necessarily lead to world mastery, as the analysis of the Indian religions demonstrates. Above all, the lack of the idea of proof and the nature of the first decisive bearer stratum of the religion drive Islam, in Weber's view, to active, innerworldly political action, making it into a "political" religion that tends toward world adjustment. On

this, cf. Weber, *Gesammelte Aufsätze zur Religionssoziologie, [1920–1921]*, 2: 220–21, where Islam, along with Confucianism, is contrasted to Buddhism, a radically world-rejecting salvation religion that leads to world flight. Weber's views are, however, too simple, even for early Islam; witness the contributions by Lapidus (in this volume) and Levtzion (in this volume).

107. Weber, *Economy and Society*, 574; *WuG*, 347.
108. Cf. e.g., John A. Hall, *Powers and Liberties: The Causes and Consequences of the Rise of the West* (Berkeley: University of California Press, 1985), 85ff., esp. 96; further, see Gellner, *Leben im Islam: Religion als Gesellschaftsordnung* (Stuttgart: Klett, 1985).
109. Weber, *The Protestant Ethic*, 126; Weber, *Gesammelte Aufsätze zur Religionssoziologie, [1920–1921]*, 1: 125.
110. Weber, *The Protestant Ethic*, 26–27; Weber, *Gesammelte Aufsätze zur Religionssoziologie*, 1: 12.
111. I thus find it difficult to take seriously the problem that moves Wilhelm Hennis: Which comes first, personality or life order? Naturally, this question has to arise if one assumes a relation of priority. However, neither Weber nor modern sociology does so (insofar as one can even speak about the latter in the singular). It is much more a state of correlation. Thus it is in principle unimportant whether the address Weber gave at Burg Lauenstein in 1917 was entitled "Personality and the Life Orders" ("Die Persönlichkeit und die Lebensordnungen") (as Marianne Weber reports), or conversely, "Life Orders and the Personality" ("Die Lebensordnungen und die Persönlichkeit") (as a participant, Ferdinand Tönnies, recorded in his notebook on September 29, 1917). It is indisputable that Weber's entire approach is based on a theory of personality that is not merely empirical but is linked to a theory of value. This has been known at least since Dieter Henrich's dissertation and was already implicit in Karl Löwith's essay on Marx and Weber. However, for Weber's "sociology," and especially for his sociology of religion, personality and life-order stand in correlation to one another. Technically, this correlation can assume all values between +1 and -1 (a favorable, indifferent, or obstructive relationship). In his review of the first published volume of the *Max Weber-Gesamtausgabe* (Weber, *Zur Politik im Weltkrieg* Series. I of vol. 15 *Max Weber-Gesamtausgabe*, ed. W. J. Mommsen in cooperation with G. Hübinger. Tübingen: J.C.B. Mohr, 1984), Hennis writes: "Whoever knows the weight the word 'personality' possessed in Weber's generation, whose language was so deeply marked by Goethe and Nietzsche, can simply not imagine that Weber could have strung them together the other way around. But a modern sociologist cannot only do so, he has to. It is almost something of an existential question for the predominant form of sociology to grant 'life orders' (vulgarly the 'society') precedence over the 'individual.' The decisive question for every Weber interpretation can only be whether that also holds for Weber's sociology." Hennis, "Im 'langen Schatten' einer Edition. Zum ersten Band der Max Weber-Gesamtausgabe," *Frankfurter Allgemeine Zeitung* 207:10. Naturally, it does not hold for it, but neither does the opposite. (Incidentally, is this a linguistic or a theoretical problem, and why is it insinuated that of all people the historian Mommsen had made manipulations in the manner of modern sociology?) On the philosophical side of the theory of personality, which, in my view, must be read against the backdrop of Kant, see Henrich, *Die Einheit der Wissenschaftslehre Max Webers* (Tübingen: J.C.B. Mohr, 1952), esp. part 2, "Die Grundlagen der Ethik" (The foundations of ethics); on the "philosophical" idea of man in Weber (and Marx), see Karl Löwith, "Max Weber und Karl Marx," in Löwith, *Gesammelte Abhandlungen. Zur Kritik der geschichtlichen Existenz* (Stuttgart: Klett, 1960), 1–67, esp. 30ff., and 65–66.

For a comprehensive account, see Schluchter, *Rationalism, Religion, and Domination*, chapter 8 and Schluchter, *Paradoxes of Modernity*, chapter 2.
112. Weber wrote to Rickert on April 26, 1920, apparently after the "Basic Sociological Terms" of the later version of *Economy and Society* were already in the press, that one could develop practically everything out of the basic concept of subjectively intended meaning (with its four orientations of meaning) and the basic concept of order (with the conception of its validity). In this way, he defines his sociology as a theory of action and order on the basis of the division between theoretical value relation and practical evaluation. As the published version of these basic terms shows, he in fact did hold fast to the concept of the theoretical value relation. Cf. Weber, *Economy and Society*, 18; *WuG*, 8.
113. This is something that especially in the Anglo-American discussion is often overlooked. Cf. n. 12.
114. Weber, *Max Weber. Selections in translation*, editor, W. G. Runciman and trans. E. Mathews (Cambridge: Cambridge University Press, 1978), 172; Weber, *Gesammelte Aufsätze zur Religionssoziologie*, 1: 205–6.
115. Weber, *The Protestant Ethic*, 128; Weber, *Gesammelte Aufsätze zur Religionssoziologie*, 1: 128.
116. Weber, *From Max Weber*, 302–22; Weber, *Gesammelte Aufsätze zur Religionssoziologie*, 1: 207–36.
117. Weber, *The Protestant Ethic*, 122; Weber, *Gesammelte Aufsätze zur Religionssoziologie*, 1: 121.
118. Weber, *From Max Weber*, 320; Weber, *Gesammelte Aufsätze zur Religionssoziologie*, 1: 234.
119. Weber, *The Protestant Ethic*, 128; Weber, *Gesammelte Aufsätze zur Religionssoziologie*, 1: 128.
120. Weber, *Economy and Society*, 439; *WuG*, 268.
121. Weber, *Economy and Society*, 1174; *WuG*, 700.
122. Weber, *From Max Weber*, 325; Weber, *Gesammelte Aufsätze zur Religionssoziologie*, [1920–1921], 1: 538.
123. Patricia Crone, *Slaves on Horses: The Evolution of the Islamic Polity* (Cambridge: Cambridge University Press, 1980), 62.
124. Weber, *Economy and Society*, 575; *WuG*, 348. Weber points to the elective affinity between the structural principle of democracy and that of the sects; he also makes references to the contribution of the ascetic Protestant sects in the development of a concept of freedom of conscience that also includes the freedom of conscience of others. Weber, *Economy and Society*, 1208–10; *WuG*, 724–26.
125. Cf. Ignaz Goldziher, *Vorlesungen über den Islam*, especially "Vorlesung 1. Muhammed und der Islam" (Mohammed and Islam); further, *WuG*, 375; Weber, *Economy and Society*, 623–24.
126. See Crone, *Slaves on Horses: The Evolution of the Islamic Polity*.
127. Becker, *Islamstudien* (Leipzig: Quelle & Meyer, 1924), 353.
128. Crone, *Slaves on Horses*.
129. Crone, *Slaves on Horses*, 10.
130. Crone, *Slaves on Horses*, 15.
131. Wellhausen, *Das arabische Reich und sein Sturz*, (Berlin: Reimer, 1902), 5.
132. Wellhausen, *Reste arabischen Heidentums, gesammelt und erläutert*, 2nd ed. (Berlin: De Gruyter, 1897), 92ff.
133. Wellhausen, *Das arabische Reich und sein Sturz*, 2.
134. Watt, *Muhammad: Prophet and Statesman* (Oxford: Oxford University Press, 1964), 96.
135. Wellhausen, *Das arabische Reich und sein Sturz*, 9.
136. Weber, *Economy and Society*, 1244; *WuG*, 746.

137. Wellhausen, *Das arabische Reich und sein Sturz*, 9.
138. Wellhausen, *Das arabische Reich und sein Sturz*, 12; Becker, *Islamstudien* (Leipzig: Quelle & Meyer, 1924), 347.
139. Naturally, this should not be understood as a regression. On this, cf. Levtzion in this volume; he shows that Islam was initially thoroughly particularistic, formulating as it did an *Arabic* monotheism. It was only under the Abbasids that it developed toward universalism, an essential component in the successful dissemination of Islam.
140. Wellhausen, *Reste arabischen Heidentums, gesammelt und erläutert*, 101ff.
141. His family was supposedly entrusted with ritual functions.
142. On this, Wellhausen, *Reste arabischen Heidentums, gesammelt und erläutert*, 68ff.
143. I have created this term following Reinhard Bendix, *Kings or People* (Berkeley: University of California Press, 1978), who speaks of "reference societies." Cf. ibid, esp. part 2.
144. Becker, *Islamstudien*, vol. I: 343, 347.
145. According to the construct, Islam is responsible for the restitution of this establishment of religion, at the same time ridding it of the aberrations it suffered under Judaism and Christianity.
146. Hall, *Powers and Liberties*, 85.
147. Weber, *Economy and Society*, 1138; *WuG*, 673.
148. Weber, *Economy and Society*, 474; *WuG*, 289.
149. Weber, *Economy and Society*, 474, 1174; *WuG*, 289, 708.
150. Weber, *Economy and Society*, 474; *WuG*, 289. Incidentally, this passage allows one to conclude that Weber did not consider Islam to be exclusively a religion of warriors. To the extent that other carrier strata move to the forefront, elements of a salvation religion can also assert themselves. In fact, Weber never unambivalently classified Islam. Cf. Schluchter, *Rationalism, Religion, and Domination*, 144 (figure 13).
151. On this, cf. Schluchter, *The Rise of Western Rationalism*, 82–138, esp. 118–38.
152. Weber, *Economy and Society*, 1015; *WuG*, 587. Weber apparently follows Becker here, who cited 833 as the turning point.
153. See the epigram prefacing the essay. Also the formulations in Weber (Weber, *Economy and Society*, 229, 239, 259; *WuG*, 131, 138, 151). On Islamic patrimonialism, see also Rodinson in Schlucther, ed, *Max Webers Sicht des Islams*, 256–71, Hardy (in this volume), Eaton (in this volume), and Eisenstadt (in this volume).
154. Weber, *Economy and Society*, 1020; *WuG*, 590, 1072.
155. Weber, *Economy and Society*, 1070; *WuG*, 625.
156. Weber, *Economy and Society*, 1082; *WuG*, 634.
157. Weber, *Economy and Society*, 232, 260; *WuG*, 133–34, 151. This was the case because the lack of all binding traditions is practically a historical impossibility.
158. Weber, *Economy and Society*, 1072–74; *WuG*, 627–28.
159. Weber, *Economy and Society*, 1104; *WuG*, 650.
160. Weber, *Economy and Society*, 1105; *WuG*, 650.
161. Weber, *Economy and Society*, 1105–6; *WuG*, 650–51.
162. See Schluchter 1996, chapter 4; and Poggi 1988 and Stefan.Breuer, "Der okzidentale Feudalismus in Max Webers Gesellschaftsgeschichte," in Schluchter, *Max Webers Sicht des okzidentalen Christentums* (Frankfurt: Suhrkamp, 1988), previously, Schluchter, *The Rise of Western Rationalism*, 139–74, esp. 153–74. Cf. Weber, *Economy and Society, 1978b*: 1051–69, esp. 1055–56; *WuG*, 611–24, esp. 613–14.
163. Weber, *Economy and Society*, 828–30; *WuG*, 480–81.
164. This is the title of the aforementioned book by Patricia Crone, *Slaves on Horses*.
165. Aside from Crone *Slaves on Horses*, see Pipes, *Slave Soldiers and Islam: The*

Genesis of a Military System (New Haven, Conn.: Yale University Press, 1981).
166. Cf. Pipes, *Slave Soldiers and Islam*, xxiii.
167. Weber, *Economy and Society*, 1015; *WuG*, 587.
168. Weber, *Economy and Society*, 1053–54; *WuG*, 613.
169. Cf. Becker, *Islamstudien*, esp. 243.
170. Weber, *Economy and Society*, 1016; *WuG*, 587.
171. Weber, *Economy and Society*, 1096; *WuG*, 644.
172. Weber, *Gesammelte Aufsätze zur Soziologie und Sozialpolitik* (Tübingen: J. C. B. Mohr, 1924b), 323ff., esp. part 3, and my study, "Modes of Capitalism: Imperial Rome and Imperial Germany," in *Rationalism, Religion, and Domination*, 281–314, esp. 305–13. Weber even conjectures that this institution originates in Islam, reaching Europe via Spain.
173. Becker, *Islamstudien*, 240.
174. Weber, *Economy and Society*, 1105; *WuG*, 650.
175. Becker, *Islamstudien*, 236.
176. Weber points to the Ottoman Empire, with its institution of the conscription of boys. Cf. Weber, *Economy and Society*, 1016; *WuG*, 588. Here, see also Perry Anderson, *Lineages of the Absolutist State* (London: Verso Editions, 1980, chapter 7).
177. Weber, *Economy and Society*, 1075; *WuG*, 628–29.
178. Weber, *Economy and Society*, 1095; *WuG*, 643.
179. Weber, *General Economic History*, 207; Weber, *Wirtschaftsgeschichte. Abriß der universalen Sozial- und Wirtschaftsgeschichte*, 239.
180. On the distinction between the principles of household and market and on the basic concepts in the sociology of the economy connected to it, see my efforts in Schluchter, *Rationalismus der Weltbeherschung*, 1980: 136–42, revised in *Rationalism, Religion, and Domination*, chapter 9.
181. Weber, *Economy and Society*, 1104–9, esp. 1108–9; *WuG*, 650–53, esp. 653.
182. Weber, *Economy and Society*, 239, 260; *WuG*, 138, 151.
183. Weber, *Economy and Society*, 240; *WuG*, 139.
184. Here, see also Hall, *Powers and Liberties*, 97.
185. Weber, *Economy and Society*, 1231–33; *WuG*, 739–40.
186. See also Schluchter 1996, chapter 4, and further, the outstanding dissertation by Song-U Chon, *Max Webers Stadtkonzeption. Eine Studie zur Entwicklung des okzidentalen Bürgertums* (Göttingen: Edition Herodot, 1985). See also Schreiner, 1986, "Die Mittelalterliche Stadt im Webers Analyse" as well as the literature cited in that publication.
187. Weber, *Economy and Society*, 1220; *WuG*, 732.
188. Weber, *Economy and Society*, 1352; *WuG*, 804.
189. Weber, *Economy and Society*, 1363; *WuG*, 811. Weber mentions the Sicilian empire under Dionysius, the Attic confederacy, the Carthaginian empire, and the Roman-Italic empire.
190. Weber, *Economy and Society*, 1239, *WuG*, 742.
191. Here Weber is thinking of the Italian *popolo* and probably Cologne as well.
192. Here, see also Weber's Vienna address on the sociology of the state as reported in the *Neue Freie Presse* (October 26, 1917): 10. The fourth concept of legitimation (in addition to the traditional, the rational-legal, and the charismatic) was here the democratic one, its "specific social carrier, however, the *sociological formation of the Occidental city.*"
193. Weber, *Economy and Society*, 1339–40; *WuG*, 796.
194. Especially succinctly formulated in Weber, *The Religion of India*, 37–38; Weber, *Gesammelte Aufsätze zur Religionssoziologie*, 2: 39–40.
195. Weber refers to the saying "Stadtluft macht frei" (town air makes one free).

Here, see above all Mitteis 1976, who points in particular to the distinction in legal position between slaves in antiquity and the medieval unfree and explains that the conception of a slave without master was an incomprehensible conception in Germanic law (Mitteis, "Über den Rechtsgrund des Satzes 'Stadtluft macht frei,'" in C. Haase, ed., *Die Stadt des Mittelalters*, vol. 2. (Darmstadt: Wissenschaftliche Buchgesellschaft:, 1976), 193–94). Thus, there are also degrees of freedom in the countryside.

196. Cf. Hurgronje, *Mekka,* vol. 1; and Weber, *Economy and Society,* 1232; *WuG,* 739.
197. Weber, *Economy and Society,* 1231; *WuG,* 739.
198. Weber, *Economy and Society,* 1016; *WuG,* 587.
199. Weber, *Economy and Society,* 1352; *WuG,* 804.
200. Weber, *Economy and Society,* 1251; *WuG,* 750.
201. Here cf. Weber, *The Protestant Ethic,* 16; Weber, *Gesammelte Aufsätze zur Religionssoziologie, [1920–1921],* 1: 3; in connection with Weber, *Economy and Society,* 1108; *WuG,* 653.
202. Weber, *Economy and Society,* 828; *WuG,* 480.
203. Weber, *Economy and Society,* 259; *WuG,* 151; in combination with Weber, *Economy and Society,* 240–41; *WuG,* 139.
204. Weber, *The Protestant Ethic,* 15–16; Weber,*Gesammelte Aufsätze zur Religionssoziologie,* 1: 3.
205. One attempt to cull a sociology of education and cultivation out of Weber is found in Volker Lenhart, "Allgemeine und fachliche Bildung bei Max Weber," *Zeitschrift für Pädagogik* 32 (1986): 529–41.
206. Weber, *Economy and Society,* 828; *WuG,* 480.
207. Weber, *Economy and Society,* 790; *WuG,* 459.
208. Weber, *Economy and Society,* 820; *WuG,* 475.
209. Weber, *Economy and Society,* 791; ,*WuG,* 460.
210. Weber, *Economy and Society,* 819, and more generally, 790; *WuG,* 460, 474.
211. Weber, *Economy and Society,* 821; *WuG,* 475.
212. Weber, *Economy and Society,* 821–22; *WuG,* 475–76. On *hijal* literature and its importance in the mutual adjustment between the law of custom and the Sharia, see Schacht, "Zur soziologischen Betrachtung des islamischen Rechts," *Der Islam* 22 (1935): 207–38, esp. 218. I use Schacht in part to correct Weber's presentation.
213. Weber, *Economy and Society,* 819; *WuG,* 474.
214. Here, see Hall, *Powers and Liberties,* 88, who generally places the opposition between the *ulama* and political domination at the center of analysis. On this problem, see also M. Rodinson, "Islamischer Patrimonialismus: Ein Hindernis für die Entstehung des modernen Kapitalismus?" in Schluchter, ed., *Max Webers Sicht des Islams* ((Frankfurt: Suhrkamp, 1987), 180–89; and Ernest Gellner, "Warten auf den Imam, " in ibid., 272–293.
215. Here see Schacht, "Zur soziologischen Betrachtung des islamischen Rechts," *Der Islam* 22 (1935): 222; and Weber, *Economy and Society,* 821; *WuG,* 476. Schacht speaks of a combination of the principle of person (*Personalprinzip*) (Muslim) and that of territory (the land of Islam).
216. Weber, *Economy and Society,* 822; *WuG,* 476.
217. Weber, *Economy and Society,* 823; *WuG,* 477. The distinction between legally immanent and legally transcendent conditions as well as the demarcation between the spheres within legally immanent conditions are central to Weber's sociology of law, just as the German distinctions between *formal* and *formell* and between *material* and *materiell* are. If one does not see this, Weber's sociology of law does in fact become an "incomprehensible" text. This is seen in Crone, *Slaves on Horses.* I have made an attempt to analyze the sociology of law taking these distinctions into account in Schluchter, *The Rise of Western*

Rationalism, 82–105. Of interest in this context is Breuer and Treiber, *Zur Rechtssoziologie Max Webers. Interpretation, Kritik, Weiterentwicklun* (Opladen: Westdeutscher Verlag, 1984).
218. Here see Weber, *Economy and Society,* 1116; *WuG,* 657. He speaks only of theocratic kadi justice. Schacht points to the necessity of differentiation. As is well known, kadi justice for Weber is not a concept restricted in application to Islam.
219. Weber, *Economy and Society,* 822; *WuG,* 476.
220. Schacht, "Zur soziologischen Betrachtung des islamischen Rechts," *Der Islam* 22 (1935): 222.
221. Weber, *Economy and Society,* 828; *WuG,* 480.
222. Weber, *Economy and Society,* 828; *WuG,* 480.
223. Weber, *Economy and Society,* 792; *WuG,* 460–61.
224. Weber, *Economy and Society,* 793; *WuG,* 461.
225. Schacht, "Zur soziologischen Betrachtung des islamischen Rechts," *Der Islam* 22 (1935): 236.
226. Weber, *Economy and Society,* 577–78; *WuG,* 349. There are also parallels between Christianity and Islam in the treatment of the usurer. A religion's orientation on such a matter per se is unimportant in this context. It is only interesting as an indicator of the existence of a dualism between in-group and out-group morals, something that appears in some form in all traditional economic ethics.
227. Schacht, "Zur soziologischen Betrachtung des islamischen Rechts," *Der Islam* 22 (1935): 237–38.
228. Rodinson, *Islam und Kapitalismus* (Frankfurt: Suhrkamp, 1986) and Turner, *Weber and Islam* (Routledge & Kegan Paul, 1974). See also Rodinson's article in *Max Webers Sicht des Islams*, which, however, follows a somewhat different line of argument in comparison to the book.
229. Rodinson, *Islam und Kapitalismus,* 26ff., esp. 32.
230. Rodinson, *Islam und Kapitalismus,* 146ff.
231. Rodinson, *Islam und Kapitalismus,* 160–61.
232. Cf. Rodinson, *Islam und Kapitalismus,* 17.
233. Rodinson, *Islam und Kapitalismus,* 115.
234. Cf. Rodinson, *Islam und Kapitalismus,* 140.
235. Rodinson appears not to be acquainted with the entire theory of objective possibility and adequate causation or with Weber's methodological writing in general.
236. Gerhard Wagner and Heinz Zipprian in particular have pointed out this question. Cf. Wagner and Zipprian, "The Problem of Reference in Max Weber's Theory of Causal Explanation," *Human Studies* 9 (1986): 21–42, where it is argued that the problem arises through adherence to Rickert.
237. Here see Schluchter, *Rationalism, Religion, and Domination,* 140–46.
238. Rodinson, *Islam und Kapitalismus,* 181.
239. Marx, *Werke-Schriften-Briefe,* 6 vols. H. J. Lieber, ed. (Darmstadt: Wissenschaftliche Buchgesellschaft, 1971), 2: 55.
240. Rodinson, *Islam und Kapitalismus,* xxx.
241. Turner, *Weber and Islam,* 8–9.
242. Turner, *Weber and Islam,* 20–21.
243. Schluchter, *Rationalism, Religion, and Domination,* chapters 3, 4.
244. Turner, *Weber and Islam,* 75.
245. Turner, *Weber and Islam,* 172.
246. Weber, *Die protestantische Ethik II. Kritiken und Antikritiken,* 325.
247. Weber, *The Methodology of the Social Sciences,* trans. and ed. E. A. Shils and H. A. Finch (New York: The Free Press, 1949), 106; Weber, *Gesammelte Aufsätze zur Wissenschaftslehre,* 4th ed. (Tübingen: J. C. B. Mohr, 1973), 208.

2

The Institutionalization of Early Islamic Societies

Ira M. Lapidus

Weber's legacy offers a special challenge for the study of Islamic civilization. It was not one of the world religions which he studied in depth. Turner's book[1] has already shown how Weber's comments about Islam were limited and scattered. Weber's views on Islam as a warrior religion, on *qadi* justice or on patrimonialism in Islamic societies are not so much wrong as they are inadequately developed and by themselves misleading caricatures of Islamic society and religion. Instead of trying to assess Islamic societies in Weber's terms or criticizing Weber from our present knowledge, we need to bypass his specific opinions and make use of the extraordinary repertoire of concepts and ideal types that Weber developed for his comparative study of civilizations to work out our own portrait of Islamic civilization in a Weberian manner. For students of Islamic societies Weber's important contributions were not his remarks about Islam, but such concepts as the forms of political domination and legitimation; his studies of charisma, of patrimonial and bureaucratic administration; his sociology of religion, and his concepts of the inner and other worldly religious orientations, and their affinity with different status groups. I have not mentioned all the important concepts, but I have deliberately left out of this list Weber's great comparative study of why capitalism developed in European but not in non-European societies. This aspect of his work was a revelation about Europe, but I think it is misleading to let the European issue define the questions for the study of non-European societies. We have to analyze these societies in terms of their own particular institutions and ethos rather than to concentrate on the relevant differences from capitalist or western societies. What I would like to do then is to avoid Weber's question of the comparison of Islamic and western societies, but use his repertoire of concepts for the analysis of early Islamic societies.

Let me begin by briefly defining the boundaries of my subject. By the institutionalization of Islam I mean the transformation of Middle Eastern societies by a religious idea—a religious idea which is understood to operate and can only be understood as it operates in a particular historical setting. Institutionalization is the process by which a religious vision represented by particular elites gives shape to the religious beliefs, the communal organization, the political regimes—indeed to the identity of societies. I mean by this definition to stress three interrelated factors: the ideas, the elites who espouse them and the sociopolitical structures in which they become embedded.

From this point of view the early institutionalization of Islamic societies took place in several successive phases and in different geographical arenas over a broad period. The first phase of course was the formation of the Arabian Muslim community under Muhammad's prophetic authority; the second was the formation of a Middle Eastern-wide Islamic society in the regions conquered by the Arabs. The institutionalization of Islam in this larger arena took place in two historical sub-periods—the period of the Caliphal empire to about the middle of the tenth century and in the Saljuq or Sultanate era to about 1400. (This is "early" institutionalization in that it precedes the later reconstruction of Islamic societies between the thirteenth (1400–1800) and the nineteenth and twentieth centuries.)

Arabian Islam

The first phase in the institutionalization of Islam is, of course, the creation of a Muslim community in Mecca and Medina under the aegis of the Prophet Muhammad. This represents the formation, of an overarching religiously defined community operating as an integrating force in a lineage society. The Prophet and his disciples are the elites who transform a segmentary society to make it serve the purposes of mediation among lineage groups, regulation of economy, state formation, and moral reform while maintaining its basic lineage structures. The coexistence of two levels of segmentary and religious organization results in a complex system of values. On the prophetic or visionary level the Quran in principle introduces a concept of transcendent reality which opposes the values of tribal culture. To the aggrandizement of tribal groups and the *areté* of warriors, it opposes a community based upon religious brotherhood and personal humility, modesty, and self-restraint. Still, the basic family and lineage structures of Arabian peoples became part of Islamic societies; pagan virtues were preserved by being vested with new meaning as Islamic ethics; and *bedouin* identity persisted alongside Islamic loyalties. The ethos, then, of the first Islamic society in Arabia was already a complex amalgam of different levels or religious transcendence, modification of worldly reality, and acceptance of non-Islamic Arabian *bedouin* civilization. In its first guise the Islamic mission became a model for how radical religious values and sectarian impulses would actually function in lineage and tribal societies.[2]

Middle Eastern Islamic Societies

The formation of the Muslim community in Arabia led to the Arab conquests and to the second phase in the institutionalization of Islam— the formation of Islamic societies in the larger Middle East. This phase was marked by the emergence of a prototypical Islamic state, the internal differentiation of the Muslim community into a number of religio-political elites and associations, the formation of Islamically defined parochial communities, and the generation of a multiple orientation toward worldly reality. In this phase the further institutionalization of Islam took place, not in the context of pastoral or oasis societies, but in an agricultural, commercial, urbanized, monotheistic and imperial civilization. For simplicity's sake we can imagine that on the eve of the Islamic era the larger Middle Eastern society was organized on several levels. Basically there were innumerable local, parochial communities built, variously, around factional, lineage, tribal and village groups. These communities were integrated by market exchanges, and by great religious associations—Jewish, Christian, or Zoroastrian. The larger scale economic network and religious associations were in turn under the umbrella of Sasanian and Byzantine empires.

Into these societies the Islamic prophetic vision and community was carried by two composite elites—the caliphs and the caliphate as an institution, and the *'ulama'* or the Islamic religious scholars, and the Sufi holy men. Each of these elites attempted to insinuate Islamic values and identities into an already complex civilization and to reshape that civilization in accord with their own ethos and interests. Thus the caliphs acting at the state level attempted to transform the existing imperial institutions into what we shall call Islamic states. The *'ulama'* and the Sufis acting upon the masses of the population attempted to form Islamic communal or sectarian associations, and to integrate Islamic symbols and identities into existing collectivities. What I will try to do briefly is look at the institutionalization of Islam at the state, the religious associational and at the parochial levels, and discuss the institutionalization of Islam as a complex process involving a multiple formation of Islamic social structures, Islamic identities and Islamic ethos. It should be clear from the outset that Islam is not a "warrior" religion; indeed that it is not a single religion in a single milieu but a world civilization representing a wide range of religious views and social ethics.

The Islamic State

The institutionalization of Islam at the state level—the creation of an Islamic form of Middle Eastern state—was the work of the caliphs who were symbols of the identity of the Muslim *umma* and bearers of the Muslim intention to transform the world in the name of the truth. From the late ninth through the eleventh century, a theory evolved which defined the qualities of person and the method of selection to the office so as to charismatically guarantee that the caliphs were the ideal persons to lead the Muslim umma. In practice, however, the caliphate did not transform the world; they were the chiefs of conquering armies, heirs to imperial administration, the heads of privileged aristocracies. They patronized a court culture which gave their regime an Islamic identity, but a version of Islam derived from Byzantine and Sasanian imperial concepts which emphasized the patrimonial authority of the caliphs and the legitimacy of the ruling elite. The Arabic poetic, historical aspects of the court culture provided an ethnic patrimonial concept of political leadership; royal arts and architecture transmitted Byzantine and Sasanian symbols of kingship; and Hellenistic philosophy provided universal justification for imperial rule. Thus, while the caliphate was the ideal succession to the Prophet and therefore a world transcending and world transforming institution it accepted the political and economic order of the Middle Eastern societies, assumed worldly power and generated a culture which was dedicated to the enjoyment and legitimation of that power. While the caliphate gave a distinctive Islamic identity to Middle Eastern imperial institutions and court cultures, it also perpetuated a pre-Islamic imperial ethos.[3]

The Institutionalization of Early Islamic Societies 143

Such glory has to pass. By the middle of the tenth century the caliphal empire was destroyed. The Middle East was conquered by Turkish nomadic warriors and by slave warlords who ruled the several Middle Eastern provinces in the tenth, eleventh, and twelfth and later centuries. These states also had a complex identity. They were in one sense Muslim because they were legitimated by Islamic symbols, such as the appointment of rulers by the caliphs, and because they upheld justice, patronized Islamic learning and waged *jihad*. But unlike the caliphate, the Turkish nomadic and slave states had no intrinsic Muslim legitimacy. After the charisma of the Prophet and the routinized charisma of the caliphs, the authority of sultans was derived largely from association rather than inherent custody of Islam. Furthermore, though Muslim in theory, the Sultanates were basically defined by Turkish patrimonial concepts of power which emphasized, either or both, the personal servitude of slaves, clients, and retainers to the ruler, and the tribal basis of the state authority; and by Persian concepts of monarchy as a mythic entity with cosmological significance. Thus, both the caliphate and the later sultanates had Islamic functions and identities, but Islamic identity was paralleled by a non-Islamic heritage of political institutions and legitimating symbols, and by a non-Islamic Persian and Turkish political ethos or concept of the purpose of government.

Islamic Religious Communities

On a second level Islam was also institutionalized in the form of religious communities in the urban centers founded and settled by the Arab conquerors, this time not under the leadership of the caliphs or as a state regime, but under the leadership of charismatic religious leaders, including the family or companions of the Prophet and their descendants, Muslim scholars such as the *qurra'* (reciters of the Quran), the *'ulama'*, and Sufi ascetics.

Muslim religious elites have their origin in the small community of people inspired by the teachings of Muhammad and dedicated to his person. While many Arab leaders became involved in war and administration, Muhammad's companions became the bearers of his religious message in the vast Middle Eastern regions conquered by the Arabs and won to their side non-Arab converts who devoted themselves to religious studies and practices. These early followers of Muhammad divided into two main tendencies. Some of them tended to conceive of the Prophet's legacy in terms of correct Muslim behavior in ritual, family, commercial, and indeed in all of life's concerns. This orientation led primarily into intellectual religious scholarship for the principle need was to "know" the teachings of the Quran and the legacy of the prophet. The Muslims whose primary concern became the exegesis of the Quran the collection of *hadith* (the stories concerning the Prophet's sayings and activities), and legal studies we call the *'ulama'* (pl.)—the religious scholars. The religious authority of an *'alim* (sing.) was based simply on his knowledge of religious teachings and his experience in attempting to implement them in the community.

The second group moved away from religious rituals and social practices to the inward cultivation of the moral and religious qualities which brought an individual closer to the spiritual quality of Muhammad and closer thereby to the divine being. This tendency was represented, in part, by the theologians and philosophers who sought rational insight into religious truths and who hoped to reconstruct their souls in accord with the truth. More important were the early ascetics, gnostics and eventually mystics who tried through renunciation of worldly concerns, poverty, piety, and spiritual exercises to wean the soul away from this world and attach it to the divine being. Such men were called Sufis. They also acquired a religious authority, not based upon knowledge, but upon spiritual experience and closeness to God.

The division between the knowledgeable scholars and the spiritual Sufis was bridged, however, by Muslims who tried to combine both. The great line of religious teachers which runs from Hasan al-Basra (d. 728) to al-Junayd (d. 911) and eventually to al-Ghazzali (d. 1111) represents the synthesis which has become the principle Islamic religious orientation. Muslim religious authority has in general come to be vested in persons who combine the knowledge of correct practice of the *'ulama'* with the immediate and personal spiritual achievement of the Sufis. However, the individual variations in replicating the religious tradition are virtually endless. Muslim religious teachers vary over the whole spectrum from legalism, intellectuality, and literalism, to extreme even antinomian spiritual self-expression.

Furthermore, the authority of individual scholars and Sufis was reinforced by a chainlike tradition of learning. The scholars of each generation, having acquired their knowledge from a chain of predecessors going back to the Prophet passed on their knowledge to their successors. Though religious knowledge was confided to books, the chain of transmission was oral. The textual knowledge had to be communicated by a living master who gave book learning spiritual meaning. Similarly, the spiritual exercises of the Sufis were passed on from generation to generation and also were assumed to be part of a chain of succession which went back to Muhammad. Muslim religious authority then combined acquired personal knowledge or spiritual insight with direct personal contact across the generations with the Prophet himself. In late Islamic times there was a tendency to identify religious insight and religious achievement with biological descent from Muhammad. In turn presumed biological descent became a basis for religious authority.

In the seventh and eighth centuries these holy men won over groups of disciples, students, and followers and thus generated numerous religious associations, including Shi'a and Khariji sects, Sunni schools of law, and Sufi discipleships. Most of these groups were small, even esoteric, cults. Some of them acquired a mass following. In opposition to the caliphs all of them claimed to embody the tradition of the Prophet and the true teachings of Islam. The Shi'a and the Kharijis at first violently opposed the caliphate, but by the ninth century the twelver Shi'a and many Kharijis had renounced world-transforming political aspirations in favor of local community affairs and pious personal lives, lived in an atmosphere of mourning for lost hopes and messianic dreams. They withdrew from transforming the world to a pious existence within the world. Even the Sunnis who supported the Caliphate in principle withdrew from public commitments and concentrated on small-scale community life and personal piety, except for the Hanbalis who openly defied the religious authority of the caliphs, a defiance which marks the emergence of a sectarian community within the Sunni fold. As a result of the sectarian associational form of Islamic organization, and its opposition to the caliphate, by the ninth century Muslim towns had become societies of religious cells distinct from the state Islamic establishment. I have argued elsewhere, and would like to emphasize again, that ever after Islamic societies have been characterized, in fact, if not in culturally recognized principle, by separate state and religious institutions.

Then in the later Sultanal or Saljuq period these early Islamic religious associations became the almost universal basis of Middle Eastern communal organization. Until the ninth century Islam was the religion of the Arab populations and assimilated urban groups, but from the ninth to the twelfth centuries the mass of the Middle Eastern peoples were converted to Islam. This was due to a number of interrelated developments which go back to the breakup of the Abbasid empire in the tenth century. The dissolution of the empire involved not only the breakdown of the state and its replacement by new foreign military elites, but also the ruin of the landowning and administrative classes and their replacement by Muslim religious leaders who converted the uprooted masses, and provided them with social and economic leadership, and with the forms of communal organization based on the religious associations created in the caliphal period. From the tenth to the thirteenth centuries the Middle Eastern masses came to be identified with the Sunni schools of law, Sufi brotherhoods, Shi'a associations, and other Muslim groups.

These were two types of Muslim associations. The first type was religious fellowships which cut across the lines of existing communities; the second were preexisting organizations which took on an Islamic identity. The schools of law and the Sufi brotherhoods were Muslim associations in the first sense. The schools of law were associations of scholars, teachers and students adhering to the law codes developed by discussion among legal scholars in the eighth and ninth centuries. Through the law schools, the *'ulama'* organized higher education, and trained teachers and judicial administrators; from the law schools came legal consultants, notaries, and judges. The students considered themselves personal disciples and loyal clients of their masters. The communities in which the schools were located provided patrons and supporters especially from the merchant and artisan classes.

Another type of Muslim religious association was based on Sufism. Sufism was collective in impulse; Sufis gathered disciples and sometimes grouped together in common residences called *khanaqas, Tariqat* or brotherhoods were formed when Sufi masters in the twelfth and thirteenth century began to reckon themselves the descendants of earlier teachers. Those who descended from the same teacher regarded themselves as perpetuating a common spiritual discipline and as units of a much larger religious movement accepting the same higher authority. Such formations became regional and even Muslim worldwide. Thus, the schools of law and Sufi brotherhoods served as confessional collectivities which could recruit individuals across the lines of existing community structures and unity smaller-scale family, clan or residential collectivities into larger units on the basis of shared allegiance to Muslim law, and to *'ulama'* and Sufi norms of religious behavior. But Muslim religious associations could also be formed within the framework of existing collective units. In urban settings schools of law, Sufi brotherhoods or Shi'a sects were often identified with a particular neighborhood, occupational or ethnic minority. As we shall see shortly, the fusion of Islamic and non-Islamic collectivities was even more important in rural societies.[4]

The Sunni Ethos

These Islamic religious associations represented very different religious orientations from those of the political elites. Muslim religious orientations varied on a spectrum ranging from other worldly ecstatic, contemplative forms of Sufism to a very worldly family and business-oriented ethos. However, there was a broad synthetic middle ground which I shall call the *sunni-shari'a*-Sufi position. This position was represented by the Hanafi and Shafi'i schools of law, the Ashari and Maturidi schools of theology, and the "sober" Sufi tradition of al-Junayd (d. 911) and al-Ghazzali (d. 1111). It attempted to integrate commitment to the principle of the caliphate as the basis of the ideal Muslim community, devotion to the fulfillment of the teachings of the Shari'a, belief in the limited use of reason for understanding religious truths, and the practice of Sufi ethical and meditational exercises in conjunction with these political, legal and moral commitments. This position attempted to combine the correct external forms of social and ritual behavior with internal emotional and spiritual awareness.

Sunnis with this orientation had a nuanced attitude to worldly actualities. They accepted existing religions as legitimate by virtue of the inherent need for order in society and they worked out routine ways of collaborating with established states. Political obedience was highly emphasized. The *'ulama'* reserved for themselves a consultative role, and the right to educate, admonish, and give moral advice to rulers, and they expected states to give them control over legal administration and patronize Muslim scholarly educational and charitable activities. Within this framework, however, Sunnis were not as much involved in politics as in community affairs. Here, too, they accepted the given clan, lineage, tribal, or clientele substructures of Middle Eastern societies, and the realities of economic life. They accepted inequalities of wealth and property and regarded social and economic justice as matters of individual behavior. Their concern was to uphold public morality, apply the *shari'a* to family and commercial affairs, educate, heal, and mediate local conflicts.

World acceptance was modified though by an attitude of detachment and refusal to be committed to the world in which they were engaged. While there was little or no impulse to change institutions there was a deep ambiguity about involvement in them. While many *'ulama'* and Sufis accepted the responsibilities of political power, held offices, accumulated land and property and served as spokesmen for the needs of their people, there was a deep strand of feeling which opposed such engagements. The companions of princes were regarded as morally corrupted; *'ulama'* and Sufis characteristically refused official positions and turned down royal gifts. Disengagement was taken as a mark of piety. The refusal to give moral assent to the world as it is was accompanied by a nostalgia for the restoration of the true caliphate and a yearning for the coming of the *madhi* (messiah). Nostalgia expressed withdrawal from the actual world; it also served to ratify things as they were.

The Hanbalis cultivated a more active stance. They took to vigilante action to enforce morality, suppress alcohol and prostitution, and attack rival sects. They rallied Muslim volunteers for holy war and on occasion (especially in the tenth and 11th centuries), attempted to restore the political power of the caliphate. This activism, however, was channeled mainly into pressuring existing regimes to uphold Muslim morality rather than being aimed at changing the political order. Thus, all Sunnis accepted the world as it was yet withheld their full engagement and assent by refusing to be directly involved in politics, by actively campaigning to improve public morals, and by nostalgic reflection and eschatological yearning. This we can instantly feel is the ethos of intellectuals.

The basic reason for this complex orientation is that Muslim religious associations were partially but never fully differentiated from other sociopolitical institutions. The Sunni position reflects a transcendent religious vision embedded in sectarian, religious and communal associations, but these existed within the overall political framework of the caliphate or sultanal regimes, and were interlocked with parochial lineage, village and other solidarities. Therefore the tension between religious and other commitments could not be absolute and the complex relationships among them had to be expressed in nuance modes of acceptance, detachment and rejection.[5]

Islamic Symbols and Rural Societies

The third and final level of the institutionalization of Islam was in rural settings.

Here Muslim religious leadership and Muslim symbols were used to unite factionalized peoples into more unified religio-political movements. Berbers in North Africa from the seventh through the thirteenth centuries were united under Kharijism, Shi'ism, Sunni reformism and later Sufism into conquering religious movements such as the Fatimid, the Almoravid, and the Almohad and into Berber states. Kharijis in eastern Arabia, Qarmatis in the fertile crescent, and Safavis in western Iran are other examples of how Muslim religious leaders and symbols became the basis of rural unification in the quest for the ever-elusive just Islamic society.

There is also evidence for the beginning of the widespread acceptance of Islamic identity by rural collectivities in the form of the veneration of Sufis and the worship of shrines. Before the thirteenth century the doctrinal basis for the veneration of Sufis as intercessors between man and God had been established. Saint worship and veneration of shrines were widely practices, and pre-Islamic magical practices and superstitions were part of popular Islam. From later epochs we know that Sufis were commonly believed to be saints and were venerated as intermediaries between the material and the spiritual worlds, and as miracle workers and dispensers of blessings. On this basis Sufis and *'ulama'* served in rural societies to mediate disputes, facilitate the selection of chiefs, organize long-distance trade, teach the young, heal the sick, provide amulets, officiate at circumcisions, marriages and funerals, celebrate festivals, do white magic, and otherwise uphold the tenuous connection of human beings with the spirits and the divine. This type of Sufism led to the veneration of the tomb or shrine, disciples and descendants of the holy man, and to a religious life of offering sacrifices and communal festivals around the tombs of saints in which Islamic and non-Islamic symbols and practices were merged. In later periods shrines came to be endowed with property and administered by the descendants of saints and by Sufi brotherhoods, and served as a center of fellowship for all people who worshipped at the tomb and believed that the saint could perform miracles. Shrine Sufism was a religion of magical protection from the arbitrary forces of nature and of acquisition of divine benefits rather than a religion of ethical or emotional self-cultivation.[6] Islam then did not necessarily lead to the formation of an organized association capable of collective action, but served as a shared identity among diverse peoples who preserved their own kinship, territorial, linguistic, ethnic and other bases of non-Islamic culture in group organization and social relations.

This rural form of Muslim belief and practice differed profoundly from both the court and the urban forms of Islam and constituted yet a third level of the institutionalization of Muslim Middle Eastern societies. Though imperial culture, *sunni-shari'a*-Sufism and shrine Sufism are all called Islam, they represent profoundly contrasting concepts of the religious life.

Conclusion

If we look back at the whole process of the institutionalization of the formation of an Islamic society in the Middle East we begin where Weber did with a charismatic leader and a visionary movement which was translated into the beliefs, practices, identities and collective communal organization not only of Arabian but of all Middle Eastern peoples from the Atlas to the Pamirs. This institutionalization occurred in a society which already had an established system of parochial, economic, religious and state institutions, and therefore involved the transformation of these established structures. Islam became part of the identity of state elites and the legitimization of Muslim empires and of numerous post-caliphal succession states. It was institutionalized in the form of urban sects and religious communities committed to particular religious beliefs, specific religious practices, veneration for particular person and to administration of communal law. Islam was also institutionalized among lineage and other parochial groups by acceptance of holy authority and Islamic beliefs or symbols which unified these groups into political movements or otherwise gave identity to inchoate populations. I should make clear that I am speaking of levels or types of institutions and that at each level there were numerous examples of states, religious associations and parochial communities. The institutionalization of Islam in all these structures and the relations among them in any given location makes up the system of an Islamic society. This brief model of early Islamic societies in the Middle East also provides a paradigm for the later evolution of Muslim societies in the Middle East and elsewhere. The concepts of Muslim state, Muslim religious associations and Muslim identity among parochial or segmentary groups are ideal types which may be used in different permutations and combinations to analyze Muslim societies in subsequent periods and in other parts of the world. Thus from Weber we can learn how to go beyond his own untutored concepts of the Islamic ethos and society and try to build a more complex model.

Notes

1. B.S. Turner, *Weber and Islam* (London, Routledge, 1974). For a full exposition of the views presented in this paper see I. M. Lapidus, *History of Islamic Societies* (New York: Cambridge University Press, 1988).
2. See I.M. Lapidus, "The Arab Conquests and the Formation of Islamic Society," in *Studies on the First Century of Islamic Society*, ed. G.H. A. Juynboll (Carbondale: Southern Ill. University Press, 1982), 49–72; I. Shahid, "Pre-Islamic Arabia," in *Cambridge History of Islam*, I. eds. P. M. Holt, A. K. S. Lambton and B. Lewis (Cambridge: Cambridge University Press 1970), 3–29. The best modern biography of the Prophet, stressing the social and political matrix of prophecy is W. M. Watt, *Muhammad at Mecca* (Oxford: Oxford University Press, 1965) and *Muhammad at Medina* (Oxford: Oxford University Press, 1962).
3. On the early Caliphate see M. G. S. Hodgson, *The Venture of Islam* I (Chicago: University of Chicago Press, 1974). A similar account of the cultural orientation appears in I. M. Lapidus, "IIslamisches Sektierertum und das Rekonstruktions- und Umgestaltungspotential der islamischen Kultur," in *Kulturen der Achsenzeit,* ed. S.N. Eisenstadt (Frankfurt am Main, Suhrkamp-Taschenbuch, 1992), II, Teil 3, 161–188.
4. On the early evolution of Muslim societies, the formation of the schools of law and other religious associations see I. M. Lapidus, "The Separation of State and Religion in the Development of Early Islamic Society," in *International Journal of Middle East Studies* 6 (1975): 363–385; "The Evolution of Muslim Urban Society," in *Comparative Studies in Society and History* 5 (1983): 21–50; "Muslim Cities and Islamic Societies," in *Middle Eastern Cities*, ed. I .M. Lapidus, (Berkeley: University of California Press, 1969), 47–79; "Ayyubid Religious Policy and the Development of the Schools of Law in Cairo," in *Colloque International sur l'Histoire du Caire*, (Cairo, 1973), 279–286; and *Muslim Cities in the Later Middle Ages*, 2nd ed. (New York: Cambridge University Press, 1984).
5. A similar statement appears in Lapidus, "Islamic sectarianism."
6. The social history of Shi'ism and shrine worship has barely begun to be studied. For an introduction see J. S. Trimingham, *The Sufi Orders in Islam* (Oxford: Oxford University Press, 1971).

3

Aspects of Islamization: Weber's Observations on Islam Reconsidered

Nehemia Levtzion

Max Weber did not write a full monograph on Islam, but he often refers to Islam in his comparative studies of world religions. Much of what Weber wrote about Islam is unacceptable to contemporary scholarship on Islam, but some of his observations offer insights into the dynamics of Islam. The purpose of this paper is to examine some of Weber's statements concerning Islam, mainly by reviewing several aspects of Islamization.

On Islamic Universalism

Weber asserted that Islam was "obviously not a universalistic salvation religion."[1] He presented the case for that statement elsewhere:

> In Islam, religion makes obligatory the violent propagation of the true Prophecy, which consciously eschews universal conversion and enjoins the subjugation of unbelievers...without recognizing the [need for] salvation of the subjugated.... The religious commandments of the holy war were not directed in the first instance to the purpose of conversion.[2]

Weber was wrong in considering holy war as antithetical to universalism. Indeed, the notion of the *jihad* "stems from the fundamental principle of the universality of Islam. This religion, along with the temporal power which it implies, ought to embrace the whole universe."[3] But, Weber was right that the holy war was not directed for the purpose of conversion. The aim of the jihad was to extend Dar al-Islam through military conquest and the imposition of Muslim rule. A country under Muslim rule is considered Dar al-Islam even if its population remains predominantly non-Muslim. In other words, the purpose of the *jihad* was a political rather than missionary, territorial expansion rather than conversion.

Islamic law recognized the existence of non-Muslim people within the Muslim state. These were the *dhimmis*, Jews and Christians, adherents of the other revealed religions. They could practice their religion if they submitted to Muslim rule, observed a number of restrictions, and paid the poll-tax (*jizya*). During the early Umayyad period the Arab conquerors discouraged conversion of the local population in the newly conquered territories, among other reasons, because they wanted to keep them as taxpaying subjects. This is why Weber says that the survival of non-Muslims in the Muslim state "was considered desirable because of the financial contribution they could make."[4]

This practice, however, was the reason for one of the most serious crises in early Islam, because it contradicted the concept of Islamic universalism, as the pious caliph 'Umar ibn 'Abd al-'Aziz (717–720) wrote to one of his governors: "I have sent you as a missionary not as tax-collector." The resentment of the local converts, known as *mawali*, who were forced to continue the payment of taxes, and were deprived of their rights as equal members of the Muslim community, fueled the 'Abbasid revolution. The rise of the 'Abbasids therefore marked the triumph of Islamic universalism over Arab particularism.

Fixed as he was on events and developments that took place in the first century of Islam, Weber believed that the Arab warriors brought about a decline in "the Islamic missionary ardor" and a recession of "those religious elements of ancient Islam which had the character of an ethical religion of salvation."[5] In fact, Arab warriors could not have made a lasting impact on the development of Islam, because by the third century of Islam they had been replaced in the Muslim armies by the Turks. More important still was the direction of the religious dynamics of Islam. Rather than a regression from an earlier, more advanced stage of an ethical universalistic religion, as implied by Weber, Islamic universalism was on the ascent. This paved the way for the acceleration of the process of Islamization, first under Muslim rule, and then far beyond the frontiers of the military expansion of the Muslims.

On Conversion Under Muslim Rule

Military conquest did not in itself bring about conversion to Islam. Conversion among the local population of the lands that came under

Muslim rule was a long process, and the number of Muslims equaled that of non-Muslims only about the middle of the tenth century, that is, a full three centuries after the conquest.

We have already referred to the policy of the Arab rulers during the first century that did not encourage conversion. Indeed, in view of the numerical superiority of the non-Muslim population, a liberal religious policy also aided the consolidation of Muslim rule and helped maintain preexisting administrative structures, where non-Muslims performed important functions.

The pace of conversion was accelerated when, following the 'Abbasid revolution, the distinction between Arabs and non-Arabs became blurred, whereas that between Muslims and non-Muslims became more pronounced. From that time one could have changed his status by converting to Islam. Since the middle of the tenth century, the discriminatory regulations, that emphasized the inferiority of non-Muslims, were more strictly applied.

Non-Muslims participated in the Intellectual, scientific and scholarly activities of the "classical age" of Islam, in the ninth and tenth centuries, which thrived in an urban society and benefited from an expanding mercantile economy. Everything changed in the transitory period to the late medieval period.

In the eleventh century the government in Muslim countries was taken over by a Turkish military elite. Weber rightly connected the creation of "the Islamic warriors' fief," and "the feudalization of the economy" through "the assignment of the tax yield of lands and subjects," to the decline and stagnation of the "oriental market economy."[6] For Weber, the Mamluk regime in Egypt, the epitome of a government by a closed military elite, represented a model of the patrimonial state.

The religion of Islam was the only bond between the Turkish military elite and the Arabic- and Persian-speaking civilian population, with the Islamic religious establishment, the *'ulama'* as mediators. The military rulers considered religious conformity essential for social and political stability, and they collaborated with the *'ulama'* in stifling creative intellectual movements, which had stirred much religious, social and political unrest of the ninth and tenth centuries. The consolidation of Sunni orthodoxy left its stamp on late medieval Islam until the eighteenth century.

Because the military elite had appropriated all the economic resources of the land, they alone were able to support religious institutions, which they did generously. They built *madaris* as colleges of learning, *khanaqhs* as hostels for Sufis, as well as mosques. Graduates of the *madaris* were appointed not only to remunerative religious posts, but also to bureaucratic offices, where they met Christian functionaries. Competition over employment added to religious bigotry. The *'ulama'* who had limited influence in all matters of state, were able to exert pressure, with popular support, for strict enforcement of the discriminatory regulations against non-Muslims, and particularly for their removal from administrative offices. Popular pogroms and official persecutions, mainly in thirteenth and fourteenth century Mamluk Egypt, resulted in waves of conversions of Christians to Islam. It was therefore under what Weber considered a feudal and patrimonial state that religious intolerance peaked, conditions of non-Muslims became harsher, and the process of conversion accelerated.

Islamization Beyond the Frontiers: On the Role of Sufism and Magic

Until the tenth-century conversion to Islam occurred only within the boundaries of the Muslim states. Even there Islam did not penetrate deep into the lower strata of society, and to peripheral groups. Only heterodox sects—Kharijis, Shi'a, Isma'ilis—developed missionary networks that operated independently of the state, which was often hostile to them, and beyond its boundaries. In this respect, the heterodox sects preceded the Sufis, who after the tenth century carried Islam into the steppes of Central Asia, to India and other remote lands. Sufis also played an important role in the Islamization, that is, in deepening the religious experience, of local societies in lands that had been conquered by the Turks after the tenth century, particularly in Anatolia and India.

Weber, who was acquainted only with the most popular unorthodox forms of Sufism, had a poor view of what he referred to as "the dervish religion, with its orgiastic and mystical elements, with its essentially irrational and extraordinary character."[7] But he does emphasize that Sufism "became influential in Islam's missionary enterprise because of its great simplicity." Weber was more specific about the success of Islam in Africa: "the propaganda of Islam in Africa rested primarily on a massive foundation of magic, by means of which it has continued to outbid other competing faiths."[8]

Muslim clerics in general, and Sufis in particular, presented Islam in terms which were familiar to the local people, playing roles similar

Aspects of Islamization: Weber's Observations on Islam Reconsidered

to those of the traditional religious experts. In rural Anatolia, the dervishes, known as Babas, were in fact the old Turkish shamans of Central Asia, who had acquired a veneer of Islam. "The credal gap between the ill-instructed Christians and the ill-instructed Muslims became progressively narrower and easier to cross" through the mediation of the Babas.[9]

For West Africa, there are numerous accounts about Muslim clerics who succeeded in winning over an African ruler, by demonstrating the omnipotence of Allah. Praying to Allah saved the country from drought, or brought victory in war, after the local priest had failed. In other words, Islam's first appeal was in competition with the traditional religion and its practitioners. The latter, however, were not eliminated, and rulers who turned to Muslim divines, also continued to seek the aid of their traditional priests. Though Muslim clerics introduced what seem to have been more sophisticated techniques, particularly through the use of the written word, they operated within a spiritual and cultural realm, which they shared with the local people, in recruiting supernatural aid.[10]

Weber pointed to "the essentially ritualistic character of religious obligations" in Islam and to "the great simplicity of religious requirements."[11]

Both statements may be related to early stages in the process of Islamization in places like Africa, where the ritual rather than the legal aspects of Islam were more important. The Quoran had first been accepted as a sacred object rather than as a source for legislation. Hence, the written word was important for its magical qualities more than for the message that it carried.

Similarly, the argument for the simplicity of Islam's religious requirements was valid only during the first encounter with new societies. At that stage Islam was not presented in all its vigor, and initial demands were minimal. But, once Islam had a foothold in a society, it began to assert itself, articulating its legal, ethical, social and political essence. Latitudinarian attitudes and tolerance of symbiotic relations with other religions gave way to the rigorous exclusiveness of a prophetic religion. This was the stage of reform that sometime took the form of a revolution or of a *jihad*.

On Clerics and Warriors

Weber seems to have been haunted by the martial character of Islam, and by the image of the Arab warriors as carrying the religion of

Islam by the sword. Hence his assertion that the ideal personality type in the religion of Islam was not scholarly scribe, but the warrior.[12] We have already mentioned that the Arab warriors ceased to play any significant role as early as the third century of Islam. Islam as we know it is a religion developed by scholars, jurists, theologians and mystics, without virtually any input of those in political authority or those who held military power.

Weber's suggestion that the warrior was "the ideal personality type" of Islam suggests that he must have had little respect for the religion of Islam, especially in view of what he himself had to say about the warriors' attitude to religion:

> The life pattern of a warrior has very little affinity with the notion of beneficent providence, or with the systematic ethical demands of a transcendental god. Concepts like sin, salvation, a religious humility have not only seemed remote from all ruling strata, particularly the warrior nobles, but have indeed appeared reprehensible to its sense of honor.... The chances and adventures of mundane existence fill [the warrior's] life to such an extent that he does not require of his religion anything beyond protection against evil magic or ceremonial rites congruent with his sense of status, such as priestly prayers for victory.[13]

These traits of the warriors in their attitude to religion may in fact be clearly demonstrated for West Africa, where there is a clear dichotomy between clerics and warriors. Clerics are thought of a peacemakers, and their houses and mosques as sanctuaries. Clerics did not carry arms, and were completely outside the arena of political competition. Clerics were therefore at the opposite end from the warriors, who held political authority, shed blood, and drank alcohol.

But, African warrior chiefs also needed the services of the Muslim clerics to produce amulets, to pray for victory, and to secure the flow of blessing. These warrior chiefs, who came under Islamic influence, began to pray and to perform other Islamic rituals. But because the term for a Muslim was synonymous to that of a cleric, and considering the dichotomy referred to above between warriors and clerics, warriors chiefs did not become Muslims. There are cases on record of princes who had become Muslims and succeeded to the throne, but facing the dilemma, they had to choose between Islam and the chieftaincy. In most cases they either resigned or were deposed.[14] Among the Wolof, in present-day Senegal, Islam had been almost fully integrated into the court. But when Muslim militants demanded that the Wolof kings convert to Islam, the kings reacted passionately, because their perception was that a converted warrior chief became a cleric, emasculating his political and warlike nature.[15] In Weber's words, quoted above, "it appeared reprehensible to his sense of honor."

The Role of Warriors in Reform Movements

In addition to what Weber has said about the warriors' attitude to religion he was aware that in certain circumstances warriors played a role in Islamic militant movements:

> As a rule the warrior nobles have not readily become the carriers of a rational religious ethic.... [But,] periods of strong prophetic or reformist religious agitation have frequently pulled the nobility in particular into the path of prophetic ethical religion.... Prophetic religion is naturally compatible with the status feeling of the nobility when it directs its promises to the warrior in the cause of religion.[16]

It is significant that another sociologist, the fourteenth century Ibn Khaldun, made similar statements concerning the role of charismatic leadership in mobilizing warriors:

> Because of their savagery, the Arabs are the least willing of nations to subordinate themselves to each other.... But when there is religion (among them) through prophecy or sainthood, then they have some restraining influence in themselves.... It is, then, easy for them to subordinate themselves and to unite.... When there is a prophet or a saint among them, who calls upon them to fulfill the commands of God and rids them of blameworthy qualities and cause them to adopt praiseworthy ones, and who has them concentrate all their strength in order to make the truth prevail, they become fully united and obtain superiority and royal authority.[17]

Warriors were not the carriers of ideas but there are historical cases that nomad warriors provided the military strength to support a charismatic leadership. The most obvious case was that of the Prophet Muhammad, who mobilized the Arab tribes to the cause of Islam. Other examples were the Almoravid movement in the eleventh century, where Ibn Yasin recruited the nomad Sanhaja of the Sahara; the Wahhabiyya of the eighteenth century, where the reformer Ibn 'Abd al-Wahhab allied himself with the Bedouin chief Ibn Sa'ud; and the Sokoto *jihad*, at the beginning of the nineteenth century, when 'Uthman dan Fodio led the Fulbe pastoralists.

Under the charismatic leadership of a prophet, a saint or a scholar the nomad warriors became united. In all these cases, the leader shared language and cultural values with the warriors, but invariably he himself was of an urban background. The military exploits of these joint ventures resulted in the creation of states that were committed to the realization of the ideals articulated by the charismatic leader. The warriors themselves, in most cases, after completing their task, returned to their old tribal ways of life on the periphery of the state, with little or no interest in the religious and political dynamics of the state.

Conclusions

Our discussion of Weber's observations on Islam began with asserting the universalism of Islam. We have argued that rather than a regression from what had first been a missionary religion, as implied by Weber's writings, there was a progression from Arab particularism to Islamic universalism. One may add in support of the universalistic character of Islam that Islam maintained a measure of uniformity in spite of its geographical expansion and its adaptation to diverse cultural environments.

We have also criticized Weber's emphasis of the martial character of Islam and the predominant role he assigned to the Arab warriors in shaping the religion of Islam. We have argued that the religion of Islam was molded through the work of jurists, scholars and mystics, without any significant intervention of the political authorities.

On the other hand, we were able to elaborate on Weber's observations concerning the feudalization of the economy of the Muslim countries. We have suggested that those remarks by Weber were relevant to the period that followed the transition from "classical" to late medieval Islam. It was during that period, in the thirteenth and fourteenth centuries, that conversion to Islam under Muslim rule peaked.

Beyond the political frontiers of Islam Sufis played an important role in the expansion of Islam. We have corrected some of Weber's remarks concerning "the religion of the dervishes," whereas his statements concerning the importance of magic in the spread of Islam are fully endorsed.

Weber viewed only part of the process of Islamization, and was not aware of the reform movements as the final stage of this process. But Weber identified the role of the warriors when they responded to the call of charismatic leaders and were recruited to provide the military power for the reform movements. It is significant that Weber's observations in this context echoed some of the pronouncements of the fourteenth century Ibn Khaldun.

Notes

1. Max Weber, *Economy and Society* (Berkeley: University of California Press, 1978), 594.

2. Max Weber, *Economy and Society,* 624.
3. Tyan, "Djihad," *The Encyclopaedia of Islam,* 2nd edition, ii: 238.
4. Weber, *Economy and Society,* 474.
5. Ibid., 344, 474.
6. Ibid., 1016, 1076.
7. Ibid., 626.
8. Ibid., 467.
9. V. L. Menage, "The Islamization of Anatolia," in *Conversion to Islam,* edited by N. Levtzion (New York: Holmes and Meier, 1979), 66.
10. Levtzion, *Conversion to Islam.*
11. Weber, *Economy and Society,* 626.
12. Ibid.
13. Ibid., 472.
14. See, for example, a case in Kano: Palmer, *Sudanese Memoirs* (Lagos: Government Publishing House,1928), iii: 108–9.
15. Colvin, "Islam and the State of Kajoor: a case of successful resistance to *jihad,*" *Journal of African History* 15 (1974): 596.
16. Weber, *Economy and Society,* 472–73.
17. Ibn Khaldun, *The Muqaddima of Ibn Khaldun,* trans. F. Rosenthal (Princeton: Princeton University Press, 1958), I: 305–6.

4

Islamization in Late Medieval Bengal: The Relevance of Max Weber

Richard M. Eaton

It is hardly surprising that Max Weber's scattered references to Islam reflect the Orientalist modes of thought current in his own day. Such references also betray his concerns with demonstrating why it was that societies not suffused with a "Protestant ethic" could not have independently developed a capitalist mode of production. Thus, in contrast to the dynamism that he found in European societies influenced by that ethic, Weber found Muslim societies to be static, if not stagnant. His characterization of Islam as a "warrior religion," moreover, was consonant with Orientalist traditions of European thought that viewed Islam as a fundamentally militant ideology.[1] His notion that the religion validated sexual license or sensual delights followed a similar frame of European thought.[2] Concerning other aspects of Islamic history, Weber was at times factually incorrect, such as, for example, in his contention that Sufism was derived from India, or that early Islam knew no quest for salvation or mysticism.[3]

Whereas Weber's specific comments on Islam were in some ways problematic, or simply wrong, it is nonetheless possible to draw fruitful insights on the evolution of Islamic institutions from some of his more general formulations on social dynamics. This is especially true in the case of the subject of this essay, Islamization, that is, the process by which Islamic societies evolved from non-Islamic ones and grew and diversified over time. I propose here to analyze three notions that Weber explicated in general terms and to test their utility in explaining Islamization in one part of the Muslim world—South Asia, and in particular, Bengal. These notions are: (a) the patrimonial state, (b) the routinization of charismatic authority, and (c) the rationalization of the pantheon so as to favor the primacy of supreme gods over lesser ones, meaning in the case of Islam, the triumph of Allah at the expense of lesser superhuman beings.

For Weber, as with most Orientalist scholars of his day, Islam really meant the Middle East; South Asia for him was a Hindu-Buddhist world, as seen in his *Religion of India*.[4] Nonetheless, South Asia contains the largest concentration of Muslims in the world and on these grounds alone would seem an appropriate area for the study of the process of Islamization. Within South Asia, the case of Bengal with its population of over a hundred million Muslims, presents itself as an especially striking instance of Islamization.

But the growth of the Bengali Muslim population, which occurred gradually between 1300 and 1800, has presented scholars both of traditional Islamic studies and of South Asian studies with something of an enigma. For Islamicists accustomed to viewing Islam as a quintessentially urban religion, and Weber was among these, the phenomenon presents difficulties since in Bengal Islam is mainly a religion of peasant cultivators. For their part, scholars of South Asia have generally explained the Islamization of Bengal in terms of a desire on the part of low-caste Hindus to escape their degraded position in a society in which caste ranking had been rigorously structured by powerful Brahman and other ritually dominant castes. Weber himself subscribed to this position.[5] But the difficulty is that eastern Bengal presents a society that has been undifferentiated in terms of both caste and kinship, and which had been only lightly exposed to Hindu political and cultural penetration prior to the Turkish conquest of the area in 1204. So, if the population that had inhabited the swamps and forests of eastern Bengal had never been integrated into a highly stratified caste system in the first place, then the question of escaping an inegalitarian Hindu order in favor of an egalitarian Islamic order, does not even arise.

What do we know about the chronology and pattern of Islamization in medieval Bengal? Scattered references by foreign travelers suggest that the growth of a Muslim community in Bengal began fairly soon after the conquest of the delta by Turkish Muslims in 1204. In 1345 Ibn Battuta met a famous Sufi shaikh, Shah Jalal, who dwelt in the far eastern region of Sylhet and who, according to the famous world-traveler, was responsible for converting the local population there to Islam.[6] From both Chinese and Portuguese travelers' accounts, recorded in the fifteenth and early sixteenth centuries respectively, it is clear that the capital city of the independent sultans of Bengal, Gaur, was largely Muslim.⁷ In 1518 Duarte Barbosa wrote that "the Heathen of these parts daily become Moors to gain the favour of their rulers," a statement sometimes seized upon as proof that Islam merely rode the back of the political changes then occurring in the delta.⁸ But Barbosa was referring to the capital city only, and not the countryside, and certainly not the vast jungle tracts of eastern Bengal, where the Islamization process was to proceed most dramatically.

It is only from the late sixteenth century that we have solid evidence of the appearance of a Muslim peasant population anywhere in Bengal, and significantly, the reports we have refer only to the eastern portion of the delta. In 1567 the European traveler Cesare Federici observed that the entire population of a large island in the southeastern delta, Sondwip Island, was Muslim.⁹ Soon thereafter, in 1599, a Jesuit missionary traveled up to the area near modern Dhaka, whose rural population were nearly all Muslims.¹⁰ In 1628–29 an Augustinian friar observed that though most of the province was still non-Muslim, conversions to Islam had been taking place ever since the Mughal conquest of the late sixteenth century.¹¹ In 1638 the Mughal governor of Bengal referred to the "masses" of Muslims inhabiting the southeastern district of Noakhali.¹² Then in the 1660s the *'Alamgir-nama* a Persian chronicle of Emperor Aurangzeb's reign, reported that most of the peasants of Ghoraghat, in Northern Bengal, were Muslim.¹³

The emergence of this peasant Muslim population coincided with two other important developments in this period, one ecological, the other political. As to the former, in ancient times the Ganges River had flowed directly down the delta's western corridor, enabling a stable agrarian society with a distinctly Hindu social system to thrive there. But from about the twelfth century A.D. the great river, by silting up its older channels, began forging ever new channels to its east, until by the sixteenth century it finally linked up with the Padma River, bringing it into the heart of eastern Bengal. The result was that it emptied into the Bay of Bengal far to the east of its original channel, which passes by Calcutta in West Bengal.¹⁴ As this happened, not only did the Hindu agrarian society decline in the West, but the "new" Ganges River fertilized the active portion of the Bengal delta, for the first time preparing the eastern delta for intensive rice cultivation.

The Mughal Empire as a Patrimonial State

The completion of these river shifts occurred roughly simultaneously with another momentous event, Akbar's conquest of Bengal of 1574, followed by the delta's integration with one of the largest empires in Indian history, the Mughals. It is against this backdrop that the above mentioned three notions of Weber become relevant.

Weber understood Islamic polity as a patrimonial state, that is, an entity in which the army, the *'ulama'* the bureaucracy, and the merchants were all dependent upon an imperial household, and whose financial and political structures depended upon the conquest and integration of new lands.[15] Analyzing the Mughal imperial household, Stephen Blake has argued that the empire conformed to Weber's patrimonial model.[16] Of special interest here is the expansive character of the Mughal state, shaped by its needs to acquire an ever larger revenue-producing base in order to accommodate an expanding nobility paid in land revenue-farming assignments (*jagir*) . Between 1574 and 1765, one clearly sees the Mughals' expansive character in eastern Bengal, where imperial authorities claimed ultimate proprietorship over new lands that were brought simultaneously within the political orbit of their expanding dominion and within the ecological orbit of the delta's expanding rice frontier.

Few North Indian Muslims had settled in Bengal in the period 1204 to 1574, since at that time the province, then ruled by independent dynasties of Indo-Turkish sultans, remained politically isolated from North India. But after 1574, when it was integrated with Mughal India, the province became exposed to new waves of immigrants. And, since the great changes in Bengal's river system that carried the course of the Ganges into the eastern delta coincided with Bengal's political integration with North India, the colonists and pioneers who moved into eastern Bengal during the sixteenth to eighteenth centuries tended not to be West Bengali Hindus, but North Indian Muslims: adventurers, Sufis, *qadis*, administrators, and so on. Many of these up-country newcomers settled in the new provincial capital of Dhaka. Indeed, one contemporary account indicates that most of the government officers and notables living in that city in the 1630s were foreigners whose ancestors or who themselves had come from places like Kashmir, Mashhad, Tehran, Badakhshan, Mazandaran, or Gilan.[17]

The influx of these North Indians dislodged an older elite group, Afghans, as the last ruling class of independent Bengal, driving many of them into more remote regions of East and South Bengal where they reestablished themselves as colonizers and local magnates.[18] Thus the new provincial capital of Dhaka became, in effect, a Mughal city, while in the countryside the pattern of settlement was mixed; some settlers

Islamization in Late Medieval Bengal: The Relevance of Max Weber

were Afghans driven into the countryside, others North Indians who were typically clients of patrons in Dhaka, who in turn were clients of the patrimonial Mughal house in Delhi. These country settlers formed, in short, the very sort of petty or "*qasba* gentry" that C. A. Bayly has described in eighteenth and nineteenth century North India, that is, small-town elites who stood between the cultivators and the state, and whose collective solidarity was formed by literacy, agrarian dependence, and adherence to Islam.[19]

Most urban-dwelling immigrants who came to Bengal in the wake of the Mughal conquest claimed high-bred origins and regarded themselves as *ashraf* or "honorable." Central to their *ashraf* identity was a refusal to touch the plow, since engaging in agricultural operations was beneath their sense of dignity and self-esteem.[20] On the other hand the great mass of Muslim cultivators of Bengal, who make up the bulk of Bengal's converted population, readily took to tilling the soil. Indeed, in their view it was mainly through cultivating the land that they could effectively articulate their identity as Muslims.[21] This reflects a culturally constructed connection between agriculture and religion, suggesting in turn that agrarian integration and religious integration were part of a single historical process.

Fundamental to this process was the political and economic expansion of Mughal power into the delta region. In 1612, when they established their provincial capital in the new city of Dhaka in the heart of the eastern delta, the Mughals placed their provincial government in the best possible position for exploiting the resources of a developing frontier zone.[22] Their success in this respect, together with the dramatitc changes in the relative fertility of different sectors of the delta, is clearly seen in the sharp increases in East Bengal's land revenue demand in the seventeenth and eighteenth centuries, compared to that of the West. Between 1595, soon after Akbar's conquest, and 1659, the revenue demand for southeastern Bengal increased by 117 percent and in northeastern Bengal by 95 percent, whereas in the southwest it increased by only 54 percent and in the northwest it actually declined by 13 percent.[23] Since land revenue demands were calculated from estimated rice production, these figures show the significant economic growth taking place in eastern Bengal, which was the younger, active portion of the delta, in contrast to the West, which was its older, ecologically moribund portion. Not even the decline of the central Mughal imperial machinery in the eighteenth century arrested the continuing process of land reclamation on the Empire's furthest frontiers. Even while palace revolutions and foreign invasions shook the rotting empire at its center in Delhi, the revenue collected by the provincial Mughal authorities in the southeastern Bengali region of Chittagong actually doubled between 1713 and 1760.[24]

In sum, it was on eastern Bengal's expanding frontier that the patrimonial character of the Mughal Empire seems most apparent. Here, where vast tracts of virgin lands were not yet populated by a settled agrarian population with an accompanying staff of entrenched officials, the Mughals had a free hand to shape a new society by vigorously exploiting the region's natural resources. By contrast, in the older portions of the Empire in the upper Ganges region, the Mughals were forced to come to terms with deeply entrenched Hindu officials and chieftains who dominated an existing Hindu agrarian society. This contrast between the Empire's older heartland and its virgin periphery proved crucial in shaping the patterns of Islamization in medieval India, which occurred far more dramatically along the Mughal periphery than in its heartland.

The Routinization of Charisma

Weber's second theory relevant to this discussion is his analysis of the routinization of charismatic authority. A close examination of the surviving data concerning the settling of eastern Bengal's rice frontier shows the important role played there by charismatic Muslim holy men, or, as was often the case, pioneering settlers who were later remembered as holy men. Locally renowned as Sufis, these men are important because the local population frequently attributes their conversion to Islam to their agency. These men are especially interesting from a Weberian perspective, since their immediate descendants or successors established bases of local influence in ways resembling Weber's conception of routinization of authority.

Very few Bengali Sufis enjoyed all-India reputations as eminent mystics; rather, the vast majority were and are popularly associated with the process of forest clearing, land reclamation, and the integration of local communities into Islam. For example, according to a local history of seventeenth century Midnapur, in about the year 1650 a Mughal administrator (*faujdar*) told a holy man named Khondkar Shah 'Ala that if he let a horse roam from dawn to noon, the enclosed jungle area would be his for life, where he would "rule" and preach Islam. The man did this and was then said to have taken the help of the local

Islamization in Late Medieval Bengal: The Relevance of Max Weber 169

people for clearing the area of forests, before settling down with his family. After having converted the local population to Islam, the man was honored as their *pir* by these people.[25]

Or again, in south central Bengal in the heart of the Sundarban forests facing the Bay of Bengal, we find the shrine of Khan Jahan 'Ali, a local hero who died in 1459. Although the epitaph on his tomb gives him military associations, according to popular traditions he came to the jungle with a large body of followers and, having reclaimed a vast tract of jungle and built roads, he converted the local people to Islam.[26] Oral traditions collected in the 1980s substantiate the thrust of these written histories. A certain Mihr 'Ali is said to have come in the early Mughal period to the forests of Jessore, also in the Sundarbans, where he helped the local population clear the jungle and make cultivation possible.[27] Again, in the seventeenth century a certain Shah Saiyid Nasir al-Din is said to have come from the Middle East to Habiganj in the Sylhet District, where he taught the local population of a dense jungle region how to cut the jungle and plant rice, as well as the rudiments of Islam.[28]

In all of these accounts the "local people" who came to comprise the Muslim peasantry were not themselves colonists, but indigenous, forest-dwelling folk whose economic and religious lives were, according to their own traditions, transformed through contact with outsiders. The most characteristic such "outsider" that emerges from these traditions is the forest pioneer, whose economic role and whose relationship with the first tillers of the soil are more sharply discernible from a review of relevant British revenue records.

The gazetteer for Noakhali District records that a certain Pir 'Umar Shah, the patron saint of *pagana* Ambarabad, which is named after him, came to the jungles of Noakhali from Iran in the early 1700s and "lived there in his boat working miracles and making multitudes of converts by whom the wastes were gradually reclaimed."[29] The area cleared by him and his local followers covered about 175 square miles of land, and in 1734 the Mughal authorities in Bengal made this area a separate *pagana*, which was the basic territorial unit of Mughal administration. Thirty years later control over revenue collection in Bengal passed from the Mughals to the British, who described this area as a virgin forest recently cleared and brought into cultivation for the first time by a number of small landholders called *jangal-buri ta'luqdar*s, that is, "jungle-clearing" landholders. These *ta'luqdar*s claimed that they had originally been independent of any governmental authority above them, but that later they "requested" the Mughal authorities in Bengal to appoint a collector, or *zamindar*, to manage the collection of their revenue due to the state. For this purpose the *ta'luqdars* allowed the collectors to have an allowance of the revenue of several of their villages in the *pagana*. Most interesting of all, the first two *zamindar* appointed were the sons of Shah 'Umar, the *pir* after whom the *pagana* had been named and who had originally converted the local people to Islam and organized them for the purpose of clearing the jungle.[30]

Analyzing the information given in this account, it would seem that the *pir* associated with these important developments, Pir 'Umar Shah, must have established contact with the forest-dwelling peoples of the Noakhali area before 1734, since that was when the Mughal authorities organized the region into a *pagana*, which is by definition a district capable of producing revenue. It is also clear that before the jungle tract became a Mughal *pagana* the forest peoples who were now cultivators and called themselves *jangal-buri ta'luqdars* had been independent of government authority. But although the *ta'luqdars*' claim to have "requested" superior revenue collector, or *zamindar*, it would seem more likely that Mughal authority in that part of Noakhali had become sufficiently strong by 1734 that the *ta'luqdars* were forced to come to terms with this authority, and so arranged that their collectors should be the sons of the man whom they credited both with organizing them to clear the jungle and with making them Muslims. In other words, as the state incorporated these forest-dwelling peoples in its orbit, the charismatic authority of the *pir* became routinized into the bureaucratic authority of the *pir's* sons, who were now government collectors, or *zamindar*.

Data in the British Indian government's village *mauda* notes collected around 1900 and preserved in the record rooms in district collectorates, reveal a similar picture. Typical is the following terse account of a village in Barisal district: "The Mahomedans owe their origin directly or indirectly to one Kazi [*qadi*: Muslim judge] who was one of the original settlers of this village. These Mahomedans have taluqs."[31] Or again, in Dhaka district we read of a village that in the early eighteenth century had not been included in the government rent rolls and was visited once by a Muslim holy man named Hazrat Daner Mau. Such was the man's charisma that the inhabitants out of reverence for the "good and popular religious man" gave him some regular stipend in the form of *nazrana*, or any gift piously bestowed upon a Muslim saint or shrine. In time, this pious gift became a fixed sum of 118 rupees. And still later, when the Mughal government incorporated the village into its rent rolls, this figure of 118 rupees became the fixed rent owed by the village to the government. At the same time, Hazrat Daner Mau, the holy man, was designated the *zamindar* of the village; that is, the state declared him the officer in charge of revenue collection.[32]

We see the same same process revealed in Persian documents concerning relations between the central government's provincial or district officers and its revenue agents at the most local levels. Dating to the mid-seventeenth century, these records attest to the systematic transfer of virgin jungle territory from the royal domain to members of a petty Muslim gentry—persons who sponsored the construction of mosques or shrines for *pir*s. These were not *waqf* grants—that is, rent-free lands given explicitly to Muslim institutions—since they were given to individuals defined by the state as trustees of mosques or shrines, who nonetheless could and did become de facto and de jure landlords over those territories alienated to them. What one sees revealed in these documents is a jungle-dwelling population, termed dependents in the documents, who were transformed into rice-cultivating peasants and thereby became both economic and religious clients of this new gentry.

One collection of such documents pertains to the colonization and settlement of Chittagong district, located in the southeastern delta facing the bay, by jungle-clearing *ta'luqdar*s, or landholders. These documents reveal a pattern by which grantees contracted with the state to organize local folk for the purpose of clearing forest lands and preparing them for agricultural operations. As this happened, the charismatic authority of these pioneers became stabilized and routinized in their successors who, claiming proprietary rights (*jangal-buri mauruthi*) over the recently cleared land, emerged as effective landlords over a peasant class of client-tenants. This is well illustrated in the case of the sons of a holy man named Shah Lutf Allah Khondkar, who bore the Sufi title *zubdat al-wasilin* ("the best of those joined with God"). In 1717 this man's sons were given about 109 acres of jungle land to cultivate, over which they came to possess hereditary rights (*jangal-buri mauruthi*). This done, they became effective landlords.[33] In a similar case, a certain 'Abd al-Wahhab Khondkar built a mosque where he himself was the *khatib*, or preacher. In 1726 he received a small parcel of land for its support. But just five years later his grandson emerged as the landlord (*chaudhuri*) of the region and was able to expand this estate by getting over seventy-five acres of additional land made out in favor of the mosque.³⁴ Or again, in 1723 two followers of a local holy man, Hazrat Shaha, were able to get twenty-five acres of jungle land for the construction and maintenance of the shrine they had built for their *pir* and ten years later that figure was increased by sixteen acres to cover the additional expenses of supporting the many dependents that they had acquired.³⁵

In these cases, the original authority of the founders of the mosques and shrines—a Sufi, a preacher, and a holy man—had been charismatic in nature. But by the time of their successors or descendants, this authority had become stabilized and routinized in new channels, typically as members of a petty gentry class enjoying direct support from the Mughal state. Weber argues that the charismatic leader is an inherently unstable category, and that his authority will tend to be routinized in the direction either of patrimonial or of bureaucratic office.³⁶ In the present instances, the routinization of the charismatic leaders' authority seems to have been abetted by the efforts of the patrimonial state, the Mughal Empire and its provincial authorities in the city of Chittagong, to encroach upon and to appropriate this local authority. One way the Empire did this was by requiring, as a condition of the grant, the successors' promise to pray for the long life of the emperor and the stability of the state. This requirement effectively brought the recipients into direct, client relationships with the emperor, which relationship is a classic characteristic of the patrimonial state. Another way the state appropriated the charismatic authority of these persons was by integrating their successors into the Empire's bureaucratic system as nontaxpaying rent-receivers.

The other important process seen in these cases is that of Islamization itself. These documents refer to the new communities of people dependent upon the mosques and shrines, the support of which provided one of the rationales of the grant in the first place. The documents also refer to the establishment of new assemblies, or circles of people for the Friday prayers, who had coalesced around these new jungle mosques (*iqamati halqa-yi jum'a*).³⁷ Finally, a deepening of Islamic identity in rural Bengal is seen in the very names of the founders and successors of these institutions. Many of them have names like Kali Shah, Jangal Pir, Kala Ghazi, and the like, suggesting their origins as purely local Bengali holy men. Significantly, though, their successors and heirs tended to bear more purely Arabic names. This pattern becomes especially clear in the mid-eighteenth century, when an increasing number of these institutions were being constructed by *hajis* and others who had more direct contact with Mecca. While such persons associated with rural leadership took the lead in adopting names identified with Islam, many amongst the masses of the Muslim Bengali peasantry retained indigenous names like Chand, Pal, and Dutt even into the twentieth century.[38] This suggests that although these jungle mosques and shrines may well have served as the original nuclei for the diffusion of Islamic rituals, the process of Islamization was anything but sudden or abrupt.

What emerges from these records, then, is a picture of an expanding culture of petty *khan*s, petty *mulla*s, and petty *pir*s all penetrating the jungles of East Bengal in the early eighteenth century, in the meantime incorporating the land along with its local inhabitants into the economic and religious orbit of the Mughal Empire. It was the patrimonial nature of the Mughal state which encouraged, in economic terms, the reclamation of thick jungle lands for rice paddy, and in social terms, the rise of new classes of rice-cultivating peasants tied to the state through extended tenure chains. Weber's notion of the routinization of charismatic authority would seem to explain how holy men, or their descendants, became established as petty revenue officials at the lower ends of those tenure chains. It also suggests why agricultural development and Islamic piety became so closely associated in the minds of today's Muslim peasantry, and why these peoples tend to ascribe their conversion to Islam to persons originally associated not only with religion but also with the reclamation of land for the purpose of rice cultivation. But this process did not necessarily begin in the seventeenth century, which is the period for which extensive paper documentation has survived the ravages of time. No doubt the process these documents reveal was typical of the entire period from the Mughal conquest in the sixteenth century, and even of earlier periods as well, as is suggested by written and oral legends concerning the case of the fifteenth-century Khan Jahan 'Ali.

The Primacy and Identity of the Supreme God

The third of Weber's notions relevant to this analysis pertains to his discussion of cosmology, specifically the pantheon and its relationship to social reality. "The decisive consideration was and remains," he wrote, "who is deemed to exert the stronger influence on the individual in his everyday life, the theoretically supreme god or the lower spirits and demons?"[39] In this connection Weber developed the notion of "rationalization," which he characterized as the crystallization of a pantheon in such a way that a supreme god tends to acquire primacy over the lesser spirits.[40] One of the forces operating to advance the cause of a single, supreme god, he argued, was the growth of empires and their incorporation of culturally heterogeneous peoples; conversely, among the forces operating to protect the cause of lesser spirits were "the powerful material and ideological interests vested in the priests, who resided in the cultic centers and regulated the cults of the particular gods."[41]

Prior to the intrusion of Islamic influence, the religious geography of medieval Bengal presented a mixed and fluid picture. In the western part of the delta a well-entrenched Brahman priesthood presided over both a fully developed Hindu pantheon and a highly stratified society. But Brahmanical influence decreased as one moved into the swamps and jungles of the eastern delta, where forest peoples subscribed to a more complex array of cults, especially those, such as Manasa or Chandi, that focused on the power of Bengali manifestations of female divinity, that is, the Goddess.[42] In this part of the delta, where the pantheon was far less clearly "rationalized"—using Weber's own notion here—than in the more Brahman-ordered western delta, Islam, which celebrates the supreme power of a single god, Allah, secured a firm footing. In medieval Bengali literature one can see how, over the course of several centuries, Islamic conceptions of the identity and nature of divine power were introduced into the Bengali religious universe.

Several interrelated aspects of this process may be observed. At first, Islamic superhuman beings were simply *included* in the existing, already dense Bengali pantheon. For example, in the invocation to a folk ballad called "Nizam Dacoit," dating probably from seventeenth-century Chittagong, we find the balladeer mentioning Bengali equivalents for the Supreme Deity, the Creator, and the Incarnation of Light. Next he invokes the Prophet Muhammad, described as a luminous figure who flashed before the Lord's eye. Then, after praising the female members of the Prophet's family, the balladeer offered his respects to the Himalayas, to Krishna, to Radha, to Mother Earth, to a local *pir*, and finally to Rama and Sita.[43] No attempt was made here either to equate or to replace any one superhuman being with any other; rather, Islamic manifestations of superhuman power—in this case the Prophet Muhammad, Light (no doubt from Sufi origins), and a local *pir*—were simply included in the invocation along with all other possible sources of superhuman power then "in the air" in rural southeastern Bengal.

A second aspect of the process was the attempt not merely to include Islamic superhuman agencies and terms in the Bengali cosmology, but to *identify* those agencies and terms with local equivalents. Such a tendency was by no means unique to Bengal. "I know of no society in West Africa," remarked Jack Goody, "which does not make an automatic identification of their own High God with the Allah of the Muslims and the Jehovah of the Christians. The process is not a matter of conversion but of identification."[44] In Bengali literature dating from the sixteenth century—romances, epics, narratives, and devotional poems—we find identifications of a similar kind. Poets of this literature not only included Perso-Islamic superhuman agencies alongside Bengali ones in a single, expanding religious universe, but actually identified one with the other. Thus the sixteenth-century poet Haji Muhammad identified the Arabic Allah with Gosain (Skt. "Master"),[45] Saiyid Murtaza identified the Prophet's daughter Fatima with Jagat-janani (Skt. "mother of the world"),[46] and towards the end of the sixteenth century Saiyid Sultan identified the God of Adam, Abraham, Moses with Prabhu (Skt. "Lord") or, more frequently, Niranjan (Skt. "One without color," i.e., without qualities).[47] Later, the eighteenth century poet 'Ali Raja identified Allah with Niranjan, Is'var (Skt. "god"), Jagat Is'var (Skt. "god of the universe"), and Kartar (Skt. "Creator").[48] Even while forest pioneers on the eastern frontier were building mosques, thereby planting the institutional foundations of Islamic rituals, Bengali poets deepened the semantic meaning of these rituals by identifying the lore and even the deities of an originally foreign creed with those of the local culture.

As Asim Roy has pointed out, the people for whom this literature was written, the Bengali masses, were ignorant of the Persian or Arabic languages and were steeped in local cults as well as in classical mythology such as the epic *Mahabharata*. By clothing Islam in a Bengali garb, then, the poets consciously sought to reach the masses.[49] One of the most masterful examples of this literature was Saiyid Sultan's epic poem *Nabi-Bamsa*, in which the author interpreted Islam not as replacing or annihilating earlier cults of Bengal, but as succeeding and perfecting them. Thus Brahma, Vishnu, Siva, and Krishna are all presented as successive incarnations (*avatar*) and prophets (*nabi*) of God, each with a "book" appropriate for his time, followed by the Hebrew prophets who propagated *tawhid*, or monotheism, finally culminating in the Prophet Muhammad. Indeed, according to this epic the four Vedas actually prophesied the advent of Muhammad.[50]

The purport of this genre of literature was thus clearly not to detach Islam from the previous religious traditions of eastern Bengal, but to *connect* it with those traditions. Some local *pir*s, identified in the indigenous literature as carriers of the new cult, became apotheosized. At the same time, masses of rural Bengalis continued to pay their devotions to the lesser spirits of the earlier pantheon, or to redefine those spirits in Islamic terms. Thus we find that Muslim cultivators were among those mentioned in medieval literature as devotees of the widespread and thoroughly Bengali cult of the snake goddess Manasa.[51] At the beginning of the twentieth century lower-class Muslims were still described as worshiping the goddess manifested as Manasa, Kali, or Lakshmi.[52] Yet another result of this use of the Bengali language and religious universe for the introduction of Islam was the heavy emphasis on feminine forms of Islamic divine power, reflecting an ancient folk Bengali vision of divine power as manifested through female agency. Accordingly Fatima, the Prophet's daughter, was addressed "mother of the world" by the seventeenth-century poet Saiyid Murtaza, and it was to her name that the poet Hayat Mahmud addressed his *jang-nama*.[53] Over the course of several centuries, then, Islamic conceptions of divine power gradually seeped into a religious universe characterized by an extraordinary fluidity. This is reflected in the medieval *mangal-kavya* literature, in which various deities—most of them manifestations of the Goddess—emerge vying with one another for the cultic allegiance of the Bengali people.

But though Islam may at first have appeared like another cult in the Bengali atmosphere, just one more "exotic flower" thriving in the delta's fertile soil, in time it acquired a rigidity and stability that helped render it autonomous from more local cults, and in time, to displace them altogether. One cannot explain this aspect of the process only in sociopolitical terms, as Weber himself would have, that is, the incorporation of Bengal into the Mughal Empire and the identification of Islam with that empire. For in the history of Islam in South Asia, political power seems to have been a necessary but not a sufficient variable patterning Islamic conversions, as is witnessed by the relatively low incidence of Islamization in Upper India, the heartland of Indo-Muslim power.

Perhaps more decisive, especially along the empire's expanding periphery, was a cognitive factor: Islam's literate basis endowed it with the capacity to be preserved and replicated far more easily than indigenous cults which, lacking such a basis, tended to be more transient and less fixed. This was especially true in eastern Bengal, whose indigenous peoples had been exposed to Brahmanical literary or social influences to a much lesser extent than was the case in the West. In the East the oral literatures associated with local cults may have praised the power or auspiciousness of this or that divinity, but such literatures were understood as human in origin. Moreover, they were nonliturgical in nature, and as such were marginal to the cults' ongoing functioning. Islam's literary basis, on the other hand, gave that religion a structural rigidity that ultimately proved decisive in its competition with rival cults, a phenomenon also noticed with respect to the advance of both Islam and Christianity in modern West Africa.[54]

This relates to the well-known fact that Islam is preeminently a religion of the Book. Not only is the Quran understood as divine in origin, but its scripture is central to Islamic liturgy. It is therefore of great significance that the diffusion of paper and papermaking technology in Bengal, which in turn provided the basis for the diffusion of the written word itself, occurred just prior to the Mughal conquest in the sixteenth century. First introduced in North India by the Turks in the thirteenth century, paper replaced the palm leaf in Bengal in the fifteenth century. It is probable that copies of the Quran were first introduced at the court of the Bengal sultanate at this time.[55] Around 1590 the poet Mukundaram referred to a section of Muslim society as "Kagozia," or papermakers,[56] meaning that by the late sixteenth-century papermaking technology had already diffused in the delta.

Among the Bengali masses in the medieval period, it seems that the earliest use of the Quran was not liturgical but magical in nature. Accordingly, in a mid-seventeenth-century poem praising the goddess Manasa, we find references to the Quran being used as a charm to ward off evil influences.[57] At that time rival cults devoted to various gods and goddesses—some derived from the Hindu pantheon, others purely local—continued to thrive side by side with Islam. But after about the mid-seventeenth century the Quran is found to be used more in a liturgical than in a magical context, and as this happened the content of the Book—above all its message of the unity and supremacy of Allah—began to acquire great fixity. Although the movement from magical to liturgical intensified in the nineteenth century under the influence of the Fara'izi reformists, on the whole it was a gradual process. Just as the adoption of Arabic personal names was very slow, as we have seen above, so also the adoption of "Allah" as the exclusive name of the Supreme God took time. As late as the beginning of the twentieth century, in fact, it was noted that "Allah" had only recently replaced "Panch Pir" and "Badar" as the divine name called upon by Muslim boatmen of Noakhali district.[58] This is a sure sign that the Islamization process was well on its way.

Conclusion

In conclusion, one finds a remarkable coincidence of three very different but interrelated types of diffusions that occurred simultaneously in late medieval Bengal—Mughal political authority, the frontier of settled agriculture, and papermaking technology. Individually, and in combination, these helped pattern a fourth diffusion, that of Islamic piety itself. It is best, however, not to disaggregate these factors into separate components, but to see them acting together as forces for the integration of a local society into a world civilization. The diffusion of paper technology, for example, strengthened Mughal bureaucratic authority; and the extension of Mughal authority, carrying with it the leaders and capital necessary for the laborious task of clearing the jungles, as well as the planting of tiny mosques and shrines in the formerly forested hinterland, was likewise critical for the growth of rice-cultivating peasant communities.

Therefore, the growth of Islam was one aspect of a larger societal transformation that took place in late medieval Bengal. This suggests that we do a disservice to our understanding of religion if we treat it as an isolate, an entity detached from larger social, economic, and even ecological processes. Max Weber seems to have understood this. Even if he did not adequately accomplish the task of describing the Islamization process in his specific but scattered references to Islam, he did provide some powerful analytical tools with which we can do the work.

Notes

1. Max Weber, *The Sociology of Religion*, trans. Ephraim Fischoff (Boston: Beacon Press: 1963), 132, 203–04, 227, 262–63.
2. Ibid., 264–65.
3. Ibid., 264, 265.
4. Max Weber, *The Religion of India: the Sociology of Hinduism and Buddhism*, trans. and ed. Hans H. Gerth and Don Martindale (New York: Free Press, 1967).
5. Ibid., 6.
6. Ibn Battuta, *The Rehla of Ibn Battuta*, trans. Mahdi Husain (Baroda: Oriental Institute, 1953), 238–39.
7. Ma Huan, *Ying-ya Sheng-lan: the Overall Survey of the Ocean's Shores*, trans. J. V. G. Mills (Cambridge: Cambridge University Press, 1970), 160; Tome Pires,

The Suma Oriental of Tome Pires, trans. A. Cortesao (London: Hakluyt Society, 1944), 1:89.
8. Duarte Barbosa, *The Book of Duarte Barbosa*, trans. M. L. Dames (London: Hakluyt Society, 1921), 2:148.
9. Samuel Purchas, *Hakluytus Posthumus, or Purchas his Pilgrimes*, 20 vols. (Glasgow: James MacLehose & Sons, 1905), 5:137.
10. H. Hosten, "Jesuit Letters from Bengal, Arakan and Burma (1599–1600)," *Bengal Past and Present*, 30 (1925), 59.
11. L. Cardon and H. Hosten, "Padre Maistro Fray Seb. Manrique in Bengal (1628–29)," *Bengal Past and Present*, 13/1 (July-September 1916), 10–11.
12. S. H. Askeri, "The Mughal-Magh Relations down to the Time of Islam Khan Mashhadi," *Indian History Congress, Proceedings*, 22nd session (1959), 210.
13. Munshi Muhammad Kazim bin Muhammad Amin, *'Alamgir-nama*, ed. Khadim Husain and 'Abd al-Hai (Calcutta: Asiatic Society of Bengal, 1868), 677.
14. N. D. Bhattacharya, "Changing Courses of the Padma and Human Settlements," *National Geographic Journal of India*, 24/1–2 (March-June 1978), 65; S. C. Majumdar, *Rivers of the Bengal Delta* (Calcutta: University of Calcutta, 1942), 65–72; W. H. Arden Wood, "Rivers and Man in the Indus-Ganges Alluvial Plain," *Scottish Geographical Magazine*, 40/1 (1924), 5–10; R. K. Mukerjee, *The Changing Face of Bengal: a Study of Riverine Economy* (Calcutta: University of Calcutta, 1938), 9–10, 164–228.
15. See Max Weber, *The Theory of Social and Economic Organization*, trans. A. M. Henderson and Talcott Parsons (New York: Free Press, 1964), 347; Bryan S. Turner, *Weber and Islam: a Critical Study* (London: Routledge & Kegan Paul, 1974), 81–82, 172.
16. Stephen Blake, "The Patrimonial-Bureaucratic Empire of the Mughals," *Journal of Asian Studies*, 39/1 (November 1979): 77–94.
17. A. Halim, "An Account of the Celebrities of Bengal of the Early Years of Shahjahan's Reign Given by Muhammad Sadiq," *Journal of the Pakistan Historical Society*, 1 (1953): 355.
18. Jadunath Sarkar, ed. *History of Bengal*, vol. 2, *Muslim Period, 1200–1757* (Patna: Janaki Prakashan, 1977), 187–88.
19. C. A. Bayly, *Rulers, Townsmen, and Bazaars: North Indian Society in the Age of British Expansion, 1770–1870* (Cambridge: Cambridge University Press, 1983), 192.
20. Risley Collection: "Reports on the Religious and Social Divisions amongst the Mahomedans of Bengal," India Office Library (European MSS. E 295), 9:88; E. A. Gait, "Muhammadan Castes and Tribes," *Census of India, 1901*, vol. 6: *The Lower Provinces of Bengal and their Feudatories*, pt. 1, "Report," 439.
21. The anthropologist John Thorp has found that among rural Bengali Muslims of the present day it is believed that God created Adam out of the earth in order that he might possess the earth and be its master, or *malik*. Thus Adam exercised his mastery of the earth by farming it, and all the groups of men descended from Adam are also considered to have farmed the land. The act of tilling the soil, then, is considered not just an occupation, but virtually a sacrament in that it symbolically connects the peasant with Adam, and thus with God. John P. Thorp, "Masters of Earth: Conceptions of 'Power' among Muslims of Rural Bangladesh" (Ph.D. dissertation, University of Chicago, 1978), 54.
22. That such exploitation lay at the heart of official Mughal ideology is reflected in the following imperial *farman* of Emperor Aurangzeb, dated 1668, which ordered that Mughal officials "should practice benevolence to the cultivators, inquire into their condition, and exert themselves judiciously and tactfully, so that

the cultivators may joyfully and heartily try to increase the cultivation, and every arable tract may be brought under tillage." Jadunath Sarkar, "The Revenue Regulations of Aurangzib," *Studies in Mughal India* (Calcutta: Sarkai & Sons, 1919).
23. Computed from data in Abu'l-fazl, *Ayn-i Akbari* (compiled 1595), as given in Shireen Moosvi, *The Economy of the Mughal Empire, c. 1595; A Statistical Study* (Delhi: Oxford University Press, 1987), 26–27; *Dastur al-'amal-i 'Alamgiri* (compiled 1659) (British Library MS., Add. 6599), fols. 120a–121a.
24. From Rs. 175,458 to Rs. 337,761. L. S. S. O'Malley, *Eastern Bengal District Gazetteers: Chittagong* (Calcutta: Bengal Secretariat Book Depot, 1980), 137.
25. Mohendra Nath Karan, *Hijli Masnad-i 'Ala*, 2nd ed. (Calcutta: Medinipur Sanskriti Parishad, 1958), 62. Cited in Sultan Jahan Ahmad, "Muslim Society in Midnapur—a Social Study of a Bengal District (1800–1919 A.D.). Ph.D. dissertation (Calcutta: Jadavpur University, 1982), 58.
26. H. Blochmann, "Contributions to the Geography and History of Bengal," *Journal of the Asiatic Society of Bengal*, 42/3 (1873): 227; L. S. S. O'Malley, *Bengal District Gazetteers: Khulna* (Calcutta: Bengal Secretariat Book Depot, 1908), 26–27; J. Westland, *A Report on the District of Jessore: its Antiquities, its History, and its Commerce*, 2nd ed. (Calcutta: Bengal Secretariat, 1870), 19–21.
27. Interview with Muhammad Sharif Husain, secretary, Jessore Public Library, Kharki Post, District Jessore, May 19, 1982.
28. Interview with Muhammad Badrul Huda, Noakhali District Collectorate Record Room, June 17, 1982.
29. J. E. Webster, *Eastern Bengal and Assam District Gazetteers: Noakhali* (Allahabad: Pioneer Press, 1911), 100–101.
30. W. H. Thompson, *Final Report on the Survey and Settlement Operations in the District of Noakhali, 1914–11* (Calcutta: Bengal Secretariat Book Depot, 1919), 60–61.
31. Barisal District Collectorate Record Room. Mauza Note Registers. Gaurnadi *thana*, vol. 1, village R.S. 696.
32. Dhaka District Collectorate Record Room. Mauza Note Registers, Narayanganj *thana*, vol. 9, No. 4269 (Narayanganj No. 437).
33. "Kanun Daimer Nathi," Chittagong District Collectorate Record Room, bundle 44, case 2792.
34. Ibid., bundle 51, case 3321.
35. Ibid., bundle 56, case 3626.
36. Weber, *Theory of Social and Economic Organization*, 379–80.
37. "Kanun Daimer Nathi," Chittagong District Collectorate Record Room, bundle 62, case 4005.38. A. K. Nazmul Karim, *Changing Society in India and Pakistan: a Study in Social Change and Social Stratification* (Dacca: Oxford University Press, 1956), 132.
39. Weber, *Sociology of Religion*, 20.
40. Ibid., 22.
41. Ibid., 23–24.
42. Abdul Majid Khan, "Research about Muslim Aristocracy in East Pakistan," *Social Research in East Pakistan*, ed. Pierre Bessaignet (Dacca: Asiatic Society of Pakistan, 1964); Nihirranjan Ray, "Medieval Bengali Culture," *Visva-Bharati Quarterly*, 11/1 (August-October 1945): 47–52.
43. D. C. Sen., trans. and ed. *Eastern Bengal Ballads: Mymensing*, 4 vols. (Calcutta: University of Calcutta, 1923–28), 2:283–84. For a discussion of the authenticity and dating of this important category of folk literature, see Dusan Zbavitel, *Bengali*

Folk-ballads from Mymensingh and the Problem of their Authenticity (Calcutta: University of Calcutta, 1963), 14.
44. Jack Goody, "Religion, Social Change, and the Sociology of Conversion," in *Changing Social Structure in Ghana*, ed. J. Goody (London: International African Institute, 1975), 103.
45. Haji Muhammad, *Nur Jamal*. Dhaka: Dhaka University Library, MS No. 374; sl. 260, fol. 6 mc. Cited in Asim Roy, "Islam in the Environment of Medieval Bengal" (Ph.D. dissertation, Australian National University, 1970), 194. 46. Saiyid Murtaza, *Yoga-Qalandar*. Dhaka: Dhaka University Library, MS No. 547: sl. 394, fol. 1a. Cited in Asim Roy, "Islam in the Environment," 299.
47. Saiyid Sultan, *Nabi-Bamsa*, ed. Ahmed Sharif (Dhaka: Bangla Academy, 1978), 1: 1 ff.
48. 'Ali Raja, *Jñana-sagara*. Dhaka: Dhaka University Library, MS. No. 146b: sl. 9, fols. 109, 215, 216. Cited in Asim Roy, "Islam in the Environment," 199, 202.
49. Asim Roy, *The Islamic Syncretistic Tradition in Bengal* (Princeton: Princeton University Press, 1983), 68–70.
50. M. R. Tarafdar, *Husain Shahi Bengal, 1494–1583 A.D.: a Socio-Political Study* (Dacca: Asiatic Society of Pakistan, 1965), 224.
51. Ibid., 164; Sukumar Sen, *History of Bengali Literature* (New Delhi: Sahitya Akademi, 1960) 52; P. K. Maity, *Historical Studies in the Cult of the Goddess Manasa* (Calcutta: Punthi Pustak, 1966), 182.
52. Risley Collection, 9:9, 249.
53. Roy, *Islamic Syncretistic Tradition*, 94.
54. Goody, "Religion, Social Change, and the Sociology of Conversion," 101–105; see also J. D. Y. Peel, "Syncretism and Social Change," *Comparative Studies in Society and History*, 10 (1967–68), 124–25.
55. Jeremiah P. Losty, *The Art of the Book in India* (London: British Library, 1982), 10–11, 40.
56. Cited in J. N. Das Gupta, *Bengal in the Sixteenth Century* (Calcutta: University of Calcutta, 1914), 91–92.
57. D. C. Sen, *History of Bengali Language and Literature*, 2nd ed. (Calcutta: University of Calcutta, 1954), 674.
58. Risley Collection, 9:417.

5

Max Weber and the Patrimonial Empire in Islam: The Mughal Case[1]

Peter Hardy

In his *Wirtschaft und Gesellschaft*, Egypt, China, and medieval Europe figure more noticeably both as locations for, and as providing distinctive specifications of, Weber's ideal types, patrimonial domination and the patrimonial state, than do areas under Muslim rule. Weber limits his methodical treatment of patrimonialism in Islam to areas under the later Abbasid caliphate, the Mamluke sultans and the Ottoman Turks, and even for those areas he provides, advisedly, few tools for understanding how patrimonial regimes developed in them. In *Wirtschaft und Gesellschaft*, Mughal India is barely even mentioned.[2] Nevertheless, elsewhere, in *Gesammelte Aufsatze zur Religionssoziologie* II, *Hinduismus und Buddhismus,*[3] Weber sets out a fuller account of a "host" society which accommodated Muslim patrimonial regimes than those he offered for Abbasid Iraq, Mamluke Egypt, or Ottoman Turkey. Moreover, *Gesammelte Aufsatze*, II betrays Weber's belief that the features Indian society he depicts as existing before any Muslim conquests, persisted into the period of Mughal domination.[4]

In "Die 'Objektivitat' sozialwissenschaftlicher und sozial-politischer Erkenntnis," Weber warns against the danger, as he sees it, of imputing causative force, genetic power, in history to ideal constructs of a developmental sequence and abstract concepts of stable relationships perceived to exist in human society amid the flux of events.[5] Any such ideal constructs and abstract concepts ("ideal types") as Weber advances in *Gesammelte Aufsatze*, II, *Hinduismus und Buddhismus*, have, as have all "ideal types," a heuristic value rather than an empirical reality. All that one is allowed to conclude (in order to remain faithful to Weber), is that before the Mughal, indeed before any Muslim, regime was established, Indian society with such and such general characteristics, witnessed the emergence of forms of political domination that Weber would describe as patrimonial.

Weber views the story of Indian society and civilization in the ancient and medieval periods, as one in which political allegiances were limited in social range; India was a region of ever-present warfare, the participants in which were able to form geographically extensive stable political units only intermittently. He sees early India as the home of allegiances and relationships organized on the principle of the charisma of the well-born, of the kin, a charisma[6] of lineages claiming outstanding magical powers and other efficacies by reason of descent from charismatic chieftains. This principle, at first strong among warriors, extended in course of time beyond warriors to those engaged in priestly, agricultural, craft and commercial activity. With those who exercised military and priestly power becoming stratified according to special efficacies inhering in particular lineages, all social groups tended to follow suit; Indian society settled into an hierarchical mould wherein hereditary, endogamous groups were, at least in part, ranked according to relative ritual status with accompanying gradations of purity and impurity. These and other considerations determined the social circles within which connubium and commensality were permissible. Weber contends that the social distances between strata inhibited the possible development of political community, notably urban political community; they gave warrior kings opportunities for dividing and ruling.

War, politics (as the rallying of wills) and rulership (as the management and distribution of resources) were, in these circumstances, the specialism of a professional stratum, claiming a high ritual status, that of the *kshatriya*. Organized principally in tribes, clans and sibs, *kshatriyas* competed for control of the major resource of agricultural production. Successful warrior groups assigned land to their members; the latter either undertook cultivation themselves or employed others (sometimes drawn from members of conquered lineages) to cultivate for them as "tenants." Or members of the dominant lineage might settle in villages and organize jointly the distribution of landholdings among themselves and others. The tribal, clan, or sib chief would, from outside the village, claim a proportion of the production of the village's landholdings, the collection of which could be organized by a local notable drawn from the locally dominant lineage, or by an agent appointed from outside by the chief.

Weber does not specifically contend, in *Hinduismus und Buddhismus*, that political entities in India which manifested, perhaps demanded, other wider allegiances than those of tribe, clan, or sib (such political entities as the Mauryan and Gupta empires), were necessarily patrimonial political entities, that is, entities created and maintained by personal ties between masters and servants, patrons and clients, benefactors and beneficiaries. In *Hinduismus und Buddhismus* he does, however, note a number of features in Indian polities that he specifically associates with patrimonialism: indeed some of them persist, he writes, into Mughal times. Thus Hindu kings confined the interest of their administration essentially to the raising of manpower for the army and to the raising of taxes. Patrimonial rulers, in so far as they operate in the interstices of inherited kin or group allegiances, have an interest in seeking legitimation from religious authority: the great Hindu patrimonial empires looked to the Brahman in this context. Patrimonial rulers, for similar reasons, need to avoid becoming dependent for resources on potentially overmighty interest groups, particularly those with some independent financial standing. Weber depicts patrimonial rulers in ancient India as cooperating with Brahmans in order to deny guilds high status and as looking to merchant monopolists of royal creation to counterbalance independent financiers. Then Weber writes of kingly administration becoming bureaucratic and patrimonial but with the indeterminate spheres of jurisdiction that in *Wirtschaft und Gesellschaft,* he regards as characteristic of patrimonial regimes as such. Also characteristic was the use of officials from a variety of status groups.

However, there were two features of the patrimonial ideal type which Weber sees as manifested most particularly by the Mughals, though those features were, he indicated, not without precedent in earlier Indian history. They were the "military prebend" and the tax prebend. With the first, the king commissioned an individual to recruit soldiers on his behalf and assigned him, or leased to him, the yields from (principally) the land revenue necessary for the maintenance of those soldiers in the royal service; with the second, the king farmed out the right to collect taxes on condition that the tax-farmer paid the king an agreed or set lump sum.[7]

In *Wirtschaft und Gesellschaft* Weber conceives patrimonial domination as a decentralized form of patriarchal domination which emerges when younger members of a patriarchal household, dependants as well as members of the patriarch's family, are settled on lands some distance from, but still under the control of, that household. Certainly the two first Mughal chiefs in India, Babur and Humayun, devolved upon members of their family and other members of their highly mobile households military charges and revenue collecting assignments over wide areas of northern India. In Akbar's period, as Stephen P. Blake has underlined, Abu'l Fazl gives an account of the royal household where officers exercising geographically wide-ranging military and administrative functions, are depicted as members of the royal household; in that account too, a distinction between household finance and "government" finance is often not made.[8] The society of the Mughal elite never lost a patriarchal flavor in that the great nobles always organized the conduct of their duties and the pursuit of their interests, around and through their household establishments. Furthermore, for many Mughal notables, the code of service to the emperor was evoked by a single term *khanazadi,* "being born of the house," connoting devoted familial service from generation to generation.[9]

Central to Weber's "ideal type" of patrimonialism, is the intensely personal, man-to-man character of allegiance and the absence of any formal limits to, or conditions of, that allegiance. Once a patrimonial servant or client has acknowledged a master or a patron, then all the former's time and energy is to be devoted to service, any service. Other worldly loyalties, to kin and to ethnic group, for example, come second. Now a succession of modern historians has demonstrated[10] how Akbar and his successors cultivated personal relationships of loyalty through direct intercourse with a wide variety of men, at court, on the battlefield, in the hunt, in personal interviews: how, by the beginning of Jahangir's reign (1605–1627), in the so-called *mansabdari* (appointment-holding) system, Akbar had succeeded in creating a corps d'elite embracing immigrants from Iran, Central Asia, Indian Muslims, Hindu Rajputs. Recruitment was widened in the seventeenth-century to include Muslims from the Deccan, Marathas and high-status Hindus with administrative and financial skills such as Brahmans and Kayasthas. Although Mughal *mansabdars* (appointment-holders) were graded according to a known hierarchy of statuses and paid according to fixed scales related, in part, to military obligations (where imposed), they were not under contract, were not confined to precise spheres of office and jurisdiction in a bureaucratic mode (though there was inevitably some specialisation), but were individually and often directly responsible "day and night," to the emperor, irrespective of status. John Richards has pointed to the Mughal officers' practice of referring to themselves as *banda-i dargah* (slave of the court) and to the Mughal emperor's assertion of a right to seize the estates of his officers.[11] In that Mughal *mansabdars* were usually free men in terms of Islamic law, we have here exemplified a feature of the patrimonial model.

In many respects the Mughal military system manifested the patrimonial characteristics set out in *Wirtschaft und Gesellschaft*. Abu'l Fazl's *Ayn-i Akbari* displays Akbar's regime as able to raise mercenary troops out of supplies and revenues belonging to the ruler: individual troopers already possessing horses, men of good social standing who were recruited directly by officers of the royal household and paid directly from the royal treasuries; contingents raised by *mansabdars* who were paid either directly from the Mughal treasuries, or by revenues assigned to the *mansabdars* (the military prebends) of *Hinduismus und Buddhismus'* horsemen and infantry of lower standing too poor initially to supply their own mounts or equipment, who were recruited by officers of the royal household and paid in cash from the central treasury for the most part. The Mughal *padshah* was supposed to enjoy a monopoly of the control of artillery and elephants.

The manner in which the Mughals employed, or attempted to employ, their servants in the control of their empire, manifests several of the strategies that, in *Wirtschaft und Gesellschaft* [12] Max Weber represents patrimonial rulers as having followed in order to perpetuate their regimes. The Mughals required *mansabdars* (and others) to attend them at court, to take part in festivals and ceremonies, and not to leave court without permission. Those appointed to the principal "provincial" and "district" offices in the empire, the *subadars* and *faujdars*, held their appointments at pleasure and tended to move around at intervals whether by way of promotion, transfer or demotion. Those granted assignments of revenue (*jagirs*) so that they may support the responsibilities of *mansabdari* appointments (or other employment) received their assignments also at pleasure, on a temporary tenure, for the most part. The Mughals split up spheres of jurisdiction and sought to route lines of responsibility running from lower-status appointees directly to themselves, rather than routing them necessarily or inevitably through the principal military and administrative agents in "provincial" areas. Thus, for example, the principal finance officer (*diwan*) or principal "muster master" (*bakhshi*) of a Mughal province, could and did report direct to the centre, and not necessarily through the *subadar*, the so-called provincial governor. And so too in lower spheres of authority where, for example, the district military commander and executive, the *faudjdar* and the district finance officer, *'amalguzar* or *'amil*, reported separately if need be to different departments at the centre, sometimes indeed to the emperor himself. The Mughal ruler tried to retain control of the levy of resources from his subject population by, for example, regulating the manner in which land revenue was assessed and collected, the rate of assessment and, also, the kind of persons by whom the revenue was collected. Assignees (prebendaries) or their agents, were supposed only to collect the revenue in accordance with rules and authorizations made by officials at the center:[13] tax farming was far from being a favoured Mughal practice in the "high" period of Mughal rule, although *jagirdars* themselves sometimes resorted to it. The Mughals acted in a patrimonial idiom, in relation to their servants when they adopted systematic methods of gathering intelligence about the conduct of their agents, by the appointment of *waqi'a-i navis* and *sawanih-nigar*, so called reporters and newswriters. Stephen P. Blake has also pointed out that the Mughals spent a great part of their time as rulers moving about the country; he shows that Akbar spent a fifth of his reign away from a fixed capital, Shah Jahan nearly a half, and Aurangzib about two-thirds.[14]

The India over which the Mughals had gained power displayed several of the social and political characteristics which, in *Wirtschaft und Gesellschaft*, Weber saw to be associated with forms of patrimonial domination (and some of which, in *Hinduismus und Buddhismus* he saw as existing in ancient India many centuries before the Mughal conquests). The Mughals lorded it over an armed countryside: in the *Ayn-i Akbari*, Abu' I Fazl writes[15] of over 4,400,000 armed men, men not recruited and paid by the Mughal regime, under *zamindars* (landholders), many of whom fitted Weber's category of local patrimonial powers or *honoratiores*. Many of these *zamindars* could be described as chiefs of charismatic lineages, clans, and tribes, with power and influence extending in some instances over small kingdoms, in others over a small cluster of villages. To Nurul Hasan, Irfan Habib, to B. R. Grover and to Ahsan Raza Khan[16] we owe awareness of the several different shapes and sizes of *zamindars*' power and privilege; but in two characteristics they were all, rivals of the Mughal patrimonial ruler—they all enjoyed power to redistribute the produce of the soil, and they all could exercise some force, however circumscribed, in relation to other elements of the general population.

A second characteristic of society under Mughal supremacy was the existence of what Weber calls "a consensual community," composed of those who are not the personal servants, officers or retainers of the patrimonial lord and who, whatever limitations upon their freedom of movement and occupation and possession may be imposed by custom and convention, are free of the ruler's sanctions in these respects, unless perhaps they fail to meet certain traditional obligations (such as paying taxes), which arise outside any relationship of personal dependence upon the patrimonial ruler. A "consensual community" is "consensual" in that its members believe that the ruler's powers are legitimate insofar as they are traditional, (or so Weber explains).[17] Prima facie, the components of such a "consensual community" existed in Mughal India. They would, in my view, include: all those who, without previous connection with the Mughals, voluntarily presented themselves for service; all those members of religious communities, sects, orders, who accepted Mughal pensions and grants, whether in cash or as revenue-free lands; all those Muslim jurists and Hindu *pandits* who advised the Mughals on Islamic or Hindu legal norms; all those merchants, who sought favors from the Mughals; all those moneylenders who lent money to Mughal officers so that they could fulfil their obligations, fiscal and military, to their emperor; all those grain dealers who purchased the cultivators' crops so that the latter could pay the land revenue demand when made in cash; all those *zamindars* who offered their loyalty to the Mughals of their own volition, perhaps to steal a march on other *zamindars* with whom they were engaged in local rivalry; all those cultivators who, without duress, paid land revenue in the *khalisa* (areas reserved for direct management by officials of the royal finance department) in the knowledge that the revenue was for the emperor's own exchequer rather than for that of an intermediary.

Weber characterizes the authority of the patrimonial ruler not, in relation to his own retainers and servants, limited by binding contracts; any regulations the ruler may issue for his relations with his subjects outside his own clientage, are also not binding on him. Nevertheless in practice (though vis-à-vis groups rather than individuals), he is disinclined to shock old loyalties and to inhibit the growth of new ones, by open breaches with inherited tradition. In what terms then, could the Mughal regime give impressions of acting according to, or within, traditional norms for rulers in India? The "high command" of the Mughal empire was, after all, predominantly Muslim by profession and India's population mainly non-Muslim; many historians[18] and others since the creation of Pakistan in 1947 (and some before), have pointed to the obstacles religion would seem to place in the way of Muslims and non-Muslims sharing political traditions, obstacles such that rule by followers of Islam was unlikely to be accepted as authoritative by followers of other religions.

Mughal rulers displayed themselves (or were displayed by others who supported their regime), in many different guises and in several different lights, as ruling in accordance with received tradition. The names stamped on coins, and other coin legends, would show them professing to be Muslims and their chief and mint towns to be "abodes of the *khilafat*." The exordia to most of the Persian histories written in Mughal times in India, described Mughal rulers as, "shadows of God," and as agents of God into whose hands had been entrusted the furtherance of Islam and the protection, if not the direct enforcement of Islamic law. Armed opposition to them by any who had entered into obligations of servanthood and allegiance to them, was excoriated by historians as "treachery and ingratitude"—an idiom redolent of that used in the Qur'an of unbelievers who show ingratitude to God for the blessings He has conferred upon them.[19] Willingness to acknowledge a master appears, in the language historians use, to involve willingness to enter into a one-sided covenantal relationship with him, in which all the obligations flow from the servant to and master of man as in the primeval covenant of man with God (Quran, VII, 171–172). Violence against Mughal rulers (as against their predecessors the Sultans of Delhi) is often depicted as schism in language which calls up thoughts of the great schisms and rebellions afterwards considered by partisans to threaten the very existence of the early Muslim community and the integrity of the religious message it bore. The implication of such use of language is that the Mughals were in the line of rightful Muslim rulers entitled to the conscientious obedience of fellow Muslims.

The appeal to Muslim traditions of rulership was made at other levels. Mughal rulers patronized Muslim scholars, jurists and members of the Sufi orders. Sometimes Mughal armies were described as armies of Islam and sometimes their opponents were described as unbelievers. Aurangzib was eulogised for imposing the tax on unbelievers (*jizya*) and for authorising the destruction of temples. Abu'l Fazl, in an essentially Islamic linguistic idiom, praised Akbar as a figure of cosmic significance, a recipient of divine light, a possessor of esoteric knowledge of the divine realities, and the expression, if not the fulfilment, in his person, of many of the ethical and religious aspirations of the contemporary Islamic world. Akbar and his successor, Jahangir, were proclaimed to be Sufi guides (*murshid*), Shah Jahan a renewer of Islam in his, the tenth-century after *hijra*.[20]

The Mughals evoked traditional values in actions which could and did endow them with authority among politically important groups of the non-Muslim population. Akbar's taking of wives from great Rajput lineages in Rajasthan, attracted to him the sentiments of fellowship and solidarity felt by Rajputs towards kin by marriage. Norman Ziegler has shown that in Rajput tradition, as a warrior king, the Mughal emperor was equated with Rama, "the preeminent *kshatriya* cultural hero of the Hindu Rajput." [21] The Mughals by their actions towards *zamindars*, great chiefs as well as towards village notables, acted within traditions going back to ancient India in that they usually left a *zamindar* with his local status and authority provided that he made due acknowledgment of Mughal superiority. The Mughals preferred to win over opponents and potential opponents by generosity, or by "bribes," before resorting to force. The outward and visible signs of Mughal grandeur and prowess were very much in a traditional Indian idiom—a magnificent court, lavish public spectacle on festive occasions, awesome buildings and fortifications, impressive public works such as bridges and caravansaries. Then the rulers themselves often gave the appearance of being "larger than life," with their large *harams*, manly distinction on the field of battle and in the hunt, and their lavish generosity.

Learned groups of non-Muslims could also see the Mughal ruler to behave traditionally. Brahmans as well as Muslim scholars received patronage, though probably less. Brahman astrologers (as well as Muslim) were consulted in decisions on auspicious times and days. Brahmans and Kayasthas were prominent in the Mughal patrimonial bureaucracy. *Pandits* advised the Mughal courts on *dharmasastra* (the Hindu science of duty and law). Although Akbar is reported to have attempted to interfere with Hindu marriage customs and to prevent self-immolation by Hindu widows, and although Aurangzib is reported to have encouraged conversion to Islam, such royal interventions into Hindu society appear to have been whimsical and irregular, if we survey Mughal rule in the round. In common with most premodern regimes, the Mughal regime accepted the social structures it encountered. It gave the impression of wanting to make the most of India as she was. If, partly as a result of the Mughal ability, through its revenue system, to transfer resources from the countryside to the towns, or from one region of the empire to another and distant region, social change occurred (as for example, an enlargement in size or an increase in prestige of certain brokering, credit-providing or long-distance trading groups) then that social change might go unremarked as an unintended by-product of the demands of Mughal public finance.

To recapitulate in order to proceed. Weber sees the successful working of a patrimonial polity as contingent upon the maintenance of three skeins of relationships between the patrimonial chief and specific elements of the peoples of his realm. Those skeins are, first that linking the ruler as patron with the clients who manage his affairs beyond his personal reach (administrative officers), second that linking him with those ready and organized to fight for him (his armed forces) and third, that linking him with those who are themselves chiefs able to lead followings and command privileges as autochthonus notables. As has been explained, these three skeins of relationships constituted the Mughal regime in India as Akbar had, by his death in 1605, constituted it. And now to proceed. During the last quarter of the seventeenth century and the first quarter of the eighteenth, all three of these skeins in Mughal India loosened, indeed, individual threads within those skeins were severed and not replaced.

From the early 1680s when the emperor Aurangzib and his court moved, in the event permanently, to the Deccan, the Mughals were engaged in continuous and spreading conflict south of the river Tapti. Although the Mughals destroyed the sultanate of Bijapur in 1686 and that of Golkonda in 1687, they failed to overcome the challenge offered by the Maratha Bhonsle family, whose great hero Shivaji had set himself up as a consecrated Hindu king in 1674. Although Mughal forces captured and killed Shivaji's grandson Sambhaji in 1689, at no time did Aurangzib achieve pacification before he died in 1707. The concentration of imperial armies for the taking of Marathat hill-forts (achieved only after lenghtly sieges) left many hintherlands unprotected against depredations by Maratha raiding bands led by small Maratha land-holding gentry turn warrior chiefs.[22]

Aurangzib's demand for revenue and resources from the "peaceful" regions of his empire became dangerously exigent. In north India where governors of provinces, "district commissioners" and finance officers now had no opportunity for particiapting in the ceremonies of personal commitment and loyalty to an imperial patron sitting in court *durbar* or public audience, the mechanisms of central control began to falter. Officers successful in meeting demands for the transfer of revenues to the Deccan were patronized, kept in place and given an extended authority for long periods. The customary disciplines of control, transfer to new and unfamiliar provinces and districts, regular inspection of revenue accounts, personal summons to court for the accounting for performance, began to relax. Officers allowed to remain long "in post" were able to form local connections, acquire clients as if they were patrimonial chiefs and, moreover, develop allegiances to royal princes envisaging an interfamily war of sucession on Aurangzib's death.[23]

The stresses of the Deccan conflicts and of the Mughal wars of succession between 1707 and 1720 weakened and sometimes broke the threads of relationship between the Mughal ruler and his military. The strength of the Mughal army lay in its heavy cavalry raised for the most part by appointed officers (*mansabdars*) who were also commissioned, on appointment to recruit and command a contingent of specified number, with pay according to set scales. That pay would be disbursed to the *mansabdar* either directly from a royal treasury with income from taxes collected directly by treasury appointees, or from collections made by the *mansabdar's* own agents where he had been assigned a revenue-yielding area of source (e.g., internal customs) called a *jagir*, assessed as yielding sum sanctioned. Clearly, receipt of the sanctioned pay would be problematical where, for example, Maratha incursions interfered with revenue collections and receipts, or where the Mughal emperor or his headquarters agents were making more appointments or promotions with levels of pay for which revenue yields, whether from directly managed or assigned areas and sources were inadequate.

These problems first presented themselves in the Deccan. In the effort to win over Maratha chiefs, Aurangzib made many expensive appointments of *mansabdars* with accompaninq assignments with, as it proved, only paper value.[24] After the fall of Bijapur and Golkonda, Auranzib enrolled many Muslim dignitaries from those sultanates, leading to resentment, and rivalry for profitable assignments, affecting especially the officers boasting long family service to the Mughal ruler (*khanazads*).

After the death of Aurangzib, the rivalry for the throne between his descendants multiplied the strains upon the Mughal military systems. Mughal princes bargained for support of military officers by lavish appointments and promotions, without regard for the revenue resources available to finance them. Royal henchmen and favorites (or great nobles usurping control) flouted imperial regulations. Areas of the empire previously reserved for direct management by royal treasury officials, were converted into assigned areas with no independent supervision of their administration. Increasingly the Mughal ruler was bargaining, with wasting assets, for military support, not commanding it. Increasingly Mughal officers could envisage a future where their personal advantage no longer lay in loyal acceptance of, and willing obedience to, the wishes and requirements of their royal patron and commander-in-chief.

The Mughal regime's military power rested upon its ability to dominate the revenue-yielding countryside from urban and sometimes fortified strongpoints. The steady conversion of autochthonous patrimonial chiefs, of greater and less power and privilege, into willing clients and collaborators, into generals and revenue collectors, was what the micrometer of Mughal political success measured. From the 1670s that micrometer began to show more negative than positive readings. Aurangzib's unmistakable espousal of orthodox Islam, with the imposition of the poll-tax (*jizya*) on non-Muslims, suggested that only Muslims were regarded as participating fully in the regime. Aurangzib's handling after 1679 of the succession to the major Rajput principality of Marwar in Rajasthan cooled relations with many Rajput chiefs for the remainder of his reign. His successor Bahadur Shah was obliged to campaign in Rajasthan against alienated chiefs of major clans.

The smaller chiefs in the countryside needed the inducements of Mughal protection and patronage and assurance of a privileged exemption from the full weight of Mughal tax demands in order wholeheartedly to cooperate with district Mughal officers in keeping the peace. Mughal failures against the Marathas and a diversion of Mughal resources from the north gradually led to chiefs making their own accommodations with the Mughal regime's enemies or, indeed "going it alone" themselves. A striking example of Mughal inability to control or overawe relatively modest local patrimonial chiefs was the Jat "rebellion" in the 1690s in the districts of Agra and Aligarh.[25] In these "heartland" areas the Jats were able to interfere with the movement of treasure and supplies along one of the principal Mughal trunk routes from north India to the Deccan. A dramatic illustration of growing inability of Mughal district officers to protect clients and allies, notables and privileged interest, in the countryside was furnished by the rising of the Sikh, Banda, in the Panjab between 1709 and 1715.[26] His peasant and lower-caste following turned successfully upon non-Muslim local chief and landholder as well as local Muslim notable. Major Mughal forces under Bahadur Shah himself had to reconquer large areas of the Panjab plains. The third skein of relationships, that between patrimonial leader-in-chief and lesser patrimonial chiefs and local privileged notables can be seen to be weakening along with the other two of Weber's skeins.

So, the Mughal regime exemplifies the major specifications of Weber's ideal type of patrimonial domination. So too does the South Asian society over which the Mughals ruled, or attempted to rule, share the characteristics of other societies in premodern Asia which were under patrimonial control—notably the persistence of autochthonous ritual, occupational and political grouping within a state that only intrudes into the life of such gouping when and where that state's overall military and fiscal dominance was threatened. But are we to expect therefore and ethic of power for its own sake or rather for the savor of its wielders?

The patrimonial order of political domination embraces, as we have seen, a range of relationships, and of techniques for managing those relationships, for ensuring that a ruler may possess supporters and resources, political "goods" in what is necessarily a highly competitive market, where the medium of exchange is influence and power, backed by a banker's reserve of force. These assets may endow the participants with the credit-worthiness of "authority." In this political market, the assumption might be that one participant has, another has not, or what one has more of, the other has less of—and that the object of such greater or lesser possession are "benefits." These "benefits" may take various forms, ability to enjoy material goods and personal services, prestige, deference, obedience, and affection. Richard B. Barnett defines politics as the way societies determine how these benefits are to be distribruted.[27] He has set up a model for the encounter between "political systems that are congruent with self-aware social communities on the one hand—ranging from administrative, kinship or linguistic networks covering large regions to more intensely conscious small localities—and political systems that are on the other hand either supraregional or altogether external to the above societies." An exchange of resources occurs between the two political systems, the local political system may have to yield up tribute and troops in return for confirmation of its "right to exist," but the "super-system" has to yield up some of what it hoped to receive in return for an easier life and an acknowledgement of its high status. What is seen as occurring is a parcelling out of packages of political power of different sizes and with different amounts of the same variety of contents. Perhaps this model is best described as an economic model of politics. Certainly Weber's typology of political life in a patrimonial society as essentially an encounter between juvenile and adult members of the same political species, that is chiefs with smaller or larger followings, can be treated as a simile of the encounter of a small firm with a big firm in an open market.

But this free-market image of politics, with each buyer and seller trying to corner the market in "benefits" by every trick in the game, including that of appeal to "right," "truth," and "reality," that is, to ideology or religion, was not the image that either Mughal publicists or others in India, including their most deadly rivals, the Marathas, saw when they raised their eyes from scenes of actual conflict. They saw a reality that, though it embraced politics as a necessary activity, encompassed it, making that activity not finally legitimate, but only a means to an end beyond itself. This was the image of society as organic, as a body, not as an assemblage; and of a dominion that is not political because it is universal, living a universal harmony.

At the beginning of the *Ayn-i Akbari*, Abu'l Fazl presents Akbar as physician to the (social) body or person (*shakhs*) of the age, the equilibrium and health of which is to be attained by (appropriate) adjustment of ranks and degrees. The multitude (of Akbar's subjects) is composed of four groups (*guruh*) to be likened to the four elements of which the cosmos is composed—fire, air, water, and earth. The groups are, first, warriors, second, merchants and artisans, third, men of the pen, and fourth, cultivators. The indispensable ruler is he who keeps each group in its place, devoting himself to making the world flourish through his knowledge of affairs and of the (real) worth of people; he sets himself to doing away with the forces of disintegration of the time and to leading the age towards equilibrium.[28] Abu'l Fazl portrays Akbar as endowed with the perception that enables him to so change a man's acquired moral traits that performs, without the dissatisfactions of vain ambition, those functions in life that Akbar's insight into the realities of a man's nature detects he should perform. Now Akbar's "reach" as ruler is cosmic because he has received, and is continually receiving, a unique endowment from the Creator. Akbar is the recipient of divine light, he has been trusted with sway over the world of symbolic forms and meanings, the esoteric and the exoteric; he is an epiphany of the divine realities, a sharer of secrets with God; he receives divine inspiration in the manner of a *Sufi* seeker. Indeed, Abu'l Fazl comprehensively describes Akbar as "an intimate of the house (or courtyard) of the divine unity."[29] But if Akbar is a witness of the Divine Unity on a cosmic plane, he is also a witness to the divine unity on the terrestrial plane. For Akbar's function is not only to bring about equilibrium between men, but also to ensure through (the transmission) of a ray of unity and concord to men's hearts, that they become one body. Unity among men is to be a homologue in terrestrial society of the cosmological unity created by the One God.

Now the unity that Abu'l Fazl (in his single work devoted to Akbar, divided by modern editors into the *Ayn i Akbari* and the *Akbar-Nama*) portrays (with Akbar as both its disclosure and its servant), appears to be an hierarchical form of unity: there are hierarchical relationships within the human social order and hierarchical relationships between human society, Akbar and cosmic reality. Within human society, unity is (as between Abu'l Fazl's four "groups") organic, that is, the four groups are associated with each other by reason of their differences, differences which are seen by Abu'l Fazl as complementary. The agriculturalist needs the warrior to give him security (of tenure as well as of person). But the relation is also hierarchical in the manner that Louis Dumont considers integral to a full concept of hierarchy, that is as the encompassing of the contrary.[30] The cultivator is (often) opposed to feeding and supporting the warrior (as Abu'l Fazl's account of the regime acknowledges). On the granary floor, where the encounter between warrior and cultivator occurs, unity between them is not achievable—one takes, the other gives—unless both recognize an encompassing principle of unity outside their immediate relationship. This principle is that both complement each other in a social order that serves a good greater than that of mere material possessions and resources, namely justice and truth. At another level, Akbar and his armed opponents, Rajput chiefs, other Muslim political prospectors in India such as the Afghans or the sultan of Gujarat might appear as equal in status with nothing but Akbar's military success to distinguish between them. But that equality is, for Abu'l Fazl, mere appearance: once the higher, transcendental level is considered, then all can see Akbar and his opponents to be in a hierarchy: Akbar's success is that of a ruler whom God has singled out as His *khalifa* of the age, His shadow on earth, an epiphany of the divine power to act, and a metaphor of God on earth (*Khuda -yi-majazi*).[31]

Abu'l Fazl is not expressing an ideology of free competition, whether for political benefits, or for material goods. Indeed he depicts, in the *Ayn-i Akbari*, the successful conduct of a wide range of social activity to be contingent upon the existence, and humanity's acknowledgment of the existence, of a charismatic, divinely guided ruler. Economic activity, cultivation and trade may be engaged in at the initiative of husbandmen and traders, but, without the activity of the true ruler (who is a repository of the Divine blessings), they will not be secure from human malevolence. Economic society cannot subsist of its own: nor should it. The wholly unoriginal *Tahzib al-Akhlaq* of Aurangzib's reign (located in a tradition of Muslim ethical thinking reaching back to the tenth-century intellectual Miskawaih) testifies to an Indo-Muslim acceptance of life as the proper orientation of human activities towards a hierarchy of ends of which none but the last and highest, nearness to God, is an end in itself. Man, states the anonymous writer of the *al-Akhlaq*,[32] has, in his deepest ground, been created capable of perfection. In his species nature as man, he unites this capacity for perfection with a yearning toward perfection, so that he acts to realize his potentiality. By nature, man is made for civil society; indeed he cannot assure himself a subsistence without living in society with its occupational specializations, its exchanges of goods and services, its cooperative activities. All created beings have some unique quality or distinctive characteristic. Man's unique quality is his ability to comprehend that this world is created by God and that man must act always in recognition that not only God has created for man a habitation, but also that God does not leave it to man to live in that habitation in any way he pleases. Man is not on earth for his own pleasure and advantage as ends in themselves, he is on earth to seek a perfection which God has revealed through his Messengers. Man must not seek that perfection through discarding or emasculating the faculties with which God has endowed him, but rather by using them to achieve a qualitatively graded series of satisfactions, satisfactions which prepare man for the onward and upward passage through a life of steady moral maturation to the final satisfaction, that of being near to God.

Most of the world's major religions deny that man, in his basic being is constituted by his social relations. Even if it is acknowledged that a man's social relatinships actually render him a moral being, in that he cannot have duties towards others, or recognize the rights of others unless there are others, most religious traditions seek definitions of those rights and duties in terms of the kind of "real being" they conceive man to have. Now, in the Indian religious and social context, there is some minimum, indeed perhaps minimal "meeting of minds" over the relationship of man's "real being" to his social being. For Islam, Allah endows man with a soul—a "fundamental being or essence"—with a, propensity to return to God. Whether that return journey is successfully accomplished depends on whether man's other faculties, the rational, the temperamental and the appetitive, are placed in proper hierarchical harmony, with reason at the top and appetite at the bottom. Should the individual fail to order himself aright, he may fall into unbelief—the victory of appetite over reason. The unbeliever, *kafir*, is to have a different temporal status from the believer, one who has achieved a better relationship between his faculties and, therefore, the state of being Allah demands of him. He who does not believe in the truth of the Prophet Muhammad's mission (i.e., the *kafir*) but who is a monotheist, is admitted to a lower status in a temporal world that is hierarchical as embracing different degrees of commitment to truth, within a universal order that is monotheistic. As a *zimmi* or person under protection, the monotheistic *kafir* enjoys security of life, property and discreet religious observance, but has to pay a poll tax (*jizya*) that Muslims do not.

Now there are certain homologies in notions of hierarchy to be found in Hindu tradition. In the *Gita*,[33] man is to be seen as a multidimensional being at whose center is a timeless monad, the self, the *jiva*, a "minute part" of the God Krishna, attached to a psychosomatic organism possessing (an individual) soul, an ego, discursive intellect and the senses. There is a state of internal war in every human being between the self and its ally the soul, on the one hand, and the other components of the human psyche. According to the "balance of power" between the different elements which essentially constitute man (and which form a hierarchy), so will man act. Man has to struggle within himself to "hierarchize" the elements of which for the *Gita* all nature is composed—purity, passion and darkness (the three *gunas: sattva, rajas,* and *tamas*). Whether man enjoys success or suffers failure, he will build up a stock of *karma*, of deeds, stretching back over many lives. This stock of deeds will affect his future births. But the world into which, for the *Gita*, he is born, is one wherein human society is composed of four classes, Brahmans, warriors, peasants and artisans, and "serfs." Certain virtues inhere in each of the four classes, virtues that are arranged in a hierarchy. Each virtue (for example, self-restraint in the Brahman, ardour in the warrior, spirit of willing service for the serf) is excellent in its own class, contradicts but also complements the virtues in other classes. There is, therefore, not a universal and uniform virtue for all classes but rather a hierarchy of virtue under which what is good at one level is not good at another level. One should not seek or practice a virtue that does not belong to one's class or code of duty, but rather do one's duty in that situation of life which one's stock of deeds have so far placed one.

The foundation deeds, the processes of change and development, the conceptual contents and the practices of the cultures of Mughal India were, as every observer conveys, polymorphic. Yet in the daily relationships of members of these different cultures, some mutual comprehension, perhaps some empathy, betrayed itself. Those who belonged to the literate traditions appear to have acted upon the presupposition or cluster of presuppositions, that social living should be shaped by a vision or image of what was ultimately a cosmic reality. It was no South Asian tradition's ideal that the conduct of terrestrial affairs, the adjustments of human being to human being, even if peaceful and amiable, should be for egoistical worldly gratification. Agreements and disagreements, cooperation and rivalry should have a "moral" function and peace should have a tilt towards the recognition of the essence of the real. Temporal power and its instruments should be in the hands of the "right minded." A universal order of being should have its earthly metaphor in the universal ruler, in whom legitimate authority to manage human relations (where such management needed human intervention) should be grounded. The universal ruler, the "lord of the earth," would need to delegate to more local agents in more immediate communication with local populations, the task of achieving local stability and equilibrium. The end should be the achievement of universal harmony. Within this schema, earthly politics was to be conceived as the activity of discovering the fittest agents who could be endowed with authority to manage subordinate realms within the universal lordship.

Success in any rivalry for localized sovereignties and rulerships, success in any rivalry between patrimonial chiefs for clients, should demonstrate the successful rival's fitness of psyche, moral character, mental aptitude and right "stance before reality." Throughout the history of India, a presupposition that outward performance shows forth inner worth, underlay the devising of high-status genealogies for lower-status political adventurers, or the ascription of an ideal obedience to Allah and service of Islam to successful rebels against Muslim sultans. The ethos of a competitive free-market politics, in which patrimonial chiefs and possible clients are to be seen selling and buying personal advantages as ends in themselves, was as foreign to Indian traditions as it was to the traditions of the other civilizations wherein Max Weber saw patrimonial regimes in cultural settings which proclaimed values of wholeness and harmony: those of ancient Egypt, of Confucian China, of medieval Europe and of the Ottoman empire.

In eighteenth-century India, as a governing institution, the Mughal regime was steadily reduced to near impotence. But as the source and registrar of legitimate authority, the occupant of the Mughal throne had never before been so widely accepted within the sub-continent. This seeming paradox has long been commented upon. C.A. Bayley, in his seminal *Rulers, Townsmen and Bazaars: North Indian Society in the Age of British Expansion, 1770–1870*,[34] has shown that this phenomenon provided an illusion of continuity in a very fluid political situation. Muslim notables who would have, in the seventeenth century been restricted and transferable local commisioners, now sought Mughal titles and offices in order to legitimize control of their provincial satrapies.

The Marathas abandoned any claim to establish an independent Hindu kingdom. At the same time as they were effectively removing Mughal control of whole provinces, Balaji Baji Rao, the Maratha Peshwa (first minister) sought and accepted from the Mughal emperor Muhammad Shah, the formal office of *na'ib-subahdar*, deputy governor of the province of Malwa (1741). In 1784, after the Maratha chief Sindhia had occupied Dehli, the residence of the emperor Shah 'Alam, the latter conferred the office of *wakil-imutlaq* or "agent with full powers" upon the then (infant) Maratha Peshwa. In texts in Marathi the Mughal emperor was referred to as "lord of the earth."[35] When the Marathas began to take a portion of the land revenues from Mughal territories they had overrun, they claimed to do so as *zamindars* who were providing traditional services to a patron and protector. In effect when the Mughal emperor formally accorded, in imperial *farmans* these powers of revenue collection, he was not surrendering sovereignty but according justice to the seekers of justice.

Richard Barnett has reminded us that an ideology as a structuring of men's perceptions of reality or of their arguments for changing that reality, is itself capable of becoming a political resource. It may assist in "acquiring or maintaining political legitimacy, or delegating authority, mobilizing support or attacking an opponent. Those in possession of 'correct' or accepted views on numerous issues...have an advantage, however impermanent, over those displaying novel, foreign, or deviant public behaviour."[36] Now, for eighteenth-century India it is certainly arguable that those engaged in political competition might gain some advantage (the advantage, for example, of not being seen to be abrasive) from acting publicly in accordance with an ideology of hierarchy. In other, nonpolitical, social activities in India, the expectations and the experience of life were that everyone had a place in a group that had a place. To gain its ends, perhaps political egoism has to pass itself off as something else—but the eighteenth century is not unique in that respect. Why, however, in India, should a nonpolitical ideal, that of a universal rule over a society in complete political harmony have political force? One answer that has been given is that such an ideal legitimates the actual use of force if the force-user purports to be trying to establish universal dominion. But the Marathas did not so purport, nor did the *nawwab* of Awadh, nor did the Nizam of Hyderabad, for they already acknowledged the Mughal as universal ruler. We need to look at the evidence for what considerations actually weighed with the takers of particular political decisions in eighteenth-century India.

This banal sounding conclusion is one with which Weber himself would, I believe, have been comfortable. As is well-known, he was opposed to explaining social and historical reality by reference to some supposed "real essence behind" surface experiences. For Weber, social and historical reality is always capable (in principle) of being represented in an infinite number of modes; moreover, he believed that for human actors, social and historical reality is as constituted by their representations of it. Recent demonstrations[37] that Indian historical reality in the eighteenth century is not fully describable by his representations, would have reassured him that his work is being taken by present-day historians of India at least for what it is: an expression of a transcendent imagination, which itself, through its power, has defied other and later historians and sociologists to reduce its insights into dogmas masquerading as ultimate truths.

Notes

1. Parts of this paper have drawn heavily upon the pioneer article: Stephen P Blake, "The Patrimonial-Bureaucratic Empire of the Mughals," *Journal of Asian Studies* 39 (November, 1979): 77–94. Dr. Blake advisedly limited himself to a discussion of the institutions, bureaucratic and military, of Mughal rule. In so far as this present paper concentrates more on the political, social and ideological setting in which Mughal domination was located, it is to be seen as supplemental to Dr. Blake's work.
2. Max Weber, *Wirtschaft und Gesellschaft: Grundriss der verstehenden Soziologie*, 5th revised edition, edited by Johannes Winckelmann (Tubingen: J. C. B. Mohr, 1976), I: 151, 152.
3. Max Weber, *Gesammelte Aufsatze zur Religionssoziologie*, Bdn, *Hinduismus und Buddhismus* (Tubingen: J. C. B. Mohr, 1921), 1–133.
4. See *Hinduismus und Buddhismus*, 70.
5. Max Weber, "Die 'Objekjectivat' sozial wissenschaflicher und sozial polilischer Erkenntnis," in *Gesammelte Aufsatze zur Wissenschaftslehre von Max Weber*, 3rd edition, edited by Johannes Winckelmann (Tubingen: J.C.B. Mohr, 1968), 192–196, 203–204.

6. Der Gentilcharisma (*Hinduismus und Buddhismus*, 51–57) das Charisma Sippe, (*Hinduismus und Buddhismus*, 57); "Wie das Gentilcharisma die Kaste, und Kaste widerum das Charisma der Sippe," 57).
7. *Hinduismus und Buddhismus*, 70, 72, 74–75, 87, 89.
8. "The Patrimonial-Bureaucratic Empire of the Mughals," 83–84.
9. J. F. Richards, "Norms of comportment among Imperial Mughal Officers," in *Moral Conduct and Authority: The Place of Adab in South Asian Islam*, ed. Barbara Daly Metcalf (Berkeley: University of California Press, 1984), 238–260. 262–263.
10. For example, M. Athar Ali, *The Mughal Nobility under Aurangzeb* (Bombay: Asia Publishing House 1966); idem, The *Apparatus of Empire* (Calcutta: Oxford University Press, 1984); J. F. Richards, "The Formation of Imperial Authority under Akbar and Jahangir," in *Kingship and Authority in South Asia*, edited by J. F. Richards (Madison: South Asian Studies, University of Wisconsin-Madison, Publication Series-Publication no. 3, 1978), 252–288.
11. "Norms of Comportment Among Imperial Mughal Officers," 264.
12. *Wirtschaft und Gesellschaft*, 2: 605–607.
13. Irfan Habib, *The Agrarian System of Mughal India, 1556–1707* (London: Asia Publishing House 1963), 295; Norman Abmad Siddiqi, *Land Revenue Administration under the Mughals 1700–1750* (London: Asia Publishing House, 1970), 112–114.
14. "The Patrimonial-Bureaucratic Empire of the Mughals," 91.
15. Abu'l Fazl, *Ayin-Akbari*, ed. H. Blochmann (Calcutta: *Bibliotheca Indica*, 1872), I: 175.
16. S. Nurul Hasan, "Zami dars under the Mughals," in *Land Control and Social Structure in Indian History*, ed. R.E. Frykenberg (Madison: University of Wisconsin Press, 1969), 17–31; Irfan Habib, *Agrarian System*, 136–189; B.R. Grover, "The Nature of Land Right in Mughal India," in *The Indian Economic and Social History Review* I , no.1 (1963): 10–11; Ahsan Raza Khan, *Chieftains in the Mughal Empire during the Reign of Akbar* (Simla: Institute of Advanced Study, 1977).
17. *Wirtschaft und Gesellschaft*, 2: 590–591.
18. For example, Ishtiaq Husain Qureshi, *The Muslim Community of the Indo-Pakistani Subcontinent* (610–1947) (The Hague: Mouton & Co. 1962), 102–103, 168; R. C. Majumdar, ed., *The Delhi Sultanate* (Bombay: Bharaty Vidya Bhavan, 1960), preface, xxix; main text, 617–623.
19. P. Hardy, "Force and Violence in Indo-Persian Writing in History and Government in Medieval South Asia," in *Islamic Society and Culture: Essays in honour of Professor Aziz Ahmad*, ed. Milton Israel and N.K. Wagle (New Delhi: Manohar, 1983), 173–176, 182–183, 188.
20. For accounts and analyses of the claims made for Akbar see: Richards, "The Formulation of Imperial Authority under Akbar and Jabangir," and P. Hardy, "Abu'l Fazl's Portrait of the Perfect Padshah: A political philosophy for Mughal India—or a personal puff for a pal?" in *Islamic Indian Studies and Commentaries*, ed. Christian W. Troll (New Delhi: Vikas 1985), 114–137. For claims made by Jahangir on his own behalf see *Tuzuk-i Jahangiri* (Aligarh 1863/4), 30. For claims made on Sbah Jahan's behalf, see, for example, Abd al-Hamid Lahauri. *Badshah Nama*, vol. I (Calcutta, *Bibliotheca Indica* 1867), and Muhammad Salih Kanbo Lahaur, '*Amil-i Salih*, vol. I (Calcutta *Bibliotheca Indica* 1923), 2; Hamid al-din Khan, *Ahkam-i 'Alamgiri*, second ed. (Calcutta M.C. Sarkar & Sons 1926), I: 5.
21. Norman P. Ziegler, "Some Notes on Rajput Loyalties during the Mughal Period," in *Kingship and Authority in South Asia*, 235.

22. A recent survey of Aurangzib's imbroglio in the Deccan is, John F. Richards, *The New Cambridge History of India* I, 5 (*The Mughal Empire*) (Cambridge: Cambridge University Press, 1993), chapters 10 and 11.
23. Muzaffar Alam, *The Crisis of Empire in Mughal North India: Awadh and the Punjab, 1707–48* (Delhi: Oxford University Press, 1986), chapter 1: Breakdown of Imperial Organization.
24. Athar Ali, *The Mughal Nobility under Aurangzeb* (Bombay: Asia Publishing House, 1966), 92–94.
25. Richards, *The Mughal Empire*, 250–252.
26. Muzaffar Alam, *The Crisis of Empire*, 134ff.
27. Richard B. Barnett, *North India Between Empires: Awadh, The Mughals and the British 1720–1801* (Berkeley: University of California Press 1980), 6–11.
28. Abu'l Fazl, *Ayn-i Akbari*, 1: 3–4.
29. Abu'l Fazl, *Akbar-Nama*. edited by Agha Ahmad 'Ali and 'Abd al-Rahim (Calcutta: *Bibliotheca Indica*, 1877), 1:4–5.
30. Louis Dumont, *Homo Herarchicus*, complete revised English edition (Chicago: University of Chicago Press, 1980), "Postface: Towards a Theory of Hierarchy," 239–245.
31. Abu'l Fazl, *Akbar-Nama*, I: 17 (*Khilafat-i-zaman*); *Akbar-Nama*, vol. III (Calcutta, 1883), 465 (*zill-ilahi*), 1:6 (*mazhar-i-qudrat-i ilahi*); vol. III: 84, (*Khuda-yi majazi*).
32. *Tahzib al-Akhlaq*,(anonymous) (Delhi Persian Collection: India Office Library, [London]), no.909, fols. 88b, 92b.
33. The *Bhagavad-Gita* with a commentary based on the original sources by R.C. Zaehner (Oxford: Oxford University Press, 1979), 11–12, 15–17, 21–23.
34. Richard B. Barnett, *North India Between Empires*, 56.
35. C.A. Bayly, *Rulers, Townsmen and Bazaars: North Indian Society in the Age of British Expansion 1770–1870* (Cambridge: Cambridge University Press, 1983).
36. Andre Wink, *Land and Sovereignty in India: Agrarian Society and Politics under Eighteenth-century Maratha Svarajya* (Cambridge: Cambridge University Press, 1986), 187–189.
37. *North India Between Empires*, 7.
38. For example by Bayly, *Rulers, Townsmen and Bazaars*, 187–189.

6

Paradise or Hell?
The Religious Doctrine of Election in Eighteenth and Nineteenth Century Islamic Fundamentalism and Protestant Calvinism

Rudolph Peters

Throughout Islamic history there have been scholars and preachers who, with an appeal to the core notions of Islam, that is, the dogma of God's unity and the example of the Prophet, have militated against the religious and political status quo. This phenomenon is usually referred to as fundamentalism,[1] a term which I shall presently try to define more precisely. This essay will study fundamentalist thought and contrast it with mainstream Islam in order to construct an idealtype of fundamentalist doctrine. This will be done with the ultimate aim of testing Weber's thesis concerning the relationship between the Protestant ethic and the rise of capitalism. The empirical material examined here is based primarily on fundamentalist movements in the eighteenth and nineteenth centuries so that a picture of a purely Islamic tradition, not yet affected by Western thought might be presented.

An authoritative interpretation of Weber's studies on world religions holds that they must be regarded as a series of experiments through which Weber sought to show that the religious factor was crucial in the development of capitalism. According to this interpretation, Weber maintained that while the social and economic prerequisites for the development of capitalism were present in many societies, the varieties of values and attitudes produced by different religions accounted for the rise of capitalism in some places and not others. As Talcott Parsons has phrased it: "In embarking upon comparative studies, Weber attempted to hold the factor of economic organisation constant and treat religious orientation as his independent variable."[2]

This idealistic view has recently come under attack, both by those who address their criticism to Weber himself and by those who, claiming that Weber ought to be read differently, address their criticism to his exegetes. With special reference to Islam, Maxime Rodinson, in *Islam and Capitalism*, follows the first line and shows that many elements of the Protestant ethic, considered of crucial importance for the development of capitalism by Weber, had their parallels in Islam. Consequently, in Rodinson's reasoning the explanation of the fact that capitalism did not originate in the Islamic world has to be sought elsewhere.[3] Bryan Turner comes to the same conclusion in his *Weber and Islam*, but he claims that this is in agreement with Weber's views. His contention is that Weber certainly noted the importance of social and economic structures in this connection and attached much weight to patrimonial domination and the structure of the city in explaining why capitalism did not arise in the Islamic world.[4]

Weber did not publish a full-scale, systematic study of Islam, as he did on ancient Judaism and on the religions of India and China. But from his scattered observations and remarks his ideas on Islam can be easily assembled.[5] In Weber's view Islam was founded as a world rejecting, ethical religion that promised its adherents salvation by faith. However, after Mohammed's emigration to Medina and his being invested with political authority, its character changed. Owing to the importance of warfare for the Islamic community and the increasing influence of the old ruling families Islam developed into a feudally oriented warrior religion. As in Calvinist Protestantism the doctrine of predestination provided Muslims with a strong motive to carry out God's will. But because of its character as a warrior religion, this did not give rise in Islam to innerworldly asceticism and a rational, methodical quest for salvation, but to excessive zeal in fighting. And later, after the Islamic conquests, the doctrine of predestination provided the basis for the widespread fatalism among the Moslem masses. This was also partly due to the rise of dervish mysticism as the religion of the small bourgeoisie. This kind of orgiastic and mystical religiosity opened the door to saint veneration and magic and was therefore non-innerworldly and irrational.

Puritanism, in Weber's view, did not develop in Islam because of its feudal orientation. The ruling warrior class that came to dominate Islam was given to worldly pleasures, sensualism, and luxuries. Under its influence the elements of ethical salvation religion of the first Meccan period were pushed to the background. Islam became a religion of world accomodation and if there was some form of asceticism it was the asceticism of the military camps and army barracks. Thus official Islam became characterized by simple and traditionalistic ethics that posed only external and ritual demands. Because of this, Weber had doubts whether Islam could be classified as an ethical salvation religion. But in his view Islam lacked innerworldly asceticism and a rational, methodical quest for salvation, owing to its character as a warrior religion, to its feudal orientation that resulted in ethics of world accommodation, and finally to its dervish mysticism that was non-innerwordly and irrational.

Weber's ideas on Islam reflect the state of—especially German—scholarship at the beginning of this century, which considered the revealing of the "essence" or "spirit" of Islam as one of its major tasks. Because of the increased knowledge of Islam, Islamic culture and Islamic history, present-day scholars tend to pay more attention to the diversity to be found in Islam and are often averse to formulating broad generalization. Thus, in criticizing Weber's ideas on Islam, one must be careful not to replace his sweeping and sometimes almost contentless views with equally global and general ones, but to take into account the great variety of religious experience subsumed under the notion of Islam.

In the following I shall concentrate on Weber's thesis concerning the relationship between Calvinist Protestantism and the development of capitalism. I shall try to refine the criticism of Weber's idealistic view, or of the idealistic interpretation of his writings, but pointing out that a certain tradition in Islam—namely Sunnite fundamentalism of the eighteenth and nineteenth centuries—offers a number of striking resemblances to sixteenth- and seventeenth-century Calvinism in that it also promoted innerworldly asceticism, rationalism and austerity. My contention is that, if one assumes that religion can have such an important impact on economic life, such differences as exist between Calvinist Protestantism and fundamentalist Islam are too minor to account for the enormous difference in the economic and social development in the regions where these forms of religion were dominant.

Before we go further it is appropriate to state more explicitly what I mean by Islamic, Sunnite fundamentalism. I shall, therefore, try to construct an idealtype of Islamic fundamentalism, based on its eighteenth- and nineteenth-century manifestations.[6]

Fundamentalist thought revolved around two pairs of concepts, namely *sunna* (the normative example of the Prophet) as opposed to *bi'da* (unwarranted innovation, deviation from the *sunna*) and *tawhid* (monotheism) as opposed to *shirk* (polytheism). These are rather abstract principles. Yet they find expression in two more concrete doctrines, one of a theoretical and the other of a practical nature. The first is the fundamentalists' insistence on *ijtihad*, on having direct recourse to the sources of religious knowledge, namely the Quran and *hadith*, in order to establish what is *sunna*. This ran counter to the established view that after the fourth century A.H. (tenth century C.E.) all Muslims had to follow the opinions of the great jurists of the first centuries (*taqlid*) and that no scholar, however learned he might be, was entitled to practise *ijtihad* anymore. Thus the fundamentalists rejected the principle of *taqlid* and claimed the right to *ijtihad* for anyone with a modicum of religious learning. The second doctrine is their rejection of the veneration of saints or holy persons and their prohibition of all cults connected with it. This is because they regard the veneration of human beings as contrary to the principle of *tawhid* and the cults pursuing it as *bi'da*. Though these doctrines can be regarded as landmarks for recognizing fundamentalist thought, in order to understand its structure, the notions of the *tawhid* and *sunna* must be further elaborated. The fundamentalist concept of *tawhid* emphasizes the existence of one, transcendental God who stands above His creation and is separate from it and who is the only Being which may be worshipped and venerated. Mankind can only know of His existence and His commands via the revelations He has sent down to prophets. Complementary to this notion of divinity is the view that all believers are basically equal and differ only in degrees of piety.

With regard to this concept there exists a clear tension between fundamentalism and mysticism. The notion of *wahdat al-wudjud* (unity of existence) of Ibn 'Arabi (d. 1240 C.E.), so popular among mystics through the ages, is condemned outright by fundamentalists on the grounds that it opens the door to pantheism. For, according to this immanent concept of divinity, God is the only real being and, therefore, essentially one with the universe, including man. Moreover, fundamentalist authors denied the possibility of obtaining direct, intuitive knowledge of God via mystical experience (*'ilm laduni*) and rejected all other forms of occult knowledge not based on revelation. This, however, does not mean that fundamentalism and mysticism are totally incompatible. There have been fundamentalist sufi orders. Their members tried to achieve self perfection through union with the spirit of the Prophet, by concentrating on his example (*sunna*) and following it.

They were averse to ecstatic activities and, although they did practise meditation, they attached great importance to action in this world.[7]

Fundamentalists did not deny the possibility of miracles performed by human beings. In line with orthodox doctrine they maintained that the faculty of working miracles (*karamat*) is a gift conferred by God on the very pious in order to honor them. However, they insisted that this faculty ceases after death, that the dead have no special powers, and that it is useless to seek favours from them or to ask their intercession with God. Fundamentalists typically condemned this as polytheism (*shirk*) since it involves ascribing special powers to a human being and placing him between oneself and God. In order to prevent this they prohibited the erection of ornate tombstones and mausolea, the holding of *mulids* (periodical festivals commemorating the birth of a holy man), and all other forms of veneration of dead persons.

Fundamentalist egalitarianism is reflected in the notion that the gate of *ijtihad* is not closed. The traditional view that after the fourth century A.H. nobody was entitled to full *ijtihad* and that *taqlid* had become obligatory was commonly justified by pointing to the extraordinary gifts of the founders of the legal schools, correctly referred to by Weber as "the charismatic powers of prophet-legislators."[8] Against this view, fundamentalists asserted that the revelation is clear and that anyone with a certain amount of learning can have access to it and can therefore practise *ijtihad*. More mundane aspects of this egalitarianism can be detected in the general ban on demonstrations of excessive respect like the kissing of hands or the use of special forms of address such as *sayyidi* (sir) or *mawlana* (my lord) that some fundamentalist movements enforced. Sometimes egalitarianism led to the application of sumptuary laws with regard to attire and jewelry. This enhanced the puritanical character of fundamentalist movements, already existing in their prohibition of tobacco in addition to the general Islamic ban on alcohol.

The principal aim of fundamentalist concern with the *sunna* was the establishment of an authentic Islamic community. By recourse to the revelation via *ijtihad*, the *sunna* can be properly defined and followed. Conversely, any practice or custom opposed to it, and therefore regarded as *bi'da*, can be banned. These actions will restore Islamic unity, another fundamentalist concern in the light of which a number of other fundamentalist doctrines must be viewed too. Thus, fundamentalist opposition to saintly cults, which are usually regional in scope, also reflects the aversion to localism, just as fundamentalist rejection of *taqlid* reveals an attempt to abolish or at least diminish the importance of the legal schools, which keep Islam divided.

The issues so far mentioned are those dealt with by fundamentalist authors. On other doctrines, such as the doctrine of predestination or the attributes of God, they were generally silent. In these instances we can assume that their views coincided with current orthodox opinion. Leaving aside the subtle dogmatic controversies, the prevailing position on predestination can be summarized as follows: God has decreed all acts in advance and predestined all men to either Paradise or Hell. The former are guided by Him to good works, the latter to evil deeds. A *hadith* reporting the words of the Prophet Mohammed illustrates this point very clearly and also emphasizes that man nevertheless must make efforts to act well:

> Then the Apostle of God said: "There is no living soul for which God has not appointed its place in Paradise or Hell, and the decision of happy or unhappy has already been taken." Then a man said: "O Apostle of God, shall we not then leave all to what has been decided for us and give up works ?" Mohammed answered: "Whosoever belongs to the people of happiness will come to the work of people of happiness, and whosoever belongs to the people of unhappiness will come to the works of the people of unhappiness." Then he said: "Perform works, for everyone is guided: the people of happiness are guided to the works of the people of happiness, and the people of unhappiness are guided to the works of the people of unhappiness." Thereupon he recited: "As for him who gives and is godfearing and confirms the reward most fair, We shall surely ease him to the Easing. But as for him who is a miser, and self-sufficient, and cries lies to the reward most fair, We shall surely ease him to the Hardship."(Quran 92:8)[9]

Fundamentalist doctrine as typified above is not very different from "mainstream" Islam. In fact, Ernest Gellner considers most of the elements mentioned here—strict monotheism, emphasis on scriptural revelation, egalitarianism, and puritanism—as belonging to the central tradition of Islam, which he argues is in this respect totally different from Christianity.[10] What distinguishes fundamentalism from other forms of Islam is not so much related to doctrine—although there have been fierce debates on special doctrinal points—as to attitude. Fundamentalism regarded Islamic society as having deviated from *sunna* and *tawhid* in the direction of *bi'da* and *shirk* and strove to redress this situation. Fundamentalist movements, therefore, are typically missionary movements aimed at spreading and implementing a calling. They are committed to changing the world and subjecting it to their ideals based on *sunna* and *tawhid*. Depending on the radicality of each separate movement, this activism is either called "commanding what is reputable and forbidding what is disreputable" (*al-amr bi-l ma 'ruf wa-l-nahy 'an al-munkar*, cf. Quran 3:110) or "holy struggle" (*jihad*).

Let us now examine to what extent this Islamic fundamentalism resembles Calvinist Protestantism, especially with regard to those doctrinal and attitudinal traits that Weber thought to be related to the development of capitalism in Western Europe. These then are the doctrine of predestination, innerworldly asceticism, rationalism and puritanism.

In Calvinist Protestantism God is viewed as a remote transcendental Being who acts as He pleases and whose decrees cannot be influenced by deliberate human action like magic working or the intercession of priests or saints. His acts are beyond human criteria of justice and man is therefore incapable of understanding them. Neither can man know what God, in His infinite wisdom, has decreed with regard to his fate in the hereafter, that is with regard to his salvation or damnation. One is of the elect or one is not and no mortal can fathom the motives of His judgment. Yet every believer must act as if he knows that he is elected and saved, and must attempt to live according to the prescriptions of his religion and follow his vocation, his responsiblity in this world.

If we compare this with fundamentalist Islam, we find a number of similarities and some differences. The conception of God as an unattainable, transcendental Being, impervious to magic and intercession is very similar, as is the notion that His decrees are beyond human comprehension. Orthodox, Sunnite Islam rejected the Mu'tazilite view that God cannot commit an injustice and that therefore His decrees concerning man's reward or punishment in the world to come had to be just, with the argument that such a view would constitute an inadmissible restriction of His omnipotence. This reasoning, however, was not pursued to its final consequences as in Protestant Calvinism. The opinion prevailed that God has preordained all events, including human behavior and every individual's fate in the hereafter and that there is basically a clear relationship, that can be understood by human beings, between man's acts and his going to Paradise or Hell. On the Day of Judgment every individual's acts will be weighed and according to the outcome, which, of course, is already known to God, he will be rewarded or punished. Believers who have committed sins will not remain in Hell eternally and in His Kindness He even can send sinners to Paradise immediately.

In Calvinist Protestantism man cannot know whether he is chosen or not, nor can he influence this by committing good works or sins. Yet he is enjoined to act as if he were elected and not to resign himself passively to his fate. Here we can note a clear doctrinal difference. For, in spite of the doctrine of predestination, Muslim theologians asserted that there was some scope for free will and human responsibility. Ibn Taymiyya (d. 1328 C.E.), a religious scholar who became very popular with later fundamentalist movements, has expressed this in the following, somewhat ambiguous words:

> The belief in predestination (*qadar*) has two levels, each of which contains two things. The first level is the belief that God, through His uncreated knowledge which is His pre-existent and eternal attribute, knows what [His] creatures will do, that He knows all their pious deeds and sins, their possessions, and the moments of their deaths; and [secondly] that God has recorded the destinies of the created beings.... God has said: "Didst thou not know that God knows all that is in heaven and earth? Surely that is in a Book; surely that for God is an easy matter." (Q 22:70), and: "No affliction befalls in the earth or in yourselves, but it is in a Book, before We create it." (Q 57:22)... When He creates the body of an embryo, before the entrance of the soul in it, He sends an angel to it, who is given four commands and to whom is said: "Record his possessions, the moment of his death, his deeds, and whether he will be happy or unhappy [i.e. saved or damned]... The second level is related to God's effective will and His omnipotence. It is the belief that what God wills, occurs and what He does not will, does not occur, that nothing moves or is at rest in heavens or on earth except through God's will...and [secondly] that men act in reality, whereas God creates their deeds. Men have the power and the will to perform acts, but God has created them [the men], their power and their will, just as He has said: "It is naught but a reminder unto all beings] for whosoever of you who would go straight; but will you shall not, unless God wills, the Lord of all Beings." (Q 81:29)[11]

Even without going too deeply into the theological implications of Ibn Taymiyya's stance—which, as a matter of fact, was in this respect very close to mainstream Islam—it will be clear that he attempts to reconcile two basically irreconcilable tenets: predestination and *liberum abitrium*. Since the Muslim believer, in Ibn Taymiyya's perspective can be reasonably certain of his ultimate salvation as long as he follows the legal and ethical prescriptions of his religion, he does not suffer from the deep anguish that is so characteristic of Calvinism and is caused by the Calvinist believer's uncertainty concerning his fate in the world to come. Yet the practical consequences of both doctrines in the present world are very similar: the Muslim will endeavour to follow the commands of his religion because this is the only road to salvation, whereas the Calvinist will do so, because he is enjoined to act as if he were saved. Thus, in both cases the result is active ethical behavior in this world.[12]

This is intimately related to a second trait that Weber ascribed to

Calvinist Protestantism and that he considered of paramount importance for the development of capitalism: innerworldly asceticism. By this term he refers to an attitude toward salvation characterized by a methodical procedure for achieving it, whereas salvation is viewed as the gift of active ethical behavior performed in the awareness that God directs this behavior, that is, that the actor is the instrument of God. This asceticism is innerworldly if this active ethical behavior must take place within or against the world order. The world then becomes a responsibility in the sense that it must be transformed according to the ascetic ideals. This is very much what Islamic fundamentalist movements were about. As in mainstream Islam, salvation was seen as a gift of ethical (in addition to ritual and legal) behavior performed in the awareness of God's guidance. But what distinguished fundamentalist from mainstream Islam was that the former wanted to change the world and subject it to its ideals based on *sunna* and *tawhid*. One could even say that fundamentalist movements pursued two kinds of salvation: individual salvation, connected with following the commands of religion, in the hereafter and collective salvation in the present world, the result of establishing a community that organizes its life according to the Islamic ideals. The underlying idea is that God will grant such a community prosperity and strength. Fundamentalist movements therefore often arise from a widespread feeling of malaise, in a society that perceives itself as being in decline, morally and, as a consequence, politically and economically.

The next question we have to ask is whether this activity aimed at salvation can be described as rational and methodical. This is a crucial point since, in Weber's view, the genesis of the capitalist spirit is closely linked to rationalism and methodical behavior. Rationality and methodicalness in achieving salvation imply—as in Calvinist Protestantism—the absence of intercession and magic in general. One cannot be saved through the intercession of persons (e.g., holy men) or institutions (the church), but only by God and/or by one's own behavior, that is through obeying the ethical and ritual rules of religion by meticulously following the Prophet's example. All this is very true of fundamentalist Islam with its vehement attacks on the cults of saints and its prohibition of magical practices.

A second element in fundamentalist Islam conducive to the inculcation of rationalism in the minds of its followers, is its insistence on the authenticity of the religious norms to be followed. This entails a continuous preoccupation with the revelation in the form of *ijtihad*, consisting in study, rational interpretation and discussion of the relevant texts. It is significant in this respect that fundamentalist authors have emphasized that this was not the exclusive domain of highly qualified specialists, but that anybody with a minimal knowledge of the revelation and the propaedeutic sciences was entitled to it. Fundamentalism, however, was not only a matter of study and theoretical interest in the revelation. The authentic norms were to be followed, not only in ritual, but also in daily life, since Islamic law covers all kinds of mundane activities. Thus there was among fundamentalists a continuous endeavour to live according to the authenticated commands of the *sunna*. At the same time their brand of Islam had to be spread, which involved a constant process of preaching and discussion, an eminently rational task.

Weber apparently subscribed to the common nineteenth-century misconception that Islam is a religion that stimulates sensualism and hedonism. This view was usually put forth with a reference to Islamic law that, it would seem, allowed a man to satisfy his lust almost without restrictions by taking up to four wives and an unlimited number of concubines and gave him the freedom to discard them at will. This was of course an exaggeration and a distortion of reality. Interestingly enough, nowadays the restrictive character of the Islamic sexual code is usually emphasized, which only shows that the prevailing image of Islam in the West changes more under the influence of developments in Western society, than as a result of transformations in Islamic society itself.

Weber's view of Islam ignored the strong tradition of piety and asceticism (*zuhd*) in Islam and the puritanical laws like the ban on alcohol (by fundamentalists also extended to tobacco), on music and dance, on the representation of living beings, on the use of gold plates and cups, the wearing of silk and jewelry by men and on extravagant wedding and circumcision parties. Admittedly, these laws often remained a dead letter, but the fundamentalists attached great value to them and tried to enforce them. This was connected not only with their respect for the *sunna*, but also with their fear that ostentatious display of wealth might lead to the worshipping of human beings. Austerity, then, is a marked trait of the fundamentalist life-style and, if fundamentalism does not entirely subscribe to the Calvinist view that everyting pertaining to the flesh is corrupt, it is certainly not a form of religion that condones revelling, luxuriating and the unbridled satisfaction of sexual appetite.

The conclusion must be that all those doctrinal and attitudinal characteristics of Calvinist Protestantism that Weber regarded as consequential in connection with the development of capitalism, can be detected in fundamentalist Islam too. It is true, they did not exist in exactly the same form or the same degree, for both forms of religion were not identical. Yet these similarities and these parallels raise serious doubts about the importance of the religious factor in explaining why capitalism developed in North Western Europe and not the other parts of the world.

Notes

Here I would like to thank Dr. Charles E. Butterworth for reading the first draft of this article. His stimulating remarks and criticisms, many of which we could discuss during our memorable Nile to Red Sea desert hike, have been very helpful to shape my thought.

1. Fundamentalism, revivalism and *integrisme* are all terms originally coined for tendencies within Christianity and therefore rather imprecise if applied to Islam. If the main distinguishing feature of Christian fundamentalism is its scripturalism and its rejection of historical criticism of the text of the Bible, most Muslims would, *mutatis mutandis*, be fundamentalists. As I shall presently explain, Muslim fundamentalism has other characteristics. That I use this imprecise term is due to the fact that it seems to have acquired *droit de cite*, more than the modern Arabic term *salafi*.
2. In the introduction to his translation of the chapters on religion from Weber's *Wirtschaft und Gesellschaft*: M. Weber, *The Sociology of Religion,* tr. Ephriam Fischoff and intr. by Talcott Parsons Boston: 1963), xxxii.
3. M. Rodinson, *Islam and Capitalism*, trans. Brian Pearce (Austin: University of Texas Press, 1978), chapter 4.
4. Bryan S. Turner, *Weber and Islam: A Critical Study* (London: Routledge and Kegan Paul, 1974), chapter 1.
5. Max Weber, *Wirtschaft und Gesellschaft*, ed. J. Winckelmann (Koln und Berlin: Kippenheuer & Witsch, 1964), 372, 412, 445, and 480–3.
6. For general literature on eighteenth and early nineteenth century fundamentalism see, Derek Hopwood, "A Pattern of Revival Movements in Islam," *Islamic Quarterly* 15 (1971): 149–158; John Voll, "The Sudanese Mahdi, Frontier Fundamentalist," *International Journal of Middle East Studies* 10 (1979): 145–166; John Obert Voll, *Islam, Continuity and Change in the Modern World* (Boulder, CO: Westview Press, 1982), chapters 3 and 4; Rudolph Peters, "*Idjtihad* and *Taqlid* in eighteenth and nineteenth Century Islam," in *Die Welt des Islams* 20 (1980):132–145; Rudolph Peters, "Erneuerungsbewegungen im 18. und in der ersten Halfte des 19 Jahrhunderts," in *Der Islam in der Gegenwart* , eds. Werner Ende und Udo Steinbach (Munchen: C.H. Beck ,1984), 91–105. A problem for the research on Islamic fundamentalism is the exclusively legal and theological character of the available texts. To the best of my knowledge, no collections of sermons, which could provide us with a better insight into the ethical views of fundamentalism, are existant.
7. Cf J. Spencer Trimingham, *The Sufi Orders in Islam* (London: Oxford. Uniersit.Press, 1971), chapter 4; Voll, *Islam*, 36–7, 55.

8. Weber, *WuG*, 607.
9. Muslim, *Sahih* (al-Qahira: Maktabat Subayh n.d., vol. VIII), 46–7. Engl. trans. in W. Montgomery Watt, "Free Will and Predestination in Early Islam," *Moslem World* 36 (1946): 131–132.
10. Cf. Ernest Gellner, "A Pendulum Swing Theory of Islam," in *Sociology of Religion*, ed. Roland Robertson (New York: Penguin Books 1969), 127–138; Ernest Gellner, "The Unknown Apollo of Biskra: the Social Base of Algerian Puritanism," in *Muslim Society*, (Cambridge: Cambridge University Press, 1981), 149–173.
11. Ibn Taymiyya, "Al-Risala al-Wasitiyya", in Ibn Taymiyya, *Madjmucat al-Rasa'il al-Kubra* (al-Qahira: Maktabat Subayh 1375/1966), vol. I: 404–405.
12. The claim that Islam is basically a ritualistic and legalistic religion cannot be upheld in view of the rich ethical component of Quran, *hadith*, and the *shari'a*. Fundamentalist concern with the *sunna* was partly a search for authentical ethical precepts.

7

Weber and Islamic Reform

Barbara D. Metcalf

Is Weber relevant to the study of modern Muslim reformist movements? Most scholars who study such movements accept Weber's problematic of the relationship between religious change and economic and social life. Indeed, some have explicitly looked to Weber and in particular to *The Protestant Ethic and the Spirit of Capitalism* as a model for explaining the religious and social changes they have sought to understand. Yet Weber's approach has been increasingly questioned, often implicitly, by a selective use of his insights and a bracketing of some of his central questions, not least his overriding interest in why modern capitalism emerged first in the West and nowhere else, a question whose formulation belies the complex interdependence of world interconnections, particularly in the capitalist world system and its committed colonial structures. Weber's ideal-typical approach focused on civilizations as a whole, minimizing not only these interconnections but, outside Europe, change over time.[1] Nonetheless, Weber's interest in the role of religion, specifically the role of religion in modernization, has inspired considerable work on Islamic movements and continues to do so.

In my comments, I would like to give an example of one recent Muslim reform movement. Then, I will offer an interpretation of what I take to be characteristics of Islamic reformist movements in general, drawing on studies of a number of other Islamic movements, and raise some points about the application of a Weberian analysis, suggesting elements in such an approach that appear to me to be fruitful and relevant to students of Islamic reform.

The reformist movement I will use as an example in this essay is often called the "Deobandi movement" after the northern Indian town,

Deoband, where a new-style, bureaucratically organized seminary was established in 1867 during the period typically regarded as the height of British imperial rule.[2] Until recently most observers posited a monolithic and stagnant "Islamic orthodoxy" in the period of European expansion, challenged only by the outflow of Enlightenment and progressive ideas associated with "the West." Hence, significant change was associated with those "modernists" who knew cosmopolitan languages like English and French and who often, themselves, wrote in these languages. The Deobandis, by contrast, while clearly responding to the new conditions of colonial rule, worked in vernacular languages and drew on historic, internal models of change. Indeed, the modernists, far from merely mimicking the West, often shared that same indigenous intellectual milieu. The Deobandi movement is one of many, broadly similar reformist or scripturalist movements widespread among Muslims in the last two centuries.[3]

In briefly describing the Deobandis in this essay, I will draw in particular on a text which is in itself an example of the newly important vernacular religious literature which was such a significant tool of the movement's spread, *The Jewelry of Paradise* (*Bihishti Zewar*), written by Maulana Ashraf 'Ali Thanawi (1863-1943) in the first years of the twentieth century.[4] The metaphor of the work's title underlines for the reader the importance of laying up "jewels"—the reward of faith and good deeds—for the afterlife and of not cultivating the material jewels of this world and the self-indulgence they represent. This particular book was written specifically for women, but it was also read widely by men.

The book encourages an active and vigorous life, and it enjoins believers to manage their worldly affairs as they do their spiritual affairs. Thus, women should manage their household efficiently, keep careful household accounts, save money each month, and exercise thrift and order throughout. Women should avoid business dealings that would be complicated by status considerations and not conducted in a straightforward and rational manner. The book urges its readers, members of the well-born classes—literate, landed, often in trade or in government service—to arise early in the day, to work with their own hands, and to avoid idleness. Women should have the skills to earn their own way against a time when they may find themselves widowed or impoverished. A section of the text legitimates manual work by the example of the prophets who were herders, shepherds, builders, carpenters or, like Muhammad himself, a trader. Whatever the source, money was to be legitimately earned on the basis of fair dealing with everyone, the book taught, for even a small amount of "forbidden" wealth could taint the whole.

The book sets out the ideal of a sober life of simplicity and responsibility to duties—to oneself, one's fellows and to God. Children should not be tossed in the air or accustomed to swinging or dressed elaborately. They should avoid attachment to any one person. They must be set to learning in a disciplined and regular way. The soul of each person, young or old, is to be systematically disciplined away from the vices of greed, envy, and anger toward a life of virtue. No one should make a habit of taking fine food and drink. The book opposes ceremonial customs to mark occasions of joy and sorrow, for these are seen as invitations to endless sin, expense, intermingling, gossiping, and ostentation. Over and over the author warns the reader of the sinfulness of debt incurred for such a purpose:

> Almighty God has declared, "Do not waste wealth. Without doubt Almighty God does not love those who waste wealth." And in another place He declared, "Those who waste wealth are the brothers of Satan and Satan is ungrateful to His God."[5]

How much better, he writes, to set a newly married couple up in business or to buy them land than to waste one's wealth on banquets and parties! In a summary of principles for correct behavior toward other people *(mu'amalat)*, Maulana Thanawi's first point is scrupulosity in acquiring money and restraint in spending it:

> Do not be so greedy that you fail to distinguish what is prohibited and what is permitted. Do not squander the money God gives you. Refrain from spending money unless there is a genuine necessity.[6]

The remaining ten rules provide a gloss on this: the need to be generous to those who sell in distress or are your debtors, the error of taking someone's possessions as a joke, the evil of underpaying laborers, the reward for generosity to those who need cooking fire or food or drinking water. Debt should be avoided, but if a necessity, it should be carefully recorded for one's heirs should death precede repayment.[7]

In this text, wealth is taken as a mark of virtue and the means of fulfilling religiously enjoined responsibilities. Poverty is likely to be a result of sin. Likely, because there is always the chance that God is testing someone he particularly loves or that a saint has chosen to live with nothing. A section of the book lists "Worldly Losses Caused by Sin," among them difficulty in one's affairs, a bad harvest, and a short life. A parallel section lists "Worldly Gains Won through Obedience." First on the list is an increase in livelihood, supplemented by the promise of honor and respect, and increased gain in wealth if there should be temporary reverses. Life-giving rain is promised only to the just.[8]

Here we have a fellowship of believers, each enjoined to take individual responsibility, guided by the learned and wise, in living what can only be called a godly, righteous, and sober life characterized by frugality and hard work. Each believer was enjoined to engage in self-reflection and willed external conformity to proper behavior should desires direct otherwise. Here is a sample conversation to be held with one's own self, using the relationship to worldly goods as metaphor:

> O Self [*nafs*], you must recognize that in this world you are like a trader. Your stock-in-trade is your life. Its profit is to acquire well-being forever, that is, salvation in the afterlife. This is indeed a profit! If you waste your life and do not gain your salvation, you suffer losses that reach to your stock-in-trade. That stock-in-trade is so precious that each hour—indeed, each breath—is valuable beyond limit, [for it earns] paradise forever and the joy and vision of God.[9]

The frugality, the positive value put on business dealings and trade, the piety and personal morality of the movement all resonate broadly with what is often usually called "puritan."

Those who shared this orientation self-consciously set themselves apart from the common religious practices of dependence on the mediatory powers of saints and their blessed tombs, in particular from pilgrimage and customary ceremonies of propitiation and intercession. These teachings served well the more mobile and politically integrated population that was emerging in the late nineteenth century. Those who shared reformist teachings had codes of behavior and forms of worship that transcended parochial customs and differences. Thus adherents of reform were far more likely to be associated with cities, education, business and trade, and government service than with a rural agricultural life. Opponents of the Deobandis, who crystallized as a distinctive religious style outsiders called "Barelvi" (after the birthplace, Bareilly, of their leader) celebrated the more custom-laden, shrine-focused religion of the countryside but, over time, developed a more systematized, universal framework for those teachings and a more heterogeneous following.[10]

It is Muslims like the Deobandis, however, discussed in books with such titles as *Muslim Puritans*, who would seem best able to offer rich resources for searchers after what has been called the Protestant ethic "analog."[11] It was with the maxims of Benjamin Franklin and common-sense observations about the worldly success of Protestants that Max Weber began his study of the Protestant ethic. Similarly, the explicit assumption of many scholars has been that there must, similarly, exist a natural affinity between reformist Islam on the one hand and modern business and trade on the other. This suggests at least two questions. Is there in fact a link between reformist Islam and capitalism and, if so, does this affinity serve to explain the reformist movements? Does the presumed "analogy" do justice to Weber's approach to the Protestant ethic?

To answer the first question it is important to examine these movements in detail. Such an examination will show that these movements exist in a variety of socioeconomic contexts, not only in situations of modern capitalism. The assumption that the reformist movements represent a response to modern economic conditions is, however, not surprising. Some are in fact associated with modern economic change. Moreover, the teachings of reformist Islam do look puritanical and their idiom is often one of trade and commerce. This is in part because early Islam took shape in an urban society characterized by growing trade and economic integration; and the reformist movements attempt to return to the teachings of that day. Islam is, in its origins, a rational and law-minded religion so that whether a reform movement arises in the context of some specific economic development or in the context of some other social and cultural crisis, the teachings will use the original language and idiom.[12] There are unities in the movements, but they are not found in social origin or sociological form.

While outside observers might describe them as voluntary social reform movements,[13] proto-nationalist movements,[14] or neo-Sufi movements,[15] from the perspective of the participants themselves, the movements are not defined by their sociological form or milieu at all, but only by their teachings. The participants see beyond external forms to their essence. They identify that by the Arabic word *tajdid*—pointing to "renewal" of the authentic teachings of the faith. The same religious orientation thus has the potential of being associated with a variety of social groups and of finding a wide variety of practical expressions.

Three characteristics define the reformist movements, despite their evident diversity. One is that their leadership comes from the classical academies or the sober Sufi brotherhoods. In this they offer a contrast to the twentieth century "fundamentalist" or Islamic "statist" movements which are often in the hands of the secularly educated. Second, the movements invariably respond to some sense of injustice in the world, although they vary in the extent to which they focus on individual morality in contrast to a focus on new social or political institutions. Here is, again, a contrast with the European Puritan vocation to control and re-form the world. The Deobandis, for example, focus wholly on individual regeneration.

Finally, the Sunni movements, from the time of Ibn Taymiyya (d. 1328), focus on the corruption of the true faith by errors that have crept in through false Sufism and emulation of the Shi'a (and much less on reaction against external influence of, say, Hindus or the West as is often assumed). The want to return to the fundamental sources of the faith. They see themselves in the image of the first great reform movement, that of the Prophet himself, who saw a world in which rulers were unjust, the rich and corrupt oppressed the poor, and humans lived by false values. His mission was to show the straight path of Islam.

If understood from within, such movements are not merely imitative of Western forms or values.[16] Nor are they due solely to economic upheaval, colonial oppression, or modern political and social change. It is true that the reformist movements have become a major trend in the modern period, but, in fact, they have occurred throughout Muslim history and represent an enduring discourse in their goals and styles of reasoning of reform.

The movements exhibit a similarity of doctrine but they arise in very diverse social and economic contexts. William Roff has analyzed, for example, four movements of the late eighteenth and early nineteenth centuries that are often labelled "Wahhabi."[17] The term suggests that the movements stemmed from the militant eighteenth-century Nejdi reform of Muhammad ibn 'Abd al-Wahhab (1703–87). Roff argues, however, that the connection among them is incidental and that each arises in very different circumstances: the Nejdi movement was connected to warring segmentary tribal lineages in Arabia; the Padri movement in Sumatra rose among traders caught up in new opportunities for wealth who experienced new forms of social differentiation with the introduction of the cultivation of coffee; the Fara'izi movement took hold among weavers and peasants in Bengal in a context of the elimination of Muslim rule and changed patterns of economic prosperity; and the Fulani jihad rose in a context of enhanced slave raiding and population growth in West Africa that produced new internal conflicts and patterns of migration. Despite the differences of context, their leaders shared the intellectual orientations then current in the Hijaz where many of them had studied in the course of the pilgrimage. The similarity of their teachings rested far more, however, on the widely diffused model of Islamic reform briefly described above. All saw the world to be awry, and blamed current problems, whatever their nature, on a failure to adhere to the pristine teachings of Islam.

Three of the movements, to be sure, took place in the expanding commercial and political arena of Western colonialism, but it would be misleading to conclude that the reformist teachings were even implicitly supportive of an accommodation to a capitalist economy. In the case of Bengal, for example, the loss of Muslim political power seems to have been of overriding importance. In both Bengal and Sumatra, the crisis was seen in the terms that the Prophet saw the Mecca of his own day: the newly rich, whether landed *zamindars* prospering from the favorable tax standard of the Permanent Settlement (1793) or compradors finding new wealth through dealings with European traders, or traders and carriers enriched by the coffee trade, all were judged to show a crude individualism and a disregard for the moral underpinnings of society. The movements were thus morally and religiously based.

The best case for a conjunction of economic situation and acceptance of reformist principles has been made for the Padri movement in the writings of Christine Dobbin.[18] Led by reformists in the *surau* (schools of the brotherhoods), the movement fostered teachings that were clearly functional in the newly prosperous coffee areas. They offered "guidelines of broader range and applicability, and providing more easily enforceable sanctions, than those of traditional *adat* [customary practice].... Moreover, Islamic law paid greater attention than did *adat* to the rights of the individual as opposed to the lineage." Having shown from area to area an overlap between coffee cultivation and Padri support, Dr. Dobbin concludes with an excellent statement of the position that, at least in this case, a material base determined the spread of reformist Islam:

> It can be seen that those engaging in a network of market relations far wider than the earlier exchange relationships among a group of villages required a mutually acceptable code of conduct which would facilitate business transactions and assist "mutual recognition." Islam and its legal system were at hand to provide the foundation of such a moral community, enabling commercial networks to function on the basis of both trust and law.[19]

The theme of the association of reformist Islam with societies moving toward a more comprehensive scale, societies increasingly integrated economically, socially, and politically, is a central one in the modern period. In my own study of the Deobandi 'ulama', who pioneered a newly bureaucratized and formal style of madrasa education to carry their teachings, it was a core group of government servants and traders who supported the movement, people for whom parochially defined cults and ceremonies had increasingly little meaning.[20] Still, an increase in economic scale is not identical with the development of a capitalist economy or a capitalist mentality.

Other cases show clearly that reform need not be limited to periods of economic change and that they are not "a religiously colored expression of bourgeois interests." Mitsuo Nakamura's study of the Muhammadiya, a voluntary association founded in 1912, explicitly challenges Geertz's argument of an "elective affinity" between Islam and trade in Indonesia.[21] In the area of south central Java which Nakamura studied, the Muhammadiya spread in a period of rising prosperity among people who had long been traders but unreformed. It was, however, no less strong in later decades of economic decline when it served as a source of self-esteem and solidarity. In this analysis, Nakamura sees himself as a Weberian who recognizes that a religious movement has implications and consequences far beyond the groups who initially brought it about. He insists on "the generative, formative and transformative aspects of religion" which make it independent of economic context.[22] My own work on Deoband bears this out, for its teachings became a mark of respectable status and were embraced by the upwardly mobile in a process wholly outside the experience and expectations of the founders.

Despite the evidence for a lack of close connection between reformist movements and economic situation, many Western and Asian scholars in recent decades have, nonetheless, focused exclusively on the economic context of religious movements. The prominence of this theme forms in itself an interesting chapter in the historiography of the non-Western world. Detlev Kantowsky has argued that in relation to India it became a matter of imperialist concern and nationalist pride to find a potential for capitalist development inherent in South Asia's cultural traditions; and there began the search for "functional equivalents" to the Protestant ethic among economically prosperous Jains, Parsis, or others.[23] In Southeast Asia, beginning with the Dutch, there was a similar concern to show that a capitalist mentality could arise endogenously and not only in imitation of the West.[24] Development specialists envisaged a manipulation of cultural tradition to emphasize the appropriate ethos. This search for an analog would not have been congenial to Weber whose concern, as noted above, was with the genesis of civilizational traditions and their institutionalization, each in its own terms (an approach with problems, of course, of its own as Said[25] warns and Huntington proves.[26] One should, further, be clear that Weber himself did not see industrialization as an unqualified good. As is well known, he had a profound insight into its limitations. Indeed, Kantowsky suggests, the construct of "development" should be turned back on to a Weberian analysis of Europe. The concept can then be seen as a theodicy, a way of justifying suffering and deprivation in the world, by which the "underdeveloped" are not only poor but morally defective, and thus, following Weber, the fortunate are able to know that they deserve the goods they enjoy.[27]

The quest for the analog, moreover, errs significantly in not seeing, as Weber would put it, that ideas become "ideal interests" and that those interests serve multiple ends beyond the merely economic. Thus the easy linking of religious reform to capitalist economic change does justice neither to the phenomenon nor to the theories of Weber so often invoked.

Despite certain evident similarities of the teachings of Islamic reform and of European puritanism, Islamic reform, one must add, differs from European puritanism in one dimension that is central to Weber's argument. Only in exceptional cases does Islamic reform give rise to the kind of psychological tension that generates sustained rationalized action in the political, let alone the economic, sphere. In its many forms, Islamic reformism seems to offer far more certainty than did Calvinism of the efficacy of human action, both ethical and ritual, in securing divine favor, and hence it generates far less anxiety about ultimate salvation. The *Jewelry of Paradise* described above, for example, provides hundreds of pages of guidance in correct ritual and legal principles in the conviction that such observance leads to ultimate reward. Calvinists had no such resource. Many of the reform movements, moreover, exist in situations of relatively little tension with their larger societies and are accepted as legitimate styles of religious orientation.

Is the "Weber thesis," then, of use in the study of Islamic reform? Weber, unlike many who invoke him, does more than establish a correlation between reformist religious beliefs and modern capitalist society. His approach requires more than a description of the material social and economic conditions that provide the context for reformist beliefs, but looks to issues of sequence and causality.

Weber actually posits two stages in his concern to explain modern economic change: first the creation of a spirit or mentality and second the role of that mentality, under special economic and political circumstances, in pointing the direction to economic development. If there are, as a recent critic has argued, "tautological leanings with respect to the effects and status of the spirit of capitalism,"[28] in subsequent work, and in fact in his original writings themselves, Weber places doctrine as prior. Three scholars, all explicitly invoking Weber in their study of Muslim reform, address this issue of sequence and cause. Alatas, looking at Malaysia, places the origin of ideologies in local material contexts, contrasting the entrepreneurial behavior of migrant Indian Muslims with local Malay Muslims.[29] This offers a nice contrast to Weber who never accepted the argument of critics who suggested that social marginality was more decisive in Protestant behavior than theology: Weber, in turn, invoked examples of displaced Roman Catholics who manifested no economically rational behavior at all. Hefner, studying the recent Islamization of a non-Muslim community in Indonesia, emphasizes the importance of sociopolitical configurations in studying religious change and illustrates the limitations of what he terms an "intellectualist" approach.[30] Peacock takes Weber as his model, but in discussing commerce and reformist beliefs, disarmingly writes that he "has no idea which comes first."[31]

For Weber, the key to the spirit of capitalism—ethical dealing, rational means, and the increase in capital as a duty—is found in the Calvinist doctrine of the elect and its relentless and chilling doctrine of divine election. The church included both the saved and the damned: membership alone was not the key to the state of the soul. No assiduity in rendering good works could modify the decree preordained. The believer was, however, called on to demonstrate his election by behaving as though he were saved: any other orientation would betray his only purpose in life, the glorifying of God. The believer was to recognize work as vocation, measure and manage time deliberately, and live with frugality and utmost simplicity. Since worldly success was the outer sign of this disciplined and holy life, alms and charity could only be seen as distorting what should be a clear relation between behavior and worldly condition. The doctrine and its psychological sanction were inextricable.

While the doctrine of predestination was set by John Calvin, it attained its significance as rational and ethical pursuit of gain coupled with a puritanical style of consumption, only in the seventeenth-century sermons of English clergy. By the eighteenth century, capitalist accumulation and the underlying values that sustained it had gained a life of their own. Writings like those of Benjamin Franklin gave no evidence of their presumed genesis in the theology of Geneva. The Weber thesis is about the psychological consequences of certain doctrines and their implications for everyday conduct. Doctrine is the source of the capitalist mentality and not a rationalization of it, although Weber was in principle also concerned about how ascetic Protestantism could in turn be influenced by social conditions.

The lesson from Weber, I would suggest, is twofold. First, to face up to issues of causality and not be satisfied with congruence. No question is harder. We all grope after what James Clifford calls "a multiply motivated model," often contenting ourselves with a collage.

The second lesson is to share Weber's taste, nurtured in the German Historical School and so evident in the *Protestant Ethic*, for concrete phenomena. Weber, for all his demurrals, mastered, in his quest for a key to psychological attitudes and behavior, theological detail and nuance as few among us ever do. If we want to be true to the phenomena we study, we must be prepared for a depth of penetration into the culture that social scientists, often concerned with the broad and generalizable picture, rarely are. We cannot be content with saying that our Javanese informant quoted the Quran: we must know chapter and verse and why he quoted the words he did. Peacock—who invites this attention by his explicit Weberian stance—is in this respect not true to his master. He uses only one part of Weber—the association of reformed beliefs with psychological rationalization—and neglects the larger picture. He ignores religion in its own terms and is puzzled by the place of ritual in Muhammadiya life.

In conclusion, Weber invites us to study specific cases not only with exhaustive study of the contextual factors in which they take place, but to textual factors as well, as they play a part in everyday lives. We may disagree with much in Weber's explicit writings on Islam. We may object to the partial, even misleading use of Weber that finds modernization or even a Puritan Ethic where the actors themselves find only Islam. But the Weberian commitment to causality and to textual as well as contextual specificity—the lessons of *The Protestant Ethic* even if not of Weber's more comparative work—is critical if we are to begin to understand the Islamic movements and reforms that have been so pervasive in recent history.

Notes

I am grateful to Ira Lapidus and Guenther Roth for their thoughtful comments on a first draft of the earlier version of this paper.

1. Among recent writings see Talal Asad, *Genealogies of Religions: Discipline and Reasons of Power in Christianity and Islam* (Baltimore, MD: The Johns Hopkins University Press, 1993); *Weber's "Protestant Ethic": Origins, Evidence, Contexts,* eds. Hartmut Lehmann and Guenther Roth (New York: Cambridge University Press, 1994); and *Nation and Religion,* eds. Peter van der Veer and Hartmut Lehmann (Princeton, N.J.: Princeton University Press, 1999).
2. Barbara Metcalf, *Islamic Revival in British India: The Deobandi Ulama, 1860–1900* (Princeton, N.J.: Princeton University Press, 1982).
3. I use the term reformist for those movements often called, following Geertz, "scripturalist" in the sense that they systematically analyze customs and practices to show their distance from textual norms (See Geertz, *Islam Observed* [New Haven, CT: Yale University Press, 1968]). In my discussion I exclude, as I explain in the text, the "modernists." I also do not discuss the movements often lumped with them which are often called "fundamentalist." Although the fundamentalist movements do share important characteristics of the reformist movements in their return to basic sources of the faith, that term can usefully be reserved for those movements of the twentieth century that (1) seek control of the modern national state; (2) define themselves as a system in opposition to other ideological systems explicitly associated with the West; and (3) are typically led by the secularly educated. In South Asia, the preeminent example of a "fundamentalist" Islamic movement is the Jama'at-i Islami (See Seyyed Vali Reza Nasr, *The Vanguard of the Islamic Revolution: The Jama'at-i Islami of Pakistan*, Comparative Studies on Muslim Societies, 19 (Berkeley: University of California Press, 1994). For a more inclusive view of "fundamentalism" see the volumes edited by Martin E. Marty and R. Scott Appleby (including *Accounting for Fundamentalisms: The Dynamic Character of Movements* [Chicago: University of Chicago Press, 1994]).
4. Barbara D. Metcalf, trans., *Perfecting Women: Maulana Ashraf'Ali Thanawi's Bihishti Zewar* (Berkeley: University of California Press, 1991). The earliest printed edition of this work is available in the British Library, catalogued with a date of 1906 although the various sections were printed in varying years at about that time. It has been widely reprinted and translated into other languages from the original Urdu.
5. Ibid., 136.
6. Ibid.
7. Ibid., 182.
8. Ibid., 77–78.
9. Ibid., 234.
10. Usha Sanyal, *Devotional Islam and Politics in British India: Ahmad Riza Khan Barelwi and his Movement, 1870–1920* (New York: Oxford University Press, 1996).
11. James Peacock, *Muslim Puritans: Reformist Psychology in Southeast Asian Islam* (Berkeley: University of California Press, 1978).
12. Ruth T. McVey, "Islam Explained: A Review Article," in *Pacific Affairs* (1982): 279.
13. Kenneth W. Jones, *Socio-Religious Reform Movements in British India* (New York: Cambridge University Press, 1989).

14. Hafeez Malik, *Moslem Nationalism in India and Pakistan* (Washington, DC: Public Affairs Press, 1963).
15. Fazlur Rahman, *Islam* (Chicago: University of Chicago Press, revised edition 1968).
16. Bryan S. Turner, *Weber and Islam* (London: Routledge, 1974).
17. William R. Roff, "Islamic Movements: One or Many?" In *Islam and the Political Economy of Meaning*, ed. William R. Roff (London: Croom Helm, 1987), 31–52.
18. Christine Dobbin, *Islamic Revivalism in a Changing Peasant Economy: Central Sumatra, 1784–1847* (London: Curzon Press, 1983).
19. Christine Dobbin, "Economic Change in Minangkabau as a Factor in the Rise of the Padri Movement, 1784–1830," in *Indonesia* (1977): 38.
20. Barbara D. Metcalf, *Islamic Revival in British India: The Deobandi Ulama, 1860–1900* (Princeton, NJ: Princeton University Press, 1982), chapter 6.
21. Mitsuo Nakamura, *The Crescent Arises over the Banyan Tree: A Study of the Muhammadiyah Movement in a Central Javanese Town* (Yogyakarta:Gadjah Mada University, 1976), 98.
22. Ibid., 23.
23. Detlef Kantowsky, "Max Weber on India and Indian Interpretations of Weber." A paper presented to the Seventh European Conference on Modern South Asian Studies, School of Oriental and African Studies (London, July 7–11, 1981).
24. Sayed Hussein Alatas, "The Weber Thesis and South East Asia," *Archives de Sociologie des Religions* (1963): 21–24.
25. Edward Said, *Orientalism* (New York: Pantheon, 1978).
26. Samuel Huntington, "The Clash of Civilizations," *Foreign Affairs* 72(3)1993: 22–49.
27. Kantowsky, "Max Weber on India," 39.
28. Gordon Marshall, *In Search of the Spirit of Capitalism: An Essay on Max Weber's Protestant Ethic Thesis* (New York: Columbia University Press, 1982), 40.
29. Alatas, "The Weber Thesis and South East Asia," 33.
30. Robert W. Hefner, "The Political Economy of Islamic Conversion in Modern East Java," in *Islam and the Political Economy of Meaning*, 53–78.
31. Peacock, *Muslim Puritans*, 94.

8

Secularization, Weber, and Islam[1]

Francis Robinson

For the hundred years preceeding the Muslim revival of the late twentieth century, the Islamic world seemed to be following a path of secularization similar to that on which the Western Christian world embarked some centuries before. Law derived from revelation had been increasingly removed from public life; religious knowledge had steadily lost ground in education; more and more Muslims had come forward who were Islamic by culture but made "rational" calculations about their lives in much the same way as Christians formed in the secular West might do. The development of this "rationaliality" and rationalization within Christianity, according to Max Weber, brought the secular world into being. This essay is concerned to explore how far Weber's theory of secularization, which is derived specifically from the experience of Western Europe, can help us both to make sense of this process in Islamic society and, perhaps, to reach some understanding of what the measure of secularization might be in an Islamic environment.[2]

Weber's process of secularization is a unique Western development, its roots deep in ancient Judaism, and its trunk in Protestantism and in the growth of capitalism. At the heart of the process lie the concepts of rationality and rationalization. We discern the growth of rationality in increasing human capacity to calculate and to control all aspects of life without appeals either to traditional norms or to charismatic enthusiasm. As bureaucracies come to embrace all the activities of the economy and of the state, opportunities for individual initiative, and dependence on traditional loyalties, are reduced. Social relationships are rendered steadily more impersonal. As rational legal systems, in which lawyers make the law, come more widely to be adopted, the hold of sacred traditions and all forms of arbitrariness in law is loosened, and individuals contemplate their prospects with greater precision. Society grows more like a machine, the individual like a cog in that machine, and human actions come more and more to be rationally calculated. The individual gains a growing sense of control over life.[3] There flow from this substantial consequences for religious understanding.

There is that famous "disenchantment of the world"; Weber uses Schiller's term *entzauberung*, meaning literally "the driving out of magic from things". The human being no longer dwells in a great enchanted garden. To find direction, and to win security in this world and the next, the human being no longer needs either to revere or to coerce the spirits; there is no longer need to seek salvation through ritualistic, idolatrous or sacramental procedures.[4] Human beings lose their sense of providence in life. "Once upon a time," declares Owen Chadwick in surveying the secularization of the European mind, "the wood was bewitched, and goblins and fair spirits dwelt in the trunks of trees and among the roots. But now the wood is administered by the Forestry Commission, and although romantic men may still hear a goblin running in the undergrowth and glimpse beauty behind a bush, they know when a subjective experience is subjective."[5]

Closely associated with disenchantment there is a fragmentation of human understanding of the world. The development of science reveals how the world consists of natural and cultural processes; humans learn that a religious understanding of it is partial, indeed, subjective. The growth of a functionally differentiated society leads to the steady relegation of religion from public life; it is forced out of the realms of economic, political, and even social conduct, and into the further recesses of private life in which its function is merely to interpret and to organize the relationship of the individual human being to the sacred. Thus, the unified vision, in which all human experience was understood through Christian revelation, is replaced by a fragmented vision in which no one set of values either embraces both public and private life, or is shared by citizens in their individual existences.[6]

This is Weber's path of secularization. From his sociology of the great religions he takes us down a path of disenchantment which culminates in the sociology of the intelligentsia, amongst whom, like as not, each human is a god unto his\herself.[7] We should note, nevertheless, that Weber's theory is regarded as offering only one possible perspective over secularization in the West. It does not explain, so Turner claims, the American case of immigration, religious revival and the secularization of theological content; nor does it account for the East

European path of secularization from above.⁸ Then, again, it does not satisfy those heirs of Comte and Durkheim who find religion deep-seated in humanity and in the consensus which makes up human society. They suspect those who talk of secularization of presupposing some golden age in the past as compared with an over-secularized present; they feel they ignore a continuing interaction between Christian revelation and Western civilization, a continual working and reworking of the Christian message through the lives and minds, the societies and institutions of Western man.⁹

These reservations noted, let us see what Weber's theory can tell us about secularization in the Islamic world. Our evidence will be derived in the main from the Islamic world of South Asia, although we shall reach out, where appropriate, to seek parallels and comparisons elsewhere. Our approach will be founded on one adopted by Peter Berger. In exploring Weber's perspectives of disenchantment and fragmentation we shall use Berger's distinction between structural secularization, that is the evacuation of religion from society's institutions and its consequences, and subjective secularization, that is the evacuation of the religious from the consciousness of man and its consequences.¹⁰

First, we consider structural secularization, the driving out of Islam from the frameworks of law, of knowledge, and of power in British India. In the case of law, we find that in the century which followed the 1770s the Islamic criminal and civil law was first encroached upon, and then replaced outright, by British codes of law. By the 1870s the Muslims of British India found that their Islamic law, the *shari'a*, accounted for no more than their personal law, that is the law relating to matters such as marriage, divorce, and inheritance. Moreover, that law was no longer strictly Islamic in its rules of procedure but slowly being reshaped, as Islamic doctrines of strict adherence to established authorities were set aside in favor of English doctrines of equity and binding precedent, by the procedures of that limited form of Weberian *qadi*-justice, the Anglo-Muhammadan law.¹¹ We can discern fragmentation in at least two senses. There was fragmentation between public and private worlds, between a public world ruled by law derived from the West, and a private world ruled by law derived from Islamic sources. There was also fragmentation between the world of the British courts, whether they applied the British codes of public law or the Anglo-Muhammadan personal law, and the world of the *'ulama,'* the traditionally learned men of Islam, who strove to offer as full guidance in the ways of the *shari'a* as they could. Beneath the framework of British justice the *'ulama'* sustained a limited system of Islamic legal guidance represented by institutions such as the *Dar al-Ifta* of the Deoband School and the *Amir-i Shari'at* organization of Phulwari Sharif, Bihar.[12]

In the case of learning, an entirely new system was erected, which owed nothing to Islam. The knowledge taught was knowledge which would enable men to work modern bureaucracy, it was not knowledge which would make God's revelation through Muhammad work more successfully in the world. The peaks of achievement in the new system were peaks of achievement in Western scholarship and science, which were usually reached in British universities, they were not peaks of achievement in *tafsir* (Quran commentary) or *fiqh* (jurisprudence) to be scaled in Cairo or an-Najaf. Education in Islamic knowledge was increasingly relegated to a minor position and increasingly became less relevant to the broad purposes of society and state. Here, too, we can discern fragmentation. There were differences between government educational institutions, which taught Western knowledge in an anglicized environment, and Muslim institutions, like Aligarh College, which to some degree at least wished to hold Western knowledge within a Muslim cultural frame. There were greater differences between all such colleges, which produced swelling streams of trousered graduates able by and large to think in Western terms and to serve the purposes of Western civilization and the Islamic madrasas, which produced a dwindling stream, relatively at least, of turbaned graduates able to see the world only through the prism of revelation.[13]

In the case of power, the only association between Islam and power which remained after the British abolished Muslim judges, or *qadis*, in the 1860s was the Anglo-Muhammadan law. Nevertheless, there did develop an association between Muslims and power. At each stage, as the British slowly devolved power on Indians between 1909 and 1947, a separate Muslim political identity was further entrenched in the modern political framework they were fashioning for India. Muslims gained separate electorates; they gained guaranteed numbers of seats; and ultimately some won an Islamic state of Pakistan. We seem to witness in the first fifty years of twentieth-century British India that somewhat paradoxical process, which also took place in Victorian Britain, that while the disenchantment of learning and other institutions goes on apace the political importance of religion remains strong.[14] Of course, we can also find fragmentation in the wake of disenchantment. There was the development of both a secular and a communal framework for politics within the colonial state. More significantly, there was the growth of a fundamental distinction between those Muslims for whom freedom meant removing the British and taking over the framework of the colonial state and its law, either in a secular India or in a Muslim Pakistan, and those Muslims for whom the only real form of freedom was the imposition of the *shari'a*, a true marriage between law derived from revelation and the machinery of the modern state.[15]

British India, therefore, reveals a moderate structural secularization; Islam was to various degrees disentangled from the frameworks of law, of learning and of power. Indeed, we might understand the situation best in terms of a kind of structural dualism. On the one hand, there was the developing fabric of the modern colonial state onto which, admittedly, some Muslim preferences had been imposed. On the other, there were the residual Islamic institutions of law and learning and the political vision which they fostered. By comparison, Turkey between the nineteenth-century reform period of the Tanzimat and the death of Ataturk had achieved a total disentangling of Islam from the frameworks of law, learning and power. But in Iran, up to the abdication of Riza Shah in 1941, or in Egypt, up to the Free Officers Revolution of 1952, we must talk more in terms of structural dualism along the lines of British India. Indeed, by the mid-twentieth century this was the pattern in most of the Islamic world.[16]

We now turn to consider subjective secularization, the disentangling of the religious vision from the consciousness of human beings. Here, too, we seem to be able to see the realization of a Weberian perspective. There seem to be processes of disenchantment in the emergence of a protestant or puritan Islam. This had its immediate origins in the great movement of revival and reform which swept through the Islamic world in the eighteenth and nineteenth centuries.[17] Barbara Metcalf analyzes one of its Indian manifestations in her study of the context and the emergence of the Deoband school in the second half of the nineteenth century. She notes the growth of Islamic practice based more firmly on the Quran, the Hadiths and the *shari'a*. It is an Islam based on scripture; it is one which is rationalizing the sense of making religion self-conscious, systematic and based on abstract principles. Groups of Muslims come forward who, while they do not in the main reject saints and Islamic mysticism (sufism), increasingly see themselves as following religious practice which is different from that of the sufi shrines, indeed, they often define their Islam in contrast to the parochial forms of the shrines. Their's is a universal form in which Muslims all over India, indeed, all over the Muslim world, could share.

It is one, moreover, whose growth and development is closely interwoven, as in the emergence of European protestantism, with the translation of scripture into the vernacular languages and the harnessing of the printing press to the spreading of religious knowledge.[18]

Thus, there came to be established among the forms of Indian Islam a puritan form, which in its extreme manifestation of the *Ahl-i Hadiths* (People of the Traditions) was stripped to the bare essentials of Quran and Hadiths. These puritan Muslims began to dispense with the great network of saints and ancestors through whom they once came close to God. They came to live less in a world penetrated through and through by sacred beings and forces. God was firmly transcendant and humans had no comfort, no guidance except God's revelation through Muhammad to help them live in this world so that they might be judged favourably in the next. These Muslims increasingly seemed to find the world a cold, bleak, disenchanted place. It is a process which in protestant Christianity many see to be preparing the way for secularization. Once the channels between humankind and God had been narrowed down to His Word, belief in God became dependent on the credibility of that Word. Once that credibility was undermined, the floodgates of secularization were open.[19]

We do not wish to suggest that the outcome for Islam will be the same, only that there are some similarities in the path travelled. For the moment, we would note that the emergence of a puritan Islam is not confined to India but is also to be found in other parts of the Islamic World. The closest parallel is probably the Muhammadiyah of Indonesia. A less close one is that of the Salafiyah of North Africa, whose assertion of the ideal of a reformed Islam as against that of a saintly Islam in the context of the urbanization of Algeria has been set out by Ernest Gellner in his somewhat misleadingly entitled essay, "The Unknown Apollo of Biskra." Some of the same drives and concerns, on the other hand, have also been expressed through the framework of a sufi order as in the case of the Nurcular of Turkey.[20]

If we can see disenchantment in the processes of subjective secularization, we can also see fragmentation and growing conflict of world views. The very emergence of the new puritan Islam in the towns and qasbahs of nineteenth-century India led to bitter conflict with those for whom the world was still enchanted; it led to those endless battles over behaviour at saints' shrines which Deobandis and Barelvis have carried with them from India to Pakistan to the towns and cities of midlands and northern Britain.[21] It also led to conflict, often no less, bitter, in letter, tract, newspaper and debate, among the reforming sects themselves. Then, there was further conflict between the various traditionalist groups and those called Islamic modernists. Islamic modernists grew from the same stock as the puritan traditionalists but strove somehow to hold elements of Western knowledge and understanding within an Islamic frame. Their line began with the great theological and historiographical efforts of Sayyid Ahmad Khan and the Aligarh movement. It moved through the crises of pan-Islamism from the late nineteenth century to the great Indian movement of 1919–24 to preserve the Turkish caliphate. Then it came to a peak, on the one hand in Abul Kalam Azad and the genesis of the idea of a composite Hindu-Muslim Indian nationalism as the political counterpart to a continuing Islamic universalism, and on the other hand in Muhammad Iqbal and the genesis of the idea of the Islamic state of Pakistan as the realistic answer to the political failure of Islamic universalism.[22] Further development led to Fazlur Rahman, that most creative of Pakistani thinkers, who was once head of the Islamic Research Institute established under his country's constitution but whose challenging thought led him to die in exile on the shores of Lake Michigan.[23]

All these thinkers, whether traditionalist or modernist, understood the world within an Islamic frame. Their vision of world history was bound by Islam: the Quran was their starting point. But, there also came those who espoused visions which challenged Islam as an all-inclusive moral, social and political system, men whose understandings of the world were distinctly secular in a Western sense. There are those, like K. M. Ashraf and Sajjad Zaheer and other supporters of the Progressive Writers Movement of the 1930s and 1940s, who espoused a primarily socialist vision of progress.[24] There are also those, both in India and in Pakistan, who have espoused a nationalist vision of past and future: there is Zulfiqar Ali Bhutto's transient vision of five thousand years of Pakistani history; there is also Mushirul Hasan's vigorous advocacy on behalf of a secular nationalist future for India in general and India's Muslims in particular. For such men Islam is no longer the explanation of the beginning and end of things; it is just another form of culture.[25]

This process of fragmentation and conflict, of the emergence of multiplying strands of conflicting thought among Muslims, which come eventually to include those that challenge Islam as total ideology, can be seen yet more distinctly in the world outside South Asia. Here the nationalism of Ataturk and Riza Shah Pahlavi stood both more confident and better developed. Here the socialism of Nasserite Egypt and Baathist Iraq was more fully thought through and realized. But here, of course, Islam was only threatened by Western domination from without, as opposed to the South Asian Muslim's fear of the pincer threat of Western domination from without and Hindu domination from within.

Thus, we find within the Islamic world much evidence of the growth of secularization along the lines that Weber traced in Christian Europe. Disenchantment and fragmentation takes place in structural terms; it also takes place in subjective terms. From almost any Western point of view the signs of secularization are plentiful. Yet, one reflection gives pause for thought about just how much weight we should attach to what we find. This secularization was a consequence of the projection of Western capital and power into the Islamic world from 1800 onwards. The steady disenchantment and fragmentation of the structures of law, learning, and power was either the direct result of the impact of Western imperialism, as in British India, or as in Turkey and Iran the result of deliberate attempts to copy European ways and institutions to make the state strong enough to keep the foreigner out. These processes were in large part forced on Muslim societies from outside or imposed from above; they were only to some extent the result of new economic and social formations within these societies. We could, moreover, argue along similar lines in dealing with those Muslims who espouse secular ideologies which deny the all-inclusive vision of Islam. That they were able to espouse these ideologies seems mainly a function of the extent to which they were caught up within a web of Western economic influence, power, and thought. They embraced a Western secularism rather than developing an Islamic one.

Some might counter this reflection by pointing to those processes of religious change in the recent Islamic past which bear comparison with similar processes in Christian history. We think of that development of a Muslim puritanism out of the internal dynamics of Islamic civilization which developed a modernist aspect as it came into contact with the West. There are certainly aspects of rationalization here, aspects of Weberian disenchantment and fragmentation. But they do not seem as yet to threaten to undermine the Islamic world view from within. Indeed, these processes seem more aspects of religious change, a reduction in the sufi element in Islam and an increasing emphasis on the law. They seem as much spurs to find a new relationship between revelation and history as a notable manifestation of secularization within an Islamic environment. It may be that this is in large part because Muslims have contemplated the meaning of Western knowledge in the context of overwhelming Western power, which has made it particularly difficult critically to explore their own world and to risk turning it upside down. More time, perhaps, is needed. On the other hand, it may be that there are limits to what a theory of secularization derived from the experience of the Christian world can tell us about religious change in the Islamic world.

So we turn from exploring the potential of Weber's theory of secularization in the Islamic context to considering the problem of secularization in Islamic terms, in fact, to considering the problem as Weber might have done, in terms of the unique "developmental history" of Islam, that is, in terms of the development of Islam as a form of rationalization of world views.[26] We start from the position that the orientation of Islam to the world is different from that of Christianity, and thus its pattern of development will be so too. As Weber suggests, Islam is particularly concerned with this world.[27] It is much more concerned with how men behave than with what they believe, in fact, all that they need believe is contained in the one sentence of the *shahada*, the confession of faith. In most of its fundamental rituals Islam concentrates on the creation and support of a community of believers on earth. There is to be communal prayer, communal fasting, alms-giving to support the community, pilgrimage to affirm the community. Indeed, a Muslim life is primarily significant as being lived as part of the community, that best community, as the Quran declares, raised up for men.[28] A prime function of the community is to support the power which will enforce the *shari'a*. This is ideally, though not wholly in fact, the distilled essence of the Quran and the life of the Prophet which offers guidance for every aspect of human life. It is ideally, and certainly in fact, the constitution of the Muslim community, as Gibb describes it, which stands "for all that the Constitution stands for the United States of America and more."[29] It embodies both the patterns of behaviour which the Muslim should strive to realize in his own life and the patterns of behaviour which the state should try to impose upon him. Muslim society is Islamic to the extent that it follows the *shari'a*. Muslim states are Islamic to the extent that they support the *shari'a*. Here we have a possible criterion of secularization in Islamic societies and states: if they are Islamic to the extent to which the *shari'a* is followed and applied, then they are secular to the extent that it is not followed and applied.

Let us see what we can learn if we use this criterion in the case of

South Asia. We have already noted that by the 1870s the application of the *shari'a* in British India had been reduced to the personal law, and that in its distorted Anglo-Muhammadan form. Nevertheless, there were important developments in its shape and in its support up to the mid-twentieth century. Throughout the history of Islam in South Asia, as in that of other Muslim societies, the *shari'a* had tolerated the continuing existence of customary laws, the non-Islamic laws of new, and not so new, entrants to the Islamic milieu. But, by the time of the Shariat Application Act of 1937, almost all toleration of these customary laws came to an end. As far as their personal lives were concerned, Indian Muslims lived under the *shari'a* alone.[30] Then, in the past, the reach of the state, particularly into rural communities, had always been limited; so had been its capacity to apply the law. But the superior machinery of the colonial state, and later of the national states of India and Pakistan, was able to bring the *shari'a* much closer to the lives of each individual Muslim. By the mid-twentieth century Muslim personal law, that point where the Quran is most explicit, that point where Muslims feel, in Anderson's telling phrase, that the *shari'a* partakes most intimately in the very warp and woof of their lives,[31] had come to be more completely applied than ever before in South Asia. Similar developments can be traced in Malaysia and Indonesia, for instance, and even in Saudi Arabia.[32]

If we now turn to examine how the *shari'a* might have been followed, it seems that, up to the eighteenth century, although many knew they were Muslims, not so many knew how to behave as the holy law might direct. Islamic knowledge, knowledge of what Muslims should and should not do, was hard to come by.[33] We know, as Bulliet, Geertz, Eaton, and many others have demonstrated, that through much of the Islamic world the process of Islamization, the patterning of society after some version of the *shari'a*, has been painfully slow. Many centuries divide the first confession of faith from the wide mastery of the scriptural tradition.[34] We also know that the early nineteenth-century movements of revival and reform in Kerala, in Bengal, and in Northern India, all suggest how large the gap was between the practice of rural and even qasbah society and the preference of an alert, reforming Islam. But the nineteenth and twentieth centuries have seen unprecedented drives, fuelled by continuing movements of reform, by vast increases in the availability of Islamic knowledge, and by favourable economic and social changes, which have brought Muslims to live lives closer to the *shari'a*.[35] Just as the application of the personal law by the state is more rigorous and more widespread than before, so equally is knowledge of the *shari'a*, and perhaps the following of it, in Indo-Muslim society at large. This, too, is not a development confined to South Asia. It is also expressed, for instance, in the popularity of the Muslim Brotherhood throughout much of the Middle East, and, in spite of the determinedly secular face of the Turkish state, or perhaps because of it, in the extraordinary thirst for Islamic knowledge among the Turkish people in recent times. It is, in fact, a feature of the late twentieth-century revival of Islam that has touched every Muslim society.[36]

We are left with contrasting perspectives. If we take that derived from Weber's theory of secularization, it does seem that Indo-Muslim society, indeed Muslim societies in general, has advanced some way down the path of disenchantment and fragmentation, the path of secularization. But, if we respect the integrity of the "developmental history" of Islam as a rationalization of world views, we have a picture which is more complex. Certainly, the exercise of European power in the nineteenth and twentieth centuries drove the *shari'a* out of the public and into the private sphere of Muslim life. Certainly, it undermined the Islamic world view of Muslim elites. Yet, on the other hand, the modern state and the modern technology, which the European brought, helped to draw many Muslims closer to the *shari'a* than before. In recent times, moreover, the retreat of the European, and some failures of the state machinery left behind, have often been accompanied by a reassertion of Islamic world view and a reinstatement of the *shari'a* in public life. A continuing process of islamization, following Weber's understanding of developmental history, seems as notable a feature of recent Islamic developments, as one of secularization, following Weber's theory of secularization.

* * *

Reviewing the argument of this essay some thirteen years after it was first written, and in the light of recent developments in the Muslim world, there is an additional reflection. We have noted above that in terms of the unique developmental history of Islam the faith was particularly concerned with this world. This is, of course, true if it is approached in a sense that veers in an orientalist/essentialist direction. But, if we consider the effective practice of Islam in many societies over much of the past 1,400 years, it has had powerful otherworldly dimensions. Most believers have attended saints' shrines and implored the saint to intercede for them with God.

The great event of Islamic history over the past two hundred years has been the attack by the movement of revival and reform on all ideas of saintly intercession for humankind with God and the new emphasis on the this-worldly dimension of the faith. The many movements of Islamic reassertion have been, and are, impelled by the consciousness of the need to act in this world to achieve salvation. There is evidence that these manifestations of "willed Islam" have come to develop new strands in Muslim consciousness that bear resemblance to similar outgrowths of European protestantism. There is a new sense of empowerment that comes with the knowledge that it is humanity that fashions the world. There is a new sense of personal autonomy and individual possibility that comes with the knowledge that individuals are able to make choices. There is a steady transfer of the symbols and centres of meaning in life from the signs of God and the friends of God to the mundane things of life—family, home, love, sex, food. There is the "inward turn" as the individual comes to examine and to reflect upon the self. In sum the individual becomes more and more focused on earthly activity and earthly fulfilment.

If we take Islam as widely practised through time as the basis of our understanding of the developmental history of Islam, strands are emerging which would appear to point in similar directions to those of protestant Christianity. We recognize, of course, that the new individualism derives some of its impetus from the influence of the West as well as having firm roots in this-worldly Islam. This said, there is growing tension between demands for individual fulfilment and the requirements of obligation to community, a tension felt most acutely in many Muslim societies by women. It is worth considering whether this tension may not be at the cusp of a process of secularization in Muslim societies.[37]

Notes

1. The first draft of this paper was given at the conference on Weber and Islam held under the auspices of the Werner-Reimers-Stiftung, Bad Homburg, in June 1984. I am particularly grateful for comments made then and later by Professors Guenther Roth and Wolfgang Schluchter. This version of the paper is in large part the same as that originally published in German, except for minor changes in the text to bring it up to date and some additions to the supporting notes.
2. It is important to emphasize that Weber's theory of secularization sees the process as an historical one. It is not a model, or ideal type, like patrimonialism, feudalism, or charismatic domination, which is meant to be applicable in different places and at many times.

3. Bryan S. Turner, *Weber and Islam: A Critical Study* (London: Routledge and Kegan Paul, 1974), 151–52.
4. Max Weber, *Economy and Society: An Outline of Interpretive Sociology*, eds. Guenther Roth and Claus Wittick (Berkeley: University of California Press, 1978), 1: 630.
5. Owen Chadwick, *The Secularization of the European Mind in the Nineteenth Century* (Cambridge: Cambridge University Press, 1975), 258.
6. This perspective, with a particular emphasis on the role of functional differentiation, is discussed by Wolfgang Schluchter in "The Future of Religion," in *Religion and America*, eds. Mary Douglas and Steven M. Tipton, (Boston: Beacon Press, 1983), 64–78. Strikingly, although he mentions Weber not once, the controversial, but also moving, work by the Anglican theologian Don Cupitt, *The Sea of Faith: Christianity in Change* (London: British Broadcasting Corporation, 1984), seems much in harmony with Schluchter's Weberian perspective.
7. This broad sweep is outlined by Guenther Roth in "Religion and Revolutionary Beliefs," in Guenther Roth and Wolfgang Schluchter, *Max Weber's Vision of History: Ethics and Methods* (Berkeley: University of California Press, 1979), 166.
8. Turner, *Weber*, 158–59.
9. See, for instance, David Martin, "Towards eliminating the concept of secularization," in Julius Gould, ed., *The Penguin Survey of the Social Sciences* (Harmondsworth: Penguin Books, 1965), 169–82; this position would also seem to underpin Chadwick, and especially his concluding statement in *Secularization*, 264–66.
10. See the chapter entitled "The Process of Secularization," in Peter L. Berger, *The Social Reality of Religion* (Harmondsworth: Penguin Books, 1973), 111–30.
11. *Qadi*-justice is justice which knows no rational rules of decision. It is one of Weber's ideal types. See, Weber, *Economy and Society*, II: 976–78. For the Anglo-Muhammadan law and the impact of its rules of procedure see, N.J. Coulson, *A History of Islamic Law* (Edinburgh: Edinburgh University Press, 1978), 165–71.
12. Tahir Mahmood, *Muslim Personal Law: Role of the State in the Subcontinent* (New Delhi: Vikas, 1977), 67–69; at the end of its first one hundred years the *Dar al-Ifta* of Deoband reckoned that it had issued 269,215 legal decisions—the work of this office and the nature of its decisions are discussed in Barbara Daly Metcalf, *Islamic Revival in British India: Deoband, 1860–1900* (Princeton, NJ: Princeton University Press, 1982), 146–54.
13. Two excellent books enable us to enter these very different worlds under British rule: David S. Lelyveld, *Aligarh's First Generation: Muslim Solidarity in British India* (Princeton, NJ: Princeton University Press, 1978), and Metcalf, *Islamic Revival*.
14. Alan D. Gilbert, *The Making of Post-Christian Britain: A History of the Secularization of Modern Society* (London: Longman, 1980), especially chapter 4.
15. Aspects of these attitudes are dealt with by Francis Robinson, "Islam and Muslim Separatism," in *Political Identity in South Asia*, eds. David Taylor and Malcolm Yapp (London: Curzon Press, 1979), 78–112; Peter Hardy, *Partners in Freedom—and True Muslims: The Political Thought of Some Muslim Scholars in British India, 1912–1947* (Lund: Scandinavian Institute of Asian Studies, 1971); Aziz Ahmad, *Islamic Modernism in India and Pakistan, 1857–1964* (London: Oxford University Press, 1967).
16. For a general survey of these processes see, Francis Robinson, *Atlas of the Islamic World since 1500* (Oxford: Phaidon, 1982), 130–56.
17. Ibid., 118–29.

18. Francis Robinson, "Islam and the Impact of Print in South Asia," in *The Transmission of Knowledge in South Asia: Essays on Education, Religion, History and Politics*, eds. Nigel Crook (Delhi: Oxford University Press, 1996), pp. 62–97; Metcalf, *Islamic Revival*, especially chapters 4 and 5.
19. A sense of this more demanding, disenchanted, world is expressed in the famous guide for women, but whose advice was equally applicable to men, published by the Deobandi scholar, Ashraf Ali Thanawi, at the beginning of the twentieth century, Barbara D. Metcalf, *Perfecting Women: Maulana Ashraf 'Ali Thanawi's Bishishti Zewar: A Partial Translation with Commentary* (Berkeley: University of California Press, 1991).
20. For a local study of this development in Indonesia see, Mitsuo Nakamura, *The Crescent Arises over the Banyan Tree: A Study of the Muhammadiyah Movement in a Central Javanese Town* (Yogyakarta: Gadjah Mada University Press, 1983); for Algeria, Ernest Gellner, "The unknown Apollo of Biskra: the social base of Algerian puritanism," in his *Muslim Society* (Cambridge: Cambridge University Press, 1981), 149–73; for the Nurcular, Serif Mardin, *Religion and Social Change in Modern Turkey: the case of Bediuzzaman Said Nursi* (Albany: State University of New York Press, 1989).
21. Metcalf, *Islamic Revival*, 232–34, 309–11, 355–60; Philip Lewis, *Islamic Britain: Religion, Politics and Identity among British Muslims* (London: I.B. Tauris, 1994).
22. Ahmad, *Islamic Modernism*, 141–94.
23. Fazlur Rahman was professor of Islamic thought in the department of Near Easter Languages and Civilization at the University of Chicago. The final statement of his thinking was *Islam and Modernity: Transformation of an Intellectual Tradition* (Chicago: University of Chicago Press, 1982).
24. For a detailed study of this group and their ideas see, Khizar Humayun Ansari, *The Emergence of Socialist Thought among North Indian Muslims (1917–1947)* (Lahore: Book Traders, 1990).
25. One attempt to develop Bhutto's vision was Ahmed Abdulla, *The Historical Background of Pakistan and its People* (Karachi: Tanzeem Publishers, 1973); Hasan's advocacy appears most powerfully in Mushirul Hasan, *Legacy of a Divided Nation: India's Muslims since Independence* (Delhi: Oxford University Press, 1997).
26. Guenther Roth has shown how fruitful it is to see Max Weber as a "developmental" historian working amongst other German developmental historians who competed hotly with each other. "Developmental History" in Max Weber's time and work," unpublished paper.
27. Weber, *Economy and Society*, I: 623–27.
28. Maulana Muhammad Ali, *The Holy Qur'an*, 6th ed. (Lahore), chapter 3, verse 109.
29. "Structure of Religious Thought in Islam," in Hamilton A.R. Gibb, *Studies on the Civilization of Islam* (Princeton, N.J.: Princeton University Press, 1962), 200.
30. Mahmood, *Muslim Personal Law*, 20–33.
31. Norman Anderson, Law Reform in the Muslim World (London: Athlone Press, 1976), 17.
32. See, for instance, Daniel S. Lev, *Islamic Courts in Indonesia: A Study in the Political Bases of Legal Institutions* (Berkeley: University of California Press, 1972); Moshe Yegar, *Islam and Islamic Institutions in British Malaya*; Donald Powell Cole, *Nomads of the Nomads: the Al Murrah Bedouin of the Empty Quarter* (Illinois: AHM Publishing Corporation, 1975), 123–25.

33. Metcalf emphasizes the difficulties which even *'ulama'* experienced in finding books in the days when they were reproduced by hand and consequently the great change made by the introduction of the lithographic printing press in the first half of the nineteenth century, *Islamic Revival*, 198–215.
34. Richard W. Bulliet, *Conversion to Islam in the Medieval Period: An Essay in Quantitative History* (Cambridge, MA: Harvard University Press, 1979); Clifford Geertz, "Modernization in a Muslim society: The Indonesian case," in *Religion and Progress in Modern Asia*, ed. R. N. Bellah, (New York: The Free Press, 1965), especially 96–7; Richard M. Eaton, *Sufis of Bijapur 1300–1700: Social Roles of Sufis in Medieval India* (Princeton, NJ: Princeton University Press, 1978) and *The Rise of Islam and the Bengal Frontier, 1204–1760* (Berkeley: University of California Press, 1996); a general argument regarding islamization is advanced in Francis Robinson,"Islam and Muslim society in South Asia," *Contributions to Indian Sociology* (n.s.), 17, 2 (1983): 185–203.
35. See, Stephen F. Dale, *Islamic Society on the South Asian Frontier: The Mappilas of Malabar 1498–1922* (Oxford: Clarendon Press, 1980); Rafiuddin Ahmed, *The Bengal Muslims 1871–1906: a quest for identity* (Delhi: Oxford University Press, 1981); Metcalf, *Islamic Revival*; S. A. H. A. Nadwi, *Life and Mission of Maulana Muhammad Ilyas* (Lucknow: Academy of Islamic Research and Publications, Nadwat-ul Ulama, 1993) and M. Anwarul Haq, *The Faith Movement of Mawlana Muhammad Ilyas* (London: George Allen & Unwin, 1972).
36. For a recent assessment of the popularity and influence of the Muslim Brotherhood see, John Obert Voll, *Islam: Continuity and Change in the Modern World* (Boulder, CO: Westview Press, 1982), 174–76, 251–52, 314–15, 318–19, 339–40; and for developments in Turkey, see, Annemarie Schimmel, "Islam in Turkey," in *Religion in the Middle East*, ed. A. J. Arberry (Cambridge: Cambridge University Press, 1969), 2:68–95; Jacob M. Landau, *Radical Politics in Modern Turkey* (Leiden: E.J. Brill, 1974), 171–93; Hamid Algar, "Said Nursi and the Risala-i Nur: An Aspect of Islam in Contemporary Turkey," in *Islamic Perspectives: Studies in Honour of Mawlana Sayyid Abul A'la Mawdudi*, eds. Khurshid Ahmad and Zafar Ishaq Ansari (Leicester: The Islamic Foundation, 1979).
37. This argument is developed in Francis Robinson, "Religious Change, the Self and Community in Muslim South Asia since 1800," *South Asia* 20,1(1997): 1–15.

9

Weber, Islamic Law, and the Rise of Capitalism

Patricia Crone

Weber's *Rechtssoziologie* (hereafter RS) is a section of his *Wirtschaft und Gesellschaft* which has generated relatively little discussion.[1] This is not surprising. Law is a technical subject best left to lawyers, who tend to leave sociology to sociologists, and Weber himself (a lawyer turned sociologist)[2] must be said to have done his best to perpetuate these tendencies by burying his theories in a general handbook as notable for its obscurity as for its erudition.[3] In the first instance the RS is a work for glossators.[4] It also has a certain appeal to exegetes who, in an attempt to find or supply overall coherence to Weber's thought, explicate its theories at a level so exalted that they cease to have much bearing on law.[5] But down-to-earth historians and sociologists of law tend to ignore the RS altogether or, at best, to limit themselves to occasional criticism of its better known propositions and occasional use of the minor insights in which it abounds. It is hard to blame them: to the non-Weberite, the RS is not only a difficult but also a profoundly unilluminating work. Still, it remains one of the most ambitious attempts since Bodin's *Six Books of the Commonwealth* to explore the relationship between law and society,[6] a subject on which neither sociologists nor lawyers tend to have much to offer;[7] and historians of Islamic law are certainly among those in need of typological and developmental schemes for the evaluation of the object of their study.[8] It is thus worth examining what is wrong with the RS and how we might reformulate its questions.

What is wrong with it (its obscurity apart) is essentially that it is formulated as a contribution to the problem of Western "rationality."

Throughout Weber's work rationality is the characteristic which has distinguished the European evolution from that of the rest of the world, and throughout he is concerned to explain how and why this evolution took place. Nowhere, however, does he explain exactly what rationality is. It stands for "a whole world of different things," as he unhelpfully observes,[9] and one gathers that it has to do with being rule-bound, regular, systematic, logical, calculating, purposive, controlled by the intellect, secular, impersonal, disenchanted, orientated towards mere *Zweck* as opposed to *Wert*, and so forth.[10] But these and other epithets merely provide a loose description of modernity, and it is by no means obvious that they add up to a single characteristic. Rationality is thus too untidy a concept to serve as a tool of analysis. Moreover, it is never clear whether it stands for the outcome of the European evolution or on the contrary for its cause. In practice Weber treats it as both cause and effect, with the result that he tends to argue in circles: rationality caused rationality to prevail in Europe whereas traditionalism prevented it from emerging elsewhere. But rationality in the sense of modernity necessarily came out of something irrational and premodern, and the enduring appeal of the *Protestant Ethic* lies in the fact that Weber here suggests how something very rational and modern could have emerged from something very traditional: here he makes bread out of ingredients such as flour, yeast and water which do not look in the least like bread on their own. But in his comparative work, including the RS, he makes his bread of proto-bread.[11] The great civilizations are here tested for their degree of rule-boundness, regularity, systematization and so forth on the assumption that it is rational rather than traditional features which combine to make modernity; and the unsurprising conclusion that rationality in the sense of modernity was absent from the premodern world is then adduced in explanation of the failure of modernity to emerge from this world. The reader does not feel illuminated. Why did *traditional* ingredients fail to produce modernity outside Europe? Given that the concept of rationality is both untidy and conducive to circularity, it should be abandoned. The trouble with the RS is that if one does so, one abandons most of the work.

The Typology of Law in the RS

Weber construes a typology of law by using rationality as a classificatory principle. All legal systems and forms of adjudication, he says, may be either rational or irrational in either a formal or a substantive sense.[12] A legal system is rational in the formal sense when it is based on a set of general principles from which all concrete rules can be deduced, as and when required, by purely logical means without regard for extralegal factors such as social, moral and political considerations. When adjudication consists in the application of such rules with strict regard for legal logic and no regard at all for the concrete setting of the case, then it is formally rational too. Formal rationality is incarnate in modern European law, or at least in the civil law tradition, the most rational of all European law being that elaborated by the German Pandectists. All non-European law, by contrast, is only rational in a substantive sense in so far as it is rational at all. Legal systems are substantively rational when, though fairly systematized, they lack freedom from extralegal concerns, that is, when legal logic tends to be overruled by social, political or religious considerations. Religious legal systems (such as Islamic law) can never be more than substantively rational because they are bound by tradition and orientated towards the maintenance of sacred institutions. Secularity is thus a precondition for formal rationality too. Adjudication is substantively rational when the application of legal rules is biased by extralegal factors. It may also be substantively irrational, meaning bound by no rules at all. Adjudication not based on rules is "qadi justice," qadis being judges who consider each case on its merits and resolve it in the light of common-sense notions regarding justice and expediency after the fashion of patrimonial rulers (such as Solomon) and laymen. Weber assumed much dispensation of justice in Islam to be of this variety,[13] but the etymology of the expression notwithstanding, he did not associate qadi justice specifically with Islam.[14]

The remaining ideal type, formal irrationality, need not concern us here, though there are what Weber would have called formally irrational elements in Islamic law.[15] Of all four types it may be said that they have an immediate appeal which does not survive prolonged exposure to thought. The classificatory concepts change meaning in the course of the classification,[16] and the outcome of the scheme is two impossible ideal types as far as legal systems are concerned. One of these (substantively irrational law) need not concern us here.[17] The other is of major importance to us in that it renders the scheme unable to isolate the major difference between Western and Islamic law.[18]

There can be no such thing as a formally rational system of law. Weber envisaged such a system as a kind of algebra or pure mathematics, that is, as a logical system which is created in isolation from the external world but which nonetheless happens to be applicable to this world.[19] But law is created for the regulation of the external world, so that however abstract its rules may be, it is the external world which generates its contents. Law may be *lebensfremd* in the sense of given to the pursuit of legal logic at the cost of practicality, but all creators of legal systems take as their starting point an inherited set of social forms and another of legal notions which they use to endorse or reshape the social forms in question. The *Bürgerlisches Gesetzbuch* may have been the most rigorously logical of all codes,[20] but it was no less substantive in orientation than any other system: far from being conceived in freedom from extralegal concerns, it was simply born somewhat out of date.[21] In short, all legal systems are substantively rational in so far as they are rational at all, as has been pointed out before.[22]

The fact that all legal systems are substantively rational does not of course mean that all are marked by the same degree of logical coherence, and Weber's formal rationality could be retained as an ideal type for systems marked by a high degree of systematization *within* the substantive boundaries. As such it is perfectly acceptable, but also perfectly useless for the task assigned to it in that it ceases to mark off Europe from the rest of the world. As Weber himself observes, a high degree of systematization is characteristic of the Romano-German family, Islamic law and other religious systems, but not of English law, the reason for this difference being that the former systems were elaborated by scholars (academic jurists, *fuqaha,* rabbis, priests) whereas the latter was shaped by judges, who tend to regard law more as a craft than as an intellectual enterprise.[23] If the objective is to identify a fundamental difference between European and non-European law, formal rationality obviously has to be something unique to Europe; conversely, if the objective is to identify a difference within European law, the inquiry into the rationality or otherwise of non-European systems is redundant.[24] In practice Weber treats formal rationality *both* as a characteristic which for well known reasons differentiated civil law from common law *and* as a characteristic which for unknown reasons differentiated European law from that of the rest of the world. This is impossible. Naturally Islamic law is less systematic than *Pandektenrecht,* and the modes of thought differ too. But if rationality is logical and coherent thought, then both are rational; and if formal rationality is the mode of thought characteristic of the "jurisprudential doctrinaire," then both are formally rational too.[25] The different modes of thought have nothing to do with formal versus substantive orientation. We could of course eliminate Islamic law from the domain of formal rationality by including secularity in the preconditions of entry; but Roman law would still slip through for all that a system which is only ancestral to modern European law, not identical with it, ought not to be admitted. In short, Weber's typology fails to differentiate what should be differentiated.

This is not surprising. Legal systematization is a clue above all to the social locus of the law; secularity relates mainly to its cultural origins, while imperviousness to extralegal concerns (an impossibility in the case of legal systems) is primarily related to the political conditions under which justice is administered. Weber's concept of rationality thus brackets three unrelated characteristics: it is a chimaera made up, like most chimaeras, of real features in unreal combination.[26] However much the features may be deemed to have "elective affinity," we need to separate them if we are to understand how and why European and, say, Islamic law developed so differently.

Law and Capitalism in the RS

Weber at one point uses his typology to construe an evolutionary scheme in which law moves from irrationality to rationality through four major stages.[27] This scheme merely lists the four ideal types in their order of rationality and Weber makes no attempt to show that history has followed it; in fact, he drops it as soon as he has set it out. The bulk of the RS is devoted to a host of other questions treated in apparently haphazard order. In so far as major themes stands out, they are the influence of rulers and *honoratiores* on the formation and administration of the law (viz. law and the sociology of domination) on the one hand and the relationship between law and economic behavior (viz. law and the rise of capitalism) on the other.[28] The reader infers that legal and economic rationality (viz. modern capitalism) are related phenomena, but Weber makes it clear that the relationship is not a directly causal one. On the one hand, he repeatedly stresses that economic factors only play a minor role in the development of law: legal development is marked by a "high degree of independence,"[29] the crucial factors behind it being "intra-juristic conditions" such as the prevailing type of legal education,[30] though political factors have also been of major importance.[31] Indeed, he explicitly states that "capitalism has not been a decisive factor in the promotion of that form of rationalization of the law which has been peculiar to the continental West ever since the rise of Roman studies."[32] On the other hand, he nowhere makes the converse claim that legal rationalization has been a decisive factor in the rise of capitalism, though he does argue that "those aspects of the law which are conditioned by political factors and by the internal structure of legal thought have exercised a strong influence on economic organization."[33] His basic point seems to be that a certain degree of legal rationalization is a precondition for the rise of capitalism and that legal systems which fail to reach this degree may act as barriers to it.[34] One infers that scholars who systematize the internal structure of legal thought for their own intellectual reasons exercise a strong influence on economic organization by inadvertently making the law a suitable instrument for the bourgeoisie. For the bourgeoisie needs a rational, that is calculable, law: capitalism, according to Weber, rests above all on the ability to calculate and predict the consequences of economic behavior; capitalists engage in *rational* calculation, as he puts it in his inimitable fashion. The more systematized the law, the more calculable it will be. If it is formulated as a set of abstract propositions from which further rules are derived by vigorous use of logic, then it will form a gapless whole from which the legal consequences of any transaction can be predicted by the further use of logic, however unforeseen the transaction may have been by the legislators; and if further the judges are reduced to mere slot machines spewing out verdicts in response to information fed into them, then one can also be sure that the courts will decide as logic predicts.[35] In sum, industrial capitalism and mechanized law go together in Weber's work.

To the extent that this is what Weber argued, he was wrong. Most obviously, the hypothesis does not fit the facts. Eighteenth-century English law was both unsystematized and characterized by qadi justice according to Weber himself.[36] He got round this problem by arguing that the dual nature of the administration of justice in England was such that qadi justice, though normally inimical to bourgeois interests, favoured the propertied, especially the capitalistic classes; more precisely, there was formalistic (though not rational) justice for the rich and qadi justice for the poor. England could thus be said to have developed capitalism both because and in spite of its judicial system.[37] But, he said, where no such dual administration of justice is possible, "capitalism will fare best under a rigorously formal system of adjudication"; bourgeois strata have normally wanted "a systematized, unambiguous, and specialized formal law."[38] Yet, he noted, where common law and civil law have been in competition in modern times, common law has tended to win out,[39] for all that Anglo-American law is so unsystematized as to lack a fundamental concept such as that of *dominium:* modern capitalism, he concluded, prospers under legal systems which "differ profoundly from each other even in their ultimate principles of formal structure."[40] If so, what is left of the theory? And modern capitalism did not just flourish in England. This was where it first appeared. If it first appeared in a country characterized by unsystematized law and an irrational judiciary, it is obvious that legal rationality was no precondition for its emergence.[41]

The facts do not fit because the reasoning behind the theory is wrong: the apparent affinity between algebraic law and capitalist calculation is spurious. A logically formulated system may make it easier for a lawyer to work out the answer to a legal puzzle, but it will not make it easier for him to predict the outcome of a real case. Since legal logic only governs the rules which are imposed on behavior, not the behavior itself, the behavior at issue has to be translated into legal logic before it can be judged, that is, it has to be construed to fit the rules. The more abstract the rules, the more drastic the translation required, or in other words the wider the scope for judicial interpretation. In principle a logically formulated system is thus *less* predictable in real life than a casuistically formulated one; in practice a host of secondary rules will soon reduce the difference to insignificance.[42] Moreover, the notion of a gapless system is meaningless in sociological terms.[43] All legal systems are full of gaps in the sense that unforeseen situations keep arising, and all are gapless in the sense that they cope with such situations by construing them to fit such rules as exist and are likely to yield the desired result. Courts dispensing unsystematized law are not in the habit of refusing to deal with unforeseen cases on the grounds that there are gaps in it, while conversely those which dispense supposedly gapless law are in the habit of construing their unforeseen cases on the basis of extralegal considerations such as public policy on a par with everyone else. To this must be added that businessmen do not in practice consult their pocket editions of the latest codes before engaging in business transactions. Where legal advice is needed, legal experts are called in; and such experts usually have a fair idea of what the legal consequences of a particular action are likely to be because they are familiar with both the law (unsystematized or other) and prevailing mode of adjudication (by qadis or others). In short, the degree to which legal systems are rational in the sense of endowed with the logical coherence characteristic of the great civil law codes is not likely to be a factor of much significance in the explanation of the rise, spread or subsequent fate of modern capitalism. No doubt the manner in which the law is administered matters, but this has to do with social and political organization, as Weber himself showed in his discussion of England and elsewhere, not with the nature of the law.

At this point a Weberite may object that Weber's argument has been misrepresented, and this is not entirely untrue. There are passages in the RS which add up to a very different theory from the one just examined. According to these passages, formal rationality as incarnate in the civil law tradition owes its existence to the joint efforts of rulers desirous of order, uniformity and unity, bourgeois elements desirous of rules without privilege and arbitrariness,[44] and scholars desirous of logic;[45] but the scholarly contribution was *not* to the advantage of the bourgeoisie, for legal logic leads to disregard of practical needs,[46] so that systematization without loss of practical adaptability was achieved only in those fields which the bourgeoisie had autonomously adapted to its needs such as commercial law and the law of negotiable instruments.[47] In short, it was the substantive interests of rulers and bourgeoisie which gave European law its historically significant features; formal rationality is irrelevant except for its negative effects. No wonder that capitalism first emerged in England where the bourgeoisie was shielded from the ravages of legal algebra.

The reader may well throw up his hands in despair. If formal rationality is basically an irrelevance from a socioeconomic point of view, why make it the hero of a work on economy and society? And if legal and economic rationality are actually at loggerheads, why present them as inseparable companions in both typological and evolutionary terms? As Cain notes, it is hard to avoid the impression that Weber cheats.[48] Presumably his heart was in that theory for which he is generally criticized and for which this paper has criticized him again, but it is the one just outlined which has explanatory potential: the peculiarity of European law here lies, not in its supposed freedom from extralegal concerns, but on the contrary in the extent to which political and social groups have been able to use it as an instrument for their own substantive concerns.[49]

Islamic Law and Capitalism

What light, then, does the RS cast on the relationship between law and the non-rise of capitalism in the Islamic world?[50] As might be expected in view of the above, the answer is not a great deal.

Islamic law was shaped by "bourgeois elements," in the sense of people overwhelmingly engaged in one form of commerce or other; it could be seen as an instrument of bourgeois interests;[51] and its concrete provisions look highly conducive to capitalism in some respects, if in others the reverse.[52] They look conducive to capitalism in that all persons have been reduced to identical legal units except for slaves[53] and, in more limited ways, women, Arabs and descendants of the Prophet.[54] Slaves are the only significant exception to the rule that the law applies to all regardless of status differentials. Further, all contracts other than marriage are what Weber would call purposive contracts rather than status contracts, that is to say they commit the parties to the performance of a specified action without otherwise affecting their social position.[55] All things have similarly been reduced to identical legal units except for land, which, though certainly marketable, is not quite a commodity like any other.[56] All things are susceptible of full ownership as long as they are ritually pure,[57] and the distinction between ownership and possession is fully developed.[58] The right to dispose of private property is subject to no limitation except on the approach of death (and, in the case of land, pre-emption), the ancient rights of the family to the patrimonial property having been reduced to a claim to two thirds of a dying kinsman's estate.[59] But the law is unconducive to capitalism in that it is highly protective. There is no freedom of contract, specifically no freedom to engage in transactions involving risk or other features enabling one party to extract unearned profit from another. Thus there are neither aleatory nor promissory contracts, no contracts involving things uncertain, unidentified or known, no sale of future, unseen or unspecified goods except in so far as concessions were made to practice,[60] and no interest except in so far as the prohibition could be circumvented;[61] and the attitude to negotiable instruments and the assignment to contractual rights is restrictive.[62] Several facilities are absent simply because nobody seems to have thought of them: thus there are no damages, no corporations and no juristic persons.

In Weberian terms Islamic law is thus rational to the extent that it treats human beings and things on a uniform basis. Its commercial facilities must also be described as advanced by the standards of its time of emergence,[63] and its restrictive rules clearly did not inhibit economic activity in medieval times: on the contrary, it is well known that premodern capitalism flourished in medieval Islamic society.[64] Weber does not deny this. He does however intimate that the law acted as a barrier to further rationalization of economic activity because it was a holy law and thus bound by tradition, orientated towards the maintenance of sacred institutions, given to moral rather than legal evaluation of human acts (a source of incalculability), and particularist in that it only applied to believers. (He also suggests that qadi justice played a role.)[65] To the extent that this hypothesis rests on the alleged correlation between legal and economic rationality it has already been refuted. It does however also raise the question how far or in what sense one can credit law with autonomous force.

A law is a body of rules enacted (or "found") by appropriate authorities and backed by sanctions. The rules have no force on their own, but simply reflect the views of those who are in a position to shape them. Since society at large rarely has much stake in their particular formulation, legal systems tend to reflect the views of professionals, with the result that "intrajuristic" factors such as legal education and the availability of foreign models play a more conspicuous role in their development than social, political or economic change.[66] In a more indirect way, legal systems will also reflect the views of the larger society to which the professionals belong, and thus social, political and economic changes too, but this relationship is more complicated: the professionals may endorse general norms or wish to change them, favour one segment of society rather than another, resist recent developments or seek to speed them up, and so forth.[67] But whatever it reflects, law is always a mirror. Though it is backed by sanctions against those who do not conform, it is a poor instrument of change: if it articulates the views of a minority, the majority cannot be made to adhere to it.[68] It follows that it is also a poor barrier against change. It cannot stop things happening unless it has strong social, political or economic backing.

Law has a spurious appearance of autonomy thanks to its notorious conservatism. It is conservative because a law is an observed regularity: if the regularity disappears there is no law, whence the fact that legal change has everywhere tended to take place in disguise.[69] Since moreover a regularity can only be observed over time, the man-made nature of law has frequently escaped the observers, who have often declared it both immutable and divine. All law is thus apt to lag behind socioeconomic and political developments, and holy laws more so than most. This, one assumes, is what suggested to Weber that law in general and holy law in particular could put a brake on such developments. But even a legal system endowed with divine immutability such as that of Islam cannot resist change unless the sociopolitical order in which it is embodied wishes to protect it against it. If socioeconomic or political developments render its rules unacceptable to its adherents, they will be changed by reinterpretation, tacit or explicit, or relegated to a legal limbo in which, though not struck out, they can be ignored or forgotten while man-made rules apply.[70] The autonomy of the law, in short, does not lie in the system itself, but rather in the social order in which it is embedded.

Islamic law was above all an account of a sacred order. It describes the right relationship between human beings, and between humans and the divine, formulating the social implications of a great and eternal truth. This endowed its premodern guardians with immense prestige and influence, further heightened by the fact that the masses were mostly illiterate. The religious scholars thus had a vested interest in the maintenance of the law: nobody could pronounce on it without membership of their ranks, and nobody could gain membership of their ranks without mastery of the law; for a scholar to question its provisions was to raise doubts about the very membership he had so laboriously acquired.[71] A holy law, once formed, cannot be hijacked by socioeconomic or political groups to serve their ends as could the secular law of Europe; much socioeconomic and political change will register outside it.

Now if we had known of significant changes in the direction of modern capitalism outside the law in the premodern Islamic world, and if further the religious scholars had been known to ignore the new transactions, or to take action against them, instead of offering legal assistance, then we would have had reason to pay serious attention to Weber's claim that Islamic law, or rather its guardians, acted as a barrier to the full development of economic "rationality." But no such developments are known. There does not appear to have been anything for the law or its guardians to impede. In order to save Weber's thesis one would have to argue in much broader terms that the law bred a society so traditional that economic developments in a modern direction could not even be conceived. But this would be a poor hypothesis, partly because it is huge and unmanageable, partly because it smacks of circularity and partly because one would not have expected medieval Islamic capitalism to change from traditional to modern forms by a quantitative leap; the process would have been cumulative and traditionalism cannot explain why it stopped where it did. All in all, discussing the possible role of the law in the nondevelopment of modern capitalism in the Islamic world is somewhat like discussing, say, the possible role of wind direction in the nonevolution of palm trees in Scandinavia. There are more obvious factors to consider first. In the Islamic case one would have thought that political conditions were such that modern capitalism was a nonstarter in whatever the direction the legal winds may have blown.

Reformulating Weber

What then do we do with the rest of the RS? This amounts to asking what we do with the concept of rationality, and since this concept has already been assigned to the dustbin, it might be thought that there is no more to be said on the matter. But behind Weber's endless invocations of rationality there is a genuine vision.[72] What, in non-Weberian terms, was it that he had seen?

What he had seen was the fundamental fact that whereas primitive societies systematically conflate all social functions, modern society systematically separates them. In primitive societies the same group will serve as the unit of child-bearing, production, defense and worship, or the various groups to which these functions are assigned will be nested so that some make up others which make up the rest; and the entire society will be underpinned by a single set of beliefs in which the social, moral and natural orders appear as identical. By contrast, modern society has deprived such groups of practically all their functions, assigning each to a special organization of its own, so that child-rearing is now the only function left to the truncated version of such groups known as the nuclear family (and, social workers apart, science fiction regularly assigns child-rearing to special agencies too). As each function has been separated from the undifferentiated bundle of activities, it has ceased by to underpinned by the original set of beliefs; and this has enabled it to be seen as a calling of its own, or in other words as a profession with its own particular aims and rules to be followed by every practitioner of this activity however badly it may fit with the rest of his social and moral world. It is this feature, among others, which Weber tried to bring out with the term rational. The modern world is no more rational, rule-bound, calculating, purposive (let alone reasonable) than any other, but the purpose is now determined from *within* the activity in question, not from the vantage point of some overall human aim: science must progress even if it going to below us up. Each activity has acquired diplomatic immunity from traditional goals and their religious underpinning.⁷³ This is what reduces *Wert* to *Zweck* and disenchants the world, making it rule-bound, calculating and so forth in the evocative rather than purely descriptive sense of these words: cold, heartless, bureaucratized, and meaningless.⁷⁴

What Weber had in mind when he spoke of Western "rationality" was thus the final outcome of that process which began with the emergence of the state. For the state emerged when communities which had hitherto helped themselves assigned the task of maintaining internal order and external defence to members who were taken off the production of food in return for services—rulers. And the emergence of the state went hand in hand with that of organized religion: communities which had hitherto saved themselves assigned the task of making sense of the world to others, who were similarly relieved of the need to produce—priests. The emergence of modern capitalism marks stage three of this process in that yet another crucial function, that of organizing production, was now assigned to specialists—entrepreneurs joined rulers and priests. And this time the change went hand in hand with the emergence of organized science. In all four cases the outcome was the creation of a special institution—state, church, factory and university—at the cost of hitherto self-sufficient groups; and in all four cases the reorganization proved so potent that the rest of the world had to follow suit. (Needless to say, all this happened via intermediary stages omitted from this scheme.) One might have expected the last stages of this process to have been incompatible with the first: the emergence of modern science and economy could well have destroyed both state and church, as Marx predicted. But in fact it was only the church which was destroyed (or more precisely reduced to a purely private affair of no consequence for the actual running of the world). State, factory and university go very well together once the state has been reorganized to cope with the new institutions, and in combination they have created a tightly integrated society superficially reminiscent of the one with which we set out. But the modern nation rests on mass participation in a variety of institutions with specialized functions, not on mass participation in a single one combining these functions; and much overall co-ordination notwithstanding, each institution still requires its own set of rules (social, cognitive or other) in order to function. There has thus been no recreation of that single overarching set of beliefs which used to validate society. The world thus remains as rational and disenchanted as Weber perceived it to be.

The Role of the State

Why then was it in Europe that stages three and four of this process were enacted?[75] Part of the answer must lie in the fact that Europe espoused a plurality of ultimately incompatible traditions. Europe was trying to be traditional according to *three* quite different models and so failed in the attempt altogether.[76] But another part of the answer undoubtedly lies in the peculiar nature of the European state.

The state plays a fundamental role in the emergence of industrial capitalism in that it has to perform three roles in order for it to become possible. First, it has to draw the teeth of such semi-autonomous groups as exist within it: people must be reduced to so many subjects before they can be seen as so many suppliers of nothing but labor (as opposed to suppliers of the services normally expected of friends and allies). Secondly, the state must pacify society so as to enable the economic experiments of entrepreneurs to go on undisturbed. Finally, it must itself learn to refrain from despoliating the experimenters.[78] But the typical pattern of political organization in the preindustrial world outside Europe is one in which the state is loosely superimposed on more or less autonomous groups: the state coexists with such groups instead of drawing their teeth. Since the state limits itself to a supervisory role, it never has enough control for a genuine pacification of society, so it coexists with robber barons too. And since its power is both limited and unstable, its own conduct tends to be arbitrary and rapacious as well. In short, there is no neutral labor, no stability and no freedom from extortion. Whoever acquires wealth accordingly invests it in membership of the ranks of the extorters rather than in industry or commerce.

In Europe, however, the state was never an apparatus loosely superimposed on semi-autonomous groups, for all that it was feeble to the point of nonexistence at times. This striking fact presumably has something to do with the extraordinary shallowness of European kinship organization, which may have something to do with Christianity in turn (as Weber surmised), but which remains basically unexplained.[78] In the absence of tribes, clans, and other descent groups to take over when the Roman state collapsed, feudal Europe saw an extreme *vertical* dispersal of power to which there can be few parallels. Given this vertical dispersal on the one hand and the failure to reestablish the imperial form on the other,[79] the subsequent recovery took European rulers far deeper into society than their counterparts elsewhere had ever gone and forced them to provide more services than normally required too. The ultimate result was that Europe was pacified and bureaucratized to a degree unheard of by a state which represented society instead of merely sitting on top of it. Unlike legal rationalism, the modern state is certainly a precondition for industrial capitalism: it does not explain why the economic reorganization took place, but it does explain why no such reoganization was attempted elsewhere.[80]

The Role of the Law

Like other institutions, modern law has been detached from the overarching values around which society used to be shaped. Contrary to what Weber's concept of formal rationality suggests, however, it has not acquired a purpose defined from within itself; rather, it has become a mere instrument of mundane concerns, as he himself suggests too.[81] Europe is unique in the degree to which the state came to take it over: law is the command of the sovereign, as Austin said, and as an aphorism about modern Europe his dictum is apt.

In historical terms, however, Austin's dictum hardly ever fits. If we start with our undifferentiated bundle of functions, we note that there is law although there is no sovereign.[82] Law and other norms serve to keep the group together; it is one out of several instruments of group cohesion, and it is frequently a conscious emblem of it too, in the sense that it is both known and applauded as something which distinguishes the group from others.[83] If we now add a sovereign, we observe that although rulers have often been regarded as ultimate dispensers of customary law, they have tended to leave its formulation to its customary propounders (priests, heads of tribes, clans, castes, families, and so on), except in so far as the law impinges directly on public affairs: criminal and public law go Austinian to the exclusion of the rest. This is the patter which obtained in China[84] and, less neatly, in Greece[85] and elsewhere.[86] Alternatively, customary law is taken up by intellectuals, be they priests (such as brahmans and the propounders of Canon law) or laymen (such as the Roman jurists, their European successors, the rabbis and the Muslim *fuqaha*). At the hands of such scholars, customary rules of a diverse and local kind will be sifted, explicated, systematized, and turned into a single coherent whole (or, given the tendencies of scholars to form schools, several versions thereof). In Weber's words, the law will be "rationalized." But as Weber saw, it will not be rationalized in the modern way, for the law remains a group emblem. It ceases, of course, to be an emblem of the groups who supplied the raw material: these typically persist in their unrevised ways. But instead it becomes an emblem of that educated elite which is thinly spread over such groups within a great civilization and which constitutes the locus of the civilization in question. Law becomes part of the classics, that is, that body of literature which enshrines the constitutive values of a particular civilization and knowledge of which serves to mark off the educated man from the masses underneath. The law is henceforth studied in the same way as nonlegal classics: famous works are glossed, explicated, epitomized, and learnt by heart regardless of whether they are of practical interest or not. The area over which the educated elite is spread may or may not be coterminous with a single state, and the jurists may or may not collaborate with such states as exist. Either way, they regard the law as the expression of sublime and eternal truths, not as a mere instrument to social and political ends. Where the law is taken over by such *honoratiores* (as Weber called them), there is typically a threefold division of labour: the sovereign issues his decrees in matters of interest to the state (mere *siyasa* in the Muslim view); the *honoratiores* expound their view of what they consider to be the only True Law (*shari'a* in the Muslim case), generally concentrating on private law to the exclusion of, or with perfunctory attention to, the areas of interest to the state; and the masses continue to live by their customary law (mere *urf* in the Muslim view) except in so far as the *honoratiores* have got them under cultural or judicial control. This is the pattern which obtained in classical Rome, classical Islam, medieval Europe, Iran before the Arab conquest,[87] India[88] and elsewhere.[89]

The law in its entirety went Austinian in the late Roman empire and, in a more extenuated sense, also in early Islam. (It nearly did in the ancient Near East as well.) But it did not remain Austinian for long. In the case of Rome, the state gradually absorbed the *honoratiores*, who had always collaborated closely with it, and eventually codified their wisdom in a single imperial compilation, Justinian's (thus destroying Roman legal science); Europe duly inherited the view that law is the prerogative of the prince, but the traditional division of labour returned to the Roman empire itself when the church reclaimed the core of private law as True Law, that is, Canon law.[90] In the case of Islam, the sovereign appears initially to have been perceived as the ultimate authority on God's law, much as other rulers have been regarded as the ultimate dispensers of customary law; but here the *honoratiores* quickly dissociated themselves from the state (thereby giving birth to Muslim legal science).⁹¹ The law in its entirety is not normally Austinian, it would seem. (Nor does state-controlled law normally seem to coexist with legal science.)

Two things follow from this. First, Weber's evaluation of the relative rationality/modernity of English and German law should be reversed. If legal modernity resides in a state-controlled law, then modernity was first incarnate in England, where the sovereign neither tolerated customary law nor left it to *honoratiores*, but on the contrary displaced it through a state-controlled judiciary from which the first common law in Europe was in due course to emerge. In the centuries after the Norman creation of a *lex terrae* the administration of justice was frequently as decentralized and dominated by local powers as the state itself, but in principle the highest law of the land was the command of the sovereign, not that of God or Rome. By contrast, in Germany the highest law was that True Law which knows of no political boundaries, the truth being true wherever it is found; here *honoratiores* were busy revising customary law in the light of this law, that is, Roman law, until the end of the nineteenth century. The intense legal culture of Pandectist Germany, and the intellectually most impressive legal studies which ensued therefrom, turn on the fact that the Pandectists were the last survivors of that educated elite which, thinly spread over Europe at large, used to be the carriers of Western culture; for the Pandectists expounded Roman law to Romanists wherever they might be found until their wisdom was distilled into national codes with attendant university courses, whereupon the last bastion of medieval culture collapsed and whole libraries turned into wastepaper.⁹² The most rational of all European law in Weber's eye turned out to have been an archaism.

Secondly, it is clear that modern European and Islamic law are polar opposites: where European law has been dissociated from the constitutive values of European civilization, Islamic law by contrast epitomizes those of Islam; where European law has been wholly taken over by the state, Islamic law has been wholly withdrawn from its control. Like other sacred systems, Islamic law is first and foremost an emblem of group membership, that is membership of the Muslim community, not merely an instrument to such sociopolitical aims as the state (or anyone else) may see fit to pursue; and the Muslim jurists may be unique among the *honoratiores* in the degree to which they have refused to come to terms with both state-made and customary law (though their attitudes have varied considerably over time and place). Weber might have argued that the relationship between the state and the law in Islam was bad for the former, and thus indirectly for the chances of modern capitalism too: this would be hard to deny. The bad relationship is the outcome of the failure of early Muslim rulers to persuade the educated elite which had emerged within their domain to collaborate with them in their ventures. More precisely, a community which had reached the pinnacle of success under religio-political sovereigns turned its back on these sovereigns and reconstituted itself under its own religious leaders.[93] This fact has certainly shaped much of Islamic history, but it is a fact about history, not about the law as such.

Weber Today

Are down-to-earth historians and sociologists of law then well advised to leave the RS alone? The answer would seem to be yes, but with one proviso: they are not well advised to ignore Weber's *agenda*, be it that of the RS or his other works. The questions which he raised about the impact of the great religions, the nature and function of law, the evolution of Europe and so forth are as alive and as pressing today as when he wrote. Weber's agenda has however passed into the general literature to the point that it is possible (apparently) to be a practising Weberite without having read a word of what he wrote;[94] and he can no longer be said to have the best answers or approaches to his own questions. Evidently, one can learn a good deal from a work such as the RS (not to mention the annotations); Weber's capacity for insight into matters on which little information was available in his time is amazing. But his insights are not lucidly structured around overall theories. One is left with bits and pieces which one has to assemble more or less for oneself with the conceptual tools offered; and since the conceptual tools are defective, there are various ways in which one can try to repair them and fit the pieces together. Why persist at the attempt? We are never going to produce that magic constellation in which all the pieces have fallen into perfect order. Nor is the ever-growing literature on Weber encouraging to those who are interested in his problems without being interested in him: does one have to devote one's life to a study of Weber in order to use his ideas? If studies such as these can strip him to his agenda, then so much the better. But what we really need is more work in Weber's spirit, not more on Weber himself.

Notes

This is a modified version of the paper submitted for translation in 1984. Retyping led to some recasting, reformulation and shortening of the argument, but no attempt has been made to bring the literature up to date. I remain indebted to John Hall, Martin Hinds and Guenther Roth for comments on the first draft. Three abbreviations have been used: *EI*²: see note 53; *ES*: see note 4; *WuG:* see note 12.

1. For a helpful introduction see M. Rheinstein and E. Shils, eds. and trans., *Max Weber on Law in Economy and Society (*Cambridge Mass.: Harvard University Press, 1954). Other works include K. Engisch, "Max Weber als Rechtsphilosoph und als Rechtssoziologe," in K. Engish and others (eds.), *Max Weber* (Berlin: Duncker and Humbert, 1966); D. M. Trubeck, "Max Weber on Law and the Rise of Capitalism,"*Wisconsin Law Review* 1972:720–753; M. Albrow, "Legal Positivism and Bourgeois Materialism: Max Weber's View of the Sociology of Law," *British Journal of Law and Society* 1 (1975):14–31; P. Beirne, "Ideology and Rationality in Max Weber's Sociology of Law," *Research in Law and Sociology* 2 (1979): 103–31; M. Cain, "The Limits of Idealism: Max Weber and the Sociology of Law," 3:53–83; A. T. Kronman, *Max Weber* (London: Edward Arnold, 1983).
2. He had full legal training and practised from 1887 to 1891.
3. Both features have often attracted comment, cf. for example Kronman, *Max Weber*, 1–2.
4. Of whom the most important are M. Rheinstein (cf. above, note 1) and J. Winckelmann. The former's annotations have been reprinted with minor changes in Max Weber, *Economy and Society,* ed. G. Roth and C. Wittich (New York: Bedminster Press, 1968 [hereafter *ES*]); the latter's annotations are to be found in the fifth edition of Max Weber, *Wirtschaft und Gesellschaft* (Tübingen: J. C. B. Mohr, 1978,) vol. iii (not accessible to me).
5. Thus for example Kronman, with recourse to philosophy (cf. *Max Weber,* 2).
6. Cf. J. H. Franklin, *Jean Bodin and the Sixteenth-Century Revolution in the Methodology of Law and History* (New York: Greenwood Press, 1963), chapter 4. Maine and Durkheim made similar attempts but primarily with reference to primitive law.
7. The former devote themselves to the nature of the legal process in the West while the latter construct jurisprudential theories based on the Western concept of law, but their findings rarely mesh or allow for cross-cultural comparison. Anthropological studies tend to be more helpful, but mostly with reference to simple societies rather than the great civilizations.
8. For an attempt to analyse it in Weberian terms, see J. Schacht, "Zur soziologischen Betrachtung des islamischen Rechts," *Der Islam* 22 (1935): 207-38.
9. M. Weber, *The Protestant Ethic and the Spirit of Capitalism,* trans. T. Parsons (New York: Scribner's, 1958), 78.
10. Sixteen different meanings can be isolated according to some (R. Brubaker, *The Limits of Rationality: an Essay on the Social and Moral Thought of Max Weber* [London: George Allen and Unwin, 1984], 2, with reference to further literature).
11. The proto-bread hypothesis also figures in the English translation of the *Protestant Ethic,* where the introduction suggests that proto-rationality may be part of the biological make-up of Europe (30). But Weber wrote this introduction fifteen years after the *Protestant Ethic* as an introduction to the entire *Religionssoziologie*.
12. The typology is set out in M. Weber, *Wirtschaft und Gesellschaft,* fourth edition, ed. J. Winckelmann (Tübingen: J. C. B. Mohr, 1956 [hereafter *WuG*])ii, 395ff = *ES,* ii, 654ff (on the categories of legal thought) and 571f = iii, 976ff (on forms of adjudication [in the sociology of domination, not the RS]). The summary

given here is based on the way the typology gets handled throughout the RS, not simply on these pages.
13. The definition of qadi justice is given in *WuG,* ii: 665 = *ES,* iii: 976 (in the sociology of domination). The concept is used in an Islamic context in *WuG,* ii: 477 = *ES,* ii: 823, where we are told in a section on Persian law that "here as elsewhere" the administration of justice aims at "material" justice rather than at formal regulation of conflicting interests and that such qadi justice stands in the way of capitalistic developments, as can be seen for example in Tunisia.
14. The term was coined by R. Schmidt in a legal essay of 1908, not by Weber himself, and Weber uses it of any kind of "irrational" adjudication, be it Solomonic, Attic, Oriental, English, or other.
15. Formally irrational law is law which, though perfectly rule-bound, invokes the supernatural through ordeals, oracles and the like. There are neither oracles nor ordeals in Islamic law, but there is considerable reliance on oaths.
16. When formal rationality is contrasted with formal irrationality, "formal" means rule-bound while "rational" means derived from human reason rather than supernatural sources. But when formal rationality is contrasted with substantive rationality or irrationality, it is "rational" that means rule-bound; "formal" now means free of extralegal concerns ("substantive" meaning shaped by them).
17. Given that a law is a rule, there can be no such thing as law based on no rules at all. To say that a legal system is substantively irrational is merely to say that it does not exist. Conversely, to say that "every formulated law is (at least relatively) formally rational" is, as Andreski points out, very much like saying that "every flower is (at least relatively) flowery" (S. L. Andreski, "Understanding, Action and Law in Max Weber" in A. Podgorecki and C. J. Whelan, eds., *Sociological Approaches to Law* (London: Croom Helm, 1981), 63, with reference to *WuG,* first edition, ii: 395 (= *ES,* ii, 656, where the translation is slightly different). It is only the dispensation of law that could in principle be substantively irrational, that is, entirely based on political, religious, emotional or other considerations rather than legal rules, though in practice it is hard to imagine.
18. The typology has also been criticized on the grounds that the term "rational" has connotations such as "sensible" and "effective" and that systems and procedures classified by Weber as irrational are perfectly rational in that sense: "if you assume that God speaks through the oracles, then it is perfectly rational to consult them...the recourse to oracles in African tribal law seems much more effective (and therefore rational) than the taking of statements sworn 'by Almighty God' in Britain in 1981 when the opinion surveys have shown that most people are not at all afraid of God's punishment" (Andreski, "Understanding, Action and Law," 63). This is true, but unfair to Weber, for he does not suggest that "irrational" legal procedures are irrational in Andreski's sense of the word: nothing is said or implied about their reasonableness, effectiveness or otherwise (nor is any moral judgement passed on them).
19. Cf. *WuG,* ii: 397 = *ES,* ii: 657, setting out the five postulates of the most formal and rational of all legal systems, that based on German *Pandektenrecht.* The crucial postulate is the second, "that it must be possible in every concrete case to derive the decisions from abstract legal propositions by means of legal logic." Weber does not say that he believes the five postulates to be true, but this is irrelevant: he did use them to illustrate the nature of formal rationality. As Rheinstein points out, throughout the RS it is clear that formal rationality stands for *Begriffsjurisprudenz* and that this is the mode of thought which Weber regarded as unique to Europe (*Max Weber on Law in Economy and Society,* xlixf).
20. Cf. K. Zweigert and H. Kötz, *Einführung in die Rechtsvergleichung auf dem*

Gebiete des Privatrecht (Tübingen: J. C. B. Mohr 197), i: 175 ("die juristische Rechenmaschine par excellence").

21. Though enacted in 1900, it reflected the society of the Bismarck period without much attention to the forces which had long been undermining it (ibid., 174).
22. "A legal system in which all concepts are of a purely formal character has never existed in the world and can hardly be even conceived as a theoretical possibility," as Rheinstein observes. Rheinstein nonetheless exonerates Weber's formal rationality on the grounds that it is a purely ideal type; but an ideal type which is *theoretically* impossible has no place in any typology (*Max Weber on Law in Economy and Society*, lvi–lvii). Albrow rightly notes that Rheinstein lets Weber off too lightly here ("Legal Positivism and Bourgeois Materialism," 28f); and Cotterell agrees that Weber's scheme is inadequate for the task to which it is applied because formal rationality is defined in such a way as to exclude consideration of the values of the law (R. Cotterell, "The Development of Capitalism and the Formalisation of Contract Law," in B. Fryer and others, eds., *Law, State and Society* [London: Croom Helm, 1981], 62).
23. This (perfectly valid) point is discussed at length in *WuG*, ii: 456–67 = *ES*, ii: 784–802.
24. For an interesting account of how the civil law acquired its special characteristics, see A. Watson, *The Making of the Civil Law* (Cambridge, MA: Harvard University Press, 1981), which agrees with Weber's in many respects (though it does not make the point referred to in the previous note).
25. Cf. *WuG*, ii: 459, 461 = *ES*, ii: 789, 792, where Weber somehow discerns a difference between the "uninhibited intellectualism of scholars" (characteristic of sacred systems) and the "logical ambitions of the jurisprudential doctrinaire only interested in the demands of legal logic" (which such systems lack).
26. Semantic relationships take on the guise of theoretical ones, as Cain rightly notes ("Limits of Idealism," 81).
27. *WuG*, ii: 504 = *ES*, ii: 882.
28. The RS is sometimes assumed to be devoted primarily to the latter question (thus Rheinstein, *Max Weber on Law in Economy and Society*, p. l; Trubek, "Max Weber on Law and the Rise of Capitalism," 721–2; B. S. Turner, *Max Weber and Islam* (London: Routledge and Kegan Paul, 1974), ch. 7. For a better appreciation, see G. Roth, "Rationalization in Max Weber's Developmental History," in S. Whimster and S. Lash, eds., *Max Weber: Rationality and Modernity* (London: Allen and Unwin, 1986).
29. *WuG*, ii: 392; cf. 395 = *ES*, ii: 650, 654f.
30. *WuG*, ii: 412, 427, 493, cf. 395 = *ES*, ii,: 776, 687f, 855, cf. 654f.
31. *WuG*, ii: 395, 482ff, 572 = *ES*, ii: 654f, 839ff; iii: 977.
32. *WuG*, ii: 511 = *ES*, ii: 892.
33. *WuG*, ii: 395 = *ES*, ii: 655.
34. Cf. M. Weber, *The Religion of China*, trans. H. H. Gerth (New York: the Free Press, 1968), ch. 6 ("The Patrimonial Structure of the Law"), where this point is made with greater clarity than in the *RS*.
35. Cf. Albrow, "Legal Positivism and Bourgeois Materialism," 28f. Compare *WuG*, ii: 573 = *ES*, iii: 979, where Weber himself uses the slot machine image, noting that this conception of the modern judge has been heavily criticized.
36. *WuG*, ii: 471, 571 = *ES*, ii: 814; vol. iii, 976; and *passim*.
37. *WuG*, ii: 471: "nicht durch, sondern zum Teil auch trotz der Struktur seines Rechtes gewann England den kapitalistischen Primat." The "zum Teil auch" is missing in the English translation with the result that Engand here gains capitalistic supremacy entirely despite its judidical system (cf. *ES*, ii, 814). Weber

says much the same at *WuG*, ii: 572 = *ES*, iii: 977, and again in *The Religion of China*, 102.
38. *WuG*, ii: 471 = *ES*, ii: 814.
39. *WuG*, ii: 511 = *ES*, ii: 892.
40. *WuG*, ii: 509 = *ES*, ii: 890.
41. That England is a problematic case to Weber has been noted many times before, cf. Rheinstein, *Max Weber on Law in Economy and Society*, lviii; Trubek, "Max Weber on Law and the Rise of Capitalism," 746–8 (a very fair discussion); Albrow, "Legal Positivism and Bourgeois Materialism," 22; Cain, "Limits of Idealism," 72, and no doubt others too.
42. This is well known to civil law scholars, see for example R. David and J. E. C. Brierley, *Major Legal Systems in the World Today*, second edition (London: Stephens and Sons, 1968), 78–80.
43. Weber himself notes (in the sociology of domination) that the idea of a gapless law has been heavily criticized (*WuG*, ii: 573 = *ES*, iii: 979).
44. *WuG*, ii: 487f = *ES*, ii: 846–8.
45. *WuG*, ii: 491ff = *ES*, ii: 852ff.
46. *WuG*, ii: 458–9, 491, 493, 506 = *ES*, ii: 789, 853, 855, 885.
47. *WuG*, ii: 495 = *ES*, ii: 858.
48. Cain, "Limits of Idealism," 72.
49. This could also be said to be the major point to emerge from M. E. Tigar and M. R. Levy, *Law and the Rise of Capitalism* (New York: Monthly Review Press, 1977).
50. On this relationship, see also M. Rodinson, *Islam and Capitalism* (Harmondsworth: Penguin Books, 1974); Turner, *Weber and Islam*, ch. 7.
51. Cf. S. D. Goitein, *Studies in Islamic History and Institutions* (Leiden: E. J. Brill, 1966), ch. 11 ("The Rise of the Middle Eastern Bourgeoisie in Early Islamic Times").
52. Weber does not say much about the concrete provisions of Islamic law. When he does descend to the level of detail, he is usually wrong or off target, but his general impression of the law is right.
53. Cf. *The Encyclopaedia of Islam*, second edition, Leiden: A. J. Brill, 1960– (hereafter *EI²*), s.v. " *'abd*." For manuals of Islamic law, see the helpful bibliography in J. Schacht, *An Introduction to Islamic Law* (Oxford: Clarendon Press, 1964).
54. Women are under the guardianship of men and cannot, in most schools, contract themselves in marriage or repudiate their husbands at will; they inherit less than men and count for less as witnesses. They are however fully endowed with the capacity to own and dispose of property and to engage in all contracts other than marriage on their own. Some schools hold that Arab women may only marry Arab men and that female descendants of the Prophet may only marry other descendants of his. Some schools penalize the slander of Arabs, and all hold the descendants of the Prophet to be too pure to receive grants of alms-tax (*zakah*, conceived as "dirt" of which people have purified themselves).
55. Cf. *WuG*, ii: 416 = *ES*, ii: 672.
56. Land is divided into various categories defined by the manner in which it has passed under Muslim control; land taken by treaty is regarded as private property, that taken by forcible conquest is deemed collective property administered by the state; they are subject to different rates of taxation. The two categories are further complicated by the various terms on which land could be granted by the state (for details, see *EI²* s.v. '*kharadj*' and the literature cited there). The free sale of land was also restricted by pre-emption (cf. *EI²*, s.v. '*shuf'a*'; note the tenth-century lawyer who rejected it on the grounds that it clashed with the

individual's freedom to sell). There are no studies of the degree to which land was commercialized in practice.
57. This criterion excludes commodities such as wine, pigs and products thereof, with much casuistic detail.
58. The contrary is asserted in the first edition of the *Encyclopaedia of Islam* (Leiden and London 1913–34), s.v. *"milk,"* but see for example L. Milliot, *Introduction a l'étude du droit musulman* (Paris: Sirey, 1953), ch. 5; *EI*², s.v. *"milk."*
59. Bequests and gifts in death sickness are restricted to one third of the estate (N. J. Coulson, *Succession in the Muslim Family* [Cambridge: Cambridge University Press, 1971], chs. 13, 15). On the historical roots of this restriction, see P. Crone, *Roman, Provincial and Islamic Law* (Cambridge: Cambridge University Press, 1987), 93ff. On preemption, see above, note 55.
60. By way of exception to the general rules all schools endorse the contract known as *salam* which involves future goods; and some concession to the practice of buying unseen goods is made by some of the schools.
61. For the means of circumvention see J. Schacht, "Die arabische Hiyal-Literatur," *Der Islam* 15 (1926): 211–32; *EI*², s.v. *"hiyal."*
62. Cf. *EI*² s.v. "hawala" and the literature cited there.
63. Cf. A. L. Udovitch, *Partnership and Profit in Medieval Islam* (Princeton: University Press, 1970), 259–61.
64. Cf. Rodinson, *Islam and Capitalism*, ch. 3.
65. Cf. above, note 13. His views on qadi justice in Islam are deemed "totally erroneous" by A. Ghani, "Disputes in a Court of *Shar'a*, Kunar Valley, Afghanistan, 1885–1890," *International Journal of Middle East Studies* 15 (1983): 353–67 at 365. Weber did not, however, say that Islamic justice was *always* qadi justice, and cases from nineteenth-century Afghanistan do not prove that it *never* was. What mirrors for princes recommend (for rulers rather than judges) is precisely qadi justice of the Solomonic type described by Weber (*WuG*, ii: 486 = *ES*, ii: 845). But we need more work of Ghani's type before anything much can be said about the question. There is also the problem of the extent to which rulers would force judges to give verdicts in their favour or interfere with the execution of verdicts they disliked (which is not the same as qadi justice). Turner offers some views on the matter (*Weber and Islam*, ch. 7), but again our knowledge is too limited to make speculation worth while.
66. Cf. A. Watson, *Legal Transplants: An Approach to Comparative Law* (Edinburgh: Scottish Academic Press, 1974); idem., *Society and Legal Change* (Edinburgh: Scottish Academic Press, 1977); idem, *The Making of the Civil Law*. For Weber on "intrajuristic" factors, see above, note 30.
67. Watson's stimulating work (cited in the preceding note) can be criticized for ignoring this aspect. It is devoted to the proposition that the relationship between law and society is far less close than usually supposed, society at large having little stake in it, that much law is out of step with society without any harm being done thereby, and that legal borrowing ("transplantation") has been the most important element in legal development: even marriage laws have been transplanted, for example, from Rome to Europe and from there to the rest of the world. Watson does not however take much account of the fact that Rome and Europe both happened to be monogamous, that Roman rules which did not fit were not taken over, that transplantation from Europe to America or New Zealand is transplantation within the same culture, that transplants rarely thrive where society is not ready for them, for example, in different cultures, that social change has generated enormous changes in (for example) British family law in recent years, that massive sociopolitical changes underlie the decisions of Third World countries to import foreign law wholesale, and so forth.

68. Cf. A. Allott, *The Limits of the Law* (London: Butterworths, 1980).
69. If scientists were to announce that the law of gravity no longer applies, one would not conclude that it had changed, but rather that it had never been true. We now distinguish between natural and human laws, but even in modern Britain "when the Lords overrule a decision of the Court of Appeal in an earlier case, they do not say that they are changing the law; they say that the earlier case was wrongly decided. It follows that all cases decided in accordance with the decision in the earlier case have also been wrongly decided" (P. Stein, *Regulae Iuris: From Juristic Rules to Legal Maxims* [Edinburgh: University Press, 1966]), 6, with the comment that if it were not for the procedural rules which restrict the time within appeals can be made, this theory would lead to manifest inconvenience!).
70. An obvious example is slavery in Jewish and Islamic law. The institution has not been abrogated, but it has lost all practical relevance and nobody is bothered by this any more (if pressed, most people would probably adopt a historicizing interpretation of its presence in the law). The *Shari'a* rules regarding the sale of unseen, unidentified and future goods have quietly gone into limbo too: few Muslims are even aware of their existence (the one rule of commercial law to have retained emblematic status being the prohibition of usury). In premodern times, much of the public law laid down in the *shari'a* was likewise suspended.
71. Cf. P. Crone and M. Cook, *Hagarism, The Making of the Islamic World* (Cambridge: University Press, 1977), ch. 13.
72. The sheer frequency with which he uses this word suggests that he had seen something which he could not express. It figures on practically every page on the RS, often several times (as also in the chapter on law in *The Religion of China*), usually in a manner apt to drive the reader mad: just as one thinks that the difference between X and Y is going to become clear, the word rational is thrown in again to explain what it is.
73. Cf. E. Gellner, "The Savage and the Modern Mind," in R. Horton and R. Finnegan (eds.), *Modes of Thought* (London: Faber and Faber, 1973), 162–181; (reprinted in a slightly different form in his *The Legitimation of Belief* [Cambridge: University Press, 1974], 152–67), on the cognitive aspect of this. Now that the idea of progress has lost its legitimating force, this diplomatic immunity is under threat.
74. Weber specialists may not agree, cf. Brubaker, *Limits of Rationality*, 50–52, for a different explanation of the difference between *Wert* and *Zweck*. But if Weber is taken literally, there does not seem to be any (cf. Andreski, "Understanding, Action and Law," 53). The meaning is conveyed by the overtones.
75. For a longer attempt to answer this question written after the original version of this paper, see P. Crone, *Pre-industrial Societies* (Oxford: Basil Blackwell, 1989), ch. 8.
76. Cf. Crone and Cook, *Hagarism*, ch. 14; Crone, *Pre-industrial Societies*, 161ff.
77. Cf. E. Gellner, "A Social Contract in Search of an Idiom: the Demise of the Danegeld State," in his *Spectacles and Predicaments: Essays in Social Theory* (Cambridge: University Press, 1979), 285f.
78. Cf. J. Goody, *The Development of the Family and Marriage in Europe* (Cambridge: University Press, 1983) (where the Christian influence is however different from that envisaged by Weber); Crone, *Pre-industrial Societies*, 151f.
79. Cf. J. Hall, *Powers and Liberties* (Oxford: Basil Blackwell, 1985), 133ff; Crone, *Pre-industrial Societies*, 161f.
80. Weber of course also stressed the crucial role of the state in the emergence of modernity, but then he stressed the importance of everything (cf. the rude comment in Tigar and Levy, *Law and the Rise of Capitalism*, 302).

81. Cf. above, 254.
82. The extent to which primitive law can be termed law is of course a moot point. The identifying features of legal rules and procedures are variously given as the use of formulaic language and/or ritual, the existence of "secondary rules" (cf. H. L. A. Hart, *The Concept of Law* [Oxford: Clarendon Press, 1961], ch. 5, on the presence of courts, the availability of sanctions and the like. Few societies on record have been so primitive as not to single out some rules and procedures from other norms and actions in one way or the other.)
83. Mosaic law is the best known example.
84. Cf. D. Bodde and C. Morris, *Law in Imperial China* (Cambridge MA: Harvard University Press, 1967); or the concise account by H. McAleavy, "Chinese Law" in J. D. M. Derrett, ed., *An Introduction to Legal Systems* (London: Sweet and Maxwell, 1968), 105–130.
85. Dracon, the first Athenian lawgiver, made penal laws for which he has become proverbial; according to another account, he established a constitution: either way, he was concerned with public rather than private law. The same is true of Solon. But when the Athenians took to ruling themselves, it was apparently only sacred law (in the sense of law pertaining to religious worship) which remained completely in the hands of its traditional exponents (cf. D. M. Macdowell, *The Law of Classical Athens,* [London: Thames and Hudson, 1978], 192–4).
86. Thus Vietnam reproduces the Chinese pattern, though the Vietnamese codes include more family than their Chinese models (M. B. Hooker, *A Concise Legal History of South-East Asia* [Oxford: Clarendon Press, 1978], ch. 3). Japan also began by replicating the Chinese model (though here it generated legal science, unknown in China itself). Fidelity to this model was shortlived, but the distinction between state-made penal and administrative law on the one hand and customary law of various kinds on the other is a constant in Japanese history (Y. Noda, *Introduction au droit japonais* [Paris: Librarie Dalloz, 1966]; English tr. Tokyo: University Press, 1976, ch. 2).
87. A. Perikhanian, "Iranian Society and Law" in *Cambridge History of Iran,* vol. iii (2), ed. E. Yarshater (Cambridge: Cambridge University Press, 1983).
88. R. Lingat, *Les sources du droit dans le systeme traditionnel de l'Inde* (Paris: Mouton & Co., 1967; English tr. Berkeley: University of California Press, 1973).
89. Cf. Hooker, *Concise History,* ch. 1, on the countries that accepted the Indian model; cf. also M. Maung, *Law and Custom in Burma and the Burmese Family* (The Hague: Martinus Nijhoff, 1963; for a specific example); D. M. Engel, *Law and Kingship in Thailand during the Reign of King Chulalongkorn* (Ann Arbor: Center for South and Southeast Asian Studies, the University of Michigan, 1975)—illustrating the extent to which even True Law can be combined with royal control.
90. Strangely, the relationship between imperial and Canon law in Byzantium does not seem to have attracted much attention. H. J. Scheltema, "Byzantine Law" in *Cambridge Medieval History,* iv (2), ed. J. M. Hussey (Cambridge: Cambridge University Press, 1967), writes as if Canon law did not exist.
91. Cf. P. Crone and M. Hinds, *God's Caliph: Religious Authority in the First Centuries of Islam* (Cambridge: Cambridge University Press, 1986).
92. E. J. Cohn and W. Zdzieblo, *Manual of German Law,* second edition (London: Oceana Publications, 1968–71), i, 26. Quite apart from the fact that the national codes destroyed the legal unity of the civil law countries, it is "one of the great glories of codified law that it makes possible...adequate law teaching at a very low level of competence" (Watson, *The Making of the Civil Law,* 173.
93. P. Crone, *Slaves on Horses: the Evolution of the Islamic Polity* (Cambridge: University Press, 1980), esp. 62f.

94. One reviewer of Crone and Cook's *Hagarism* judged Weber's influence to be manifest throughout the work (thus H. Lazarus-Yafeh in *Asian and African Studies* 14 [1980]: 295). But though both authors had general knowledge of Weber's views, neither had read much or (speaking for myself) any of his work, and neither was conscious of paying attention to him in the course of writing.

10

Weber and Islamic Sects

Michael Cook

There are two ways in which one might approach the theme of this paper. One strategy would be to take the copula in the title as establishing a union of two sets. One might thus begin by invoking Weber and end by disinvoking him; in the intervening stretch one might say whatever one had it in mind to say about Islamic sects. Such an approach would have its attractions, not least the ease with which the resulting paper could be recycled at future conferences on the theme of "X and Islam." The alternative strategy, and that adopted here, is to construe the copula as establishing an intersection, however slight; an incidental advantage of this approach is that it enables us to be exceedingly brief.

The specific task assigned to me by the organisers of the conference was to examine the applicability in the Islamic context of Weber's notion of a "sect" (*Sekte*) as opposed to a "church" (*Kirche*). How far do the groups which an Islamicist unthinkingly regards as sects deserve that designation in a specifically Weberian sense? And if not, why not?

Let us begin by attempting to pin down Weber's distinction between church and sect. The main points would seem to be the following:

1. *Membership*. A church is a compulsory and comprehensive institution; it embraces the whole of society, and in general you enter it by being born into it. A sect, by contrast, is a voluntary and elective association (*Verein*); you are in it by choice—yours and its.[1]

2. *Structure of authority*. A church is a hierarchical organisation. A sect, by contrast, is an egalitarian congregation. Thus a church is "the bearer and trustee of an office charisma,"[2] and is dominated by a "professional priesthood,"[3] whereas a sect is "a community (*Gemeinschaft*) of personally charismatic individuals,"[4] and this is reflected in the struc-

ture of power within it: "Consistent sects subscribe to the principle of the absolute sovereignty of the congregation (*Gemeindesouveränität*)."[5] The contrast is admittedly not always so stark—churches can be somewhat congregational,[6] and sects can "establish regular offices for economic and pedagogic reasons."[7] Yet the principle is firm: pure sects insist on "direct democratic administration" by the congregation.[8]

(3) *Political character.* A church, by its nature, is too much entangled with society as a whole to be a non-political institution. A sect, by contrast, is in a "peculiar and highly important relationship to the political power"—albeit of a negative kind. For the sect is "a specifically antipolitical or at least apolitical group."[9] Essentially, this is because what a sect wants is to be left alone; it is "simply not concerned with outsiders." Hence sectarian advocacy of "tolerance" and the "separation of church and state."[10]

Weber, in sum, is offering us the following schema:

	church	sect
1. membership	compulsory (comprehensive)	voluntary (select)
2. structure of authority	hierarchical	congregational
3. political character	politically involved	antipolitical or apolitical

This may look like a clearcut distinction. But before we attempt to apply it to the Islamic data, we should perhaps reach for a jug of cold water. The first thing to note is that Weber is not putting forward an *exhaustive* set of categories for classifying structures of religious organisation. If we come across such an organisation in the real world, it might be a church or a sect, but it could just as well be something else—say a "hierocracy." Secondly, Weber does not offer us *definitions* of his key terms; he simply gives an account of the differences. On other conceptual frontiers, other aspects of his ideas of church and state will be relevant—as when he distinguishes between a "church" and a "hierocracy."[11] Thirdly, Weber nowhere presents a *formal* account of his distinction between church and sect. In the tripartite schema presented above, the ideas are Weber's, but the listing is mine. This leaves us in some uncertainty. Have I missed something? Have I misplaced the frontier between stipulation and empirical finding? Have I missed or misconstrued the relationship between the three elements?

A case in point is the first criterion on my list membership. Weber, as we saw, stresses that membership of a sect is voluntary. Do we then insist that a closed religious community is not a sect? Logically we have no choice; yet Weber himself cheerfully refers to Indian "sects" (*Sekten*) as examples of groups closed by endogamy.[12] Perhaps, then, we should construe the voluntary characteristic as a secondary manifestation—and not a necessary one—of something deeper. And indeed Weber suggests something of the kind in a passage in which he explains that a sect "requires the free consensus (*freie Vereinbarung*) of its members, since it aims at being an aristocratic group, an association of persons with full religious qualification."[13] If the essential point of the membership criterion is that the group is select—you are there because you are one of the few who belong there—then even the metempsychotically closed Druze community might qualify as a Weberian sect. But Weber himself leaves us in the dark.

There is also a more general point to be made about Weber's distinction. Given the softness of his categories, we have a right to suspect that his apparently general concepts may be only imperfectly abstracted from the specific contexts which gave rise to them. General concepts naturally tend to originate in the study of particular things. Weber's idea of a "church" is transparently the product of his study of the Christian church; and in the absence of formal definition, what he means by it might well be expressed as "things like the Christian church." His notion of a sect derives just as transparently from his interest in such Protestant splinter groups of the early modern period as the Baptists;[14] sects, for Weber, are by the same token "things like the Baptists." Now there is nothing amiss in the fact that Weber's general concepts have particular origins, nor does any stigma attach to the circumstance that these origins lie in Europe. The question at issue is whether, in the process of generalization, the concepts in question have been successfully emancipated from the specificity of their origins. If not, there may be hidden historical premises lurking behind the apparent generality. We shall come to a case in point.

What Weber does is accordingly to alert us to a suggestive distinction, but no more. Whether it will be of any assistance to us when we venture out into the empirical jungle remains to be seen.

Let us look first at the way in which Weber himself applies his distinction in the Islamic context—in so far as he does so.[15]

On one point Weber is explicit: we are fully justified in speaking of an Islamic "church."[16] At the same time, there are clearly sects to be found in Islam—though this appears only from incidental references. Weber refers to the followers of the Sudanese Mahdi as a sect.[17] He likewise speaks in passing of the "distinctly intellectualist character" of "a few heterodox sects" in Islam, but without stopping to identify them.[18] But are the Shi'ites a sect (or sects)? One passage suggests that they are: in a discussion of law, Weber remarks on "the rigorous sectarianism (*die streng sektiererische Eigenart*)" of the Shi'ites.[19] But another passage suggests the contrary, referring to Shi'ite Islam as a church.[20] And what of the other major heterodox grouping in Islam, the Kharijites To my knowledge, Weber does not refer to them.

What are we to make of these views? We can leave aside the question whether Sunni Islam can qualify as a Weberian church, though Weber, as we have seen, was in no doubt that it did.[21] On the question of sects in Islam, the *obiter dicta* collected above can hardly be made to yield a considered position. Weber clearly thought that Islamic sects existed, but beyond that he gives us little guidance.

If we set out on our own with Weber's distinction in our baggage, we immediately encounter a striking misfit between his notion of a sect and the groups which an Islamicist would naturally call by this term. These groups are in many, perhaps most, cases intensely *political*. The religion of Muhammad, as Weber noted, "is fundamentally political in its orientation,"[22] and sacred politics constitutes the classic domain of sectarian self-definition in Islam—it is here that the deepest and most enduring cleavages have arisen. It follows that the sects of the Islamicist are not sects in a Weberian sense—and equally that Weber's distinction fails to bite on the most arresting single feature of religious schism in Islam. Did Weber perceive or intend this consequence? Probably not; the passage in which he speaks of "the Mahdists and other sects in Islam" is specifically concerned with their doctrine of "the obligation to bring about a revolution in behalf of the faith (*Glaubensrevolution*)."[23]

A further point, already adumbrated in Weber's *obiter dicta*, is that his concept of a sect does not sit well on Shi'ite Islam, even if we leave aside the question of politics. We can perhaps contrive to nudge the Shi'ites through the membership criterion. Membership of a Shi'ite community is not, on the whole, markedly less voluntary that that of other such Islamic groups. (Doubtless it was in practice more voluntary in the early Islamic period than it became later on.[24]) And a certain

Weberian elitism, a sense of constituting a community of the elect, is articulated in Shi'ite thought. (Though again, it can hardly have the same meaning for a solidly Shi'ite population, such as has existed in Iran since the sixteenth century, as it has for a Shi'ite minority.) The real trouble comes with the second criterion, the structure of authority. If Sunni Islam is perhaps a bit too congregational to be a convincing Weberian church, Shi'ite Islam has too much of a tendency to hierarchy to be convincing as a Weberian sect or sects. There is too much charisma of office, and too much respect for persons be they imams, 'Alids or mollahs. On this criterion it is Shi'ite rather than Sunni Islam which has the better title to the rank of a Weberian church.

This leaves us with the Kharijites as the most promising candidates for Weberian secthood in Islam. Again, we have to leave aside the political criterion. That said, it is in the Kharijite context that Weber's concept is most evocative. With regard to membership, we find among the Kharijite groups indications of a marked emphasis on the elective character of the community,[25] together with notable parallels to the sectarian Christian idea of *an ecclesia pura*.[26] With regard to the structure of authority, Kharijite communities display a certain congregational character which is reflected in the downgrading of the charisma of office in Kharijite doctrines of the imamate. But for their strongly political character, these Kharijite groups would be well worth considering as Weberian sects.

What are we to conclude from these findings? On balance, it is hard to avoid the conclusion that Weber's distinction between church and sect is not an illuminating one for the analysis of the groups we know as Islamic sects. The categories fail to engage on the Islamic phenomena. Why is this so?

At this point it may be useful to return to the Weberian status of the Kharijites. It is, as we saw, the political orientation of the Kharijite groups that disqualifies them as Weberian sects. Now in Weber's conception, the apolitical character of a sect is a product of its desire to extricate itself from the society which envelops it. Such extrication was not easy to bring about in sixteenth-century Europe; indeed some of the sects in question eventually went so far as to remove themselves from Europe altogether. But the central image is that of a sect seeking to shore up an inner space within an uncongenial society. The conditions under which the Kharijite communities of early Islam took shape were a different story. Several factors conspired to make it commonplace for a group to extricate itself physically from a society perceived as religiously alien, and to embark on a political life of its own, often in violent confrontation with the rulers of the society it had left. In other words, if we accept Weber's view that a fundamental purpose of a sect is to disentangle itself from the surrounding society, then whether the sect seeks to achieve this by shoring up an inner space or by removing itself to an outer one, in other words by renouncing or by embracing politics, can be seen as a matter of historically conditioned strategy.[27] Here, then, we have exposed one of those hidden historical premises of Weber's sociology at which I hinted above. A contingent feature of the history of Europe has been smuggled into a supposedly cross-cultural concept.

We could go on from here to rework Weber's distinction in the light of this exposure, and thereby greatly improve the fit between Weberian categories and Kharijite realities. But to do this would be to rethink Weber's ideas, not to apply them. Is it in fact worth our while to rethink Weber's concepts? In the case in point, my own answer would be negative. Weber is neither so obviously right, nor so interestingly wrong, as to provide a useful starting-point for our own attempts to understand the peculiar groups we know as Islamic sects.[28]

Notes

1. "It is its character as a compulsory association (*"Anstalts"-Charakter*), particularly the fact that one becomes a member of the church by birth, which distinguishes the church from a "sect." It is characteristic of the latter that it is a voluntary association (*"Verein"*) and admits only persons with specific religious qualifications." (Max Weber, *Economy and Society: An Outline of Interpretive Sociology*, ed. G. Roth and C. Wittich [New York: Bedminster Press 1968] [hereafter ES], p. 56 = Max Weber, *Wirtschaft und Gesellschaft: Grundriss der verstehenden Soziologie*, fifth edition, ed. J. Winckelmann, (Tübingen: J. C. B. Mohr, 1972 [hereafter *WuG*]), p. 30).
2. *ES*, 1164 = *WuG*, 693.
3. *ES*, 1164 = *WuG*, 692.
4. *ES*, 1164 = *WuG*, 693.
5. *ES*, 1205 = *WuG*, 722.
6. *ES*, 455f = *WuG*, 277f.
7. *ES*, 1208 = *WuG*, 724.
8. *Loc. cit.*
9. *Loc. cit.*
10. *ES*, 1208 = *WuG*, 725.
11. *ES*, 1164 = *WuG*, 692.
12. *ES*, 386 = *WuG*, 235.
13. *ES*, 1204 = *WuG*, 721. A sect is a "*visible* community of saints, from whose midst the black sheep are removed;" a church, by contrast, includes the righteous and the unrighteous alike (*ES*, 1204 = *WuG*, 721f).

14. The Baptists are for Weber "one of the most typical sects in the sociological sense: (*ES*, 1204 = *WuG*, 721).
15. In what follows, I may have been an occasional victim of the useful but imperfect indices of *ES* and *WuG*.
16. "In the full sense of the term, churches have arisen only in Islam and Lamaist Buddhism, apart from Christianity" (*ES,* 1164 = *WuG*, 693).
17. *ES,* 56 = *WuG*, 359, referring to "the Mahdists and other sects in Islam." This passage was pointed out to me by Nehemia Levtzion.
18. *ES*, 512 = *WuG*, 311.
19. *ES*, 823 = *WuG*, 476. In a further passage, the English translation makes Weber speak of the "Shi'ites sect" (*ES*: 456), but the German has simply "Schi'iten" (*WuG*, 278).
20. *ES*, 1205 = *WuG*, 722.
21. The problem is, of course, Weber's second criterion, the structure of authority.
22. *ES*, 444 = *WuG*, 271.
23. *ES*, 596 = *WuG*, 359.
24. It could be argued that a true Weberian sect is likely to exist only in the process of formation; compare charisma.
25. Cf. the view held by some Kharijites that children are not to be regarded as members of the community, but are to be called to Islam on reaching puberty (Ashar, *Malaqat al-islamiyyin*, ed. H. Ritter, second edition [Wiesbaden: Franz Steiner Verlag 1963], p. 93).
26. Cf. the general Kharijite view that the grave sinner is excluded from the community (*ibid.*, 86), and the Azraqite examination of candidate entrants (*ibid.*, pp. 86, 87, with which compare *ES*, 1205 = *WuG*, 722f).
27. There are, of course, Muslim groups which sought an inner rather than an outer space, notably the Imam Shi'iten this too is susceptible of a measure of historical explanation.
28. I would like to thank the organisers of the conference for giving me the opportunity to write this short paper, and Louise Marlow for fortifying me against any temptation to make it longer.

11

Weber's Analysis of Islam and the Specific Pattern of Islamic Civilization

S. N. Eisenstadt

The Problematique of Weber's Analysis of Islam

Weber's analysis of Islam—fragmentary as it is—evinces the same basic problems that can be found in his analysis of those civilizations to which he devoted full treatises—the Jewish and above all the Chinese and Indian ones. We have seen[1] that in the analysis of all these civilizations he was torn between, on the one hand, their recognition as Great Civilizations or—to use Jasper's later term—"Axial Age Civilizations," with special dynamics of their own which distinguished them from the pre-Axial one and, on the other hand, the emphasis of prevalence within them of "traditional" "pre-Axial" characteristics which could seemingly explain why these civilizations have not developed the Western rationalism and capitalism.

The same is true, in principle, of his analysis of Islam—fragmentary as it is. On the one hand he fully recognizes Islam as a Great Religion or Civilization as what would be later designated an Axial civilization, one of those civilizations characterized by a very strong emphasis on the tension between the transcendental and the mundane world and by the concomitantly very strong urge to reconstruct the world according to the premises of such a basic transcendental vision. At the same time, preoccupied as he was with his main problematique—why modern civilizations, rationality, capitalism and the like developed only in the West—he looked for explanations as to why it had not developed in Islam—despite seemingly propituous preconditions which could indeed seemingy be found in it—especially its being the purest monotheistic and universalistic religion with a very strong potential for rationalization of human behavior.

As with other civilizations, he looked here, in the case of Islam, for the explanation of this problem, above all at the persistence within it of "pre-Axial" or "traditional" social formations and ideological tenets—singling out the weakening of the universalistic orientations through the persistence of magic and ritual behavior; the predominance of (the Arab) warrior class as well as withdrawal from the world among many of the sects or orders in Islam.

However, as Nehemia Levtzion has shown in great detail in his essay in this volume, Weber was probably wrong in many—certainly not all—details of this description of Islam.[2] His misunderstanding of many of these features of Islamic civilization was, to some degree, of the same kind as when he described the Chinese Imperial system as patrimonial. It was not due only to the state of Islamic (or Chinese and the like) scholarship of his period, but above all because of his tendency to find in such traditional elements—and not so much in the internal dynamics of these civilizations as Great Civilizations—the reasons for the lack of development in the direction of Western rationality. This tendency was, of course, in contradiction to his seminal, unique, contribution to the analysis of the internal dynamics of the Great Civilizations—be it Chinese, Indian or Buddhist, or Jewish ones—especially to the very detailed analysis between their basic premises, structure of elites, of orthodoxies and heterodoxies, and of their respective institutional dynamics, and his work was indeed—as we have shown with respect to his analysis of Chinese, Indian and Buddhist civilizations[3]—torn between these two tendencies. This is even more true of his analysis of the Islamic civilization, probably because of the fragementary nature of his work on Islam.

In order therefore to confront Weber's original problematique—namely that of the lack of original development within Islam of those symbolic and institutional tendencies which in the West were connected with the development of the modern world—it is necessary to analyze some of those aspects of this civilization which are most pertinent for the understanding of this problematique in terms of the dynamics inherent in the very ideological and institutional premises of the Islamic civilization, of Muslim societies. The best starting point is probably that aspect of Islamic society which Weber did indeed point out as one central—and yet in some ways anomalous—aspect of this civilization, namely the prevalence within it, of what he called the sultanic mode of government and which he attributed to the traditional predominance of the traditional warrior class as the carriers of Islam.

There can, of course, be no doubt that most of Islamic polities evinced some very strong sultanic-patrimonial characteristics. This seems to be a rather anomalous fact from the point of view of the basic premises of this civilization, especially its strong transcendental visions, its strong emphasis on the active reconstruction of the world. Given these premises, the political regimes that crystallized within the realm of Islamic civilization should have developed in the direction of Imperial regimes or, given the continuous expansion of this civilization in the direction of something akin to Imperial-feudal regimes that developed in Europe. And yet in fact only very few Muslim regimes—the Abbysid, the Fatimid, to a smaller degree the Safavid, and above all the Ottoman ones—have indeed developed relatively strong Imperial characteristics—even if of "traditional" Imperial regimes with strong patrimonial characteristics. At the same time, although many "feudal components"—such as the famous *Iqta*—could be found in the realm of Islamic lands, there never developed in Islamic lands that combination of political and economic forces which characterized European feudal and postfeudal society—namely the multiplicity and continuous impingement of centers and sub-centres and the possibility—even if limited—of the conversion of economic into political power.

All this was not due—or certainly not mainly due—to the prevalence within Islamic lands of many "traditional" elements. It was rather much more inherent in the very mode of the institutionalization and expansion of Islam. Here of special interest is one crucial and unique aspect of many of these regimes—namely that they were ruled, to use Daniel Pipes' expression—by military slaves, or to use Patricia Crone's expression, by "Slaves on Horses,"[4] slaves imported by the rulers which became converted to Islam and incorporated into it. Let's accordingly proceed now to the analysis of the basic premises of Islamic civilization and the mode of its expansion.

The Basic Premises of Islam in Civilization: Sectarianism and the Social and Political Dynamics in Muslim Societies

Among the cultural orientations that crystallized in the Islamic realm, of special importance from the point of view of our analysis is the following: the emphasis on overcoming the tension inherent in the chasm between transcendental realm and the mundane one by total submission to God; the principled autonomous access of all members of the community to the attributes of the transcendental order, to the sacred, through such submission to God; the closely connected emphasis on the principled political equality of all believers; the strong universalistic element in the definition of the Islamic community; the ideal of the *umma*—the political-religious community of all believers, distinct from any ascriptive, primordial collectivity and the strong emphasis on thisworldly, above all, political and military—activity.

This ideology entailed a complete fusion of political-religious dimensions of collectivities and collective identity. The pristine vision of the *umma*, probably only implicit in the very formative period of Islam, assumed complete convergence between the sociopolitical and religious communities.[5] The possibility of attaining the pristine vision of Islam, of the ideal fusion between the political and the religious community, of constructing the umma, was actually given up from relatively early periods in the formation and expansion of Islam. But although it was never fully attained it was continually promulgated, as Aziz Al Azmeh has shown with a very strong utopian orientation, by different scholars and religious leaders, in the later periods.[6] Given the continual perceptions of the perfect age of the Prophet as an ideal, even utopian model, the idea of renovation constituted a continual component of Islamic civilization or religion. Muhammed's state in Medina became as Henry Munson, Jr. has aptly put it—the Islamic "primordial utopia."[7]

In implementation of all these basic premises of Islamic ideology, Islamic societies evinced, as Maxime Rodinson has put it, the characteristics of a "totalitarian movement," as if it were a political party strongly oriented to the reconstruction of the world and very militant in this pursuit[8]—albeit needless to say without having all the modern technological and administrative means of totalitarianism.

The emphasis on the reconstruction of a combined political-religious collectivity was connected in Islam with the development of a strong ideological negation of any primordial element or component within this sacred political-religious identity. Indeed, of all the Axial Age civilizations in general, and the monotheistic ones in particular, Islam was, on the ideological level, the most extreme in the denial of the legitimacy of such primordial dimensions in the structure of the Islamic community—although de facto of course the story was often, as Bernard Lewis has shown, markedly different.[9] In this it stood in opposition to Judaism with which it shared other characteristics, such as the emphasis on the direct unmediated access of all members of the community to the sacred. It differed however also from Judaism in its basic conception of the relations between man and God, in the strong emphasis—as the name Islam connotes—on the total submission to God and in the lack of a conception of any possible contractual relation between God and man.

True enough, two primordial aspects have indeed very forcefully persisted in the development of Islam in very central areas—namely the strong emphasis on descent from the Prophet as a source of legitimation of rulers, and the emphasis on the Arabic language as the sacred language of Islam, of the Quran, of prayer, and also to a large degree, legal exegesis. This was in contrast to Judaism where the Bible was read in Greek in Alexandria (and in English in many synagogues in the United States); or to Christianity where the liturgy was naturally read in Greek (or other languages) in the East, and later on also in Europe (Latin Christendom) after the Reformation. But beyond these two primordial elements (descent from the Prophet and the use of Arabic) there developed in Islam no sanctification of any "ethnic" primordial-communal elements or symbols and it was the universalistic ideology of the *umma* that became predominant.

Yet the very strong universalistic ideology which became dominant in Islam was, from the very beginning, torn by a tension between the particularistic primordial Arab elements which constituted the initial carriers of the Islamic vision and the universalistic orientation which has become more important with continuous conquest and continuous incorporation of new territorial entities and ethnic groups.[10] Hence there developed strong tensions between the particularistic primordial Arab elements or components, which were the initial carriers of the Islamic vision, and the universalistic orientation—tensions which became more important with continual conquest and incorporation of new territorial entities and ethnic groups. The final crystallization of this universalistic ideology took place with the so-called Abbasid revolution, which, as M. Sharon has shown,[11] involved a shift in the legitimation of rulers in Sunni Islam from direct descent from the prophet and consensus of the community to seniority and ultimately to the ability to fulfill the prophet's will.

It was also in this period, however, that in close relation to the institutionalization of this universalistic vision, there developed within Sunni Islam a de facto separation between the political and the religious elites as analyzed by H. A. R. Gibb and more recently by I. Lapidus.[12] It was in close relation to this situation that there developed in the late Abbasid history the separation between the Khalif and the actual ruler (the Sultan) heralding de facto separation between the rulers and the religious establishment ('ulama'). The *khalif* who became de facto powerless did yet continue to serve as an ideal figure—insofar as he appeared to be the presumed embodiment of the pristine Islamic vision of the *umma*, and as the major source of legitimation of the Sultan—even if usually he had no way to refuse such legitimation.

This separation was connected with the rise to that unique type of ruling group—most intimately connected with Islamic patrimonial sultanism, but to be found also in Islamic Imperial regimes—namely, the military-religious rulers, who emerged from tribal and sectarian elements. It also gave rise to the system of military slavery, which created special channels of mobility such as the *qulam* system in general, and the Mamlukes and Ottoman deoshime in particular, through which the ruling groups could be recruited from alien elements.[13] It is these dynamics of the institutionalization and expansion of Islam that explains why it was only under very special circumstances that imperial or imperial-like regimes developed in Islam, whereas most Islamic regimes were of the patrimonial-sultanic kind.

In close relation to this separation—and to the continual quest for the "true" ruler, there developed in Muslim societies two major types of legitimation of rulers. One type, most prevalent above all in the mainstream of Islamic (Sunni) religious thought, stressed the legitimacy in the Muslim community of any ruler who assures the peaceful existence of the Muslim community and the upholding of the Islamic law (the *shari'ca*—but at the same time emphasizing the coercive nature of such rulers, of the political order and its basic distance from the pristine ideal. This type of legitimation and accountability of rulers was also closely connected, as was the case in other Axial civilizations, with the acceptance of the legitimacy of mundane concerns, be they utilitarian or power-seeking ones, of many sectors of the population and of the rulers. Whatever the extent of the acceptance of such legitimation, it usually entailed the duty of the rulers to implement justice—and hence entailed also the possibility of scrutinisation of their behavior by the *'ulama'*—even if such scrutinization did not usually have direct and clear institutional political effects. It was indeed in many ways the *'ulama'*, however weak was their organization, that constituted the guardians of the pristine Islamic vision, of the normative dimensions of the *umma*, and their moral force was very great.

It was in close relation to the characteristics of the *'ulama'* that the Muslim regimes evinced several important characteristics that distinguish them from other "traditional" "classical" patrimonial regimes in Southeast Asia or the early Near East, namely the relatively high symbolic—but with much smaller organizational—autonomy of the religious elite. Although this highly autonomous religious elite did not develop into a broad, independent, and cohesive organization, and although religious groups and functionaries were not organized as a distinct separate entity; nor did they constitute a tightly organized body— except when, as in the Ottoman Empire, they were organized by the state or in different modes in Shi'ite Islam. Yet, at the same time it was these religious leaders, the *'ulama'* and the sufi-Sheikhs, who were the custodians of the law and through it of the boundaries of the Islamic community. The *'ulama'*—even the relatively highly controlled *'ulama'* as in the Ottoman empire—were always seen as guardians of the Islamic community. As guardians of this community the *'ulama'* performed important juridical functions and could also provide, especially in the patrimonial regimes some autonomous sphere of life not entirely controlled by the rulers. It is in this that they differed greatly from religious groups in "usual" traditional patrimonial or tribal regimes.

These specifically Islamic groups—the *'ulama'* in general and the legal specialists in particular—were universal in the historical experience of classical Islam. It is these groups that created major networks cutting across the boundaries of any specific political regime. Indeed, in general Islam, above all through the networks of the *'ulama'* brought together, under one religious—and often also social-civilizational— umbrella, varied ethnic and geopolitical groups, tribal, settled peasants, urban groups, creating mutual impingement and contacts between them which otherwise probably would not have developed among them.

It is these distinctive Islamic groups that were central in the construction of the major public spheres which have been distinctive of Islamic societies, namely—to follow M. Hodgson—the arenas of schools of law; the waqfs and the religious orders which provided autonomous arenas of life not entirely controlled by the rulers.[14]

These public spheres were largely autonomous in that they constituted arenas constructed according to distinctual criteria of recruitment and action. They were also areas in which different sectors of the society could voice their demands in the name of the presumed basic premises of Islamic vision. These public spheres were, of course, de facto often highly dependent on the ruler and there could develop from within the confrontational stances with the ruler. Yet their development was to a very large extent autonomous, creating also wide, trans-state, often clientilistic networks. But their autonomy did not on the whole move in the direction of autonomous participation in the central political era—in the Western sense.

The second type of legitimation and accountability promulgated the vision of the ruler as the upholder of the pristine, transcendental vision, embodied, if not in the figure, at least in the ideal of the *khalifs*. The continuity of their existence epitomized the continuity of the ideal of the pristine Islamic vision. Many of the later rulers (such as the Abbasids and Fatimids and other Muslim rulers came to power on the crest of religious movements that upheld this ideal, legitimized themselves in such religious-political terms, and sought to retain popular support by stressing the religious aspect of their authority and by courting the religious leaders and religious sentiments of the community. Concomitantly, political problems constituted the central problem of Islamic theology.[15]

Such a conception of rulers, especially when combined with messianic or eschatological orientations, could become promulgated, and embodied, in the figures of Mahdis, messianic-like renovators which appeared in many Muslim societies throughout history. Many rulers, as for instance the Moroccan sultans Sidi Muhammed and Mowlay Suleiman, attempted, especially if they could claim to be descendents of the prophet, to portray themselves as such *khalifs*—to be challenged by different sectors of the *'ulama'* and various popular secterian-like movements.[16] It was especially within Shi'ite Islam that a stronger potential for the implementation of such visions by the ruler continually existed in the image of the hidden imam, even if in a subterranean fashion, but it constituted also a very strong component of various sects in mainstream, sunni, Islam.[17]

The impact of the continuity of this utopian vision on the original Islamic period and ideal, and the fact that this ideal was both never fully implemented and never fully given up, became evident in some specific characteristics of the political dynamism of Islamic regimes and of Islamic sects, or rather movements with sectarian tendencies. One has of course to be very careful in using the term sect—with its Jewish and especially Christian roots—with respect to Islam, or with respect to Hinduism. One of the distinct characteristics of Christian sectarianism—the tendency toward schism—has been, after the great break between the Shi'ites and the Sunnis, barely applicable to Islam.

But sectarian-like tendencies existed in the continual social movements that developed in Muslim societies. In the vision promulgated by many of these movements, the political and/or of the renovative orientations, very often in some combination of the two aiming at the restoration of the pristine vision of Islam, was never given up. Such renovative visions or orientations were embodied in the different versions of the *Mujaddid* tradition—the tradition of reform—and possibly even innovative reforms.[18]

Such movements of renovation and reform could be focused on the person of a "mahdi" or be promulgated by sufi orders as well as tribal groups, such as the Wahhabites, and in some of the schools of law. As Emanuel Sivan has pointed out:

> Islamic Sunni radicalism was born out of the anti-accommodative attitude towards political power which had always existed within this tradition as a vigilante-type, legitimate, albeit secondary strand. Its most consistent and powerful paragon over the last seven centuries was the neo-Hanbalite school of Islamic law. When modern Sunni radicals looked in the 1920s and 1960s for a tradition to build upon, they turned quite naturally, like their predecessors in the late eighteenth century (the founders of Saudi Arabia) to neo-Hanbalism.[19]

Such restorative protofundamentalist tendencies were very often connected with very strong utopian eschatological orientations. As Aziz Al Azmeh has put it:

> The Medinan Caliphate can thus be regarded, with Laroui, as a utopia, What Laroui omits is an important complement without which consideration of this matter would remain incomplete: this is eschatology. Unlike activist, fundamentalist utopia, this finalist state of felicity and rectitude associated with the future reigns of the Mahdi (the Messiah) and of 'Isab. Maryam (Jesus Christ) is not the result of voluntaristic action. Like the medinan regime and the prophetic example, it is a miraculous irruption by divine command onto the face of history, although it will be announced for the believers by many cosmic and other signs. Not only is the End a recovery of the Muslim prophetic experience, it is also the recovery of the primordial Adamic order, of the line of Abel, of every divine mission like those of Noah, Abraham, Moses, David, Solomon, Jesus and Muhammad, who incorporates, transcends and consummates them all in the most definitive form of primeval religiosity, Islam. The End, like the beginning and like the periodic irruptions of prophecy, is really against nature; it is the calque of the beginning so often repeated in history, and is the ultimate primitivism.[20]

This political and/or renovative component could be oriented towards active participation in the political center, its destruction or transformation, or towards a conscious withdrawal from it. But even such withdrawal which developed both in Shi'ism and Sufism, often harbored tendencies to pristine renovation. Such withdrawal could also often entail, as was the case with the Sufi orders in the eighteenth century, the reconstitution of the public sphere with many implicit, sometimes even explicit, political implications.

True enough, within Islam there never developed, as Bernard Lewis has shown, a concept of revolution.[21] Indeed, within any single Muslim polity there did not develop, despite the potential autonomous standing of members of the 'ulama', any continual institutional mechanisms—beyond the possible impact of rebellions or threats thereof for calling the rulers to accountability, and especially of deposing them.

In stable Islamic regimes the various religious sects and popular movements did not provide fully institutionalized effective checks on the political authority, and there was no machinery other than revolt for enforcement of any autonomous political demand of various groups—but the potentiality for revolt was endemic in Muslim societies.

But at the same time, as Ernest Gellner indicated in his interpretation of Ibn Khaldun's work, a less direct yet very forceful pattern of indirect accountability of rulers arose. Such possibility did develop in the combination, rooted in the development of various social movements with the resurgence of tribal revival against "corrupt" or weak regimes,[22] rooted in the mode of expansion of Islam. Indeed, a very important characteristic of Islamic societies was that the political impact of such movements with their sectarian tendencies was often connected with processes attendant on the expansion of Islam and especially with the continuous impingement on the core Islamic politics of tribal elements who presented themselves as the carriers of the original ideal Islamic vision and of the pristine Islamic polity. Significantly enough, many tribes (e.g., the Mongols), after being converted to Islam, transformed their own "typical" tribal structures to accord with Islamic religious-political visions, presented themselves as the symbol of pristine Islam, with strong renovative tendencies oriented to the restoration of pristine Islam.

This tendency was indeed closely related to the famous cycle depicted by Ibn Khaldun—namely, the cycle of tribal conquest motivated by strong internal tribal solitary and religious devotion, giving rise to the conquest of cities and settlement in them, followed by the degeneration of the ruling (often formerly tribal) elite and its possible subsequent regeneration out of new tribal elements from the vast—old or new—tribal reservoirs. Such new "converts," along with the seemingly dormant tribes of the Arabian peninsula, of which the Wahhabites constitute probably the latest and most forceful illustration of how such groups became a central dynamic political force in Islamic civilization.[23]

It was because of these distinct characteristics of its expansion that Islam was probably the only Axial civilization within which sectarian-like movements—very often in combination with tribal leaders or councils—often led not only to the overthrow or more frequently downfall of existing regimes but also to the establishment of new political units oriented, at least initially, to the implementation of the original pristine primordial Islamic utopia.

It was the Wahhabites that constituted, as John Voll has indicated, the last—and very forceful—case of a "traditional" Islamic proto-fundamentalist movement. To follow him: "The vision of creating a society in which the Quran is implemented means that Ibn Abd al-Wahhab's mission would inevitably entail political consequences. It was the local rulers who forced him to leave the town where he began teaching, and it was another local ruler, Ibn Sa'ud, who provided necessary support. The political system created by the Wahhabis did not place the inspirational teacher in a position of political rule. Instead, the Wahhabi state was based on the close cooperation of a learned ruler (shaykh) and an able commander (*emir*). The combination reflected a long-standing perception of the proper relations between the institutions of the scholars and those of the commanders. Such a system of institutionalization reflected a reduced emphasis on charismatic leadership among Sunni fundamentalists and was also an important aspect of the great Sunni sultanates of the medieval era.

"Wahhabism" is thus a term used today to indicate the type of reformism elucidated in Abd al-Wahhab's opposition to popular religious superstitions and innovations, his insistence on informed independent judgment over against the rote reliance on medieval authorities, and his call for the Islamiziation of society and the creation of a political order which gives appropriate recognition of Islam. Wahhabism represents an important type of fundamentalism that continues to operate within the modern world but was not initiated as a result of conflict with the modernized West. The Wahhabis succeeded in establishing a state which, while imperfect, has nonetheless been recognized by many in the Islamic world as consonant with the fundamentalist vision to create an Islamic society. It is the most enduring experiment within the broader mission and as such has provided a standard against which other movements and states could be measured.[24]

Insofar as such movements did not create, in the Ibn-Khaldunian mode, new regimes—their impact on the Muslim societies, as that of many other groups in Islamic society was through the continual reconstruction of the major public spheres—especially of those three to which we have referred above and which the late Marshall Hodgson[25] has pointed out in his incisive analysis as the distinctive characteristics of the Islamic societies, namely the schools of law, the *waqf* and the Sufi-orders.

It was indeed in these contexts that the construction of such autonomous public spheres gave rise to some of the distinct patterns in the historical experience of Muslim societies, especially to the specific patterns of pluralism characteristic of these societies. Such pluralism was characterized, even in Imperial Islamic societies, by very strongly *patrimonial* features, such as the existence of segregated regional, ethnic and religious sectors,[26] and to a relatively weak permeation of the center to the periphery and impingement of the periphery on the center; as well as the prevalence—especially in these sectors—of multiple patterns or bases of legitimation. But in contrast to more classical patrimonial regimes which developed in such non-Axial Civilizations as Mesoamerica, Ancient Near East (Hinduized) South Asia, the Muslim patrimonial regimes were in constant tension with the more sectarian tendencies and they could be undermined by the more extreme protofundamentalists, which could attempt like, for instance, the Wahhabis to establish new "pristine" regimes.

It is but natural that these tensions and confrontations between the pluralistic and protofundamentalist became intensified in Muslim societies with the establishment of modern polities rooted in the ideological premises of modernity with their strong emphasis on relatively homogeneous territorial states. The contemporary scene in the Muslim societies can be seen as moving between these poles of attempts to establish territorial states with some elements of pluralism that binds on their earlier historical sequence; and strong anti-pluralistic tendencies in the form of either extreme secular oppressive, often military regimes or extreme Jacobin fundamentalist ones.

Notes

1. S. N. Eisenstadt, "Innerweltliche Transzendenz und die Strukturierung der Welt. Max Webers Studie über China und die Gestalt der chinesischen Zivilisation," in *Max Webers Studie über Konfuzianismus und Taoismus*, ed. W. Schluchter, 363–411 (Frankfurt 1983); S.N. Eisenstadt, "Die Paradoxie von Zivilisationen mit außerweltlichen Orientierungen. Überlegungen zu Max Webers Studie über

Hinduismus und Buddhismus," in W. Schluchter, ed., *Max Weber Studie über Hinduismus und Buddhismus* (Frankfurt 1984), pp. 333–360.
2. N. Levtzion, chapter 3 in this volume.
3. See the reference in endnote 1.
4. D. Pipes, *Slave Soldiers and Islam* (New Haven: Yale University Press 1981).
5. M. Cook, *Mohammad* (Oxford: Oxford University Press, 1983); M. Hodgson, *The Venture of Islam* (Chicago: University of Chicago Press 1974).
6. Aziz Al Azmeh, *Islams and Modernities* (London: Verso 1993).
7. Henry Munson, Jr., *Islam and the Revolution.*
8. M. Rodinson, *Mohammed* (London: Allen Lane, 1971).
9. B. Lewis, *Islam in History* (London: Alcove Press, 1973).
10. Ibid.
11. M. Sharon, *Black Banners from the East* (Jerusalem: Magnes Press, 1983).
12. H. A. R. Gibb, *Studies in the Civilization of Islam* (Boston: Beacon Press, 1962) and I. M. Lapidus, *A History of Islamic Societies* (Cambridge: Cambridge University Press 1988); Idem, "State and Religion in Islamic Societies," *Past and Present*, No. 151, (1996): 3–27.
13. P. Crone, *Slaves on Horses. The Evolution of the Islamic Polity* (Cambridge: Cambridge University Press, 1980); M. Itzkowitz, *Ottoman Empire and the Islamic Tradition* (New York: Alfred A. Knopf,1972).
14. M. Hodgson, *The Venture of Islam* (Chicago: University of Chicago Press, 1974).
15. H.A.R. Gibb, *Studies in the Civilization of Islam*; I. M. Lapidus, *A History of Islamic Societies*; H. Laoust, *Les Schisms dans l'Islam* (Paris: Payot, 1965).
16. I. M. Lapidus, "Islam and Revolution in the Middle East," op.cit.
17. See the references in endnote 16.
18. E. Landau-Tasseron, "The 'Cyclical Reform': A study of the mujaddid tradition," in *Studia Islamica* 70 (1989): 79–118. H. Lazarus-Yafeh, "'Tajdid al-Din': A Reconsideration of Its Meaning, Roots and Influence in Islam," *The New East*, 31 (1986): 1–10. N. Levtzion, "Eighteenth Century Renewal and Reform Movements in Islam," *The New East* 31 (198): 48–70; idem and J. O. Voll, eds., *Eighteenth Century Renewal and Reform in Islam* (Syracuse, NY: Syracuse University Press, 1987); idem and Gideon Weigert, "Religious Reform in Eighteenth-Century Morocco," *Jerusalem Studies in Arabic and Islam* 19 (1995): 173–197; John Voll, "Fundamentalism in Sunni Arab World: Egypt and the Sudan," in *Fundamentalisms Observed*, eds. M. Marty and R. Scott Appleby, 345–403 (Chicago: University of Chicago Press, 1991).
19. E. Sivan, "In God's Cause," in the Erasmus Ascention Sympoisum, *The Limits of Pluralism. Neo-Absolutism and Relativism* (Amsterdam: Praemiuim Erasmianum Foundation, 1994), p. 16.
20. Aziz Al Azmeh, *Islams and Modernities*, 98.
21. B. Lewis, "Islamic Concepts of Revolution," in *Islam in History,* 253–266 (London: Alcove Press 1973).
22. E. Gellner, *Muslim Society* (Cambridge: Cambridge University Press, 1981); also A. S. Ahmed, *Millenium and Charisma among the Pathans* (London: Routledge & Kegan Paul, 1979).
23. J. Voll, "Fundamentalism in Sunni Arab World: Egypt and the Sudan."
24. Ibid, 351.
25. M. Hodgson, *The Venture of Islam*, op.cit.
26. D. Eickelman and J. Piscatori, *Muslim Politics* (Princeton, NJ: Princeton University Press, 1996); Ann E. Mayer, "The Fundamentalist Impact on Law, Politics, and Constitutions in Iran, Pakistan, and the Sudan," in *Fundamentalisms and the State*, eds. Martin E. Marty and R. Scott Appleby (Chicago: University

of Chicago Press, 1993), 110–151; Timur Kuran, "The Economic Impact of Islamic Fundamentalism," in *Fundamentalisms and the State*, eds. Martin E. Marty and R. Scott Appleby, 302–341; James Piscatori, "Accounting for Islamic Fundamentalisms," in *Accounting for Fundamentalisms*, eds. Martin E. Marty and R. Scott Appleby (Chicago: University of Chicago Press, 1994), 361–373; S. A. Arjomand, "Unity and Diversity in Islamic Fundamentalism," in *Fundamentalisms Comprehended,* eds. Martin E. Marty and R. Scott Appleby (Chicago: University of Chicago Press, 1995), 179–198; Valerie J. Hoffman, "Muslim Fundamentalists: Psychosocial Profiles," in *Fundamentalisms Comprehended*, 199–230.

Bibliography

Abdulla, Ahmed. 1973. *The Historical Background of Pakistan and its People*. Karachi: Tanzeem Publishers.

Abu'l Fazl. 1877–1883. *Akbar-Nama*, edited by Agha Ahmad 'Ali and 'Abd al-Rahim Calcutta: Bibliotheca Indica.

Abu'l-fazl. 1987. *Ayn-i Akbari* (compiled in 1595). See S. Moosvi.

Abu-Rabi', Ibrahim M. 1996. *Intellectual Origins of Islamic Resurgence in the Modern Arab World*. Albany: State University of New York Press.

Ahmad, Aziz. 1967. *Islamic Modernism in India and Pakistan 1857–1964*. London: Oxford University Press.

Ahmad, Sultan Jahan. "Muslim Society in Midnapur—a Social Study of a Bengal District (1800–1919 A.D.). Ph.D. dissertation: Calcutta: Jadavpur University, 1982.

Ahmed, Rafiuddin. 1981. *The Bengal Muslims 1871–1906: A Quest for Identity*. Delhi: Oxford University Press.

Ahmed. A. S. 1979. *Millenium and Charisma among the Pathans*. London: Routledge & Kegan Paul.

Alam, Muzaffar. 1986. *The Crisis of Empire in Mughal North India: Awdh and the Punjab, 1707–48*. Delhi: Oxford University Press.

Alatas, Syed Hussein. 1963. "The Weber Thesis and South East Asia." *Archives de Sociologie des Religions*: 21–24.

Albrow, M. 1975. "Legal Positivism and Bourgeois Materialism: Max Weber's View of the Sociology of Law." *British Journal of Law and Sociology* 1:14–30.

Albrow, M. 1975. "Legal Positivism and Bourgeois Materialism: Max Weber's View of the Sociology of Law." *British Journal of Law and Society* 1: 14–30.

Alexander, Jeffrey. 1982/1983. *Theoretical Logic in Sociology*. 4 vols. Berkeley: University of California Press.

Algar, Hamid. 1979. "Said Nursi and the Risala-i Nur: An Aspect of Islam in Contemporary Turkey." In *Islamic Perspectives: Studies in Honour of Mawlana Sayyid Abul A'la Mawdudi*, edited by Khurshid Ahmad and Zafar Ishaq Ansari, 313–33. Leicester: The Islamic Foundation.

Ali, M. Athar. 1966. *The Mughal Nobility under Aurangzeb*. Bombay: Asia Publishing House.

Ali, M. Ather. 1984. *The Apparatus of Empire*. Calcutta: Oxford University Press.

Allott. A. 1980. *The Limits of the Law*. London: Butterworths.
Alter, P., W. J. Mommsen, and T. Nipperdey, eds., 1986. "Max Webers Begriff der Universalgeschichte." In *Max Weber der Historiker*, edited by G. J. Kocka, ed., 51–72. Göttingen: Vandenhoeck & Ruprecht.
Amin, Munshi Muhammad Kazim bin Muhammad.1868. *Alamgir-nama*, edited by Khadim Husain and 'Abd al-Hai. Calcutta: Asiatic Society of Bengal.
Anderson, Norman. 1976. *Law and Reform in Muslim World*. London: Athlone Press.
Anderson, Norman. 1976. *Law Reform in the Muslim World*. London: Athlone Press.
Anderson, Perry. 1980 [1974]. *Lineages of the Absolutist State*. London: Verso Editions.
Ansari, Khizar Humayun. 1990. *The Emeregence of Socialist Thought Among North Indian Muslims (1917–1947)*. Lahore: Book Traders.
Arat, Yesim, 1997. "The Project of Modernity and Women in Turkey." In *Rethinking Modernity and National Identity in Turkey*, edited by Sibel Bozdogan and Resat Kasaba, 95–112. Seattle: University of Washington Press.
Arjomand, S. A. 1995. "Unity and Diversity in Islamic Fundamentalism." In *Accounting for Fundamentalisms,* edited by Martin E. Marty and R. Scott Appley, 179–198. Chicago: University of Chicago Press.
Asad, Talal, 1993. *Genealogies of Religions: Discipline and Reasons of Power in Christianity and Islam*. Baltimore: The Johns Hopkins University Press.
Ashar, Abu'l-Hasan al-Ash'ai. 1963. *Maqalat al-islamiyyin*, edited by H. Ritter, second edition. Wiesbaden: Franz Steiner Verlag.
Asim Roy. 1970. "Islam in the Environment of Medieval Bengal." Ph.D. dissertation, Australian National University.
Askeri, S. H. 1959. "The Mughal-Magh Relations down to the Time of Islam Khan Mashhadi." *Indian History Congress, Proceedings*, 22nd Session, 201–13.
Aziz, Al- Azmeh. 1993. *Islams and Modernities*. London: Verso.
Barbosa, Duarte. 1921. *The Book of Duarte Barbosa*, translated by M. L. Dames. London: Hakluyt Society.
Barisal District Collectorate Record Room. Mauza Note Registers. Gaurnadi *thana*, vol. 1, village R.S. 696.
Barnett, Richard B. 1980. *North India Between Empires: Awadh, the Mughals and the British, 1720–1801*. Berkeley: University of California Press.
Bayly, C. A. 1983. *Rulers, Townsmen and Bazaars: North Indian Society in the Aqe of British Expansion 1770–1870*. Cambridge: Cambridge University Press.
Bayly, C. A. 1983. *Rulers, Townsmen, and Bazaars: North Indian Society in the Age of British Expansion, 1770–1870*. Cambridge: Cambridge University Press.

Becker, Carl Heinrich. 1924. *Islamstudien.* Vol. I. Leipzig: Quelle & Meyer.
Beirne, P. 1979. "Ideology and Rationality in Max Weber's Sociology of Law." *Research in Law and Sociology* 2:103–31.
Bendix, Reinhard. 1978. *Kings or People.* Berkeley: University of California Press.
Berger, Peter L. 1973. *The Social Reality of Religion.* Harmondsworth: Penguin Books.
Berger, Peter. 1973. *The Social Reality of Religion.* Harmondsworth: Penguin Books.
Berman, Harold J. 1983. *Law and Revolution. The Formation of the Western Legal Tradition.* Cambrige: Harvard University Press.
Berman, Harold J. 1987a. "Some False Premises of Max Weber's Sociology of Law." *Washington University Law Quarterly* 65, 4: 758–770.
Berman, Harold. J. 1987b. "Conscience and Law: The Lutheran Reformation and the Western Legal Tradition." *Journal of Law and Religion* 17: 177–202.
Bhagavad-Gita with a commentary based on the original sources by R.C. Zaehner, Oxford: Oxford University Press 1979 (paperback reprint).
Bhattacharya, N. D. 1978. "Changing Courses of the Padma and Human Settlements," *National Geographic Journal of India*, 24/1–2 (March-June).
Blake, Stephen P. 1979. "The Patrimonial-Bureaucratic Empire of the Mughals." *Journal of Asian Studies* 39, 1 (November): 77–94.
Blochmann, H. 1873. "Contributions to the Geography and History of Bengal," *Journal of the Asiatic Society of Bengal* 42/3: 00–00.
Bodde, Derk, and C. Morris. 1967. *Law in Imperial China.* Cambridge Mass.: Harvard University Press.
Breuer, Stefan and Hubert Treiber, eds. 1984. *Zur Rechtssoziologie Max Webers. Interpretation, Kritik, Weiterentwicklung.* Opladen: Westdeutscher Verlag.
Breuer, Stefan. 1988. "Der okzidentale Feudalismus in Max Webers Gesellschafts-geschichte." In *Max Webers Sicht des okzidentalen Christentums*, edited by W. Schluchter, 437–475. Frankfurt: Suhrkamp.
Brierley, David R. and J. E. C. Brierley. 1968. *Major Legal Systems in the World Today.* Second edition. London: Stephens and Sons.
Brubaker, Rogers. 1985. *The Limits of Rationality. An Essay on the Social and Moral Thought of Max Weber.* London: George Allen & Unwin.
Bulliet, Richard W. 1979. *Conversion to Islam in the Medieval Period: An Essay in Quantitative History.* Cambridge, Mass.: Harvard University Press.
Cain, Maureen. 1980. "The Limits of Idealism: Max Weber and the Sociology of Law." In S. Spitzer, ed., *Research in Law and Sociology* 3: 53–83. Greenwich, Conn.: JAI.Press.
Cardon, L. and H. Hosten. 1916. "Padre Maistro Fray Seb. Manrique in Bengal (1628–29)." *Bengal Past and Present* 13, 1 (July-September): 10–11.

Chadwick, Owen. 1975. *The Secularization of the European Mind in the Nineteenth Century*. Cambridge: Cambridge University Press.
Chon, Song-U. 1985. *Max Webers Stadtkonzeption. Eine Studie zur Entwicklung des okzidentalen Bürgertums*. Göttingen: Edition Herodot.
Cohn, E. J. and W. Zdzieblo. 1968–71. *Manual of German Law*, second edition. London: Oceana Publications.
Cole, Donald Powell. 1975. *Nomads of the Nomads: the Al Murrah Bedouin of the Empty Quarter*. Illinois: AHM Publishing Corporation.
Collins, Randall. 1986. *Weberian Sociological Theory*. Cambridge: Cambridge University Press.
Colvin, L. G. 1974. "Islam and the State of Kajoor: A Case of Successful Resistance to Jihad." *Journal of African History* 15: 587–606.
Cook, M. 1983. *Mohammad*. Oxford: Oxford University Press.
Cotterell, R. 1981. "The Development of Capitalism and the Formalisation of Contract Law." In *Law, State and Society*, edited by B. Fryer and others, 54–69. London: Croom Helm.
Coulson, N. J. 1964. *A History of Islamic Law*. Edinburgh: Edinburgh University Press.
Coulson, N. J. 1969. *Conflicts and Tensions in Islamic Jurisprudence*. Chicago: University of Chicago Press.
Coulson, N. J. 1971. *Succession in the Muslim Family*. Cambridge: Cambridge University Press.
Crone, Patricia. and M. Cook. 1977. *Hagarism: The Making of the Islamic World*. Cambridge: Cambridge University Press.
Crone, Patricia. and M. Hinds. 1986. *God's Caliph: Religious Authority in the First Centuries of Islam*. Cambridge: Cambridge University Press.
Crone, Patricia. 1980. *Slaves on Horses. The Evolution of the Islamic Polity*. Cambridge: Cambridge University Press.
Crone, Patricia. 1987. *Roman, Provincial and Islamic Law*. Cambridge: Cambridge University Press.
Crone, Patricia. 1989. *Pre-Industrial Societies*. Oxford: Basil Blackwell.
Crone, Patricia. 1996. "The Rise of Islam in the World." In *The Cambridge Illustrated History of the Islamic World*, edited by Francis Robinson, 2–31. New York: Cambridge University Press.
Cupitt, Don. 1984. *The Sea of Faith: Christianity in Change*. London: British Broadcasting Corporation.
Dale, Stephen F. 1980. *Islamic Society on the South Asian Frontier: The Mappilas of Malabar, 1498–1922*. Oxford: Clarendon Press.
Das Gupta, J. N. 1914. *Bengal in the Sixteenth Century*. Calcutta: University of Calcutta.
Dastur al-'amal-i 'Alamgiri (compiled 1659) (British Library MS., Add. 6599), fols. 120a–121a.
Davis, Joyce M. 1997. *Between Jihad and Salaam: Profiles in Islam*. New York: St Martin's.

Dhaka District Collectorate Record Room. Mauza Note Registers, Narayanganj *thana*, vol. 9, No. 4269 (Narayanganj No. 437).
Dobbin, Christine. 1977. "Economic Change in Minangkabau as a Factor in the Rise of the Padri Movement, 1784–1830." *Indonesia*: 1–38.
Dobbin, Christine. 1983. *Islamic Revivalism in a Changing Peasant Economy: Central Sumatra, 1784–1847*. London: Curzon Press.
Dobbin, Christine. 1983. *Islamic Revivalism in a Changing Peasant Economy: Central Sumatra, 1784–1847*. London: Curzon Press.
Dumont, Louis. 1980. *Homo Herarchicus*, complete revised English edition. Chicago: University of Chicago Press.
Eaton, Richard M. 1978. *Sufis of Bijapur 1300–1700: Social Roles of Sufis in Medieval India*. Princeton, N.J.: Princeton University Press.
Eaton, Richard M. 1996. *The Rise of Islam and the Bengal Frontier, 1204–1760*. Berkeley: University of California Press.
Eickelman, Dale and J. Piscatori. 1996. *Muslim Politics*. Princeton, N.J.: Princeton University Press.
Eickelman, Dale. 1994. "Mass Higher Education and the Religious Imaginatiuon in Contemporary Arab Societies." *American Ethnologist* 19 (4): 643–655.
Eisenberg, Melvin A. 1988. *The Nature of the Common Law*. Cambridge, Mass.: Harvard University Press.
Eisenstadt, S. N. 1984. "Die Paradoxie von Zivilisationen mit außerweltlichen Orientierungen. Überlegungen zu Max Webers Studie über Hinduismus und Buddhismus." In *Max Weber Studie über Hinduismus und Buddhismus*, edited by W. Schluchter, 333–360. Frankfurt: Suhrkamp.
Eisenstadt, S.N. 1983. "Innerweltliche Transzendenz und die Strukturierung der Welt. Max Webers Studie über China und die Gestalt der chinesischen Zivilisation." In *Max Webers Studie über Konfuzianismus und Taoismus*, edited by W. Schluchter, 363–411. Frankfurt: Suhrkamp.
Engel, D. M. 1975. *Law and Kingship in Thailand during the Reign of King Chulalongkorn*. Ann Arbor: Center for South and Southeast Asian Studies, University of Michigan.
Ewing, Sally. 1987. "Formal Justice and the Spirit of Capitalism: Max Weber's Sociology of Law." *Law and Society Review* 21: 87–512.
Fakhry, M. 1958. *Islamic Occasionalism and Its Critique by Thomas Aquinas*. London: Allen & Unwin.
Frank, R. M. 1985. "Two Islamic Views of Human Agency." In *La Notion de liberté au Moyen Age: Islam, Byzance, Occident*, 37–49. Paris: Societé d'Edition.
Franklin, J. H. 1963. *Jean Bodin and the Sixteenth-Century Revolution in the Methodology of Law and History*. New York: Greenwood Press.
Fyzee, Asaf A. A. 1964. *Outlines of Muhammadan Law*. Third edition. Oxford: Oxford University Press.
Gait, E. A. 1901. "Muhammadan Castes and Tribes." *Census of India, 1901*, vol. 6: *The Lower Provinces of Bengal and their Feudatories*, pt. 1, "Report."

Geertz, Clifford. 1965. "Modernization in a Muslim society: the Indonesian Case." In *Religion and Progress in Modern Asia,* edited by R. N. Bellah, 92–108. New York: The Free Press.

Geertz, Clifford. 1968. *Islam Observed.* New Haven, Conn.: Yale University Press.

Gellner Ernest. 1979. "A Social Contract in Search of an Idiom: The Demise of the Danegeld." In *Spectacles and Predicaments,* 277–306. Cambridge: Cambridge University Press.

Gellner, Ernest. 1973. "The Savage and the Modern Mind." In *Modes of Thought,* edited by R. Horton and R. Finnegan, 162–181. London: Faber and Faber.

Gellner, Ernest. 1969. "A Pendulum Swing Theory of Islam." In *Sociology of Religion,* edited by Roland Robertson, 127–138. New York: Penguin Books.

Gellner, Ernest. 1979. "A Social Contract in Search of an Idiom: the Demise of the Danegeld State. In Gellner, *Spectacles and Predicaments: Essays in Social Theory,* 277–306. Cambridge: Cambridge University Press.

Gellner, Ernest. 1981. *Muslim Society.* Cambridge: Cambridge University Press.

Gellner, Ernest. 1974. *The Legitimation of Belief.* Cambridge: Cambridge University Press.

Gellner, Ernest. 1981. "The Unknown Apollo of Biskra: the Social Base of Algerian Puritanism." In *Muslim Society,* 149–173. Cambridge: Cambridge Univrsity Press.

Gellner, Ernest. 1985. *Leben im Islam: Religion als Gesellschaftsordnung.* Stuttgart: Klett.

Gellner, Ernest. 1987. "Warten auf den Imam." In *Max Webers Sicht des Islams. Interpretation und Kritik,* edited by W. Schluchter, 272–293. Frankfurt: Suhrkamp.

Gerber, Haim. 1994. *State, Society and Law in Islam. Ottoman Law in Comparative Perspective.* Albany: State University of New York.

Ghani, A. 1983. "Disputes in a Court of *Sharia,* Kunar Valley, Afghanistan, 1885–1890." *International Journal of Middle East Studies* 15: 353–67.

Gibb, H. A. R. 1962. "Structure of Religious Thought in Islam." In *Studies on the Civilization of Islam,* 176–218. Princeton, N.J.: Princeton University Press.

Gibb, H.A.R. 1963. *Studies in the Civilization of Islam.* Boston: Beacon Press.

Gilbert, Alan D. 1980. *The Making of Post-Christian Britain: A History of the Secularization of Modern Society.* London: Longman.

Goitein, S. D. 1966. *Studies in Islamic History and Institutions.* Leiden: E. J. Brill.

Goldziher, Ignaz. 1910. *Vorlesungen über den Islam.* Heidelberg: Winter.

Göle, Nilüfer. 1996. *The Forbidden Modern: Civilization and Veiling.* Ann Arbor: University of Michigan Press.

Goody, Jack. 1975. "Religion, Social Change, and the Sociology of Conversion." In *Changing Social Structure in Ghana,* edited by. J. Goody, 101–105. London: International African Institute.

Goody, J. 1983. *The Development of the Family and Marriage in Europe.* Cambridge: Cambridge University Press.

Grover, B. R. 1963. "The Nature of Land Right in Mughal India." *The Indian Economic and Social History Review* I, 1: 10–11.

Habermas, Jürgen. 1984/1987. *The Theory of Communicative Action,* 2 vols. translated by T. McCarthy. Boston: Beacon Press.

Habib, Irfan. 1963. *The Agrarian System of Mughal India (1556–1707).* London: Asia Publishing House.

Halim, A. 1953. "An Account of the Celebrities of Bengal of the Early Years of Shahjahan's Reign Given by Muhammad Sadiq." *Journal of the Pakistan Historical Society* vol: 338–56.

Hall, John A. 1985. *Powers and Liberties: The Causes and Consequences of the Rise of the West.* Berkeley: University of California Press.

Hallaq, Wael B. 1984. "Was the Gate of Ijtihad Closed?" *International Journal of Middle East Studies* 16: 3–41.

Halleq, Wael B. 1985/86. "The Logic of Legal Reasoning in Relgious and Non-Religious Cultures: The Case of Islmic Law and the Common Law." *Cleveland State Law Review* 34: 79–96.

Hannif, Ghulam. 1996. "The Challenge of Science and Technology to the Muslim World." In *VAST '96 Papers* 2: 284–302. Kuala Lumpur: International Islamic University Malaysia.

Haq, M. Anwarul. 1972. *The Faith Movement of Mawlana Muhammad Ilyas.* London: George Allen & Unwin.

Hardy, Peter. 1971. *Partners in Freedom—and True Muslims: the political thought of some Muslim scholars in British India 1912–1947.* Lund: Scandinavian Institute of Asian Studies.

Hardy, Peter. 1983. "Force and Violence in Indo-Persian Writing in History and Government in Medieval South Asia." *Islamic Society and Culture: Essays in honour of Professor Aziz Ahmad,* edited by Milton Israel and N.K. Wagle, 172–90. New Delhi: Manohar.

Hardy, Peter. 1985. "Abu'l Fazl's Portrait of the Perfect Padshah: A Political Philosophy for Mughal India—Or a Personal Puff for a Pal?" in *Islamic Indian Studies and Commentaries,* ed. Christian W. Troll, 114–137. New Delhi: Vikas.

Hart, H. L. A. 1961. *The Concept of Law.* Oxford: Clarendon Press.

Hasan, Mushirul. 1977. *Legacy of a Divided Nation: India's Muslims since Independence.* Delhi: Oxford University Press.

Hasan, S. Nurul. 1969. "Zamidars under the Mughals." In *Land Control and Social Structure in Indian History,* ed. R. E. Frykenberg, 17–31. Madison: University of Wisconsin Press.

Hefner, Robert W. 1987. "The Political Economy of Islamic Conversion in Modern East Java." In *Islam and the Political Economy of Meaning,* edited by William R. Roff, 53–78. London and Sydney: Croom Helm.

Hennis, Wilhelm. 1984. "Im 'langen Schatten' einer Edition. Zum ersten

Band der Max Weber-Gesamtausgabe." *Frankfurter Allgemeine Zeitung* 207:10.

Hennis, Wilhelm. 1987. *Max Webers Fragestellung. Studien zur Biographie des Werks.* Tübingen: J.C.B. Mohr (Paul Siebeck).

Henrich, Dieter. 1952. *Die Einheit der Wissenschaftslehre Max Webers.* Tübingen: J.C.B. Mohr (Paul Siebeck).

Hinneberg, Paul, ed. 1906. *Die Kultur der Gegenwart. Ihre Entwicklung und ihre Ziele.* Berlin: Teubner.

Hodgson, M. G. S. 1974. *The Venture of Islam*, 3 vols. Chicago: University of Chicago Press.

Hoffman, Valerie. 1995. "Muslim Fundamentalists: Psychosocial Profiles." In *Fundamentalisms Comprehended*, edited by Martin E. Marty and R. Scott Appleby, 199–230. Chicago: University of Chicago Press.

Hooker, M. B. 1978. *A Concise Legal History of South-East Asia.* Oxford: Clarendon Press.

Hopwood, Derek. 1971. "A Pattern of Revival Movements in Islam." *Islamic Quarterly* 15: 149–158.

Horowitz, Donald. 1994. "The Qur'an and The Common Law: Islamic Law Reform and the Theory of Legal Change." *The American Journal of Comparative Law* 42, 2–3: 233–293 and 545–580.

Hosten, H. 1925. "Jesuit Letters from Bengal, Arakan and Burma (1599–1600)." *Bengal Past and Present*, 30: 52–78.

Huff, Toby E. 1993. *The Rise of Early Modern Science: Islam, China, and the West,* New York: Cambridge University Press.

Huff, Toby E. 1997. "Science and the Public Sphere: Comparative Institutional Development in Islam and the West." *Social Epistemology* 11: 25–37.

Huntington, Samuel. 1993. "The Clash of Civilizations." *Foreign Affairs* 72 (3): 22–49.

Hurgronje, Christian Snouck. 1888. *Mekka*, vol. 1: *Die Stadt und ihre Herren.* The Hague: Nijhoff.

Ibn Battuta, 1953. *The Rehla of Ibn Battuta*, translated by Mahdi Husain. Baroda: Oriental Institute.

Ibn Taymiyya. 1966/1375. "Al-Risala al-Wasitiyya." In *Madjmuat al-Rasa'il al-Kubra* by Ibn Taymiyya. al-Qahira: Maktabat Subayh, 1: 404–405.

International Islamic University Malaysia. 1996. *VAST '96 Papers*, 2 vols. [Conference Proceedings on "Values and Attitudes in Science and Technology"]. Kuala Lumpur: International Islamic University Malaysia.

Ishtiaq Husain Qureshi. 1962. *The Muslim Community of the Indo-Pakistani Subcontinent* (610–1947). The Hague: Mouton & Co.

Itzkowitz, M. 1972. *Ottoman Empire and the Islamic Tradition.* New York: Alfred A. Knopf.

Jansen, Johannes J. G. 1986. *The Neglected Duty: The Creed of Sadat's Assassins and Islamic Resurgence in the Middle East.* New York: Macmillan.

Jones, Kenneth W. 1989. *Socio-Religious Reform Movements in British India*. New York: Cambridge University Press.
Kantowsky, Detlef. "Max Weber on India and Indian Interpretations of Weber." A paper presented to the Seventh European Conference on Modern South Asian Studies, SOAS, London, July 7–11, 1981.
Karan, Mohendra Nath. 1958. *Hijli Masnad-i 'Ala*, second edition. Calcutta: Medinipur Sanskriti Parishad.
Karim, A. K. Nazmul. 1956. *Changing Society in India and Pakistan: A Study in Social Change and Social Stratification*. Dacca: Oxford University Press.
Kennedy, E. S. 1966. "Late Medieval Planetary Theory." *Isis* 57: 365–78.
Kennedy, E. S. and Victor Roberts. 1959. "The Planetary Theory of Ibn al-Shatir." *Isis* 50: 227–235.
Khadduri, Majid and H. Liebesny, eds., 1955. *Law in the Middle East*. Washington, D.C.: The Middle East Institute.
Khadduri, Majid, trans. 1961. *Islamic Jurisprudence. Shafi'i's Risala*. Baltimore: The Johns Hopkins University Press.
Khaldun, Ibn. 1968. *The Muqaddima*, translated by Franz Rosethal. Princeton, N.J.: Princeton University Press.
Khan, Abdul Majid. 1964. "Research about Muslim Aristocracy in East Pakistan." In *Social Research in East Pakistan*, edited by Pierre Bessaignet, 21–37. Dacca: Asiatic Society of Pakistan.
Khan, Ahsan Raza. 1977. *Chieftains in the Mughal Empire during the Reign of Akbar*. Simla: Institute of Advanced Study.
Khan, Hamid al-din. 1926. *Ahkam-i 'Alamgiri*, second ed. Calcutta M.C. Sarkar & Sons.
Kocka, Jürgen. 1986. *Max Weber der Historiker*. Göttingen: Vandenhoeck & Ruprecht.
Kohler, Joseph. 1905. "Zum Islamrecht." *Zeitschrift für vergleichende Rechtswissenschaft* 17:194–216.
Kolam, Tufan, 1992. "Scientific Manpower and Economic Development." In *Science and Technology Manpower for Development in the Islamic World*, edited by F. A Daghastani, 69–85. Amman, Jordan: Islamic Academy of Science.
Kronman, Anthony T. 1983. *Max Weber* (Jurists: Profiles in Legal Theory). London: Edward Arnold.
Kuenzlen, Gottfried. 1978. "Unbekannte Quellen der Religionsoziologie Max Webers." *Zeitschrift für Soziologie* 7: 215–27.
Lahaur, Muhammad Salih Kanbo. 1923. *'Amil-i Salih*, vol. I. Calcutta: Bibliotheca Indica.
Lahauri, 'Abd al-Hamid. 1867. *Badshah Nama*. Calcutta: Bibliotheca Indica.
Landau, Jacob M. 1974. *Radical Politics in Modern Turkey*. Leiden: E.J. Brill.
Landau-Tasseron, E. 1989. "The 'Cyclical Reform': A Study of the Mujaddid Tradition." *Studia Islamica* 70: 79–118.

Laoust, H. 1965. *Les Schisms dans l'Islam*. Paris: Payot.
Lapidus, I. M. 1967. *Muslim Cities in the Later Middle Ages*. Second edition. Cambridge: Harvard University Press.
Lapidus, I. M. 1969. "Muslim Cities and Islamic Societies." In *Middle Eastern Cities*, edited by I. M. Lapidus, 47–79. Berkeley: University of California Press.
Lapidus, I. M. 1973. "Ayyubid Religious Policy and the Development of the Schools of Law in Cairo." In *Colloque International sur l'Histoire du Caire*, 279–286. Cairo: Ministry of Culture.
Lapidus, I. M. 1975. "The Separation of State and Religion in the Development of Early Islamic Society." *International Journal of Middle East Studies* 6: 363–385.
Lapidus, I. M. 1982. "The Arab Conquests and the Formation of Islamic Society." In *Studies on the First Century of Islamic Society*, edited by G. H. A. Juynboll, 49–72. Carbondale: Southern Illinois University Press.
Lapidus, I. M. 1983."The Evolution of Muslim Urban Society." *Comparative Studies in Society and History* 5: 21–50.
Lapidus, I. M. 1988. *A History of Muslim Societies*. New York: Cambridge University Press.
Lapidus, I. M. 1992. "Islamisches Sektierertum und das Rekonstruktions-und Umgestaltungspotential der islamischen Kultur." In *Kulturen der Achsenzeit* II, Teil 3, ed. S. N. Eisenstadt, 161–188. Frankfurt am Main, Suhrkamp-Taschenbuch.
Lapidus, I. M. 1996. "State and Religion in Islamic Societies." *Past and Present* 151: 3–27.
Lazarus-Yafeh, H. 1980. "Review of P. Crone and M. Cook, *Hagarism*." *Asian and African Studies* 14: 295–98.
Lazarus-Yafeh, H. 1986. "'Tajdid al-Din': A Reconsideration of Its Meaning, Roots and Influence in Islam." *The New East* 31: 1–10.
Lehmann, Hartmut and Gunther Roth, eds. 1994. *Weber's "Protestant Ethic": Origins, Evidence, Contexts*. New York: Cambridge University Press.
Lelyveld, David S. 1978. *Aligarh's First Generation: Muslim Solidarity in British India*. Princeton, N. J.: Princeton University Press.
Lenhart, Volker. 1986. "Allgemeine und fachliche Bildung bei Max Weber." *Zeitschrift für Pädagogik* 32: 529–41.
Lev, Daniel S. 1972. *Islamic Courts in Indonesia: A Study in the Political Bases of Legal Institutions*. Berkeley: University of California Press.
Levi, Edward H. 1949. *An Introduction to Legal Reasoning*. Chicago: University of Chicago Press.
Levtzion, Nehemia, ed. 1979. *Conversion to Islam*. New York: Holmes and Meier.
Levtzion, N. 1979. "Patterns of Islamization in West Africa." In *Conversion to Islam*, edited by N. Levtzion, 207–216. New York: Holmes and Meier.

Levtzion, N. 1986. "Eighteenth Century Renewal and Reform Movements in Islam." *The New East* 31:48–70.
Levtzion, N. and Gideon Weigert. 1995. "Religious Reform in Eighteenth-Century Morocco." *Jerusalem Studies in Arabic and Islam* 19: 173-197.
Levtzion, N. and J. O. Voll, eds. 1987. *Eighteenth Century Renewal and Reform in Islam.* Syracuse, N.Y.: Syracuse University Press.
Lewis, Bernard. 1973a. *Islam in History.* London: Alcove Press.
Lewis, Bernard. 1973b. "Islamic Concepts of of Revolution." In B. Lewis, *Islam in History*, 237–52.
Lewis, Bernard. 1991. *The Politial Language of Islam.* Chicago: University of Chicago Press.
Lewis, Philip. 1994. *Islamic Britain: Religion, Politics and Identity among British Muslims* London: I. B. Tauris.
Liebesny, Herbert. 1955. "The Development of Western Legal Privileges." In *Law in the Middle East*, edited by M. Khadduri and H. Liebesny, 309–333.
Liebesny, Herbert. 1985–86. "English Common Law and the Islamic Law in the Middle East and South Asia: Religious Influences and Secularization." *Cleveland State Law Review* 34: 19–33.
Lingat, R. 1967. *Les sources du droit dans le systeme traditionnel de l'Inde.* Paris: Mouton & Co; English translation: Berkeley: University of California Press, 1973.
Losty, Jeremiah P. 1982. *The Art of the Book in India.* London: British Library.
Löwith, Karl. 1960. "Max Weber und Karl Marx." In Löwith, *Gesammelte Abhandlungen. Zur Kritik der geschichtlichen Existenz.* Stuttgart: Klett, 1–67.
Ma Huan, 1970. *Ying-ya Sheng-lan: The Overall Survey of the Ocean's Shores*, translated by J. V. G. Mills. Cambridge: Cambridge University Press.
Macdowell, D. M. 1978. *The Law of Classical Athens.* London: Thames and Hudson.
Mahmood, Tahir. 1977. *Muslim Personal Law: Role of the State in the Subcontinent.* New Delhi: Vikas.
Maity, P. K. 1966. *Historical Studies in the Cult of the Goddess Manasa.* Calcutta: Punthi Pustak.
Majumdar, R. C. ed. 1960. *The Delhi Sultanate.* Bombay: Bharaty Vidya Bhavan.
Majumdar, S. C. 1942. *Rivers of the Bengal Delta.* Calcutta: University of Calcutta.
Makdisi, G. 1981. *The Rise of the College in Islam and the West.* Edinburgh: Edinburgh University Press.
Malik, Hafeez. 1963. *Moslem Nationalism in India and Pakistan.* Washington, D.C.: Public Affairs Press.
Mardin, Serif. 1989. *Religion and Social Change in Modern Turkey: The Case of Bediuzzaman Said Nursi.* Albany: State University of New York Press.

Marshall, Gordon. 1982. *In Search of the Spirit of Capitalism: An Essay on Max Weber's Protestant Ethic Thesis*. New York: Columbia University Press.

Martin, David. 1965. "Towards eliminating the concept of secularization." In *The Penguin Survey of the Social Sciences*, edited by Julius Gould, 169–82. Harmondsworth: Penguin Books.

Marty, Martin E. and R. Scott Appleby, eds. 1993a. *Fundamentalisms and the State*. Chicago: University of Chicago Press.

Marty, Martin E. and R. Scott Appleby, eds. 1993b. *Fundamentalisms and Society*. Chicago: University of Chicago Press.

Marty, Martin E. and R. Scott Appleby, eds. 1994. *Accounting for Fundamentalisms: The Dynamic Character of Movements*. Sponsored by the American Academy of Arts and Sciences. Chicago: University of Chicago Press.

Marty, Martin E. and R. Scott Appleby, eds. 1995. *Fundamentalisms Comprehended*. Chicago: University of Chicago Press.

Marx, Karl. 1971. *Werke–Schriften–Briefe*. 6 vols. H. J. Lieber, ed. Darmstadt: Wissenschaftliche Buchgesellschaft.

Maung, M. 1963. *Law and Custom in Burma and the Burmese Family*. The Hague: Martinus Nijhoff.

Mayer, Ann E. 1993. "The Fundamentalist Impact on Law, Politics, and Constitutions in Iran, Pakistan, and the Sudan." In *Fundamentalisms and the State*, edited by Martin E. Marty and R. Scott Appleby, 110–151. Chicago: University of Chicago Press.

McAleavy, H. 1968. "Chinese Law." In *An Introduction to Legal Systems*, edited by J. D. M. Derrett, 105–130. London: Sweet and Maxwell.

McCarthy, Richard J. ed. and trans. 1953. *The Theology of Ash'ari*. Beirut: Imprimerie Catholique.

McVey, Ruth T. 1982. "Islam Explained: A Review Article." In *Pacific Affairs*: 279.

Menage, V. L. 1979. "The Islamization of Anatolia." in *Conversion to Islam*, edited by N. Levtzion, 52–67.

Mernissi, Fatima. 1987. *Beyond the Veil*. Revised edition. Reading, Mass.: Addison Wesley Press.

Mernissi, Fatima. 1991. *The Veil and the Male Elite. A Feminist Interpretation of Women's Rights in Islam*. Reading, Mass.: Addison Wesley Press.

Merryman, John Henry. 1985. *The Civil Law Tradition. An Introduction to the Legal Systems of Western Europe and Latin America*. Stanford, Cal.: Stanford University Press.

Metcalf, Barbara D. 1982. *Islamic Revival in British India: Deoband, 1860–1900*. Princeton, N. J.: Princeton University Press.

Metcalf, Barbara D. ed. 1984. *Moral Conduct and Authority: The Place of Adab in South Asian Islam*. Berkeley: California University Press.

Metcalf, Barbara D. 1991. *Perfecting Women: Maulana Ashraf 'Ali Thanawi's Bihishti Zewar*. Berkeley: University of California Press.

Michaud-Quantin, Pierre. 1970. *Universitas: Expressions du movement communautaire dans le moyen-Age Latin*. Paris: J. Vrin.
Milliot, L. 1953. *Introduction a l'étude du droit musulman*. Paris: Sirey.
Mills, C. Wright. 1951. *White Collar*. New York: Oxford University Press.
Mitchell, Richard P. 1993. The *Society of the Muslim Brothers*. New York: Oxford University Press.
Mitteis, Heinrich. 1976. "Über den Rechtsgrund des Satzes 'Stadtluft macht frei'." In *Die Stadt des Mittelalters*, edited by C. Haase, ed., vol. 2:182–202. Darmstadt: Wissenschaftliche Buchgesellschaft:
Mommsen, Wolfgang J. 1989. "The Antinomical Structure of Max Weber's Political Thought." In *The Political and the Social Theory of Max Weber*, 24–43. Chicago: University of Chicago Press.
Mommsen, Wolfgang J. 1985. "Max Weber. Persönliche Lebensführung und gesellschaftliche Wandel. Versuch einer Rekonstruktion des Begriffs der Geschichte bei Max Weber." In *Geschichte und politisches Handeln. Theodor Schieder zum Gedächtnis*, edited by P. Alter, W. J. Mommsen, and T. Nipperdey, 261–81. Stuttgart: Klett.
Moosvi, Shireen. 1987. *The Economy of the Mughal Empire, c. 1595; A Statistical Study*. Delhi: Oxford University Press.
Morony, Michael. 1990. "The Age of Conversion: A Reassessment." In *Conversion and Continuity: Indigenous Christian Communities in Islam Lands Eight to Eighteen Centuries*, edited by Michael Gervers and Ramzi Jibran Bikhazi, 135–150. Toronto Pontifical Institute of Medieval Studies.
Mukerjee, R. K. 1938. *The Changing Face of Bengal: A Study of Riverine Economy*. Calcutta: University of Calcutta.
Mumtaz Ali Anwar and Ahmad Bakeri Abu Bakar. 1996. "Current State of Science and Technology in the Muslim World." *VAST '96 Papers* I: 304–327.
Munson, Henry, Jr., 1988. *Islam and the Revolution in the Middle East*. New Haven: Yale University Press.
Muslim, b. Hajji al-Qushayri. 1946. *Sahih. Al-Qahira: Maktabat Subayh*, n.d., vol. VIII, 46–47. English translation in W. Montgomery Watt, *Free Will and Predestination in Early Islam. Moslem World* 36: 131-132.
Musud, Muhammad Khahid, Brinkley Messick, and David S. Powers. eds. 1996. *Islamic Legal Interpretation. Mutifs and Their Fatwas*. Cambridge: Harvard University Press.
Nadwi, S.A.H.A. 1993. *Life and Mission of Maulana Muhammad Ilyas*. Lucknow: Academy of Islamic Research and Publications, Nadwat-ul Ulama.
Nakamura, Mitsuo. 1983. *The Crescent Arises over the Banyan Tree: A Study of the Muhammadivah Movement in a Central Javanese Town*. Yogyakarta: Gadjah Mada University.
Nasr, Seyyed Vali Reza. 1994. *The Vanguard of the Islamic Revolution: The*

Jama'at-i Islami of Pakistan (Comparative Studies on Muslim Societies, 19). Berkeley: University of California Press.

Noda, Y. 1976. *Introduction au droit japonais*. Paris: Librarie Dalloz; English tr. Tokyo: Tokyo University Press.

North, Douglass C. 1990. *Institutions, Institutional Change and Economic Performance*. New York: Cambridge University Press.

O'Malley, L. S. S. 1908. *Bengal District Gazetteers: Khulna*. Calcutta: Bengal Secretariat Book Depot.

O'Malley, L. S. S. 1908. *Eastern Bengal District Gazetteers: Chittagong*. Calcutta: Bengal Secretariat Book Depot.

Odegard, Peter H. 1928. *The Story of the Anti-Saloon League*. New York: Columbia University Press.

Palmer, H. R. 1928. *Sudanese Memoirs*. Lagos: Government Publishing House.

Peacock, James. 1978. *Muslim Puritans: Reformist Psychology in Southeast Asian Islam*. Berkeley: University of California Press.

Peel, J. D. Y. 1967–68. "Syncretism and Social Change." *Comparative Studies in Society and History* 10: 124–25.

Perikhanian, A. 1983. "Iranian Society and Law." In *Cambridge History of Iran*, edited by E. Yarshater, vol. iii (2): 627–80. Cambridge: Cambridge University Press.

Peters, Rudolph. 1980. "Idjtihad and Taqlid in 18th and 19th Century Islam." *Die Welt des Islams* 20: 132–145.

Peters, Rudolph. 1984. "Erneuerungsbewegungen im 18.und in der ersten Halfte des 19 Jahrhunderts." In *Der Islam in der Gegenwart,* edited by Werner Ende und Udo Steinbach, 91–l05. Munchen: C.H. Beck.

Peters, Rudolph. 1996. *Jihad in Classical and Modern Islam: A Reader*. Princeton, N. J.: Markus Wiener Publishers.

Pipes, Daniel. 1981. *Slave Soldiers and Islam: The Genesis of a Military System*. New Haven, Conn.: Yale University Press.

Pires, Tome. 1944. *The Suma Oriental of Tome Pires*, translated by A. Cortesao. London: Hakluyt Society.

Piscatori, James. 1994. "Accounting for Islamic Fundamentalisms." In *Accounting for Fundamentalisms*, edited by Martin E. Marty and R. Scott Appleby, 361–373. Chicago: University of Chicago Press.

Poggi, Gianfranco. 1988. "Max Webers Begriff des okzidentalen Feudalismus." In *Max Webers Sicht des okzidentalen Christentums*, edited by W. Schluchter, 476–97. Frankfurt: Suhrkamp.

Post, Gaines, 1964. *Studies in Medieval Legal Thought: Public Law and the State, 1150–1322*. Princeton, N.J.: Princeton University Press.

Purchas, Samuel. 1905. *Hakluytus Posthumus, or Purchas his Pilgrimes*, 20 vols. Glasgow: James MacLehose & Sons.

Rahman, Fazlur. 1968. *Islam*. Chicago: University of Chicago Press, revised edition.

Rahman, Fazlur. 1982. *Islam and Modernity: Transformation of an Intellectual Tradition* Chicago: University of Chicago Press.
Ray, Nihirranjan. 1945. "Medieval Bengali Culture." *Visva-Bharati Quarterly* 11, 1 (August-October): 47–52.
Richards, J. F. 1978. "The Formation of Imperial Authority under Akbar and Jahangir." In *Kingship and Authority in South Asia*, edited by J. F. Richards, 252–288. South Asian Studies, University of Wisconsin-Madison Publication Series-Publication, no 3.
Richards, J. F. 1984. "Norms of comportment among Imperial Mughal Officers." In *Moral Conduct and Authority: The Place of Adab in South Asian Islam*, edited by Barbara Daly Metcalf, 238–260. Berkeley, California University Press.
Richards, J. F. 1993. *The New Cambridge History of India (The Mughal Empire)*. Cambridge: Cambridge University Press.
Rickert, Heinrich. 1902. *Die Grenzen der naturwissenschaftlichen Begriffsbildung. Eine logische Einleitung in die historischen Wissenschaften*. Tübingen: J. C. B. Mohr (Paul Siebeck).
Rickert, Heinrich. 1907. "Geschichtsphilosophie." In *Die Philosophie im Beginn des 20. Jahrhunderts. Festschrift für Kuno Fischer*, edited by W. Windelband, second edition, 321–422. Heidelberg: C. Winter
Rickert, Heinrich. 1986. *The Limits of Concept Formation in Natural Science*, translated and edited with an introduction by Guy Oakes. New York: Cambridge University Press (An abridged version of Rickert 1902).
Risley Collection: "Reports on the Religious and Social Divisions amongst the Mahomedans of Bengal." India Office Library (European MSS. E 295) 9.
Ritzer, George. 1996. *The McDonaldization of Society*. Revised edition. Thousand Oaks, Cal.: Pine Forge Press.
Robinson, Francis. 1979. "Islam and Muslim Separatism." In *Political Identity in South Asia*, edited by David Taylor and Malcolm Yapp, 78–112. London: Curzon Press.
Robinson, Francis. 1982. *Atlas of the Islamic World since 1500*. Oxford: Phaidon.
Robinson, Francis. 1983. "Islam and Muslim society in South Asia." *Contributions to Indian Sociology* (n.s.) 17, 2: 185–203.
Robinson, Francis. 1996. "Islam and the Impact of Print in South Asia." In *The Transmission of Knowledge in South Asia: Essays on Education, Religion, History and Politics*, edited by Nigel Crook, 62–97. Delhi: Oxford University Press.
Robinson, Francis. 1997. "Religious Change, the Self and Community in Muslim South Asia since 1800." *South Asia* 20, 1:1–15.
Rodinson, Maxime. 1971. *Mohammed*. London: Allen Lane.
Rodinson, Maxime. 1978. *Islam and Capitalism,* translated by Brian Peace. Austin: University of Texas Press.
Rodinson, Maxime. 1986. *Islam und Kapitalismus*. Frankfurt: Suhrkamp.

Rodinson, Maxime. 1987. "Islamischer Patrimonialismus: Ein Hindernis für die Entstehung des modernen Kapitalismus?" In *Max Webers Sicht des Islams. Interpretation und Kritik* edited by W. Schluchter, 180–89.

Roff, William R. 1987. "Islamic Movements: One or Many?" In *Islam and the Political Economy of Meaning*, edited by William R. Roff, 31–52. London: Croom Helm.

Rosenthal, F. 1958. *The Muqaddima of Ibn Khaldun*. Princeton, N.J.: Princeton University Press.

Roth, Guenther. 1979. "Religion and Revolutionary Beliefs." In *Max Weber's Vision of History: Ethics and Methods,* edited by Guenther Roth and Wolfgang Schluchter, 144–165. Berkeley: University of California Press.

Roth, Guenther. 1987. "Rationalization in Max Weber's Developmental History." In *Max Weber, Rationality, and Modernity*, edited by S. Whimster and S. Lash, 75–91. London: Allen and Unwin,

Roy, Asim. 1983. *The Islamic Syncretistic Tradition in Bengal*. Princeton, N.J.: Princeton University Press.

Roy, Oliver. 1994. *The Failure of Political Islam*. Cambridge, Mass.: Harvard University Press.

Sabra, A. I. 1987. "The Appropriation and Subsequent Naturalization of Greek Science in Medieval Islam: A Preliminary Statement." *History of Science* 25: 223–243.

Sabra, A. I. 1994. "Science and Philosophy in Medieval Theology: The Evidence of the Fourteenth Century." *Zeitschrift für Geschichte der Arabisch-Islamishen Wissenschaften* 9: 1–42.

Said, Edward. 1978. *Orientalism*. New York: Pantheon.

Saliba, George. 1994. "Arabic Astronomy and Copernicus." *Zeitschrift fur Geschichte der Arabish-Islamischen Wissenschaften* Band 1: 73–87; reprinted in *A History of Arabic Astronomy: Planetary Theory During the Golden Age of Islam*. New York: New York University Press, chapter 15.

Sanyal, Usha. 1996. *Devotional Islam and Politics in British India: Ahmad Riza Khan Barelwi and his Movement, 1870–1920*. New York: Oxford University Press.

Sarkar, Jadunath, ed. 1977. *History of Benga: Muslim Period, 1200–1757*. Patna: Janaki Prakashan.

Sarkar, Jadunath. 1919. "The Revenue Regulations of Aurangzib." *Studies in Mughal India,* 168–97. Calcutta: M. C. Sartar and Sons.

Schacht, Joseph. 1926. "Die arabische ḥiyal-Literatur." *Der Islam* 15: 211–32.

Schacht, Joseph. 1935. "Zur soziologischen Betrachtung des islamischen Rechts." *Der Islam* 22: 207–38.

Schacht, Joseph. 1964. *An Introduction to Islamic Law*. Oxford: Clarendon Press.

Schacht, Joseph. 1974. "Islamic Religious Law." In *The Legacy of Islam*, second edition, edited by J. Schacht and C. E. Bosworth, 392–403. New York: Oxford University Press.

Scheltema, H. J. 1967. "Byzantine Law." In *Cambridge Medieval History,* iv (2), edited by. J. M. Hussey, 55–77. Cambridge: Cambridge University Press.

Schiele, Friedrich Michael and Leopold Zscharnack, eds. 1909–13. *Die Religionen in Geschichte und Gegenwart. Handwörterbuch in geminverständlicher Darstellung.* 5 vols. Tübingen: J.C.B. Mohr (Paul Siebeck).

Schimmel, Annemarie. 1969. "Islam in Turkey." In *Religion in the Middle East,* II, edited by A. J. Arberry, 68–95. Cambridge: Cambridge University Press.

Schluchter, Wolfgang, ed. 1985. *Max Webers Sicht des antiken Christentums. Interpretation und Kritik.* Frankfurt: Suhrkamp.

Schluchter, Wolfgang, ed. 1987. *Max Webers Sicht des Islams. Interpretation und Kritik.* Frankfurt: Suhrkamp.

Schluchter, Wolfgang. 1979. *Die Entwicklung des okzidentalen Rationalismus. Eine Analyse von Max Webers Gesellschaftsgeschichte.* Tübingen: J.C.B. Mohr (Paul Siebeck).

Schluchter, Wolfgang. 1980. *Rationalismus der Weltbeherrschung.* Frankfurt: Suhrkamp.

Schluchter, Wolfgang. 1981. *The Rise of Western Rationalism,* translated by G. Roth. Berkeley: University of California Press.

Schluchter, Wolfgang. 1983. *Max Webers Studie über Konfuzianismus und Taoismus. Interpretation und Kritik.* Frankfurt: Suhrkamp.

Schluchter, Wolfgang. 1983. "The Future of Religion." In *Religion and America,* edited by Mary Douglas and Steven M. Tipton, 64–78. Boston: Beacon Press.

Schluchter, Wolfgang, ed. 1988a. *Max Webers Sicht des okzidentalen Christentums.* Frankfurt: Suhrkamp.

Schluchter, Wolfgang. 1988b. *Religion und Lebensführung. Studien zu Max Webers Religions- und Herrschaftssoziologie,* 2 vols. Frankfurt: Suhrkamp.

Schluchter, Wolfgang. 1989. *Rationalism, Religion, and Domination,* translated by N. Solomon. Berkeley: University of California Press.

Schluchter, Wolfgang. 1996. *Paradoxes of Modernity: Culture and Conduct in the Theory of Max Weber,* translated by N. Solomon. Stanford, Cal.: Stanford University Press.

Schmid, Michael. 1981. "Struktur und Selektion: Emile Durkheim und Max Weber als Theoretiker struktureller Evolution." *Zeitschrift für Soziologie* 10: 17–37.

Schöllgen, Gregor. 1985. *Handlungsfreiheit und Zweckrationalität. Max Weber und die Tradition der praktischen Philosophie.* Tübingen: J.C.B. Mohr (Paul Siebeck).

Schreiner, Klaus. 1986. "Die mittelalterliche Stadt in Webers Analyse und die Deutung des okzidentalen Rationalismus." In *Max Weber der Historiker,* edited by J. Kocka, 119–50. Göttingen: Vandenhoeck & Ruprecht.

Sen, D. C. 1954. *History of Bengali Language and Literature,* 2nd ed. Calcutta: University of Calcutta.

Sen, D. C., trans. and ed. 1923–28. *Eastern Bengal Ballads: Mymensing*, 4 vols. Calcutta: University of Calcutta.

Sen, Sukumar. 1960. *History of Bengali Literature*. New Delhi: Sahitya Akademi.

Shahid, I. 1970. "Pre-Islamic Arabia." In *Cambridge History of Islam*, I, edited by P. M. Holt, A. K. S. Lambton, and B. Lewis, 3–29. Cambridge: Cambridge University Press.

Sharon, M. 1983. *Black Banners from the East*. Jerusalem: Magnes Press.

Siddiqi, Norman Abmad. 1970. *Land Revenue Administration under the Mughals (1700–1750)*. London: Asia Publishing House.

Sivan, E. 1994. "In God's Cause." In *The Limits of Pluralism. Neo-Absolutism and Relativism* (The Erasmus Ascention Symposium), 9–27. Amsterdam: Praemium Erasmianum Foundation.

Sivin, Nathan. 1983. "Chinesische Wissenschaft. Ein Vergleich der Ansätze von Max Weber und Joseph Needham." In *Max Webers Studie über Konfuzianismus und Taoismus. Interpretation und Kritik*, edited by W. Schluchter, 342–62. Frankfurt: Suhrkamp.

Stein, P. 1966. *Regulae Iuris: From Juristic Rules to Legal Maxims*. Edinburgh: University Press.

Stern, S. M. 1970. "The Constitution of the Islamic City." In *The Islamic City*, edited by A. Hourani, 25–50. Philadelphia: University of Pennsylvania Press.

Sultan, Saiyid. 1978 *Nabi-Bamsa*, edited by Ahmed Sharif. Dhaka: Bangla Academy.

Tarafdar, M. R. 1965. *Husain Shahi Bengal, 1494–1583 A.D: A Socio–Political Study*. Dacca: Asiatic Society of Pakistan.

Tenbruck, Friedrich H. 1977. "Abschied von *Wirtschaft und Gesellschaft*." *Zeitschrift für die gesamte Staatswissenschaft* 133: 703–36.

Thompson, W. H. 1919. *Final Report on the Survey and Settlement Operations in the District of Noakhali, 1914–11*. Calcutta: Bengal Secretariat Book Depot.

Thorp, John P. "Masters of Earth: Conceptions of 'Power' among Muslims of Rural Bangladesh." Ph.D. dissertation, University of Chicago, 1978.

Tibi, Bassam. 1985. *Der Islam und das Problem der kulturellen Bewältigung des sozialen Wandels*. Frankfurt: Suhrkamp.

Tigar, M. E. and M. R. Levy. 1977. *Law and the Rise of Capitalism*. New York: Monthly Review Press.

Timur Kuran, "The Economic Impact of Islamic Fundamentalism." In *Fundamentalisms and the State*, edited Martin E. Marty and R. Scott Appleby, 302–341.

Trimingham, J. Spencer. 1971. *The Sufi Orders in Islam*. London: Oxford University Press.

Troeltsch, Ernst. 1960. *The Social Teachings of the Christian Churches*, 2 vols. New York: Harper Torch.

Trubek, David. 1972. "Max Weber on Law and the Rise of Capitalism." *Wisconsin Law Review* 3: 720–753.
Turner, Bryan S. 1974. *Weber and Islam: A Critical Study.* London: Routledge and Kegan Paul.
Tyan, Edward. 1974. "Djihad." *Encyclopaedia of Islam*, 2nd edition, ii: 238.
Udovitch, A. L 1970. *Partnership and Profit in Medieval Islam.* Princeton, N.J.: Princeton University Press.
Ulrich, F. 1912. *Die Vorherbestimmungslehre im Islam und Christentums. Eine religionsgeschichtliche Parallele.* Gütersloh: C. Bertelsmann.
Valerie J. Hoffman, 1996. "Muslim Fundamentalists: Psychosocial Profiles." In *Fundamentalisms Comprehended*, edited by Martin E. Marty and R. Scott Appleby, 179–198. Chicago: University of Chicago Press.
van der Veer, Peter and Hartmut Lehmann, eds. *Nation and Religion, Perspectives from Asia and Europe.* Princeton, N. J.: Princeton University, 1999.
Voll, John, 1979. "The Sudanese Mahdi, Frontier Fundamentalist." *International Journal of Middle East Studies*, 10 (1979): 145–166.
Voll, John. 1982. *Islam. Continuity and Change in the Modern World.* Boulder, Colo.: Westview Press.
Voll, John. 1991. "Fundamentalism in Sunni Arab World: Egypt and the Sudan." In *Fundamentalisms Observed*, edited by Martin E. Marty and R. Scott Appleby, 345–403. Chicago, University of Chicago Press.
Wagner, Gerhard and Heinz Zipprian. 1986. "The Problem of Reference in Max Weber's Theory of Causal Explanation." *Human Studies* 9: 21–42.
Watson, A. 1974. *Legal Transplants: An Approach to Comparative Law.* Edinburgh: Scottish Academic Press.
Watson, A. 1977. *Society and Legal Change.* Edinburgh: Scottish Academic Press.
Watson, A. 1981. *The Making of the Civil Law.* Cambridge Mass: Harvard University Press.
Watt, W. Montgomery. 1946. "Free Will and Predestination in Early Islam." *Moslem World* 36 (1946): 131–132.
Watt, W. Montgomery. 1948. *Free Will and Predestination in Early Islam.* London: Allen & Unwin (reprint of Watt 1946).
Watt, W. Montgomery. 1962. *Muhammad at Medina.* Oxford: Oxford University Press.
Watt, W. Montgomery. 1964. *Muhammad: Prophet and Statesman.* Oxford: Oxford University Press.
Watt, W. Montgomery. 1965. *Muhammad at Mecca.* Oxford: Oxford University Press.
Watt, W. Montgomery.1985. "Islamic Alternatives to the Concept of Free-Will." In *La Notion de liberté au Moyen Age: Islam, Byzance, Occident*, 15–24. Paris: Societé d'Edition.
Weber, Marianne. 1926. *Max Weber. Ein Lebensbild.* Tübingen: J.C.B. Mohr (Paul Siebeck).

Weber, Max. 1921. *Gesammelte Aufsatze zur Religionssoziologie*, Bdn, *Hinduismus und Buddhismus*. Tübingen J. C. B. Mohr (Paul Siebeck).
Weber, Max. 1921. *Gesammelte Aufsätze zur Religionssoziologie*, 3 vols. Tübingen: J. C. B. Mohr (Paul Siebeck) [1920–1921].
Weber, Max. 1923. *Wirtschaftsgeschichte. Abriß der universalen Sozial- und Wirtschaftsgeschichte*. S. Hellman and M. Palyi, eds., Munich: Duncker und Humblot.
Weber, Max. 1924a. *Gesammelte Aufsätze zur Sozial- und Wirtschaftsgeschichte*. Tübingen: J. C. B. Mohr (Paul Siebeck).
Weber, Max. 1924b. *Gesammelte Aufsätze zur Soziologie und Sozialpolitik*. Tübingen: J. C. B. Mohr (Paul Siebeck).
Weber, Max. 1949. "Die 'Objekjectivat' sozial wissenschaflicher und sozial politischer Erkenntnis." See Weber 1949.
Weber, Max. 1949. *The Methodology of the Social Sciences*, translated and edited by E. A. Shils and H. A. Finch. New York: The Free Press.
Weber,' Max. 1949. *The Methodology of the Social Sciences,* translated by Edward Shils and Henry Finch. New York: The Free Press.
Weber, Max. 1952. *Ancient Judaism*, translated and edited by . H. H. Gerth and D. Martindale. Glencoe, Ill.: The Free Press.
Weber, Max. 1958a [1946]. *From Max Weber*, translatedand edited with an introduction by H. H. Gerth and C. W. Mills. New York: Oxford University Press.
Weber, Max. 1958b. *The Protestant Ethic and the Spirit of Capitalism*, translated by T. Parsons. New York: Charles Scribner's Sons.
Weber, Max. 1958c. *The Religion of India,* translated and edited by H. H. Gerth and D. Martindale. New York: The Free Press.
Weber, Max. 1958d. *The Social and Rational Foundations of Music,* edited and translated by Don Martindale, Johannes Riedel and Gertrude Neuwirth. Carbondale: Southern Illinois University Press.
Weber, Max. 1961 [1927]. *General Economic History.* New York: Collier (a translation of Weber 1923).
Weber, Max. 1964. *Max Weber on Law in Economy and Society*, edited and translated by M. Rheinstein and E. Shils. Cambridge Mass.: Harvard University Press.
Weber, Max. 1964. *The Sociology of Religion*, translated by Ephraim Fischoff. Boston: Beacon Press.
Weber, Max. 1964. *The Theory of Social and Economic Organization*, translated by A. M. Henderson and Talcott Parsons. New York: The Free Press.
Weber, Max. 1967/1946. *The Religion of India: the Sociology of Hinduism and Buddhism*, translated and edited by Hans H. Gerth and Don Martindale. New York: The Free Press.
Weber, Max. 1968. *The Religion of China,* translated by H. H. Gerth. New York: The Free Press.

Weber, Max. 1972. *Wirtschaft und Gesellschaft*, edited by J. Winckelmann, 5th ed. Tübingen: J. C. B. Mohr.
Weber, Max. 1973 [1922]. *Gesammelte Aufsätze zur Wissenschaftslehre*, 4th ed. Tübingen: J. C. B. Mohr.
Weber, Max. 1976. *Agrarian Sociology of Ancient Civilizations,* translated by R. I. Frank. London: New Left Books.
Weber, Max. 1976. *The Agrarian Sociology of Ancient Civilizations*, translated by. R. I. Frank. London: New Left Books. Includes a translation of "Agrarverhältnisse im Altertum," first published in *Handwörterbuch der Staatswissenschaften*, 1909, and later reprinted in the *Gesammelte Aufsätze zur Sozial- und Wirtschaftsgeschichte* (see Weber 1924a above).
Weber, Max. 1976. *Wirtschaft und Gesellschaft: Grundriss der verstehenden Soziologie*, 5th revised edition, edited by von Johannes Winckelmann. Tübingen J. C. B. Mohr (Paul Siebeck).
Weber, Max. 1977. *Critique of Stammler*, translated with an introduction by G. Oakes. New York: The Free Press.
Weber, Max. 1978a. "Anticritical Last Word on *The Spirit of Capitalism*," translated by W. M. Davis. *American Journal of Sociology* 83: 1105–31.
Weber, Max. 1978b. *Economy and Society*, edited by G. Roth and C. Wittich. Berkeley: University of California Press.
Weber, Max. 1978c. *Max Weber: Selections in Translation*, edited W. G. Runciman and translated by E. Mathews. Cambridge: Cambridge University Press.
Weber, Max. 1978d. *Die protestantische Ethik II. Kritiken und Antikritiken*, edited by J. Winckelmann. Gütersloh: Siebenstern.
Weber, Max. 1984. *Zur Politik im Weltkrieg*. Series. 1 of vol. 15. *Max Weber-Gesamtausgabe*, edited by W. J. Mommsen in cooperation with G. Hübinger. Tübingen: J.C.B. Mohr.
Webster, J. E. 1911. *Eastern Bengal and Assam District Gazetteers: Noakhali*. Allahabad: Pioneer Press.
Wellhausen, Julius. 1902. *Das arabische Reich und sein Sturz*. Berlin: Reimer.
Wellhausen, Julius. 1927 [1897]. *Reste arabischen Heidentums, gesammelt und erläutert*. Second edition. Berlin: De Gruyter.
Westland, J. 1870. *A Report on the District of Jessore: Its Antiquities, its History, and its Commerce*. Second edition. Calcutta: Bengal Secretariat.
Winckelmann, Johannes. 1986. *Max Webers hinterlassenes Hauptwerk: Die Wirtschaft und die gesellschaftlichen Ordnungen und Mächte*. Tübingen: J. C. B. Mohr (Paul Siebeck).
Wink, Andre. 1986. *Land and Sovereignty in India: Agrarian Society and Politics under Eighteenth-century Maratha Svarajya*. Cambridge: Cambridge University.
Wolfson, Harry. 1976. *The Philosophy of Islam*. Cambridge, Mass.: Harvard University Press.

Wood, W. H. Arden. 1924. "Rivers and Man in the Indus-Ganges Alluvial Plain." *Scottish Geographical Magazine* 40, 1: 5–10.

Yegar, Moshe. 1979. *Islam and Islamic Institutions in British Malaya* Jerusalem: The Magnes Press, The Hebrew University.

Zbavitel, Dusan. 1963. *Bengali Folk-ballads from Mymensingh and the Problem of their Authenticity*. Calcutta: University of Calcutta.

Ziadeh, Farhat. 1968. *Lawyers: The Rule of Law and Liberalism in Modern Egypt*. Stanford, Cal.: Stanford University Press.

Ziegler, Norman P. 1978. "Some Notes on Rajput Loyalties during the Mughal Period." In *Kingship and Authority in South Asia*, edited by J. F. Richards, 235–51.

Zweigert, K. and H. Kötz. 1971. *Einführung in die Rechtsvergleichung auf dem Gebiete des Privatrecht*. Tübingen: J. C. B. Mohr.

Contributors

Michael Cook is the Cleveland E. Dodge Professor of Near Eastern Studies at Princeton University. He has published in the fields of Ottoman economic history, early and medieval Islamic religious and cultural history, and the early history of the Wahhabi movement.

Patricia Crone is a Faculty member of the School of Historical Studies, Institute for Advanced Study, Princeton. Born in Denmark, she obtained her PhD in London (1974), and taught in Oxford from 1977–90 and in Cambridge (1990–97). Her research focuses on the first five centuries of Islamic history. Her publications include *Meccan Trade and the Rise of Islam* (1987) and *Pre-Industrial Societies (1989)*.

Richard M. Eaton is Professor of History at the University of Arizona, specializing in the history of South Asia, history of Islamic civilization, comparative history, and world history. His publications include *Sufis of Bijapur* (Princeton, 1978) and *The Rise of Islam and The Bengal Frontier* (California, 1993).

Shmuel N. Eisenstadt is Rose Issac Professor Emeritus of Sociology at the Hebrew University of Jerusalem, where he has been a faculty member since 1946. He has served as Visiting Professor at numerous universities around the world and serves on many editorial boards of academic journals. He is the author and editor of numerous books and papers and the recipient of honorary doctoral degrees from such universities as the University of Helsinki, Harvard University and the Hebrew Union College.

Peter Hardy, now retired from Cambridge University, is a historian specializing in Mughal India. He is author of several books, including, *The Muslims of British India* and *Partners in Freedom and True Muslims. The Political Thought of Some Muslim Scholars in British India 1912–1947.*

Toby E. Huff is Chancellor Professor of Sociology at the University of Massachusetts Dartmouth. He is editor of *On the Roads to Modernity: Conscience, Science and Civilizations*: *Selected Writings by Benjamin Nelson* (1981); author of *Max Weber and the Methodology of the Social Sciences*, (1984); and *The Rise of Early Modern Science: Islam, China and the West* (1993).

Nehemia Levtzion is Professor of the History of the Muslim Peoples at the Hebrew University. Beyond his major studies on Islam in Africa, he has carried out comparative studies of such aspects of Islam as conversion, socio-political roles of the '*ulama*', renewal and reform movements in the eighteenth century, as well as the structure, organization and ritual of Sufi Brotherhoods. He served as the president of the Open University of Israel, and is currently the Chairman of the Planning and Budgeting Committee of the Council for Higher Education in Israel.

Barbara Daly Metcalf, a historian, is dean of the Division of Social Sciences at the University of California at Davis. She is the author of *Islamic Revival in British India: Deoband, 1860–1900* (1982), the editor of *Moral Conduct and Authority: The Place of Adab in South Asian Islam* (1984), the translator of *Perfecting Women: Maulana Ashraf 'Ali Thaanawi's Bihisti Zewar* (1990), and the author of *Making Muslim Space in North America and Europe* (1996).

Rudolph Peters teaches Islamic studies at the University of Amsterdam. From 1982 to 1987 he was the director of the Netherlands Institute of Archeology and Arabic Studies in Cairo. He is author of *Islam and Colonialism: The Doctrine of Jihad in Modern History* (The Hague, 1979), and editor of *Jihad in Classical and Modern Islam.* (Princeton, 1995). He publishes mainly on Islamic law and Islam and politics.

Francis Robinson is Professor of the History of South Asia in the University of London, Vice-Principal Royal Holloway College, and President of the Royal Asiatic Society of Great Britain and Ireland. Among his books are: *Separatism Among Indian Muslims, Atlas of the Islamic World since 1500*, and *The Cambridge illustrated History of the Islamic World.* His special research interests lie in Muslim learned and holy families, in particular the Firangi Mahal family of Lucknow (India), and religious change in Muslim South Asia since 1800.

Wolfgang Schluchter is Professor of Sociology at the University of Heidelberg and Dean of the Max Weber Center for Advanced Studies at the University of Erfurt. He is the author of several books on Max Weber, most recently, *Paradoxes of Modernity: Culture and Conduct in the Theory of Max Weber*. He is also the editor of six books on Weber's sociology of religion and co-editor of the historical-critical works on Weber.

Index

'Abbasid revolution
  Islamic universalism and, 154
  Muslim rule and, 155
  tax payments and, 154
Abbasid regime, imperial characteristics, 283
Administrative staff
  development of, 92
  patrimonialism and, 95
  terms for, 92–93
African troops, private armies as, 105
Akbar, 165–166, 190–192, 196
'Ali, Khan Jahan, 173
'Ali, Mihr, 169
Aligarh movement, 234, 237
AliThanawi, Maulana Ashraf, 218–219
Allah
  Bengal and, 174
  elite troops of, 92
  man's social relationships, 198
  Supreme God adoption as, 177–178
  universal God doctrine, 90
Anarchy
  defined, 105
  general conditions of, 105–106
  Mecca and, 105
Anglo-Muhammadan law, 234
Aquinas, Thomas, 39
Ash'ari theology school, 147
Ashraf, K. M., 237
Aurangzib (emperor)
  Deccan relocation, 192
  eulogized acts of, 190
  Islamism and, 191
  military conquest, 192
  military system, 193–194
  Muslin dignitaries, 193
  revenue demands, 192
Authority structure
  Islamic sects vs churches, 273–274
  Kharijites and, 277
  Shi'ites and, 277
  Sunni and, 277
Azad, Abul Kalam, 237
Al-Azmeh, Aziz, 284, 289

Barbosa, Duarte, 165
Barnett, Richard, 201
al Basra, Hasan, 144
Bayley, C. A., 167, 201
Becker, Carl Heinrich, 59, 86, 97–98
Bengal
  charisma routinization, 168–173
  European vs Muslim societies, 163
  Hindu pantheon, 174
  Islamic chronology, 164–165
  Islamic notions of, 163–164
  Islam's rise in, 8
  Mughal empire in, 165–168
  Muslim political power, 223
  Muslim population growth, 164–165
  Supreme God and, 173–178
  vs Middle Eastern Islamism, 164
Berger, Peter, 233
Berman, Harold, 14, 35, 38
Bhutto, Zulfigar Ali, 237
Bi'da (heretical innovation), 208, 209, 210
Blake, Stephen P., 186

Caliphs
  charismatic leaders as, 142
  evolution of, 142
  ideal of, 288
  imperial institutions and, 142
  Mohammed succession, 142
  power returning to, 148
  vs sultans, 286
Calvin, John, 226
Calvinism
  afterlife, 30–31
  divine election, 226

election doctrine, 29, 71, 211, 226
ethics and, 73
God and, 73–77, 211
grace and, 71
man's judgement, 211–212
organization of, 115–116
personal conduct, 73
psychological effects, 73
predestination, 226
predestination vs free will, 212
proving one's self, 72–73
Puritanism vs Islam, 206–207
rational salvation, 213
religious ideas, 114
ruling nature of, 81
sexual appetites and, 214
Sunni fundamentalism and, 207
system of life, 29
vs fundamentalism, 211, 215
vs Islamism, 18, 30, 225–227
vs other religions, 114–116
Capitalism
European steps into, 33–35
evolutionary model for, 16
factors in, 9–10
Islamic law and, 254–258
Islamic reforms, 15–16
progressive development of, 10
vs objectification, 112
See also Law and capitalism; Occidental capitalism
Centralization, authority in, 92
Chadwick, Owen, 232
Christian laws, vs sacred laws, 107
Christian religions
Crusades of, 91
interest structuring, 114–115
organization of, 115–116
religious ideas, 114
Church. *See* corporations
Church-sect typology, problems of, 20–22
Clerics, vs warriors, 158–159
Clifford, James, 227
College, Islamic. See Madrasas
Constantinople, conquest of, 6
Contract, freedom of, 14
Cook, Michael, 21–22
Copernicus, 27
Corporation
church and, 35

Islamic law and, 34–35
laws enacting for, 36
powers of, 36
Cromwell, Oliver, 22
Crone, Patricia, 6, 33, 84, 86, 283
law and capitalism, 13–18
rationalism, 10–12, 14
Cults
Gods worshipped by, 174, 177
Hindu pantheon origins of, 177
vs Islamism, 177

Decentralization, authority in, 92
Deobandi movement
characteristics of, 218
Islamic reform and, 19, 217–218
puritan themes in, 19–20
scripturalist movement, 19
Deity (female)
cult allegiance to, 176
manifestations of, 174, 176
Dobbin, Christine, 223

Eaton, Richard, 8
Eisenstadt, S. N., 5, 23
Election doctrine
Calvinism and, 29, 71, 211, 226
capitalism spirit in, 226
egalitarianism, 209
fundamentalism and, 205
fundamentalism vs mysticism in, 208–209
God and, 211
grace and, 71
innerworldly asceticism, 213
Islam vs Puritanism in, 44, 206–207
Islamism establishing, 209–210
predestination doctrine, 206, 212–213
rationalism, 213–214
religious ethics, 71
salvation by faith, 206
vs Islamic "mainstream," 210
Weber's capitalism and, 205–206
English law
capitalism and, 252–253
characteristics of, 252–253
equity and binding precedents, 233
modern rationality evaluation of, 263
systematization lacking in, 250
vs Islamic law, 233–234
European law, vs Islamic law, 12–13, 263–264

Ewing, Sally, 14

Fara'izi movement, reasons for, 222
Fatalism, vs predestination, 71
Fatima, mother of the world, 176
Fatimid regime, imperial characteristics, 283
Fazl, Abu'l, 186, 188, 196–199
Feudal systems
    central power in, 93
    characteristics of, 94
    charismatic origins of, 94
    development of, 92–93
    external aspects of, 94–95
    forms of, 94
    individual rights, 93
    internal aspects of, 94–95
    law and, 32–33
    Oriental vs Occidental, 37
    patrimonialism as, 32–33
    See also Occidental feudalism; Oriental feudalism
Fragmentation
    education and, 234
    human understanding and, 232
    Islamic structural, 238
    law and, 233–234
    secularization and, 238
Franklin, Benjamin, 220, 227
Free Officer Revolution of Riza Shah, 235
Fulain jihad, reasons for, 222
Fundamentalism
    Calvinism and, 211
    Christian use of, 17
    defined, 205
    development cycle, 23
    doctrines of, 207–208, 210
    egalitarianism, 209
    goals of, 209–210
    holy war concept, 208
    Islamic use of, 17
    leadership for, 221
    rationalism and, 213–214
    salvation types, 213
    Sunni movements and, 222
    unrest sources, 213
    vs "mainstream" Islam, 210, 210–211
    vs mysticism, 208–209
    vs pluralism, 292
Fuqaha (legist), 12, 250

Gellner, Ernest, 290
German law, modern rationality evolution of, 263
Ghazi, Kala, 172
al-Ghazali, 144
Gibb, H. A. R., 285
God
    concepts of, 75–77, 80, 174–175
    connecting traditions to, 176
    cult worship, 174, 177
    empire growth, 174
    Hinduism and, 199
    identity of, 173–178
    Islamic assimilation and, 176
    Islam's literate and, 176–177
    literature and, 175
    man's relationship in, 77
    nature of, 75–77
    papermaking technology and, 177
    religious ethics and, 73–75
    universalism doctrine of, 90
    See also Allah
Goldziher, Ignaz, 59, 85
Goody, Jack, 175
Grace
    election doctrine and, 71
    religious ethics and, 77
Grover, B. R., 188

Habib, Irfan, 188
Hadith, defined, 144
Hardy, Peter, 9
Hasan, Mushirul, 237
Hasan, Nurul, 188
Hinduism
    Gita of, 199
    supreme God and, 199
Hodgson, M., 287
Holy men
    pioneering settlers as, 168
    See also Religious scholars
Holy war
    concepts of, 7
    doctrine dissemination in, 91
    economic interest during, 91–92
    fundamentalism and, 208
    goals of, 153
    Islamic universalism and, 153–154
    Oriental patrimonialism, 91–92
    political interest during, 91–92
    religious exclusiveness as, 157

religious foundations for, 79
Sufism and, 157
vs Christian Crusades, 91
Homagium, defined, 94
Huff, Toby, 46n9, 47n27
Hurgronje, Christian Snouch, 59

Ibn Khaldun, 159, 290–291
Ijtihad, 4, 7, 17, 50n18, 208, 209
    See Holy war
Imperialism
    characteristics with, 283
    Islamic states from, 142
India
    political integration, 166
    professional stratum in, 184
    society characteristics, 184
    structured secularization of, 233–234
    tribal organizations, 184
    See also Bengal
India's patrimonial empires, Weber's writings on, 183–184
India's structured secularization
    patrimonial associations, 185
    patrimonial nature of, 183–184
    professional stratum, 184
    society characteristics, 184
    tribal organizations, 184
Injustice, reform movements and, 221–222
Innerworldy asceticism, defined, 213
Institutionalization
    defined, 140
    interrelating factors, 140
    Islamic religious communities, 143–147
    Islamic state, 142–143
    Islamism (Arabian), 140–141
    Middle Eastern societies, 141–142
    phases successive in, 140
    rural societies, 148–150
Iqbal, Muhammad, 237
Islamic analysis
    comparison points of, 67–68
    cultural phenomena contrasts, 64–65
    economic attitude conditioning, 65
    methodological considerations, 64–68
    rational capitalism, 65–66
    Western capitalism, 67
    Western culture uniqueness, 65
Islamic civilization patterns
    analysis tendencies in, 282
    institutional development lacking, 282–283
    military slaves in, 283
    politics, 283
    vs Axial Age civilizations, 281
Islamic law
    autonomy appearance of, 256–257
    "bourgeois elements" shaping, 255
    capitalism, 254–257
    capitalism outside of, 257–258
    concepts missing, 41
    jurist law from, 108
    legal prophecies, 108
    rational capitalism, 111
    rational nature of, 255–256
    reformulating Weber on, 258–259
    role of, 261–264
    rules in, 256
    sacred law as, 108
    sacred orders as, 257
    sanctions backing of, 256
    Schacht conclusions on, 116–117
    state's role in, 260–261
    systematization in, 250
    theologian jurists creating, 108
    typology of, 248–251
    vs European law, 12–13, 263–264
    vs Weber's approach, 116, 264
    See also Sacred law
Islamic motivational elements
    capitalism development, 31
    casual chain of, 29–30
Islamic reforms
    association themes in, 223–224
    capitalism and, 15–16
    causality issues, 227
    characteristics of, 221–222
    "church-sect" typology, 20–22
    Deobandi movement, 19, 217–218
    economic situations and, 223
    economic vs religious contexts, 224–225
    "elective affinity," 224
    group traits of, 19–20
    leadership for, 221
    mediator power dependence, 220
    political activism, 22–23
    Protestant ethic, 220–221
    purposes of, 18
    religious doctrine roots, 19
    Sunni movements, 222–223

teachings of, 221
types of, 221
vs Calvinism doctrine, 226–27
vs European precursors, 20
vs European Puritanism, 225
vs individual responsibilities, 220
vs rural agricultural life, 220
wealth responsibilities, 219–220
Weber's thesis on, 225–226
Western powers presence and, 18–19
Islamic religious communities
group formations, 145
institutionalizing, 143
Muslim association types, 146–147
Muslim elite and, 143–144
organizations developing, 145–146
theologians and, 144–145
Islamic Research Institute, 237
Islamic sects
approaches to, 273
distinction of, 275
charities, 277–278
membership in, 275
political identifications of, 276
purposes of, 278
Shi'ites, 276–277
Sunni, 277
vs churches, 273–275
vs Islamic groupings, 276
vs Weber's analysis, 273–275
Islamic societies
Arabia and, 140–141
boundaries, 140
challenging study, 139
institutions of, 139–140
Islamic state, 142–143
Middle Eastern, 141–142
religious communities, 143–147
rural societies, 148–150
Sunni and, 147–148
Islamic state
caliphs role in, 142
city vs territorial domination, 105
institutionalizing, 142
puritanical laws, 214
Sufi symbol developing, 149
sultan's authority and, 143
Turkish conquest of, 143
Islamic universalism
holy war and, 153–154
military expansions, 154

non-Muslim religions, 154
Islamism
activist tendencies of, 80
anti-magical tendencies, 80
clerics in, 157–159
community establishing, 209–210
Constantinople conquest, 6
daily prayers, 2–3
death fears, 78
five pillars of, 3, 78
formative period of, 5–6
"Golden Age" of, 3–4
hierarchy in, 83–84
holy war concepts, 7
institutionalization of, 140
law sources of, 4–5
legal prescriptions of, 3
Middle Eastern Islamism, 5
military slaves, 6
misconceptions of, 214
Muslim rule, 154–156
organization of, 115–116
pluralism in, 5
political systems in, 7
predestination and, 77–78
reform movements, 159–160
religion vs politics in, 84
religious conversions, 6
religious doctrines confiscating, 79
religious ideas, 114
religious tolerance, 8
religious view differing in, 142
ruleship institutionalizing, 9
Sufism and, 156–157
'ulama' and, 7–8
universalism, 153–154
vs Calvinism, 18
vs great religions, 114–115
vs independent reasoning, 4
vs legal structure, 110
warriors and, 142, 157–159
world wide spreading of, 8–9
See also Bengal
Islamism (Arabian)
characteristics of, 141
institutionalizing, 140
religious community establishing, 140–141
religious complexity in, 141

Jahan 'Ali, Khan, 169

Jahiliya (age of ignorance), 22
James, William, 70
Jat rebellion, Mughal control and, 194
Jihad, see Holy War and Ijtihad
Judaism, vs other religions, 114–116
al-Junayd, 144
Jurisprudence
   basis of, 4
   purposes of, 4

Kali (female deity), 176
Kantowsky, Detlev, 224–225
Khalif. *See* Caliphs
Khan, Ahsan Raza, 188
Khan, Sayyid Ahmad, 237
Kharijites
   authority structures, 277
   church vs sect, 277
   political orientation of, 277
Khondkar, Shah Lutf Allan, 171
Kohler, Joseph, 59

Lapidus, Ira, 5, 285
Law
   administrative staff and, 106–107
   capitalism and, 9, 251–254, 261–264
   classifying of, 12
   corporation idea, 34–35
   decisiveness, 112
   European vs Islamic law, 263–264
   external factors to, 31–32
   feudalism, 32–33
   jurisdiction principles, 36
   justice outcomes form, 109–110
   Justinian's codified compilation, 262–263
   legal training types, 107–108
   modern rationality evolution of, 263
   Oriental vs Occidental feudalism, 37
   patrimonialism, 32
   rational capitalism elements, 111–112
   ruling powers purposes, 33
   secular legal development, 34–35
   sociology of, 9
   substantive-theological systemization, 108–109
   testation, 34
   types of, 106
   unified legal system impediments, 109
   value detaching, 261
   vs sovereign, 261–262
   Western law development of, 35–36, 110–111
   writings on, 9
   See also English law; European law; Islamic law; Personal law; Profane law; Public law
Law and capitalism
   algebraic law, 253–254
   Arab-Muslim withdrawals, 16–17
   economic behavior, 251–252
   English law, 252–253
   European failures, 16
   formal rationalism, 14, 254
   freedom of contract, 14
   independence degree in, 251
   institutional component of, 9
   internal motivation problems, 17–18
   intra-juristic conditions, 251
   Islamic reforms, 15–16
   legal rationalization, 13–14
   rationality stages, 251
   vs Islamic world, 14–15
   Western evolutionary model, 16
Law and cities
   Islamic secular laws, 38
   legally autonomy, 38
   Occidental vs Oriental functions, 37
   social organization emergence, 37–38
   Western and Islamic development, 38–39
Law typology
   legal systematization, 251
   legal systems coherence, 250
   rational legal systems, 249–250
   religious legal systems, 249
   vs formal irrationality, 249
Leadership
   fundamental movements sources, 221
   reform movement sources, 221
Legal equality
   Islamic cities, 104
   land vs town laws, 104
   person vs institution, 104
Levtzion, Nehemia, 6, 282
Lewis, Bernard, 284, 290

Madrasa(s), 33, 234
Mahdi, role of, 288
Mahmud, Hayat, 176
Majahideen (warrior), 7, 30

Mamluk ruleship, 6
Man, Hindu beliefs of, 199
Manasa (female deity)
    cult of the snake, 176
    manifestations, 174
    manifestations of, 176
    Quran and, 177
Marx, Karl, 43
Maturidi theology school, 147
Mecca
    Arabian Islamism and, 140–141
    clan city as, 105
    community organizations lacking, 105
    conquest of, 6
    distinctive anarchy of, 105
    Islamism and, 79–80
    nation-wide importance of, 89
    Oriental patrimonialism, 87–88
Membership
    Islamic sects vs church, 273–274
    Khariites, 277
    Shi'ites, 276–277
    voluntary nature of, 275
Metcalf, Barbara, 18–23, 23
Middle Eastern Islamic societies
    economic networks, 141
    elite in, 141–142
    institutionalizing of, 141
    multi–level society, 141
    prototypical Islamic state emerging, 141
Modernity
    law role in, 106–113
    Occidental cities, 101–106
    Oriental cities, 101–106
    political domination, 85–101
    religious ethics, 68–85
    Weber critiquing, 113–123
    Weber's analysis, 64–68
    Weber's study, 53–64
Mohammed
    Arabian Muslim community formation, 140
    death of, 90
    legal prescription and, 3
    Mecca failures, 85–86
    Medina and, 86
    Oriental patrimonialism, 85–86
    political effectiveness of, 86–87
    Quran and, 3
    succession of, 90–91, 142
    universal God doctrine, 90
    vs tribal cultures, 85
    war and peace forms of, 89
    warrior support for, 159
    "worlds" related by, 89–90
Mughal empire
    armed countryside in, 188
    Aurangzib and, 192–193
    authority acceptance, 200–201
    characteristics of, 166
    city power of, 166–168
    consensual communities, 188–189
    military systems, 187, 193–194
    patrimonial domination as, 195
    patrimonial state as, 165–168
    political legitimacy in, 201–202
    polymorphic cultures, 200
    revenue collecting, 194
    rivalry success, 200
    rules of, 190
    scholar patronizing, 190, 191–192
    sultan dignitaries, 193
    values of, 191
Muhammadiya (voluntary organization), vs elective affinity, 224
Muhammed, Sidi, 288
Murtaza, Saiyid, 176
Muslim rule
    government overtaking, 155
    conversion to, 155
    Turkish military elite, 155–156
    vs military conquest, 154–155
Muslim societies dynamics
    association types, 146–147
    Bengali population growth, 164
    fundamentalist movement, 291
    Islamic goals, 283–284
    khalifs and, 286, 288
    Mahdis and, 288
    pluralism and, 292
    pluralism vs fundamentalism, 292
    political components, 289–290
    political identity fragmentation, 234
    political-religious fusion, 284
    political-religious reconstruction, 284–285
    primordial aspects, 285
    public sphere distinctions, 287
    revolution concepts, 290
    ruler accountabilities, 290

rules types, 286
social movements, 289
totalitarianism in, 284
tribal conquest cycles, 290–291
ulama in, 287–288
universalistic vision, 285–286
utopian vision, 288–289
vs church–sect typology, 21
vs traditional patrimonial regimes, 287
Wahhabis and, 291–292
Muwaqqit (timekeeper), 10
Mysticism, vs fundamentalism, 208–209

Nakamura, Mitsuo, 224
Nau, Hazrat Daner, 170, 170–171
Nejdi movement, reasons for, 222

Objectification, vs economic activity, 112
Occasionalism, Islamic, 18
Occidental capitalism
    development of, 57–58
    identification problems, 58
    reasons for, 58–59
Occidental church, rational law making, 110
Occidental cities
    characteristics of, 102
    economic vs administrative concepts, 102
    medieval city, 103–104
    memberships status in, 104
    urban autonomy, 103
Occidental feudalism
    fealty and patrimonial feudalism, 99
    political vs economic orientation, 101
    vs oriental feudalism, 99
Occidental, knighthood in, 98–99
Occidental political development, vs fief–based feudalism, 96
Occidental rationalism
    domains in, 11–12
    meaning of, 11
Oriental cities
    characteristics of, 102
    Islamic urban development, 104–106
    Mecca as, 101
    Weber's classification criteria, 102–104
Oriental feudalism, 97
    Knight status of, 99
    monetary orientation problems, 99
    nature of, 99
    non-fealty feudalism, 99
    vs Occidental feudalism, 99–100
Oriental patrimonialism
    administrative staff establishing, 92
    centralization and decentralization in, 92
    external conditions, 101
    feudal systems, 93–95
    holy war, 91–92
    Islam succession, 90–91
    Mecca and, 87–88
    Mohammad and, 85–86
    patrimonial domination, 95
    public domination, 92–93
    slaves, 96–98
    universal God doctrine, 90
    vs Occidental patrimonialism, 99–101
    Western political formation, 95–96
Ottoman Empire, 'ulama' and, 287

Padri movement, reasons for, 222
Papal revolution, 38
Parsons, Talcott, 205
Patrimonialism
    administrative staff, 95
    associations of, 185
    central power, 93
    characteristics of, 186–187, 192
    chief skeins of, 192
    decentralizing, 185–186
    defined, 32
    domination formation in, 94
    feudalism in, 32–33
    free-market politics, 196–197
    goals of, 94
    ideal type of, 185
    individual rights, 93
    Mughal military systems, 187
    political domination, 195–196
    regimes perpetuating, 187–188
    ruler authority, 189–190
    unity hierarchical form, 197
Personal law, fragmentation in, 233–234
Peters, Rudolph, 17, 21, 23
Pipes, Daniel, 283
Pir, Jangal, 172
Political domination
    authority, 195
    benefits of, 195
    commercial enterprise growth, 100
    medium of exchange types, 195
    relationship managing in, 195
    self-aware social communities, 195

Power. *See* Feudalism; Patrimonialism
Predestination
  destination and, 75–77
  election doctrine, 206
  entanglements of, 71–72
  fundamentalism and, 210
  Islamism and, 77–78
  predetermination as, 77
  theories of, 71
  vs fatalism, 71
  vs free will, 212–213
  vs self proving, 71
Profane law
  autonomous development of, 110–111
  independence of, 110
  Roman and German traditions, 110
  vs sacred law, 107
  Western development of, 110
Progressive Writers Movement, 237
Protestant Ethic
  capitalism development, 206
  Deobandi movement, 220–221
  German Historical School in, 227
  Islamic reforms, 220–221
  rationality and, 248
Public law
  fragmentation in, 233–234
  rational capitalism, 111
Puritanism
  Islamic reforms and, 225
  vs Islamism, 44, 206–207

Quran
  bare essentials of, 236
  divine origins, 177
  God's speech as, 38
  incorruptibility, 13
  individual specialists on, 12–13
  Islamic liturgy, 177
  magical quality vs message, 157
  Muslim concerns of, 144
  puritan Muslim use, 236
  revolution and, 38

Rational capitalism
  defined, 65
  external aspect of, 100
  individual enterprise vs economic systems, 65–66
  law and, 111–112

models for, 66
Rationalism
  abandoning of, 10
  defined, 173–174
  election doctrine, 213–214
  fundamentalism, 213–214
  law typology, 249
  outcome process of, 259
  Protestant Ethic and, 248
  purposes of, 1–2
  vs modern society, 258–259
  Weber reforming, 258–259
  Weber's use of, 247–248
Religions, world great, 2
Religious ethics
  church organization importance, 83–84
  conduct and, 73
  destination vs predestination, 75–77
  economic mentality, 80
  election doctrine and, 71
  entanglement of, 71–72
  external relations, 81–82
  God conceptions, 73–75
  God to man relationships, 77–78
  idea characteristics, 69–70
  institutional resistance, 85
  Islam confiscating, 79–80
  logical vs pragmatic–psychological consequences, 70
  logical vs religious foundations, 73
  predestination, 71, 78
  proving oneself, 72–73
  psychological effects, 80–81
  response literature, 72
  values orientations, 68–69
  vs conduct, 68
  vs fatalism, 71
Religious ideas, major religion comparisons, 114
Religious scholars ('ulama')
  associations vs tribes joining, 88
  elite status of, 141
  establishing of, 87
  fragmentation of, 233–234
  higher education and, 146
  intentions of, 142
  Islamic thought architects of, 7–8
  Islamism and, 7–8
  legal studies, 144
  mediator role, 155–156
  Muslim, 287–288

Ottoman Empire and, 287
patrimonial state and, 166
purpose of, 5
rule scrutiny by, 286
rural society role, 149
Sunni and, 147
vs cults of the Gentes, 88
vs outsiders, 88–89
Printing press, 25, 236
Public sphere, 5, 45, 287, 290

Qadi justice, 13, 41, 108, 109
Qiyas (analogy), 4, 12, 108

Rechtsstaadt, 32–33, 93, 96
Richards, John, 186
Robinson, Francis, 23–26
Rodinson, Maxime, 39, 117–121, 206, 284
Roff, William, 222
Routinization
  British tax collections, 169–170
  class rise from, 173
  culture expanding from, 173
  forest-dwelling contacting, 170
  Muslim land grants, 171–172
  name style as, 172–173
  pioneering settlers role, 168–169
  tax collections, 172
Roy, Asim, 175
Rule of law, Western idea of, 96
Rural societies
  institutionalizing of, 148
  Islamic identity accepting, 149
  Islamic symbols, 148–150
  religious leadership, 149
  Sufism symbols developing, 149
  vs urban Islamic forms, 150

Sabra, A. I., 51n125
Sacred law
  effectiveness of, 109
  Islamic law as, 108
  predictability impediments to, 109
  secular relationships, 33–34
  unified legal system and, 109
  vs Christian law, 107
  vs profane law, 107, 111–112
Safavid regime, imperial characteristics, 283
Salvation, fundamental types of, 213
Schacht, Joseph, 34, 111, 113–117

Schluchter, Wolfgang, 1, 26–29, 32–33, 37–39, 42–45
Science, modern, 1, 10, 17, 27, 28, 29, 33, 39, 56, 58, 65, 67–68
  Arabic-Islamic, 10–11, 27
Secularization
  contrasting perspectives, 241
  disenchantment in, 232, 236–238
  fragmentation and, 238
  human understanding fragmentation, 232–233
  India's Puritan forms, 236
  Islamism and, 23–26, 239
  learning systems, 234
  power and, 234–235
  shari'a application and, 25–26, 239–241
  structural secularization, 24, 233–235
  subjective secularization, 24–25, 235–236
  vs religious change, 238–239
  Weber's process of, 231–233
  Western capital and power consequences as, 238
  Western colonial presence, 23
  Western model, 25
  world disenchantment and, 23–24
Shah, Bahadur, 194
Shah, Kali, 172
Shah, Khondkar, 168
Shahada, defined, 239
Shariat Application Act (1937), 240
Shi'a, identification with, 146
Shi'ites
  church vs sect, 276–277
  origins of, 3
  political participation in, 289–290
Sin, "bookkeeping" of, 76
Sivan, Emanuel, 289
Slaves
  administrative staff and, 97
  Africans as, 105
  history of, 97
  Islamic law and, 255
  military use of, 286
  payments to, 97–98
  purchasing of, 99
  rise of, 286
  vs Western based feudalism, 98
State's role
  capitalism rising, 260–261
  European kinship's organizations, 260
  fundamental role of, 260

Index   331

plurality traditions of, 260
semi-autonomous groups and, 260–261
Structural secularization. *See* Secularization
Sufism
   defined, 146
   development of, 146–147
   elite status, 141
   fundamentalism, 222
   God's intercessions, 149
   holy war and, 157
   identification with, 146
   influence of, 156–157
   Islamism and, 156–157
   law school of, 146
   missionary networks, 156
   pioneering settlers, 168–169
   political participating, 289–290
   ritualistic character, 157
   rural society roles, 149
   symbols developing, 149
   West Africa conversions, 157
Suleiman, Mowlay, 288
Sultans
   authority of, 143
   vs khalifs, 286
Sunni
   anti-corruption focus, 222
   authority structure, 277
   Calvinism and, 207
   characteristics of, 147, 285–286
   church vs sect, 277
   detachment attitude of, 147–148
   fundamentalists groups, 291
   goals of, 147, 222, 285–286
   Islamic reforms, 222–223
   law schools of, 146–147
   sources for, 222
   vs political elite, 147
   vs sociopolitical institutions, 148

Troeltsch, Ernst, 21
Turner, Bryan S., 39, 43, 121–123, 206, 232

'Ulama'. *See* Religious scholars
Ulrich, F., 30, 75
Umar ibn 'Abd al-'Aziz, 154
Umayyad dynasty, 6
Umma, predominance of, 285
Unity
   charismatic rulers, 197
   hierarchical forms, 197
   Hindu traditions of, 199
   man's social relations, 198–199
   social activity and, 197–198
Universities
   ecclesiastic control of, 106
   fragmentation in, 234
   science focus in, 107
   theology and secular law separation, 110
Urban development
   Islamic world in, 104
   Weber's analysis of, 102–104
Utility
   hierocratic power, 96
   rule of law, 96
   urban power, 96

Voll, John, 291

al-Wahhab, Abd and Wahhabhis, 291
   defined, 222, 291
   fundamentalism of, 291
Warriors
   charismatic leadership, 159–160
   ideal personality type, 158
   military movements and, 159
   role of, 158–159
   vs clerics, 158–159
   vs orthodox ethics, 122
Wealth
   patrimonial seizure of, 98
   religious responsibility and, 219–220
   research and, 220–221
Weber, Marianne, 57, 59
Weber, Max
   analysis problems, 281–283
   basic framework, 26–29
   church vs Islamic sects, 273–275
   church-sect typology of, 20–21
   circular reasoning of, 42
   death of, 2
   economic ethics vs religious orientations, 1
   economic rationalism, 1
   frame of reference for, 2
   innerworldly ethic, 45
   Islam image of, 6–7
   Islam study by, 206
   Islamic contributions, 139
   Islamic law concepts, 41
   Islamic reform thesis, 225–227

main thesis of, 42–43
patrimonial writings, 183–187
Puritanism vs Islamism, 44
rationality and, 40–41, 247–248, 250
reforming of, 258–259
relevance of, 264
religious ideas influencing, 39
routinization, 8
secularization, 231–232
theoretical emphasis of, 45–46
vs institutional factors, 43–44
Western rationalism influences, 1–2
women's roles, 44–45
world disenchantment, 17
worldview typology, 113
writings of, 54
Weber's critiques
  analysis gaps, 123
  Islamic law, 116–117
  logic difficulties, 119
  major religion comparisons, 114–116
  Marxism perspectives, 117–121
  response lacking, 117
  Rodinson and, 117–121
  Sahacht and, 116–117
  subject knowledge, 120–121
  thesis in, 119
  Turner and, 121–123
Weber's Islamic study
  article publishing, 61–62
  conclusions of, 63–64
  developing of, 53–54
  investigation reasons for, 58–59
  manuscript of, 62–63
  non-Christian interest, 54–56
  political and economical history, 56–57
  qualitative approaches, 57–58
  twofold project, 59–61
  Calvinism similarities, 30
  components basic for, 29
  conclusions of, 27
  criticism of, 39–46
  individual capitalist enterprises, 28
  internal and external factors, 28–29
  law and cities, 37–39
  law and state, 31–37
  motivational elements, 29–31
  multifocal views, 27–28
  writings on, 26–27
Wellhausen, Julius, 59, 85
West Africa
  Sufism missionary conversions, 157
  warriors vs clerics, 158–159
Western capitalism, characteristics of, 67
Western law
  church and, 35
  development of, 35–36
Women
  books written for, 218
  Islam's multiple wives, 214
  lifestyle advice to, 218–219
  Muslim feminists, 44
  polygamy and, 44–45
  role of, 44–45
  traditional role of, 44
  See also Deity (female)

Zaheer, Sajjad, 237
Ziadeh, Farhat, 36
Ziegler, Norman, 191